STUDIES IN LABOUR AND SOCIAL LAW

GENERAL EDITORS

BOB HEPPLE

Professor of English Law in the University of London, at University College

PAUL O'HIGGINS

Regius Professor of Laws, Trinity College, Dublin, and.
Fellow of Christ's College, Cambridge

Trade Union Democracy, Members' Rights and the Law

PATRICK ELIAS AND
KEITH EWING

MANSELL PUBLISHING LIMITED
LONDON AND NEW YORK

First published 1987 by Mansell Publishing Limited
(A subsidiary of The H.W. Wilson Company)
6 All Saints Street, London N1 9RL, England
950 University Avenue, Bronx, New York 10452, U.S.A.

British Library Cataloguing in Publication Data

Elias, Patrick
   Trade union democracy, members' rights and the law.——(Studies in
labour and social law).
   1. Trade-unions——Information and legislation——Great Britain
I. Title   II. Ewing, K.D.   III. Series
344.104'188   KD3050

   ISBN 0-7201-0729-6
   ISBN 0-7201-1871-9 Pbk

Library of Congress Cataloging-in-Publication Data

Elias, Patrick.
   Trade union democracy, members' rights and the law.

   (Studies in labour and social law)
   Bibliography: p.
   Includes index.
   1. Trade-unions——Law and legislation——Great Britain.
I. Ewing, K.D. (Keith D.)   II. Title.   III. Series.
KD3050.E43   1987   344.41'018   87–7645
ISBN 0-7201-0729-6   344.10418

Set in 11/12 pt Compugraphic Baskerville
by Colset Private Limited, Singapore

Printed and bound in Great Britain by
Biddles Ltd, Guildford and King's Lynn

CONTENTS

Preface   vii

List of Abbreviations   ix

Chapter 1   The historical context   1

Chapter 2   The contract of membership   23

Chapter 3   Admissions and the closed shop   62

Chapter 4   Trade union government and the courts   96

Chapter 5   Statutory regulation of trade union
             government   136

Chapter 6   Discipline and expulsion   191

Chapter 7   Discipline and industrial action   236

Chapter 8   The role of law in trade union government   260

Bibliography   291

Table of Cases   304

Index   308

Preface

In recent years trade union government has attracted detailed and sustained scrutiny by the press, by the courts, and by Parliament, with the interest of each being fuelled by the miners' strike of 1984–5. The purpose of this book is to address the major legal problems which arise in the relationship between trade unions and their members and to consider the role which law should play in this now controversial but sensitive area.

In Chapter 1 we begin with a historical introduction, tracing the different periods in the development of the law, from the Combination Acts to the Trade Union Act of 1984. In Chapter 2 we discuss the basis for legal intervention, looking especially at the contract of membership, but also at concepts such as the so-called right to work and the duty to act fairly. Chapter 3 deals with the right of unions to regulate admission to membership, particularly in the context of the closed shop. Here we consider the common law and also the statutory controls to be found in sections 4 and 5 of the Employment Act 1980.

Chapter 4 deals with the role of the courts in regulating the way in which trade unions are governed. Because of its industrial and political significance, we devote a separate section of this chapter to a study of the legal issues arising out of the miners' strike of 1984–5, clearly the major event in recent labour history. In Chapter 5 we address another important event, namely the statutory regulation of trade union government. Here we look at the Trade Union Act 1984 which introduced mandatory elections to trade union executive committees; compulsory strike ballots; and the periodic review of trade union political funds.

In Chapter 6 we consider the power of trade unions to discipline and expel members, an issue which we also address in Chapter 7. The latter is concerned, however, with the specific problem raised by the taking of disciplinary measures against members who strike-break. The study concludes in Chapter 8 with an analysis of the role which law should play in the government of trade unions. The political climate is such that it is now difficult to argue that there should be no statutory regulation of trade union internal affairs. As we try to show in Chapter 8, this is a view which appears to have adherents in the labour movement.

In the course of preparing this book for publication, we have accumulated debts to a large number of people. We wish to record our thanks first to the editors of this series, Bob Hepple and Paul O'Higgins, for their encouragement and forbearance over a number of years. Secondly, we are grateful to Paul Davies, editor of the *Industrial Law Journal*, for permission to draw on material previously published in that journal; to John Hutton, who granted permission to reproduce the table which appears in Chapter 5; and to Bill Rees for permission to draw on material published previously in collaboration with the second-named author. Thirdly, we wish to record our debt to our publishers, and to Veronica Higgs in particular, for patiently enduring an abnormally long gestation period.

Patrick Elias
Keith Ewing
31 December 1986

List of Abbreviations

ACAS	Advisory, Conciliation and Arbitration Service
ACTT	Association of Cinematograph, Television and Allied Technicians
AEU	Amalgamated Engineering Union
APEX	Association of Professional, Executive, Clerical and Computer Staff
ASLEF	Associated Society of Locomotive Engineers and Firemen
ASTMS	Association of Scientific, Technical and Managerial Staffs
AUEFW	Amalgamated Union of Engineering and Foundry Workers
AUEW	Amalgamated Union of Engineering Workers
AUEW-TASS	Amalgamated Union of Engineering Workers (Technical, Administrative and Supervisory Section)
AUT	Association of University Teachers
BALPA	British Air Line Pilots' Association
BIFU	Banking, Insurance and Finance Union
CAC	Central Arbitration Committee
CBI	Confederation of British Industry
Citrine	*Citrine's Trade Union Law*, 3rd edn by Hickling, M.A., London, Stevens, 1967
CO	Certification Officer
COHSE	Confederation of Health Service Employees
CPSA	Civil and Public Services' Association
CTU	Conservative Trade Unionists
EAT	Employment Appeal Tribunal
EEF	Engineering Employers' Federation
EEPTU	Electrical Electronic Telecommunication and Plumbing Union
EPCA	Employment Protection (Consolidation) Act 1978
ETU	Electrical Trades' Union
FDA	Association of First Division Civil Servants

GMBATU	General, Municipal, Boilermakers and Allied Trades' Union
Gower	*Gower's Principles of Modern Company Law*, 4th edn by Gower, L.C.B., Cronin, J.B., Easson, A.J. and Wedderburn of Charlton, London, Stevens, 1979.
Grunfeld	Grunfeld, C., *Modern Trade Union Law*, London, Sweet and Maxwell, 1966.
HVA	Health Visitors' Association
ILO	International Labour Organization
IOD	Institute of Directors
IPCS	Institution of Professional Civil Servants
IRC	Independent Review Committee of the Trades' Union Congress
ITGWU	Irish Transport and General Workers' Union
ITWF	International Transport Workers' Federation
MR	Master of the Rolls
NACO	National Association of Co-operative Officials
NALGO	National and Local Government Officers' Association
NAPO	National Association of Probation Officers
NALHM	National Association of Licensed House Managers
NAS/UWT	National Union of Schoolmasters/Union of Women Teachers
NASDS	National Amalgamated Stevedores' and Dockers' Society
NATFHE	National Association of Teachers in Further and Higher Education
NATSOPA	National Society of Operative Printers, Graphical and Media Personnel
NCU	National Communications' Union
NGA	National Graphical Association
NUDAW	National Union of Distributive and Allied Workers
NUFTO	National Union of Furniture Trade Operatives
NUGMW	National Union of General and Municipal Workers
NUJ	National Union of Journalists
NUM	National Union of Mineworkers
NUPE	National Union of Public Employees
NUR	National Union of Railwaymen
NUS	National Union of Seamen
NUSMW	National Union of Sheet Metal Workers
NUT	National Union of Teachers
NUTGW	National Union of Tailors and Garment Workers
POEU	Post Office Engineering Union
RSBC	Revised Statutes of British Columbia
RSO	Revised Statutes of Ontario
SCPS	Society of Civil and Public Servants

SLADE	Society of Lithographic Artists, Designers, Engravers and Process Workers
SOGAT	Society of Graphical and Allied Trades
STA	Scottish Typographical Association
STE	Society of Telecom Executives
TGWU	Transport and General Workers' Union
Treitel	Treitel, G.H., *The Law of Contract*, 6th edn, London, Stevens, 1983.
TUA	Trade Union Act 1913
TUC	Trades' Union Congress
TULRA	Trade Union and Labour Relations Act 1974
TULR (Am) A	Trade Union and Labour Relations (Amendment) Act 1976
UCATT	Union of Construction, Allied Trades and Technicians
UCW	Union of Communication Workers
UK	United Kingdom
UPW	Union of Post Office Workers
URTU	United Road Transport Union
USDAW	Union of Shop, Distributive and Allied Workers

1

The Historical Context

THE STRUGGLE FOR LEGALITY

By the beginning of the nineteenth century, trade unions were well established in Britain. They had emerged despite the range of criminal wrongs for which their members could be liable. But at the turn of the century they were subjected to an additional and comprehensive criminal liability. In 1799 a Combination Act was passed making any combination of workers illegal.[1] Initially this Act was intended to apply to certain workers employed by London millwrights only, but the Government decided to extend it and apply it to workers generally. This decision seems to have been inspired partly by fears of the potentially revolutionary nature of trade unionism — a fear possibly exacerbated by the experiences of the French Revolution in 1789 and uprisings in Ireland a few years later — and partly because industrial action was obstructing trade. The latter was particularly serious since Britain was at war with France. The Act created penalties of three months' imprisonment for trade union activities designed to raise wages or reduce hours, and provided for summary proceedings before a single magistrate. However, because of protests about the potentially arbitrary nature of such a hearing, it was replaced in the following year by another Act. This provided that there should be at least two justices, who should not be masters in the trade concerned, and it also extended the law to combinations of employers. But this latter change involved a formal equality before the law only, since the justices were from the employers' class and would likely be their close neighbours or personal acquaintances. It is not surprising, therefore, that despite the existence of employers' associations, there appears to be no record of any conviction of employers under the Act.

The Combination Acts were nothing if not comprehensive. The 1800 Act rendered criminal 'all Contracts, Covenants and Agreements whatsoever, in Writing or not in Writing, at any time or times heretofore made or entered into, by or between any Journeymen Manufacturers or other Persons within this Kingdom'[2] designed to improve wages, alter hours, reduce output or otherwise interfere with the way in which employers ran their businesses. The Webbs characterized this legisla-, tion as 'a new momentous departure',[3] a view which historians have since recognized exaggerates its importance. It did not introduce any fundamentally new principle, and the penalties it imposed were relatively light for the period. Moreover, research indicates that it was used infrequently and convictions were often quashed on technical grounds. From the employers' point of view other laws, such as the Master and Servant Acts, which made it a criminal offence to break the contract of employment, or the common law offence of conspiracy, would serve their interests equally well. Nonetheless, together with these various other criminal constraints, the Combination Acts were undoubtedly a setback to the growth of trade unionism, particularly in the newer, larger industries of cotton and wool where technological development was most rapid and class differences most marked. But many other organizations, particularly small craft unions, continued .to operate under the shadow of the criminal law, often with connivance of an employer who preferred to resolve conflicts through collective bargaining rather than through recourse to the criminal courts.

Gradually the climate of opinion changed. With the return of economic prosperity in the 1820s, the threat of widespread public disorder was less immediate. Furthermore, a number of influential people, supporters of the economic philosophy of Jeremy Bentham, took the view that workers should be at liberty to combine. One of these, Francis Place, campaigned skilfully for the repeal of the Combination Acts and finally, in 1824, following the Report of a Select Committee of the House of Commons into matters affecting industry, including the operation of the Acts, he was successful. The various Combination Acts were formally repealed. One of the factors which made this step acceptable was the view expressed by Place and other Benthamites, and subsequently endorsed by the Select Committee, that it was only the unions' illegality that attracted recruits to them, and that once the unions were made lawful, they would gradually wither away. Another, perhaps, was the fact that by this time the Combination Acts were in any event virtually a dead letter and it appears that no prosecutions had been instigated under them for a number of years. But the opinion that trade unions would gradually cease proved to be fundamentally misconceived. Feeling no doubt intoxicated with their new-found freedom, the unions greeted the repeal with a wave of strikes rather than the decline in membership which had optimistically been predicted. The government responded swiftly. In the following year, after yet another Select Committee Report, it tightened.up considerably on the 1824 Act and severely limited the legality of industrial action. The 1825 Act created a host of vaguely worded criminal offences, such as 'molestation', 'intimidation', and 'conspiracy',[4] which were subsequently very widely interpreted by the judges.[5] But at least the principle of freedom of association was left intact, though the repeal did not make all combinations of workers lawful. Section 4 of the 1825 Act merely rendered lawful those combinations whose sole purpose was to press for wage increases or changes in the hours of work. It did not include those organizations which sought to influence other conditions of employment, and the prevailing opinion was that they remained illegal.

RESTRAINT OF TRADE

It will be readily apparent then that until the repeal of the Combination laws, and even for some time thereafter, discussion of the legal status of the trade unions was dominated by the criminal law. Consideration of the rights and duties of union members was barely in issue at all. The battleground was freedom of association rather than freedom in association. But once the victory for freedom of association had been achieved, the operation of internal affairs inevitably became more important. Nevertheless, it was some time before the matter was raised in the courts. Given the formality and expense of bringing proceedings before the courts at that time, this is hardly surprising. The County Court, which was specifically established to provide a court for the people, was itself not created until 1846,[6] and even this court was too expensive for most workers. Consequently any internal disputes had to be resolved according to the union's own dispute procedure. For example, Mortimer, historian of the boilermakers' union, reports that in that union several disputes, mostly concerned with benefit rights, were settled by a procedure which involved the use of independent arbitrators.[7] In any event, when cases did come before the courts it was made clear that even though some combinations were no longer criminal, this did not make them legal in the sense of permitting them to enforce their rules.

The leading case is *Hilton* v. *Eckersley*.[8] Given the psychological and financial barriers deterring workers from resorting to the courts, it is not surprising that the case involved an internal dispute between a combination of employers rather than employees. A group of master cotton spinners had entered into a bond whereby they agreed to adopt a common policy on such matters as wages paid and hours worked, that policy to be determined by the majority. An attempt to enforce the bond against a recalcitrant employer proved unsuccessful. The Court of

Exchequer Chamber held that this limitation on the right of employers to carry on their business according to their discretion was in restraint of trade. While it was not willing to express an opinion as to whether this rendered the organization criminal, it held that the consequence was that the agreements were incapable of being enforced in law. Although the case was about an employers' association, the judgments make it clear that the court was fully aware of the potential implications of its decision for trade unions. Indeed, this factor seems to have significantly influenced its decision, as the following extract from the judgment of Baron Alderson indicates:

> We see no way of avoiding the conclusion that, if a bond of this sort between masters is capable of being enforced at law, an agreement to the same effect amongst workmen must be equally legal and enforceable: and so we shall be giving a legal effect to combinations of workmen for the purpose of raising wages, and make their strikes capable of being enforced by law.[9]

This decision was of no great consequence to the unions. They did not wish to settle their disputes in the courts, and consequently the courts' refusal to receive them was a matter of little consequence. But their legal status soon did become a matter of concern to them, though for a rather different reason. As unions became established and more wealthy, so they became increasingly vulnerable to officials who might be tempted to embezzle their funds. Naturally unions wished to be able to pursue the offender and recover their property, but their unincorporated status made this action virtually impossible. This was not a problem peculiar to unions; it was shared by all unincorporated groups. The difficulty lay not in the unions' purposes, but in the members' joint ownership of property. The theory was that since unions were unincorporated, the property belonged to all the members as joint owners, so that if a member disappeared with union funds, it was not theft since the member was merely taking personal property, albeit owned jointly with others. In order to circumvent this problem in relation to friendly societies, the Friendly Societies Act 1855 had enabled bodies registered under that Act to prosecute defaulting officials, and moreover it provided a summary procedure for that purpose. This Act applied, amongst other organizations, to 'any Friendly Society established . . . for any Purpose which is not illegal',[10] provided that it deposited its rules with the Chief Registrar of Friendly Societies. The Act was specifically framed in this way because it was intended that it should embrace trade unions. Many unions deposited their rules and confidently assumed — as did the Chief Registrar — that they had thereby gained the protection of the Act.[11]

However, this confidence proved to be mistaken, for in *Hornby* v. *Close*[12] the Court of Queens Bench held that while purposes in restraint of trade might not make an organization criminal, it remained 'illegal' within the terms of the Friendly Societies Act and so could not utilize the special procedures provided by that legislation. Consequently union funds could be stolen with impunity. Legislation was quickly passed to remedy this situation,[13] the alacrity perhaps not wholly unconnected with the fact that only a year previously the franchise had been extended for the first time to working men.

THE ROYAL COMMISSION OF 1867

In 1867, the year of *Hornby* v. *Close*, a Royal Commission was established to investigate the whole question of trade unionism, including the possibility of legal reforms. This was occasioned by allegations of widespread violence being perpetrated by trade unionists against non-unionists, especially in Sheffield and Manchester. The Commission issued both Majority and Minority Reports,[14] but it was the latter which provided the basis for subsequent legislation. This was surprising because the Majority Report was by far the more restrictive as far as the unions were concerned, and at that time there was much hostility displayed towards trade unionism. The Majority desired to curb what they saw as the unacceptable face of labour, and their proposals, if implemented, would have led to a virtual emasculation of union freedom.[15] They suggested that unions should be subject to a system of registration. Once registered, they would be immune from the threat of criminal law. But in return for this immunity, their rules would have to be approved by the Registrar of Friendly Societies, who would have to refuse registration to any organizations which had objectionable rules. These included rules designed to restrict entry into a trade, or which sought the closed shop as an objective, or which permitted the union to take sympathetic action on behalf of other workgroups. In short, the legality afforded to the unions was little wider than that found in the statutes which had repealed the Combination Acts almost fifty years earlier. In addition, the Majority recommended that benefit and trade funds would have to be kept separate. As far as internal affairs were concerned, the Majority had virtually nothing to say, merely suggesting that a registered union should be regulated in its internal affairs in a manner 'resembling in some degree that of Corporations'.[16]

The Minority Report was drafted by supporters of the unions.[17] Fortunately for them, the evidence given to the Commission indicated that violence by trade unionists, which had been the principal reason for the creation of the Commission, was dying out and had in any event been isolated in particular regions. Moreover, evidence given in support of the unions had skilfully shown them in their most favourable light, emphasizing their valuable role in providing friendly benefits and demonstrating the responsible way in which the majority of them conducted their affairs. This quelled much of the hostility shown towards the unions and helped to make the Minority's views acceptable to the government. The Minority's basic objective was that unions should be given just sufficient legal status to provide immunity from the criminal law of restraint of trade, and also to enable them to protect their funds. They suggested that their rules should be registered, but that the Registrar would have no control over their content, save where they were incomplete or fraudulent. However, they expressly rejected any suggestion that the unions' internal affairs should otherwise be subjected to the legal process. They argued that giving the unions the right to resort to the courts to enforce their agreements would at best be futile, because the prevailing hostility to them meant that the judges would not readily enforce them, and at worst could be positively harmful, because it might be made conditional on the unions accepting 'a complete law regulating the whole life of the union' with conditions which few of them could accept.[18] Presumably they had in mind here the recommendations of the Majority. Perhaps, too, they felt that legislation would place a formidable weapon in the hands of the employers, who would be able to encourage dissident union members into harassing unions with legal actions. Interestingly enough, their opponents were happy to accept this philosophy of legal abstention from internal union affairs. No doubt it was distasteful to the Victorian establishment to permit judges to enforce agreements which it found repugnant.

THE TRADE UNION ACT 1871

The outcome of this strange alliance was the Trade Union Act 1871 which adopted the principle of non-intervention in union affairs. Union autonomy was accepted as a desirable principle. Not only did Parliament reject the contention of the Majority report that union rules should be rigorously controlled, it went further in that it sought to prevent the Courts from enforcing those rules which had been autonomously drafted by the unions themselves. The core of the recommendations of the Minority Report was reflected in three sections of the Act. Section 2 provided that unions were not to be considered as criminal conspiracies merely because their rules were in restraint of trade. Section 3 dealt with the civil law difficulties and stipulated that the restraint of trade doctrine should not render trade union agreements or trusts void or voidable. Had the position been left there, the rules would have been valid and capable of being enforced in the courts in the usual way. Consequently section 4 was enacted, its rather curious drafting reflecting the intention of keeping internal union affairs out of the courts while enabling the unions to protect their property interests and enforce their agreements against third parties. This was made clear by Mr Bruce who, introducing the Bill in Parliament, quoted with approval the passage from the Minority Report where a proposal to make contracts between union members enforceable in law had been expressly and unequivocally rejected.[19] However, this intention was subsequently frustrated because of defects in the drafting of the section. It provided:

> Nothing in this Act shall enable any Court to entertain any legal proceedings instituted with the object of directly enforcing or recovering damages for the breach of any of the following agreements, namely:
> (1) Any agreement between members of a trade union as such, concerning the conditions on which any members for the time being of such trade union shall or shall not sell their goods, transact business, employ, or be employed:
> (2) Any agreement for the payment by any person of any subscription or penalty to a trade union:
> (3) Any agreement for the application of the funds of a trade union,
> (a) To provide benefits to members; or
> (b) To furnish contributions to any employer or workman not a member of such trade union, in consideration of such employer or workman acting in conformity with the rules or resolutions of such trade union; or
> (c) To discharge any fine imposed upon any person by sentence of a court of justice; . . .
> But nothing in this section shall be deemed to constitute any of the above-mentioned agreements unlawful.

Why the section was framed in this way, rather than in the form of a direct exclusion of jurisdiction over internal affairs, is not entirely clear. But it is likely that it owed its particular construction, at least in part, to the language of the Minority Report of the 1867 Royal Commission. There it had been stated with reference to the doctrine of restraint of trade that 'in all matters but the direct enforcement [of contracts in restraint of trade] and as to all matters incident to or consequential of such a contract, the doctrine should have no place'.[20] This would achieve their objective of protecting union funds while at the same time preventing the courts exercising jurisdiction over internal union rules. Perhaps the draftsmen thought that if they also used the word 'directly' they would be faithfully implementing the Minority's — and thus the Government's — intentions. But this was always an optimistic assessment. For if that objective was to be realized, the courts had to be willing to make two basic assumptions. The first was that unions operated in unreasonable restraint of trade at common law. If they did not, and were lawful bodies, then section 3 would be unnecessary to save their rules from illegality and they could be enforced in the normal way. Nor would section 4 then operate to exclude the judges. This was because that section specified that '*Nothing in this Act* shall enable any Court to entertain any legal proceedings' in relation to the enumerated agreements, so if those agreements could be enforced independently of the Act, section 4 did not operate. Section 4 fed on section 3 and if the latter was inapplicable then so was the former. The second assumption which the courts had to make if they were to adopt a self-denying ordinance was to accept that section 4 should be interpreted liberally rather than literally. Only on this basis could the specific terms of section 4 operate to provide a blanket exclusion of the judges from union affairs.

Circumventing Section 4

Initially the courts were prepared to construe section 4 so as to promote its objective. However, they soon discarded the philosophy of non-intervention and began to indicate a desire to extend control over union affairs. This was achieved by a gradual rejection of both underlying assumptions. First, in a number of cases the courts began to hold that some unions were not operating in restraint of trade at common law at all[21] or, alternatively, that insofar as some of their rules were in unreasonable restraint of trade, they could be severed from those which were not so that only the latter remained void.[22] Consequently these organizations were lawful and their rules could be enforced in the normal way. They did not rely upon section 3 to save them from illegality, and this in turn meant that section 4 was inapplicable. So neither the restraint of trade doctrine nor section 4 protected the rules of these unions from judicial encroachment. This method of bringing unions within the courts' control was, however, relatively short-lived. Subsequently the judges refused to treat unions as lawful at common law,[23] and there is no case since 1911 in which they have done so. Indeed, some unions even specifically stated in their rules that they were empowered to act in restraint of trade if necessary, thereby appearing to put the matter beyond doubt.[24] Ironically they chose to assert their illegality at common law in order to ensure that they would reap the benefit of non-intervention.

However, the courts gradually rejected the second assumption also. Initially, they interpreted section 4 very widely so as to achieve the objective of keeping internal union affairs beyond judicial control, but later they withdrew from this position. In one of the earliest cases on the section, *Duke* v. *Littleboy*,[25] the court refused to grant a union executive council an injunction to prevent the misapplication of funds by a seceding branch. It held that this would be directly to enforce an agreement for the application of the funds for the benefit of the members. But as the plaintiffs claimed, there was a fallacy in the argument. It clearly does not follow that by restraining the improper expenditure of funds, the courts are enforcing an agreement to provide benefits to members. It might increase the likelihood of such benefits being paid simply because it preserves the resources available for such payments, and the expectation of such payment might even be the motive behind the action. But an injunction in no sense compels the union to distribute its money in that way. Even if it can be said to amount to an indirect enforcement — which is by no means certain — it clearly does not constitute a direct enforcement. However, Denman J considered this distinction between direct and indirect to be 'too great a refinement'.[26] He thought that the real purpose of the action must be that the plaintiffs hoped that the funds would be used to provide benefits to them and that this objective meant that section 4 was applicable. Arguably the court here was even more reluctant to interfere than Parliament intended, since one of the policies behind the 1871 Act was to prevent the improper application of union funds.

Subsequently the courts recognized the fallacy. In *Wolfe* v. *Matthews*[27] an injunction was granted to restrain union funds being spent on a proposed amalgamation in breach of the union's rules, Fry J commenting that this at best amounted to an indirect enforcement of the agreement. Finally the issue came before the House of Lords in *Yorkshire Miners' Association* v. *Howden*[28] where *Wolfe* v. *Matthews* was approved. A union member sought to restrain the payment of strike benefit in breach of the rules, even though the union's governing body had approved the payment. The union argued that the court's jurisdiction was excluded by section 4(3)(a), but a majority of their Lordships rejected this contention. That section merely prevented members from enforcing a right to benefit. It did not stop them from restraining the improper payment of benefit. Section 4 did not permit unions to conduct their affairs in breach of their constitutions, even if that was the wish of a majority of the members. Lord Macnaghten commented 'how disastrous it might be to the funds of this union, and to trade unions generally, if there were no means of preventing the managers and masters of the union from diverting its funds from their legitimate and authorised purposes'.[29] The House of Lords also intervened later to restrain by injunction the expulsion of a trade union member contrary to the rules. The courts had earlier held that the effect of such an injunction would be to enforce an agreement to pay benefit contrary to section 4(3)(a).[30] In *Amalgamated Society of Carpenters and Joiners* v. *Braithwaite*,[31] however, Lord Wrenbury tersely commented that 'it is not enforcing an agreement against a party to grant an injunction to restrain him from tearing it up. When the injunction is granted and obeyed, the result is simply to leave the relations between the parties in *statu quo ante* without enforcing them at all'.[32]

Braithwaite was a clear indication of the significant shift in judicial attitudes to section 4 which had taken place since the early cases. An indication of this is provided in the speech of Lord Buckmaster where he said:

> Looking at the words of the section alone, unaided and unembarrassed by previous decisions, I should have thought it plain that an action which in fact asks for nothing but a declaration as to the construction of a rule as to membership and as an incident thereto, an injunction, was not an attempt to enforce directly any such agreeement as that referred to in the statute.[33]

He also said that:

> To construe a rule is not directly to enforce any agreement between the members, and I am unable to see any reason why the words of the statute should be so extended as to exclude a trade union itself or any of its members from obtaining the advantage of having obscure words construed by a wholly independent tribunal.[34]

After *Braithwaite*, section 4 did not seriously hinder judicial control of internal union affairs at all. The judges had rejected the policy behind section 4 and shown an increasing desire to intervene in union matters. Judicial abstention had gradually given way to judicial control, at least to the extent that courts would generally require adherence to the union's own constitution. But it would not be correct to say that the judges thereby distorted the section in order to achieve this control. The interpretation they adopted, although contrary to the intentions of the framers of the Act, was perfectly consistent with the statutory language.

Indeed, it might have been predicted, given the English judges' emphasis on the need to construe statutes literally, coupled with the rule of interpretation which precludes the courts from considering the Parliamentary history of an Act. As Lord Macnaghten pointed out in the *Yorkshire Miners'* case, the approach adopted by the courts in the early cases involved departing 'rather widely from the language of the enactment'.[35]

The result of this interpretation was that within fifty years of the Act being passed, union autonomy was protected within only a very narrow range. Its principal effect was to prevent members from suing the union to assert their benefit rights, provided the union pleaded section 4 in defence. Yet ironically this restriction on the enforcement of the union's friendly society functions was one of the least justifiable aspects of that section. But even here the courts occasionally became intolerant of the limited restraints which the section continued to impose. They sometimes sought to sidestep that provision by resorting to unreasonable interpretations which unduly strained the language of the Act. For example, one case relates to subsection 3 where the court was prevented from directly enforcing any rule to provide benefits to members. In *McGahie* v. *USDAW*,[36] however, the court held that a union member could successfully take legal action to compel the union to consider his application for legal aid, even though he could not have enforced his right to any legal aid which the union might have agreed to grant him. This case is not wholly typical, but it shows how keen the courts had become to extend their jurisdiction over unions' domestic affairs. In addition, the unions do not seem to have been particularly concerned to exclude the courts' intervention by relying upon the section. In one case which arose shortly before section 4 was repealed,[37] in which a member was claiming a right to legal aid under the union constitution, section 4 was not pleaded in defence even though it would appear to have been directly applicable. The section was thus easily evaded by the courts (sometimes willingly on the part of the unions, it seems) and its death knell was finally tolled when it was repealed by the Industrial Relations Act 1971,[38] a step which had earlier been proposed by the Donovan Commission.[39]

The Repeal of Section 4

The Industrial Relations Act 1971 was the beginning of a new era in the statutory regulation of union internal affairs, an era interrupted since only by the legislation of the Labour Government of 1974-9. The 1971 Act did not simply repeal section 4 of the 1871 Act. It imposed a detailed system of regulation of internal union affairs which was the complete antithesis to the policy of the 1871 legislation. The Act did not herald the first legislative intervention in trade union affairs, but it was far more comprehensive than any previous law. A variety of statutes, beginning with the Trade Union Act 1871 itself, had imposed certain limited statutory obligations on the unions. These dealt with such matters as the provision of information for members,[40] control over the operation of union mergers[41] and the creation and operation of the political fund.[42] However, the previous legislation was developed in a piecemeal fashion, regulating particular problems which required attention. It did not substantially undermine the contractual basis of the union–member relationship. The 1971 Act marked a new phase in that it provided a comprehensive regulation of the relationship between the union and its members, imposing fundamentally new duties on the unions. The first major change related to trade union status. Before 1971 trade unions did not have corporate status, though they were treated by the courts for some purposes as corporate bodies. In the *Taff Vale* case it was held that trade unions registered under the 1871 Act had sufficient corporate status to be sued in their name for the tortious acts of their officials.[43] And in *Bonsor* v. *Musicians' Union*[44] it was held that unions could be sued in contract for damages by their members. A registered union was treated by Lords Porter and Morton as a quasi-corporation,[45] a 'near corporation' in the words of Lord Porter.[46] It is clear, however, that the unions had no desire for full incorporation. Although this had been proposed by the Donovan Commission,[47] it was rejected by the Labour government's White Paper, *In Place of Strife*,[48] in the following terms:

> The Royal Commission recommended that trade unions should be given corporate status. The TUC has represented that this would be undesirable, as it would have no significant advantages and would not be appropriate to unions' constitutional structure. The Government accepts these arguments and does not propose to implement the Royal Commission's recommendations.[49]

Yet section 74 of the Conservative administration's Industrial Relations Act 1971 provided that a trade union registering under the Act 'shall become a body corporate'.

The second major initiative was contained in Schedule 4 which required unions registered under the Act to have rules about specified matters. This was not in itself a new policy. The 1871 Act had also created a system of registration — with the Chief Registrar of Friendly Societies. Registration carried with it minor legal advantages and was entirely voluntary.[50] However, registered (but not unregistered) unions had to have rules providing for a range of matters. These included the objects of the union; the purposes for which its funds could be used; the conditions under which any member may be entitled to benefit; the fines and forfeitures which might be imposed on members; and the manner of making, amending and rescinding rules.[51] Registration under the 1971 Act was also voluntary, but carried with it more significant benefits. Only registered unions could (i) enter into agency shop agreements or approved closed shop agreements;[52] (ii) use the recognition procedures established by the Act;[53] or (iii) compel employers to disclose information.[54] More importantly, unregistered unions could be sued in their own name and they had no immunity for unlawful acts committed in the course of a strike.[55] But despite these potential benefits, the unions generally refused to register, as part of the TUC boycott of the Act. Those unions which did register were expelled from the TUC.[56] So far as the substance of registration was concerned, much of this was uncontroversial. For example, registered unions were required to have rules which specified the powers and duties of the governing body and its officers,[57] the manner in which rules could be made, altered or revoked,[58] the way in which meetings could be convened and conducted,[59] and the manner in which the organization could be dissolved.[60] In practice, most unions would have had rules of this nature even before the Act was passed. What did prove contentious, however, was the obligation on unions to specify any body or official authorized to instruct members to take industrial action, and to specify the circumstances in which such instructions could be given. This applied to shop stewards as well as full-time officials.[61]

It was also the case that registered unions could have been required by the Registrar to amend their rules to comply with section 65 of the Act. This was the major initiative of the 1971 Act. In what was in historical context a far-reaching development — which applied to registered and unregistered unions alike .— section 65 established what was in effect a 'bill of rights' for union members. It made it unlawful for a union arbitrarily or unreasonably to exclude or expel a person from membership; it set out procedures to be complied with in cases of discipline; it established a right to resign; and it made it unlawful unreasonably to refuse to permit a member to vote, participate in union meetings, or stand for office. Infringement of the rights to membership and rights of membership were thus protected. This was merely a part of a package which sought to undermine union strength in a variety of ways, notably by rendering the closed shop illegal, and by restricting the circumstances in which unions could lawfully take industrial action. Since the TUC adopted a policy of total opposition to the Act, section 65 was rejected wholesale along with most of the Act's other provisions. Moreover, section 65 itself contained two particular provisions which were strongly resented by the trade union movement. One stipulated that it would be an unfair industrial practice for a union to discipline its members who refused to take part in strikes which were themselves either unfair industrial practices, or were not in contemplation or furtherance of an industrial dispute.[62] The unions saw this as undermining their collective strength just when they had to be most cohesive. The other rendered void any agreement which sought even to limit a member's right to have recourse to the courts.[63] This meant that rules requiring members to exhaust internal proceedings before taking their cases to the court could no longer be enforced at all. So far from showing a preference for the autonomous settlement of membership disputes through the unions' own domestic procedures, the Act positively discouraged it.

THE RETURN TO ABSTENTION

Section 65 and Schedule 4 were repealed along with the rest of the Industrial Relations Act in 1974. The Trade Union and Labour Relations Act 1974 (as amended in 1976) marked a sharp return to abstention by the state in the internal affairs of trade unions, though it is true that it did not revive section 4 of the 1871 Act. The first important feature of the new approach was to remove corporate status. For the first time all trade unions were put on a clear juridical basis which for most purposes placed them in the same position as that which had been enjoyed by unions registered under the 1871 Act. The position is covered by section 2 of the 1974 Act. The section begins by saying that a union shall not be, or be treated as if it were, a body corporate, and it also specifies that any purported registration under what is now the Companies Act 1985 will be void. However, having first asserted the unions' voluntary, unincorporated status, the section then gives them many of the powers and liabilities of incorporated bodies. For example, unions are given a power to contract, they can sue and be sued in their own name, any judgments against them can be enforced as though they are incorporated bodies, and they can beneficially own property. These statutory exceptions are exhaustive of the circumstances in which trade unions may be treated as bodies corporate, a point illustrated by *EETPU* v. *Times Newspapers Ltd.*[64] In that case the plaintiff union sought to bring an action in defamation, claiming that an article in the defendant's newspaper had damaged its reputation. But this tort depends upon the person defamed having a separate legal personality. Unions registered under the 1871 Act had been considered to fall into this category, and so in *NUGMW* v. *Gillian*[65] the Court of Appeal held that a registered union could sue in defamation to protect its reputation. But in the *EETPU* case it was held that this was no longer the position. The 1974 Act unambiguously forbids the courts to treat unions as if they were bodies corporate, and since there is no express provision specifying that they should be treated as having a separate legal personality for the purposes of torts involving wrongs done to a person, such as defamation, the judge denied that the union could in law have a separate personality to be protected. Parliament had in 1974 deprived trade unions of the necessary personality on which such an action depends.

The second important feature of TULRA was to abolish the duty to register and the external supervision of union rules. It is true, however, that the 1974 Act introduced the concept of 'listing', which is the functional equivalent of registration.[66] Section 8 provides that the Certification Officer (CO) (who inherited this work from the Chief Registrar of Friendly Societies) shall maintain a list of trade unions. The list shall include every trade union or every organization of workers which (a) was on September 30, 1971 registered as a trade union under the 1871 Act; (b) has since that date been formed by the amalgamation of a number of such organizations, each of which was registered; or (c) immediately before the commencement of TULRA was affiliated to the TUC. In addition, any body not falling into any one of these categories may apply to be included on the list. Listing is thus mandatory in the case of many trade unions. There are, however, no duties associated with listing, though there are benefits. A listed union may apply to the CO for a certificate of independence which may be important to acquire some of the benefits under the Employment Protection Act 1975 and the EPCA 1978. It is only independent trade unions which have the right to information,[67] to be consulted on redundancies,[68] and to time off for their officials and members.[69] An independent trade union is defined by TULRA as one which:

> (a) is not under the domination or control of an employer or a group of employers or of one or more employers' associations; and
> (b) is not liable to interference by an employer or any such group or association (arising out of the provision of financial or material support or by any other means whatsoever) tending towards such control.[70]

The Certification Officer has set out a number of criteria which he uses in applying the statutory definition to individual cases[71] which in turn have been approved by the EAT.[72] These include the history of the organization and, in particular, whether it was established or promoted by the employer in the recent past; its membership base, since obviously it is more likely to be vulnerable to interference if its members are limited to the employees of a particular employer; its organization and structure, and particularly the extent to which higher management can participate in its affairs; its finance, notably its source of income and the strength of its reserves; the extent to which it has to rely upon employer-provided facilities; and its collective bargaining record.

While there are no duties associated with listing, TULRA does not remove all state supervision of union affairs. By section 10 all unions, including listed and non-listed, are required to keep proper accounting records. Accounts in all but the smallest trade unions must be professionally audited,[73] and the auditors' independence and effectiveness are secured by a variety of provisions. They can be dismissed only by a resolution passed at a general meeting or meeting of delegates, regardless of what the rules say; they have an unrestricted right of access to all books and documents; and they may attend meetings and also require officers to give them information.[74] Finally, those unions which continue to operate superannuation funds must keep that fund separate and, save in very exceptional cases, have it periodically examined by a professional actuary.[75] A copy of the actuary's report must be supplied free of charge to any member who requests it. In addition, every union is under a duty to send in an annual return which must contain revenue accounts, a balance sheet, and a copy of the current rules.[76] However, there is no question of having to comply with model rules and there is no requirement to have rules of any particular kind dealing with specific matters — as there was not only under the 1971 Act, but also under the 1871 Act. The sanction for failure to comply with these provisions is a penal one, and both the union and the individual official responsible may be made liable. Information from these returns is collated and published by the Certification Officer in an annual report. This includes details of the membership of trade unions with over 100,000 members and a note of income, expenditure and assets. In 1985 the Certification Officer reported that 409 trade unions were listed and that at least 44 were not.[77] The total membership of listed organizations at the end of 1984 was 10.7m; the total income for the year was £374 million; and the total assets at the end of the year stood at £489 million.

The third important feature of TULRA was to remove the 'bill of rights' for union members. However, the Labour Government of the day was in a minority position in Parliament and could not reverse the Act quite as fully as it would have wished. As a result, certain statutory provisions which made it unlawful arbitrarily or unreasonably to exclude or expel a person from membership were retained on the statute book until 1976, when these too were repealed.[78] In their place the TUC established its own Independent Review Committee to hear complaints from persons excluded or expelled from affiliated unions where a closed shop operates.[79] This is not to deny the continued existence of statutory regulation. But the measures which were enacted, though important, were nevertheless marginal and not unacceptable to the unions. First, as we have seen, TULRA contained duties to provide information and keep accounting records, a duty which applies to all unions, not just listed ones, and a duty which requires an annual return to the Certification Officer.[80] The Act also provides that unions shall supply any person on request with a copy of its most recent annual return so there is a duty to inform not only the Certification Officer, but also members of the union and indeed members of the public who have as great a right to information as the members themselves. These measures contrast with the duty under the 1871 Act which enacted that the rules of registered unions had to provide for every person having an interest in the funds being given the right to inspect the book of accounts kept by the union, and also to scrutinize the list of members.[81] In *Norey* v. *Keep*,[82] a case subsequently approved by the Court of Appeal in *Dodd* v. *Amalgamated Marine Workers' Union*,[83] it was held that in order to render the requirement effective, the member could employ skilled agents, usually accountants, to inspect the accounts providing their employment was in good faith, that they were not personally objectionable to the union, and that they were willing to give an undertaking to communicate any information they discovered solely to their clients.

In one important respect, the present law is less rigorous than the 1871 Act. This required the rules of the union to permit any member to inspect its books at the office of the union.[84] This was much wider than TULRA which requires unions only to permit access by members and others to the annual returns.[85] This will fall far short of the information which could be obtained by investigating all the books at the office of the union. It is possible, however, that many union rules will bear the legacy of the 1871 Act and continue to include the rule required by that Act but not now by TULRA. If so, the member will have the right to inspect the books as a term of the contract of membership, a point illustrated by *Taylor* v. *NUM (Derbyshire Area) (No. 2)*,[86] one of the cases to arise out of the mining dispute. The plaintiffs applied for an order that the union permit them to inspect its books in the presence of an accountant. The rules continued to adopt the 1871 requirement, providing that any member or any person having an interest in the funds shall at all reasonable times be entitled to inspect the books. In this case, the plaintiffs were informed that they could consult the books unaccompanied by their accountant, on the grounds that inspection was a right granted only to members. As we have seen, however, in *Norey* v. *Keep*[87] it was held that the right to inspect the books was not a personal one and that a member could insist on conducting the inspection with the help of a trained agent. An attempt was made in *Taylor* to distinguish *Norey* on the grounds that the rule in that case had been inserted to comply with a statutory requirement,[88] whereas the rule of the Derbyshire union was purely contractual, with the result that it should be differently construed. Unsurprisingly perhaps, this argument was rejected, with Vinelott J holding that although the rule was formerly one required to be inserted by statute, 'it was nonetheless a rule and binding by contract', and that a rule 'such as this' should not be 'differently construed because it now rests solely upon contract and is one which is not required to be included by statute'.[89] Consequently, it was concluded that the members 'must be entitled to the assistance of a trained accountant who can interpret the books and who will notice points which will give rise to enquiry if not suspicion'.[90]

In one sense the disclosure provisions of TULRA were not intended for the benefit of trade union members. They are designed to make trade unions publicly accountable for their finances, and members benefit as a result. However, they benefit as members of the public, and not as union members. Indeed, the only significant intervention in this period which gave members (as members) rights against the union were the Sex Discrimination Act 1975[91] and the Race Relations Act 1976.[92] Section 12 of the 1975 Act renders unlawful discrimination on grounds of sex both in relation to the right to membership, covering admissions and expulsions, and the rights of membership.[93] The former includes the terms on which the union is prepared to admit a woman into membership, as well as a simple discriminatory refusal to admit. The latter makes it unlawful for the union to discriminate in the way in which it affords a woman access to the benefits, facilities or services of membership, and this includes refusing or deliberately omitting to afford her such access. Consequently the refusal or failure to take up the grievances of a female member, or a group of female members, because of their sex, would be unlawful. The 1976 Act, section 11, makes similar provision for discrimination on grounds of race, which means discrimination on the grounds of colour, race, nationality or ethnic or national origins.[94] Discrimination under both Acts may be direct or indirect. The former applies under the 1975 Act where a woman is treated less favourably than a man simply because of her sex (and vice versa).[95] Under the 1976 Act it applies where a black person is treated less favourably than a white person simply because of race.[96] The effect of the 1975 Act was that the few relatively small single-sex unions which were formerly to be found in the teaching profession had to merge.[97] They could not continue to recruit male or female members only without contravening the Act.[98]

Similarly, the few unions which had separate categories of membership for men and women had to restructure to combine them.

Indirect discrimination arises where the union applies a requirement or condition before membership or one of the benefits of membership can be obtained; the condition is one which applies or would apply equally to men, but the proportion of women who can comply with it is considerably smaller than the proportion of men; and the union cannot show that the condition is justifiable irrespective of sex. Where this operates to the detriment of a particular woman, because she cannot comply with it, she will be able to complain that she has been the subject of unlawful discrimination.[99] The matter was considered in *Steel* v. *UPW*,[100] the only reported EAT decision involving a claim of sex discrimination against a union. The complainant, a postwoman, alleged unlawful discrimination against both the union and her employer, the Post Office. Until the Sex Discrimination Act 1975, women did not have the status of 'permanent full-time' workers in the Post Office, even if they in fact worked permanently and full-time, as Mrs Steel had done since 1961. Seniority among employees was determined in accordance with the number of years a person was employed as a permanent full-timer. From 1975 the rule denying women this permanent full-time status was rescinded, but women could calculate their seniority as from that date. One of the benefits of seniority was that the choice of postal rounds or 'walks' was on that basis. Mrs Steel applied for a vacant walk but it was given to a man who had been employed since 1973 on the grounds that he had two years more seniority. She alleged indirect unlawful discrimination against the employer, and claimed that the union had also discriminated against her by agreeing to these rules. The EAT upheld her claim against the employer, even though the discrimination stemmed from the continuing effects of past discrimination, which was not unlawful when it was operated, but it rejected the claim against the union. Nevertheless, it accepted that the union could in principle be liable, either on the basis of section 12 or, indeed, under section 42, which makes it an offence to knowingly aid another to do an act made unlawful under the 1975 Act; but on the facts, liability was held not to exist under either section.

CONCLUSION

From this brief historical outline of the legal control exercised over the unions' internal affairs, five historical periods can usefully be distinguished. First, there was what may be termed the 'complete autonomy' model, when union autonomy reigned supreme and the policy adopted was to let the unions govern themselves. This was followed by a phase of increasing intervention, the policy shifting from one of complete autonomy for the unions to one of 'constitutional autonomy' or autonomy within their constitutions. This remains the basis of common law regulation. Here the courts will intervene to the extent that they will oblige the union to act according to its rules and will readily frustrate union policies even if supported by a majority, as in the *Yorkshire Miners'* case,[101] if the constitution has not been scrupulously followed. Thirdly, with the Industrial Relations Act came a temporary period of detailed external regulation and a rejection of the notion of the sanctity of rules. Standards of conduct were imposed on the union from without. Inevitably this phase required Parliamentary intervention since, as we shall see, the common law powers permitting the judges to regulate the union constitution itself are very limited (though not insignificant). Fourthly, with TULRA (as amended) came the forceful reinstatement of legal abstention in trade union internal affairs. This, however, has also proved to be temporary only. For the fifth and final development has seen the re-emergence of detailed external regulation. This has been done by the Employment Act 1980 and the Trade Union Act 1984.[102] Essentially there are two aspects to this new policy. The first is legal regulation of the unions' right to control membership and the second is direct statutory intervention in the way in which trade unions are governed. Together these represent intervention on a scale quite unprecedented in Britain, though there are parallels in other jurisdictions. In Chapters 3 and 6 we consider the first strategy, and in Chapter 5 the second. But first we consider the contract of membership which is the basis of jurisdiction and control in those areas of trade union government where legislation does not yet intrude.

NOTES

1. This section draws heavily on Musson, *British Trade Unions 1800–1875* (1976); Pelling, *A History of British Trade Unionism* (3rd edn., 1976); and S. and B. Webb, *The History of British Trade Unionism 1666–1920* (1919).

2. 39 & 40 Geo. 3, c. 106, s. 1.

3. *Op. cit.*, p. 72.

4. Combination Act 1825 (6 Geo. 4, c. 129), s. 3.

5. See *Walsby* v. *Anley* (1861) 3 E & E 516; *Skinner* v. *Kitch* (1867) LR 2 QB 393; *R.* v. *Druitt* (1867) 10 Cox CC 592.

6. County Courts Act 1846 (9 & 10 Vict., c. 95).

7. Mortimer, *History of the Boilermakers' Society*, Vol 1, 1834–1906 (1973), pp. 23–4.

8. (1855) 6 El. & Bl. 47.

9. *Ibid.*, at p. 76.

10. Friendly Societies Act 1855 (18 & 19 Vict., c. 63), s. 44.

11. See S. and B. Webb, *op. cit.*, pp. 261–2.

12. (1867) LR 2 QB 153.

13. Trades Unions Funds Protection Act 1869 (32 & 33 Vict., c. 61).

14. On the Royal Commission, see S. and B. Webb, *op. cit.*, pp. 264–74.

15. Eleventh and Final Report of the Royal Commission appointed to Inquire into the Organisation and Rules of Trade Unions and Other Associations. Parliamentary Papers. 1868-9, vol. xxxi.

16. *Ibid.*, p. xxiv.

17. For an account of the work of the Minority, see McCready, 'British Labour and the Royal Commission on Trade Unions 1867–1869' (1955), 24 *Univ. of Toronto Q.*, 390.

18. Eleventh and Final Report of the Royal Commission, etc., *op. cit.*, p. 1x.

19. 204 Parl. Debs. (3rd series) 266–7 (February 14, 1871).

20. *Op. cit.*, p. 1ix.

21. *Osborne* v. *Amalgamated Society of Railway Servants* [1911] 1 Ch. 540.

22. See Citrine, pp. 49–50.

23. See e.g. *Russell* v. *Amalgamated Society of Carpenters and Joiners* [1910] 1 KB 506 (CA); [1912] AC 421, *Miller* v. *Amalgamated Engineering Union* [1938] Ch. 669.

24. See *Miller* v. *Amalgamated Engineering Union*, *op. cit.*

25. (1880) 49 LJ Ch. 802.

26. *Ibid.*, at p. 804.

27. (1882) 21 Ch. D. 194.

28. [1905] AC 256.

29. *Ibid.*, at p. 266.

30. See *Rigby* v. *Connel* (1880) 4 Ch. D. 482; *Chamberlain's Wharf* v. *Smith* [1900] 2 Ch. 605; and *Osborne* v. *Amalgamated Society of Railway Servants* [1911] 1 Ch. 540.

31. [1922] 2 AC 440.

32. *Ibid.*, at p. 469.

33. *Ibid.*, at p. 448.

34. *Ibid.*, at p. 451.

35. *Op. cit.*, at p. 266.

36. 1966 SLT 74. But compare *Briggs* v. *NUM* 1969 SLT 165 and *Bernard* v. *NUM* 1971 SLT 177.

37. *Buckley* v. *NUGMW* [1967] 3 All ER 767.

38. 1971 Act, Schedule 9.

39. Royal Commission on Trade Unions and Employers' Associations 1965–1968. *Report.* Cmnd. 3623, para. 815.

40. 1871 Act, s. 14.

41. Trade Union (Amalgamation) Act 1917; Societies (Miscellaneous Provisions) Act 1940; Trade Union (Amalgamations, etc.) Act 1964.

42. Trade Union Act 1913.

43. *Taff Vale Railway Co.* v. *Amalgamated Society of Railway Servants* [1901] AC 426.

44. [1956] AC 104.

45. *Ibid.*, at pp. 128–31 and 120–8.

46. *Ibid.*, at p. 131.

47. Royal Commission on Trade Unions and Employers' Associations's 1965–1968. *Report.* Cmnd..3623, para. 792.

48. Cmnd. 3888 (1969).

49. *Ibid.*, para. 111.

50. On which, see Grunfeld, pp. 47–8.

51. 1871 Act, s. 14 and Schedule 1.

52. 1971 Act, s. 11.

53. 1971 Act, s. 45.

54. 1971 Act, s. 56.

55. 1971 Act, s. 154.

56. See Weekes, Mellish, Dickens and Lloyd, *Industrial Relations and the Limits of Law* (1975) for a discussion of the Act.

57. 1971 Act, Schedule 4(7).

58. 1971 Act, Schedule 4(9).
59. 1971 Act, Schedule 4(8).
60. 1971 Act, Schedule 4(13).
61. 1971 Act, Schedule 4(10).
62. 1971 Act, s. 65(7).
63. 1971 Act, s. 65(10).
64. [1980] QB 585.
65. [1946] KB 81.
66. TULRA 1974, s. 8.
67. 1975 Act, s. 17.
68. 1975 Act, s. 99.
69. 1978 Act, ss. 27, 28.
70. TULRA 1974, s. 30.
71. Certification Officer. Annual Report for 1976 (1977), paras. 2-16-2-25.
72. *Blue Circle Staff Association* v. *CO* [1977] ICR 224.
73. TULRA 1974, s. 11.
74. TULRA 1974, Schedule 2 (Part 1).
75. TULRA 1974, Schedule 2 (Part 2).
76. TULRA 1974, Schedule 2(2).
77. Certification Officer. Annual Report for 1985 (1986).
78. TULRA 1974, s. 5 repealed by TULR(Am)A 1976, s. 1(a).
79. TUC Annual Report 1976, p. 94.
80. TULRA 1974, s. 11(4).
81. 1871 Act, s. 14 and Schedule 1(6).
82. [1909] 1 Ch. 561.
83. [1924] 1 Ch. 116.
84. 1871 Act, s. 14.
85. TULRA 1974, s. 11(4).
86. [1985] IRLR 65.
87. *Op. cit.*
88. 1871 Act, s. 14.
89. [1985] IRLR 65 at p. 66.
90. *Ibid.*
91. 1975 Act, s. 12. But see s. 49 which allows unions to reserve seats on elective bodies for members of one sex only.
92. 1976 Act, s. 11.
93. For the meaning of discrimination on grounds of sex, see 1976 Act, s. 1.
94. 1976 Act, ss. 1 and 3.
95. 1975 Act, s. 1(1)(a).
96. 1976 Act, s. 1(1)(a).
97. The obvious example being NAS/UWT.
98. See further, Creighton, *Working Women and the Law* (1979), pp. 192-4.
99. 1975 Act, s. 1(1)(b), 1976 Act, s. 1(1)(b).
100. [1978] ICR 181. See also *FTAT* v. *Modgill* [1980] IRLR 142
101. *Yorkshire Miners' Association* v. *Howden* [1905] AC 256.
102. Employment Act 1980, ss. 4, 5; Trade Union Act 1984, ss. 10, 11 respectively.

2

The Contract of Membership

FROM PROPERTY TO CONTRACT

At common law the jurisdiction of the courts to intervene in trade union affairs will now almost invariably be based on contract. This was not always the case, however. For a long time the theory was that English courts could exercise jurisdiction to protect members' interests only where their property rights were at stake. This was not to deny the existence of a contract,[1] and indeed the wrongful interference with property rights generally took the form of a breach of contract.[2] But unless the action before the court was brought to protect a proprietary interest, the court would not intervene. This stress on property rights as the basis of jurisdiction arose from the judgment of Lord Jessel MR in *Rigby* v. *Connol*.[3] The plaintiff had asked for a declaration and an injunction to prevent the union from expelling him from membership in breach of its rules. A closed shop operated, so expulsion led to the plaintiff losing his job. Unfortunately, his statement of claim omitted to mention that he had any proprietary interest in the union. The Master of the Rolls, while dismissing the case on other grounds,[4] expressed the opinion that this lack of any proprietary interest precluded the court from exercising any jurisdiction at all:

> I have no doubt whatever that the foundation of the jurisdiction is the right of property vested in the member of the society, and of which he is unjustly deprived by such unlawful expulsion. There is no such jurisdiction that I am aware of . . . to decide upon the rights of persons to associate together when the association possesses no property.[5]

This judgment has been criticized on two counts. First, while there was some authority for the view that equitable remedies could only be granted to protect proprietary interests,[6] there was ample opportunity for his Lordship to have developed the principles of equitable jurisdiction so as to break free from the limitations of property,[7] and to provide protection for the substantial interests of the plaintiff in this case.[8] Second, even accepting that property is a prerequisite of an equitable remedy, this need not, as the Master of the Rolls intimated, have precluded the courts from granting a declaration: by this time the remedy seems to have lost its equitable origins.[9] Ultimately, however, this emphasis on property proved no real barrier in practice to the courts exercising jurisdiction,[10] partly because the property requirement was occasionally ignored by the courts,[11] but principally because they developed a very wide and flexible concept of a proprietary right so as to include such matters as the right to vote,[12] or the member's right to share the funds in any possible dissolution[13] — accurately described as 'the least significant of his interests in union membership'.[14] Nevertheless, such proprietary fictions were undesirable in principle. The real interest of the members was often to maintain their membership, or perhaps to protect their reputations, or their jobs. Yet it was necessary to stress an insignificant and extremely tenuous property right in order to persuade the courts to intervene.[15]

The Move towards Contract

Although the germ of the contract basis of jurisdiction appeared early this century, it was not until the Court of Appeal decision in *Lee* v. *Showmen's Guild of Great Britain*[16] that the courts finally retraced their steps from the false trail laid by Lord Jessel MR, and established jurisdiction firmly on contract. Denning LJ led the way:

> the power of this court to intervene is founded on its jurisdiction to protect rights of contract. If a member is expelled by a committee in breach of contract, this court will grant a declaration that their action is *ultra vires*. It will also grant an injunction to prevent his expulsion if that is necessary to protect a proprietary right of his; or to protect him in his right to earn a livelihood . . . but it will not grant an injunction to give a member the right to enter a social club, unless there are proprietary rights attached to it, because it is too personal to be specifically enforced . . . That is, I think, the only relevance of rights of property in this connexion. It goes to the form of remedy, not to the right.[17]

This was a welcome and overdue recognition of the contractual nexus, but as this judgment indicated it did not altogether do away with the necessity of establishing a fictional proprietary interest. The court re-asserted the traditional proprietary basis of the equitable remedy, thereby indicating that an injunction would still not be granted to protect reputation or a right to membership *per se*.

In practice, however, this has not affected the courts' power to grant equitable relief. This is partly because the judges have adopted a very liberal view of what constitutes a property right; partly because, as the extract from Lord Denning's judgment indicates, they have recognized that the 'right to work' deserves protection by way of an injunction, thereby ensuring that in a closed shop situation membership will be protected without the need to discover an artificial property right;[18] and also because in some cases the courts seem simply to have ignored the question of whether or not a proprietary interest was involved. In both *Leigh* v. *NUR*[19] and *Watson* v. *Smith*[20] injunctions were granted to prevent an election for office being held without the plaintiff's nomination going forward, yet in neither case did the court consider either whether the right to nomination was a property right or whether the plaintiff had any potential proprietary interest at stake arising from the office. There are also signs that the courts might explicitly recognize that injunctions can be issued to protect contractual rights alone, even in the absence of any proprietary interest. In *Hodgson* v. *NALGO*[21] the plaintiff was granted an injunction to prevent union delegates at a TUC conference voting contrary to a resolution of the union's own conference, even though the judge specifically stated that nothing in the nature of a proprietary right was involved. So the old property basis of the injunction is being severely shaken,[22] and this is not limited to the trade union context. The result is that although the absence of a proprietary right will no doubt always be a relevant factor for a judge to consider before granting an injunction, it is unlikely now to provide a complete bar to that remedy. This is particularly important in the trade union sphere since in some circumstances, including those occurring in *Hodgson* v. *NALGO* itself, damages will be a wholly inadequate remedy.

The Nature of the Contract of Membership

Contract is more satisfactory than property as the basis of jurisdiction because it provides a wider and more realistic basis for intervention. But it is still sometimes little more than a fiction providing the conceptual tool which the judges use to exercise some control over the legal relationship between the union and its members. In common with a great variety of modern contracts, the contract of membership does not reflect the traditional contractual ideology. The individual may have little option whether or not to enter into the contract and, of course, there will be no bargaining over its terms. The member enters into what Selznick has described as a contract of adherence,[23] which involves a continuing relationship of terms dictated by the union and by which the members are bound whether they approve of them or not. Indeed, the member will often have no knowledge of the terms at all. Many unions do in fact require their members to be supplied with a rule book on joining the union, and there is a statutory obligation on unions to provide a copy of the rules, either free or at a reasonable charge, to any person (whether a member or not) who requests it.[24] However, in practice a proportion of the members will not receive a rule book at all.

Despite this obvious imbalance in the bargaining power of the parties to the contract of membership, it should be emphasized that the rule-making processes which unions adopt ensure that the contract of membership is far closer to the classic contract model of free and equal bargaining parties than is the case in most standard form contracts. It is misleading to treat the contract of membership as in any sense analogous to the standard form contracts imposed upon consumers for example, despite Lord Denning's attempts to draw the comparison. It is true, as Lord Denning pointed out in *Cheall* v. *APEX*,[25] that in one sense the union membership contract is even more a fiction than the standard form consumer contract since the member may not have the option whether or not to sign the contract in circumstances where a closed shop operates. But in a more fundamental way it is very different from some contracts. Union rules do not lay down oppressive standards inflicted upon members by powerful and self-interested union officials. They are made by the members themselves, either directly or through their elected representatives. Details vary from union to union, but generally the power to amend the rules rests with the delegates at the national conference or some specially convened conference, and these delegates tend to be elected either directly by the members or indirectly through the branches. Almost invariably a majority greater than a simple one is necessary to effect a valid rule change. If any power of amendment is reserved to the union executive or its equivalent — and this is very exceptional — it will be limited to certain matters only, such as altering the benefit rates.

This is not to deny that the executive, and particularly the full-time officers, wield a significant influence on the rule-making decisions.[26] In practically all unions they have a right to recommend rule changes, a right which will not for practical reasons extend to the ordinary member (though it will generally be exercisable by union branches and other bodies within the union); and they will usually exert sufficient influence to persuade the delegates to accept their recommendations.[27] Occasionally, union rules reinforce this dominant role by giving the executive

committee the sole right to initiate recommendations for rule amendments, and denying that right to other bodies within the union. However,
this is wholly exceptional and usually either the members collectively, or
their representatives, have an opportunity both to recommend rule
changes and to vote upon them. This ensures that whatever the views of
the union officers (and it should be remembered that their collective
views are themselves the product of a compromise between the opinions
of individuals) the rules passed must receive a reasonable level of acceptance among the membership. Those imposing the terms are also bound
by them, a feature which is absent from standard form consumer contracts. It is this participatory rule-making process that prevents the
concept of a *contract* of membership from being a wholly artificial legal
fiction; it also provides a powerful reason why the courts should tread
warily before they attempt to exercise control over the substance of the
rules.

Contract and the Scope for Judicial Control

Regulating internal union affairs on the basis of contract has two particular implications of considerable importance. First, the contract can
be enforced only by the parties. The jurisdiction of the courts is limited
to granting relief to those who assert rights under the contract. This is a
trite observation, but one of fundamental importance. It asserts the
principle of union autonomy in a rather different sense, for it means that
while contract remains a basis of jurisdiction, no outsiders have any legal
interest in the operation of union internal affairs. In particular, it is not
open to any employer to object to a call for industrial action, or the
payment of strike pay, on the ground that it is not permitted by the
union rules. So an acceptance of contract as the basis of jurisdiction
imposes limitations on the opportunities of both judges and other third
parties to try to control the unions' domestic affairs. It does not, however, prevent the use of what Kahn-Freund termed the 'Trojan Horse',
whereby employers or other third-party pressure groups encourage and
perhaps finance individual union members who are in fact sympathetic
to their interests to challenge decisions or actions taken by a union.

Secondly, because the sanctity of contract requires that the terms of
the contract agreed to by the parties should be enforced, the adoption of
a contractual model of control involves the acceptance of the right of the
union autonomously to determine its own rules. Contract sets the contours of judicial control so that any intervention must be capable of
justification in terms of contract principles and doctrines. However, this
is not to deny an active role for the courts in this area. Although acceptance

of contract as the basis of jurisdiction is in theory an assertion of union autonomy, the courts have in practice adeptly fashioned the principles of contract so as to weaken that autonomy and to give themselves a considerable role to play in regulating internal union affairs. Three doctrines in particular have been used to open up the paths of control. First, the courts have claimed the right to interpret the terms of the contract,[28] even where the union constitution purports to leave matters involving construction of the rules exclusively to a union committee. Secondly, the courts have the power to add terms to the contract of membership under the guise of implied terms. This is discussed further below. Finally, the courts have managed to a limited extent to strike out union rules on the grounds that they are contrary to public policy. In this way they are able to exercise control over the substance of the rules themselves. The precise scope for intervention here is uncertain because the law is now very much in a state of flux. We shall return to this very important problem below.

On the question of power over the rules through interpretation, the courts have been ambivalent about the approach which they should adopt to construction of the rules. It is true that in *Heatons' Transport (St Helens) Ltd* v. *TGWU*[29] Lord Wilberforce, delivering a single speech for all of their Lordships, commented: 'Trade union rule books are not drafted by parliamentary draftsmen. Courts of law must resist the temptation to construe them as if they were; for that is not how they would be understood by the members who are the parties to the agreement.'[30] In a similar vein, Lord Denning has said that courts should construe union rules 'reasonably, fairly, broadly and liberally in the interests of all concerned in the association',[31] though admittedly this formulation gives less emphasis to the members' understanding of the rules than does Lord Wilberforce's approach. Even so, it is a recognition that, to use Roskill LJ's words in the same case, '[t]he rules . . . ought not . . . to be too legalistically construed'.[32] But the statements of principle do not accurately reflect what actually happens in practice. The most striking feature of rule interpretation is that the courts will construe the rules very strictly and will construe any ambiguity in favour of the member. A more accurate statement of what happens in fact is provided by Viscount Dilhorne in *British Actors' Equity Association* v. *Goring*[33] where he said, in a speech with which Lords Pearson, Salmon and Scarman concurred:

> I do not think that, because they are the rules of a union, different canons of construction should be applied to them than are applied to any written documents. Our task is to construe them so as to give them a reasonable interpretation which accords with what in our opinion must have been intended.[34]

THE TERMS OF THE CONTRACT

Express Terms

The primary source of the terms of the contract of membership is the union rule book. This constitutes the express terms of the contract. The rule book fulfils the role of a constitution, outlining the powers and composition of the various organs within the union; a bill of rights, detailing the rights of individual union members; a statement of the duties of such members; a trust document, indicating the lawful purposes on which union funds can be expended; and, more generally, a guide to the army of full-time and voluntary officers, revealing to them their powers and duties and the manner in which they should be exercised. The range and detail of the rule book varies enormously as between different unions. Some smaller organizations have a rule book comprising no more than a few dozen pages, whereas the AEU has over one hundred pages of detailed rule provisions. The content of the rules will of course reflect the policies and aspirations of the organization. They will bear the stamp of its particular character in various ways. For example, 'closed' unions (such as the print unions) which seek to restrict entry into membership will tend to have more stringent eligibility requirements and a more centralized control over admissions than the larger 'open' unions (such as the TGWU) which draw their strength from membership size, and will tend to adopt a decentralized procedure to facilitate membership growth. Again, some union rules will reflect aspects of that union's history. The ban on Communists holding office in the EETPU, a rule which was introduced following the election scandal in that union when certain Communist leaders rigged the ballots for important union posts, is an obvious example of such a provision.

The content, and more especially the structure, of rule books has also been subject to certain legal influences. For over a hundred years following the Trade Union Act 1871, registered trade unions were obliged to have rules about certain matters, the most important of which were the objects of the union, the purposes for which its funds could be used, the conditions under which members could claim benefits or be subject to fines or forfeitures, the methods of making, altering and rescinding rules, and the periodical audit of accounts.[35] However, as pointed out in Chapter 1, this law did not specify what the substance of these rules should be, so that union autonomy was not compromised by this requirement. The Industrial Relations Act 1971 followed the pattern of the 1871 Act in this respect, but it significantly extended the range of matters to be covered. In particular, it required the development of procedures for handling grievances and for allowing appeals from decisions relating to admissions and discipline.[36] More contentiously, it required the union to indicate the powers and duties of their shop stewards.[37] This was interpreted as an unwarranted interference into their domestic arrangements by some unions, and at least one deregistered largely because it felt that these requirements would force it to be too authoritarian.[38] Since most unions did not register under the 1971 Act, these provisions were of limited influence. When the Act was finally repealed, this indirect regulation over union rules was lost too, and not even the modest requirements of the 1871 Act have been retained. However, since virtually all the large unions were registered under the 1871 Act, their rule books have in practice continued to have explicit rules about the matters which were specified in that Act.

A more direct control over the substance of the rules themselves is exercised in relation to those unions adopting political objects. Under the Trade Union Act 1913, section 3, it is mandatory for such unions to ballot their members for authority to establish a political fund. The ballot must be conducted in accordance with rules to be approved by the Certification Officer, and under the Trade Union Act 1984, section 12, must be repeated at ten-yearly intervals. If the members approve the adoption or continuation of political objects, the union must then adopt or continue to operate political fund rules. These must provide that political objects (as defined) must be financed from a separate political fund. The rules must also provide that members have the right not to contribute to the fund and that they may not be discriminated against by reason of their exemption. Provided the statutory requirements are met, the unions may construct their own rules, though in practice most unions have adopted the model rules which were originally drafted by the Chief Registrar of Friendly Societies and have now been reformulated by the Certification Officer, and they incorporate these into their rule books. Similarly, unions will frequently include in their rules stipulations required by the Trade Union (Amalgamations, etc.) Act 1964 relating to mergers, though here there is strictly no statutory obligation for unions to furnish rules on amalgamations at all.

Implied Terms

While the written rules — the express terms of the contract — are the most important source of the membership terms, they do not constitute the sole terms of the contract. They will also be supplemented by implied terms and those derived from custom and practice.[39] Indeed, since there is no obligation for a union to have a written constitution at all, the whole contract could in theory be implied. However, in general, and in marked contrast to the contract of employment, implied terms have played a relatively small part in moulding the contract of membership. The striking feature about the judicial attitude to implying terms in the membership contract is that the judges will hardly ever imply terms which will extend the duties of the members as against the union. In *Spring* v. *NASDS*[40] the court declined to imply a power of expulsion to give effect to a TUC Disputes Committee award: the officious bystander would not testily suppress such a term, but would ask 'what's that'? In *Leigh* v. *NUR*[41] Goff, J declined to imply a term that candidates for office should be members of the Labour Party when the rules required the holder of the office to be a party member. This term was not necessary to give business efficacy to the contract because the candidate could obtain membership before taking up the position. A third example is *Radford* v. *NATSOPA*[42] where the plaintiff refused to comply with union policy relating to redundancies and was expelled from the union. One of the defences raised by the union in the subsequent action for unlawful expulsion was that it was an implied term of the plaintiff's contract that he would be just and faithful in his dealings with the union and his fellow members, and would comply with all reasonable and proper directions from the union as to his dealings with employers. Plowman, J rejected this. The rule book had specifically enumerated the circumstances in which a member could be expelled from the union, and his Lordship considered these to be exhaustive. There was no room for any additional implied term that the member should obey union policies.

This strict adherence to the rule book does not apply only where the union is seeking to assert power over the member. It is true that the courts have implied the rules of natural justice and the duty to act fairly into the contract of membership. Clearly these are important limitations on the powers conferred by the rules. However, as far as the terms are concerned, a recent case at the time of writing shows that the courts may be equally reluctant to imply terms to the advantage of the member. The plaintiff in *Liptrott* v. *NUM (Nottingham Area)*[43] was concerned about members of the defendant union who had participated in the miners' strike and had paid no union dues for a period of more than three months. In his view, such people ceased to be financial members in accordance with the rules and as such were ineligible to receive benefits and disqualified from standing for office. Liptrott initially sought a declaration that the strikers were disqualified from office, but later dropped this claim and sought a declaration that the unions were entitled to charge a re-admission fee from the members in question. Three striking miners counterclaimed for a declaration that although they were on strike and had paid no contributions for more than three months, they were at all times full financial members and so the question of re-admission did not arise. One of the arguments for the counterclaim was that the rule book, as a matter of commonsense, and in order to give business efficacy to the contract, must contain an implied term whereby those on strike were exempt from paying contributions. This was reinforced by the fact that under the rules striking members were entitled to benefit of 30p a week whereas weekly dues were £1.18. This led to the argument that as a matter of commonsense the rules cannot contemplate the cross-payment of both amounts contemporaneously. But although the counterclaim succeeded on other grounds, the implied term was rejected. Nolan J pointed to the express exemption from contributions for members who were sick, and the absence in the rules of any corresponding provision for strikers. He also held that the defendants had difficulty in defining an appropriate term, it being unclear whether the term proposed would cover all strikes or only those called by the union, and whether it would cover unlawful strikes. The court was prepared to decide against the defendant even though it would lead to the absurd result whereby the whole union would be destroyed by a strike lasting more than three months in the course of which the members paid no contributions.

Custom and Practice

In the everyday government of trade unions, the formal processes which are reflected in the union rules are often bypassed, and an informal system of government based upon custom and practice emerges. Legal recognition of this fact has been given by the House of Lords itself in the celebrated *Heatons' Transport* case when their Lordships approved the following section of the TUC Handbook on the Industrial Relations Act:

> Trade union government does not however rely solely on what is written down in the rule book. It also depends upon custom and practice, by procedures which have developed over the years and which, although well understood by those who operate them, are not formally set out in the rules. Custom and practice may operate either by modifying a union's rules as they operate in practice, or by compensating for the absence of formal rules. Furthermore, the procedures which custom and practice lay down very often vary from workplace to workplace within the same industry, and even within different branches of the same union.[44]

It is ironic that custom and practice should have been so fully accepted in this case, which resulted in the union being liable for industrial action taken by their shop stewards, when it has in fact been virtually ignored by the courts in the context of internal union disputes. As a result, the gap between the practical operation of the constitution and the way it works in theory, as reflected in the formal constitution, is effectively disregarded by the courts. This emphasis on the dead letter of the union rules rather than the living law of its practices is likely to give union members the impression that, at least in the sphere of internal union affairs, the operation of the law is both arbitrary and artificial, upholding formal rights but ignoring legitimate expectations.

There seems to have been no recognition that custom might modify the union rules. The judgment of Danckwerts J in *Kimberley* v. *Showmen's Guild of Great Britain*[45] is revealing. In that case the plaintiff successfully contended that a purported amendment of the union rules excluding him from membership was invalid. During the course of his judgment, his Lordship said:

> It seems to me that the rules of the Society were not observed, and if the rules of the Society were not observed it is quite idle, it seems to me, to contend that the matter is cured by the fact that for some time past the practice of the Society has been to ignore the provisions of its own rules and deal with the matter in some other way.[46]

It is contract doctrine itself that severely limits the scope for incorporating terms into the contract through custom and practice. In particular, no custom can be implied into the contract if it is contrary to an express or necessarily implied term.[47] In practice, however, it is extremely difficult to distinguish between 'customs which add to and customs which contradict' the terms of a contract.[48] However, it is clear, at least in the union context, that the courts have been reluctant to treat union practices as a modification of the rules. As *Kimberley's* case itself demonstrates, even a continual and longstanding union practice is likely to be construed as inconsistent with the written terms, so that adherence to that practice involves a breach of the agreement. This is further illustrated by *Edwards* v. *Halliwell*.[49] The union subscription rate was raised by a delegate meeting as had been the practice for several years, though the rules required a two-thirds majority in a ballot of all the members. The plaintiffs, who were union members, successfully claimed that this was a breach of their contract. The Court of Appeal held that the defect could not be cured by the acquiescence of the vast majority of the members to the informal procedures, despite their being well established.

Even where a practice is not inconsistent with other terms of the contract, it is still difficult to establish that it creates a contractually binding obligation. In *Weakley* v. *AUEW*[50] for example, the union claimed that the chairman of its executive committee had the power to exercise a casting vote in circumstances where the committee was evenly divided, and it referred to three previous occasions where this had been done. However, these incidents spanned a period of forty years and the court was not willing to hold that this power had been legally established in these circumstances. But although the courts seem reluctant to accept custom and practice as an independent source of legal obligation, they may be more willing to give it greater significance in the context of rule interpretation. Where a rule is ambiguous, it is obviously desirable that it should be construed in the light of the union's own perception of its meaning. Such an approach was in fact followed in *Brown* v. *AUEW*[51] though this is the only example of the practice having been adopted, so perhaps too much should not be made of the case. In that case there was a complex wrangle over the issue of which of two candidates had properly been elected to the post of union divisional organizer. One of the many issues arising out of that case was whether the union's final appeal body had power to hear appeals on administrative as opposed to disciplinary matters. Walton J held that it had. Although the union rules were not clear on this point, the practice for many years had been for the appeal court to include both administrative and disciplinary matters within its jurisdiction, and so the rule was accordingly construed in this way:

> . . . where you have a . . . rule . . . which is amply wide enough on its face to permit the bringing of the kind of appeal which is here in question, and you find that as a matter of practice over many years, whatever actual advice the union may have received along the way, such kinds of appeals have consistently been brought, then it seems to me that the court is fully justified in reading the rule as comprehending that kind of appeal. Per contra, in another union with precisely the same rule, it might be established as a matter of fact that such types of appeal had never been entertained; and this fact would then be at least the beginning of a tenable argument that precisely the same wording should be read in precisely the opposite sense quoad this kind of appeal.[52]

JUDICIAL CONTROL OF THE TERMS

So far the discussion has examined the way in which the contract of membership is constituted and interpreted and, as we have seen, the judges can be influential in these areas. However, perhaps the most controversial issue in the relationship between the judiciary and the unions, at least so far as internal affairs are concerned, is the question of how far the judges should be able to exercise control over the substance of the rules themselves. As long as the legal relationship between the union and its members is conceived in contractual terms, opportunities for control are, at least in theory, narrowly circumscribed. As has been mentioned, the rationale of contract is that the parties will make their own terms and the function of the law is essentially to enforce the agreement which they choose to make, subject only to the restrictions imposed by public policy. Therefore, it is not surprising to find that the courts have occasionally tried to shift the basis of jurisdiction from contract to some wider principle which will enlarge their control over the rules.

The first major attempt was in the *Osborne* case where the House of Lords equated trade unions registered under the Trade Union Acts 1871–6 with statutory corporations and held that such unions could only promote the objects referred to in the statutory definition.[53] This applied to the regulation of relations between masters and men and the imposition of restrictive conditions on the conduct of any trade or business.[54] The immediate effect of this decision was to disable unions from imposing a levy for the purpose of supporting the Labour Party. The damage was repaired, however, by the Trade Union Act 1913 which provided by section 1 that: 'The fact that a combination has under its constitution objects or powers other than statutory objects . . . shall not prevent the combination being a trade union . . .' As is well known, the 1913 Act did not reverse *Osborne* completely. While removing any general statutory *ultra vires* impediment, the Act also imposed restrictions on the freedom to raise money for political objects. Unions are required to ballot their members before promoting political objects, and individual members have the right not to contribute towards the financing of such activity. But despite this restriction, the Act was of great importance. If the statutory *ultra vires* impediment had not been removed, it would have given the judges very wide powers to strike out any rules inconsistent with the statutory objects. The matter is now dealt with in TULRA section 28 by the use of a definition of a trade union which makes it clear that equivalent of the statutory objects are merely inclusive rather than exhaustive. In other words, an organization is a trade union if its principal purposes include the statutory objects, regardless of whether it exists also to promote other objects.

A second attempt to widen the basis of judicial control has been made by Lord Denning. He has asserted on a number of occasions that union rules are less a contract than a 'legislative code', and that they should be treated analogously to by-laws.[55] In *Bonsor* v. *Musicians' Union* he followed this to its logical conclusion and argued that the courts should apply the principle enunciated in *Kruse* v. *Johnson*[56] to union rules just as they do to by-laws. This would have enabled the courts to strike out as *ultra vires* any rules they considered unreasonable in the sense that they could 'find no justification in the minds of reasonable men'.[57] Although later in *British Actors' Equity Association* v. *Goring* he rejected this analysis,[58] Lord Denning re-adopted it in *Cheall* v. *APEX*,[59] saying that union rules are 'only binding so far as they are reasonable and certain'. However, the House of Lords in *Faramus* v. *Film Artistes' Association*[60] has unequivocally rejected such a novel approach. The argument founders on its premise. As their Lordships pointed out, the concept of *ultra vires* is only applicable to bodies making by-laws because it is Parliament which confers law-making powers on such bodies and it can readily be assumed that Parliament never intended to give them authority to make rules which are unreasonable, at least in the sense in which that term is used in *Kruse* v. *Johnson*. But unions are voluntary bodies; the source of their rules is a voluntary agreement and not the authority of Parliament at all; so there is no room for any such assumption in their case. There may indeed be an implied term in the contract of membership prohibiting rule *amendments* which are fundamentally inconsistent with the original constitution. But no such term could operate to invalidate any rules which formed the basis of the original agreement itself. Courts simply cannot strike out contract terms because they think them unreasonable, for this would be in effect to rewrite the contract. The *Faramus* case merely confirmed that this principle applies as much to union rules as to other forms of contract. And despite Lord Denning's continuing crusade to reverse *Faramus*, the principle there enunciated has both logic and authority to sustain it.

The *Faramus* decision re-asserted the traditional view that unions are essentially voluntary bodies which must be regulated by normal contractual principles. Nevertheless, even within the contractual frame the courts have found a surprising degree of room for manoeuvre in controlling union rules by using the device of public policy. Some of the heads of public policy which they employ are well established and common to all contracts. These include the principles that the terms of the contract must not be illegal; that the parties cannot oust the jurisdiction of the courts; and almost certainly that the rules cannot exclude natural justice. More significantly, perhaps, although the House of Lords in *Cheall* v. *APEX*[61] appeared to echo the *Faramus* approach, their Lordships did so with one important qualification. Lord Diplock held that there was no right of individuals to associate with people who are unwilling to associate with them, but that different considerations might apply if the effect of expulsion from a trade union would be to put someone's job in jeopardy, either because of the existence of a closed shop or for any other reason. This is important for it lends support for two emerging heads of public policy, the precise status and application of which are as yet uncertain, but which would appear to give the courts additional powers over union rules. The first is the principle that union rules must not infringe the right to work, a vague doctrine which is closely linked to the notion of restraint of trade; and the even more embryonic principle that rules infringing a duty to act fairly will be void. The important feature about these two principles is that they are not generally applicable to all kinds of contracts but are being developed as a judicial response to the power which bodies such as unions and professional associations have to control access to jobs. Their emergence involves a recognition of the fact that at least one of the practices of the union, the operation of a closed shop, entitles the courts to review union constitutions more fully than traditional contractual principles would permit. Since both these principles provide criteria which potentially enable the courts to exercise a certain degree of control over a wide range of union rules, they will be considered in detail here, together with the effect of the doctrine of restraint of trade to which they are both closely related. The other heads of public policy, which are all more specific in their operation, are considered at other points in the book.

Restraint of Trade

The possibility that the doctrine of restraint of trade might be used to control the content of union rules was raised by Lord Denning in *Faramus* v. *Film Artistes' Association*.[62] It will be recalled that the Trade Union Act 1871, section 3, provided that the objects of a trade union were not to be unenforceable merely because they were in restraint of trade. In *Faramus*, however, Lord Denning expressed the view in the Court of Appeal that the statutory immunity applied only to the *purposes* of the unions but not to its *rules*. Consequently, he held that the eligibility rules of a union operating a closed shop were not protected. This was just about a tenable view at the time, albeit one which involved a particularly strict construction of the statutory provision, since the immunity then in force specifically extended only to union *purposes* and did not expressly embrace union *rules*. Nevertheless the House of Lords in *Faramus* flatly rejected such a literal construction of the statute[63] and so closed down this method of control too. Lord Evershed said that 'the effect [of the section] . . . is not merely to declare the purposes valid but to validate also ''any agreement'', that is to say, any agreement which is relevant or directed to the purposes of the union'.[64]

However, despite this decision, the Court of Appeal returned to restraint of trade in *Edwards* v. *SOGAT* where Sachs LJ attempted a rather different approach. He did not distinguish between the purposes or main objects and the rules, but rather between rules which were proper to the purposes of the union and those which were not — a distinction which could perhaps just about gain some support from Lord Evershed's dictum quoted above. Sachs LJ said:

> A rule that in these days of closed shops entitles a trade union to withdraw the card of a capable craftsman of good character who for years has been a member, even if styled 'temporary member' for any capricious reason such as (to mix conventional and practical examples) having incurred the personal enmity, for non-union reasons, of a single fellow member, the colour of his hair, the colour of his skin, the accent of his speech, or the holding of a job desired by someone not yet a member, is plainly in restraint of trade. At common law it is equally clearly unreasonable so far as the public interest is concerned. Is it then protected by either section 3 or section 4 of the Trade Union Act 1871? It cannot be said that a rule that enabled such capricious and despotic action is proper to the 'purposes' of this or indeed of any trade union. It is thus not protected by section 3 and is moreover ultra vires . . . It is thus void as in restraint of trade.[65]

His Lordship tried to distinguish the House of Lords' decision in *Faramus* by stating that the case had been concerned with eligibility and not expulsion rules — clearly a wholly artificial distinction, and not one which can be justified from the judgments of their Lordships in *Faramus*. And whatever the justification for the distinction he drew between rules directed towards proper union purposes and other rules, it is doubtful whether it can now be relied upon following the new formulation of the statutory immunity from the restraint of trade doctrine in section 2(5) of the TULRA 1974. This protects both the objects and the rules of a trade union.[66]

The Right to Work

The right to work is a nebulous and ill-defined right which has developed largely under the impetus of Lord Denning. As we have seen, he first expressed the view in *Lee* v. *Showmen's Guild of Great Britain*[67] that the courts had jurisdiction to intervene in the internal affairs of unions where a person's right to work was infringed. But there he was using the concept to mean little more than that the expelled member had lost his job following the expulsion, and that this was the most damaging consequence of the expulsion and the primary justification for judicial intervention. In *Nagle* v. *Feilden*,[68] however, the concept was given greater precision and became far more significant by being used to found a cause of action. The plaintiff had been refused a licence by the Jockey Club because of her sex. Without a licence, the opportunity for her to run her horses at race meetings was severely curtailed. This adverse consequence had been avoided by the simple expedient of granting a licence to her head lad, but she was dissatisfied with this subterfuge and claimed that the Jockey Club's action was unlawful. Her claim was struck out as disclosing no cause of action, but on appeal the Court of Appeal said that her action should proceed. They held that there were grounds for arguing that an arbitrary and capricious rule imposed by an organization exercising a virtual monopoly in an important field of human activity was actionable as an infringement of the right to work. This clearly has important implications for trade unions where a closed shop operates. However, it was thought at the time that whatever the limits of the right to work doctrine might be, it could not be transferred from the turf to trade unions because of the unions' statutory immunity from the restraint of trade doctrine.[69] The concepts are very closely related since an interference with the individual's right to work occurs only because the union is operating in restraint of trade. All such restraints by their very nature limit the opportunity of individuals to obtain work. So they would in essence seem to be two sides of the same coin, the right to work being the doctrine of restraint of trade reinterpreted from an individual standpoint.

In *Edwards* v. *SOGAT*,[70] however, Lord Denning implicitly denied that the two doctrines were the same. He declared that a rule which permitted a union to expel temporary members without a hearing was arbitrary and capricious and therefore invalid as an infringement of the right to work. The extraordinary aspect of the judgment was that he did not even consider whether the rule was saved by the statutory immunity from the restraint of trade doctrine. This provided that the purposes of any trade union shall not, by reason merely that they are in restraint of trade, be unlawful so as to render void or voidable any agreement or trust. This provision, then contained in section 3 of the Trade Union Act 1871, was re-enacted in TULRA, section 2(5) which provides also that a rule of a trade union shall not be unenforceable merely because it is in restraint of trade. Lord Denning's failure to consider this immunity could be only because he considered the right to work doctrine to be a head of public policy distinct from the doctrine of restraint of trade, a possibility which had not been anticipated by those commentators who so readily dismissed *Nagle's* case as irrelevant to the trade union movement. Presumably, therefore, it is not merely the fact that the rule is an unreasonable restraint of trade, in that it interferes with a person's employment, but also the fact that it is arbitrary or capricious which takes it outside the immunity. If the right to work is thus an independent doctrine, the immunity arguably will not apply. This provided that the purposes of a union (and now the rules) should not be treated as void *merely* (and now *only*) because they are in restraint of trade. If, however, the objects or the rules fall foul of some other head of public policy it may be that they could be struck down on that alternative ground. They are then being attacked not merely or only because they are in restraint of trade.

Apart from this uncertainty about the overlap between the right to work and the restraint of trade doctrines, the potential effects of the right to work development are also difficult to predict because the doctrine is so imprecise. As Megarry VC has observed, the 'right to work' may be an acceptable social or political catch-phrase, but it is hardly a suitable legal term of art.[71] Sachs LJ in *Edwards'* case referred to it more accurately as the 'right of equal opportunity to obtain work',[72] which is similar to, though possibly narrower than, Salmon LJ's formulation in *Nagle's* case as a 'right not to be capriciously and unreasonably prevented from earning his living as he wills'.[73] Certainly the latter approach would mean that a rule might infringe the right to work even though the scope of the closed shop was very limited. It would seem to cover any arbitrary or capricious interference, and not merely a significant interference, in a person's opportunity to obtain employment. Moreover, the doctrine could perhaps extend to embrace not merely the opportunity to obtain work but also rights arising out of work. In this way it could even apply where no closed shop operated at all. For example, it has been relatively common for unions to negotiate agreements providing that non-members will be dismissed first in the event of redundancy. Following the Employment Act 1982, dismissal of non-unionists in accordance with such an agreement will be automatically unfair. However, if that provision were repealed, could rejected applicants allege that the refusal to admit them into the union constituted an infringement of their common law right to work in the sense of a right not to be arbitrarily or capriciously prevented from having an equal prospect of long-term job security? Alternatively, would the doctrine be brought into effect if certain promotions were limited to union members only? Extensions of this kind cannot be discounted, though they would significantly expand judicial control over union activity.[74]

The Duty to Act Fairly

Clearly *Edwards'* case goes some way towards resuscitating the claim rejected by the House of Lords in *Faramus'* case, that the courts can strike out unreasonable rules, at least in the sense in which 'unreasonable' was used in *Kruse* v. *Johnson*.[75] Nor has the intervention of Parliament reflected in the new formulation of the statutory immunity necessarily stifled this revival. Moreover, two cases suggest a possible way in which the courts will be able to effect a full recovery, while of course paying suitable lip service to the rationale in *Faramus*. This potential basis for intervention rests upon the emerging doctrine of the 'duty to act fairly'. This doctrine is now well established in the field of administrative law. Initially it had procedural connotations only, and was used as an alternative expression to natural justice. Some judges were reluctant to say that the principles of natural justice applied to decisions which were analytically administrative. They preferred to limit the concept of natural justice to describe the relatively formal procedural requirements which the law demands of those exercising judicial or quasi-judicial functions. These requirements include such matters as the right to notice of any matter adversely affecting a person, and the opportunity for him or her to comment upon it before an unbiased decision-maker. In fact, the principles are very flexible and the precise requirements vary from situation to situation. Nevertheless, despite their flexibility, judges became unwilling to use the phrase natural justice to describe their application to those decisions which were administrative in nature because they thought that the phrase embaced a fuller set of procedural safeguards than they were willing to impose. At the same time, they did not wish to adopt the position that no procedural safeguards at all were required. So they developed the phrase 'the duty to act fairly' as a loose way of describing the limited, though still flexible, procedural requirements that the law would demand in these circumstances. Megarry VC has explained this development by saying that 'the further the question is removed from what may reasonably be called a justiciable question, the more appropriate it is to reject an expression which includes the word ''justice'' and to use instead terms such as ''fairness'' or ''the duty to act fairly'' '.[76]

However, in a few cases the duty to act fairly has been used to describe not merely the *procedural* standards which the courts will demand when administrative decisions are being made, but also as a source of certain *substantive* requirements which the law will impose. This is illustrated in particular by Lord Denning's judgment in *Breen* v. *AEU*,[77] an important trade union case which is also discussed in detail in Chapter 6. Lord

Denning there said that a union district committee would have to act fairly when deciding whether or not to confirm a shop steward's election to office. However, this duty to act fairly involved constraints both in relation to the procedures to be adopted and to the way in which the discretion was to be exercised. Lord Denning envisaged that the traditional grounds under which the courts can review the exercise of a discretion by a statutory body, notably that it must take into account relevant considerations, ignore irrelevant ones, act for a proper purpose, and in good faith, were all implied in the duty of the committee to exercise its discretion fairly.[78] Recently this concept of the duty to act fairly has been imposed as a requirement in a situation which in certain respects is analogous to that which arises when a member is rejected from a union. In *McInnes* v. *Onslow-Fane*[79] the plaintiff was refused a boxing manager's licence by an area council of the British Boxing Board of Control. He complained of certain procedural defects but this claim failed. We shall return to this aspect of the case when the regulation of union admissions is considered in Chapter 3. Sir Robert Megarry recognized that there could be certain limited procedural requirements in some circumstances but, more importantly in this context, he also recognized that there would be certain substantive controls over the way in which the Board exercised their powers:

> What then does the requirement of the duty to act fairly mean in this type of case? As I have said, [counsel] accepted that the board were under a duty to reach an honest conclusion without bias and not in pursuance of any capricious policy. That, I think, is right: and if the plaintiff showed that any of these requirements had not been complied with, I think the court would intervene.[80]

This shows that the vice-chancellor envisaged the 'duty to act fairly' as providing the basis for the jurisdiction of the courts if a person is arbitrarily rejected from certain organizations.

But in addition to providing the cause of action itself, the duty to act fairly is also the principle which the courts can utilize to invalidate the exercise of a discretion. It is therefore very similar to the right to work and, indeed, in *McInnes* the judge referred to *Nagle's* case as a striking example of the requirements of natural justice and fairness reaching beyond statute and contract. However, as some remarks at the beginning of his judgment indicate, he also left open the possibility that this notion of the duty to act fairly could potentially enable the courts to exercise jurisdiction in a wider range of situations than those envisaged by the right to work doctrine:

> There are many bodies which, though not established or operating
> under the authority of statute, exercise control, often on a national
> scale, over many activities which are important to many people,
> both as providing a means of livelihood *and for other reasons* . . . One
> particular aspect of this is membership of a trade union, without
> which it is impossible to obtain many important forms of work.
> (emphasis added)[81]

It is submitted that these words indicate that it is at least conceivable that
the duty to act fairly could be extended to encompass bodies which
exercise important public functions impinging upon the individual even
though they do not directly affect livelihood. If so, the path is clear for
the courts to recognize that other functions of trade unions, apart from
the closed shop, justify the application of the doctrine. For example, a
recognition of the vital role of collective bargaining and of the importance which that institution has for the individual in moulding the terms
and conditions of his or her employment contract could well tempt the
courts to apply the duty to act fairly even where no closed shop existed.
So the possible ramifications of this decision are extremely important,
for although it was conceded in this case that the Board could not pursue
any capricious policy, it is clear that Sir Robert Megarry would have
been willing to interfere on this ground in the absence of any such
concession. But if the exercise of discretion can be challenged on the
basis of public policy in this way, then surely rules can likewise be
attacked. After all, they are merely policy choices made binding. The
duty to act fairly could, in other words, be used to invalidate union rules
themselves. And though the *McInnes* case itself concerned admissions,
the argument for striking out capricious rules in an expulsion context
would appear to be even stronger, for there the member is being
deprived of a right to membership and not a mere possibility or a hope of
being admitted into membership.

   It is possible, therefore, that the duty to act fairly could enable the
courts to strike out union rules as well as to control the exercise of
discretion and powers, and that it could operate even where the union
has not control over access to employment. If the step is taken of
extending the duty beyond the closed shop context, then a wide range of
union rules could come under scrutiny. For if collective bargaining is
considered a sufficiently important function to attract the duty, then it
could open up control not merely over the right to membership, which
would involve the regulation of union admission and expulsion rules,
but also over rights of membership. For example, insofar as the right to
vote, or to nominate or stand as a candidate in union elections are the
methods whereby the union member is able to influence union policy

and its strategy for collective bargaining, rules which arbitrarily or capriciously interfere with these rights could come under scrutiny. It should be emphasized, however, that the *McInnes* case certainly does not go this far and it is quite possible that the judges would be unwilling to recognize that this duty arises in any situation save that where the union operates a closed shop. In effect, this involves limiting the concept to those areas already regulated by the right to work doctrine. Even so, the decision is still not without significance for although the judges might yet be persuaded that the concept of the right to work is inapplicable in view of the statutory immunity from the doctrine of restraint of trade, they are more likely to treat the duty to act fairly as springing from a different soil. If the doctrine is constrained in this way, its practical significance will be limited by the effect of the Employment Acts 1980 and 1982. This would not, however, make any such development any more justifiable. Admittedly any such control over the closed shop would be residual: it would cover capricious rules and policies only. But this is a vague phrase and would give the judges a wide discretion in practice. It is not so different from rules which could 'find no justification in the minds of reasonable men' — the description given by Russell CJ to those by-laws which are so unreasonable that they can be attacked under the *Kruse* v. *Johnson* principle.[82] If so, the extension of the notion of the duty to act fairly in this way would virtually re-activate the doctrine which Lord Denning adopted in the Court of Appeal in *Bonsor's* case, but in a different guise. This duty would replace the by-law analogy as the mechanism for exercising control over union rules. The development of the law in this way would lead to the danger cautioned by the conservative Donaldson LJ in *Cheall* v. *APEX*[83] where he said that judges must not fall into the trap of confusing political with public policy.

ENFORCING THE CONTRACT

The Limits of Contractual Enforcement

The first problem which arises in the area of enforcement is that there are limits to the general principle that the member may enforce the terms of the contract. It is possible, first, that the member may be unable to enforce rights which arise under the constitution where membership is really incidental to the operation of these rights. A company shareholder can only sue qua shareholder and not in some independent capacity, such as a director or solicitor,[84] and a similar principle probably applies to trade unions. *In Nisbet* v. *Percy*[85] a union member was dismissed from his post as a national organizer. The union rules provided that the post would run for three years but the member was dismissed during that period and he sought a declarator that he had been wrongfully dismissed, and damages. The Inner House of the Court of Session found against the pursuer but indicated that he might have had more success had he chosen to sue in his capacity as a member rather than as an employee, and had he claimed that the action was *ultra vires* the union's rules. This would provide the only method of enforcing the relevant rules if they were not incorporated into his contract of employment since then he would be unable to enforce them qua employee. In a subsequent case, *Milton* v. *Nicolson*,[86] which involved basically the same issue brought against the same union, the pursuer called on the advice in *Nisbet's* case and sought to bring his action in his capacity as a member. Lord Fraser was prepared to assume that the pursuer was competent to sue in that capacity, but it was not necessary to determine the matter since he found that the action taken by the union was not in any event *ultra vires*. It is to be questioned however, following the company law authorities, whether the courts should in fact have permitted the pursuer to sue qua member. The company law authorities suggest that the courts would not permit a member who also has a contract of employment with the union to sue in his or her capacity as a member where in essence he or she is trying to enforce provisions of the constitution which affect him or her qua employee.

The second restriction arises from the fact that in some instances statute itself prevents certain rules from being enforced in the courts. As we have seen, this legislative restriction was quite extensive when section 4 of the Trade Union Act 1871 was in force, but since its repeal the statutory prohibitions are narrower and relate to specific matters only. One arises under the Trade Union (Amalgamations, etc.) Act 1964. It is there provided that 'the validity of a resolution approving an instrument of amalgamation or transfer shall not be questioned in any legal proceedings whatsoever . . . on any ground on which a complaint could be, or could have been, made to the Certification Officer'.[87] Consequently, even though an allegation of invalidity will frequently involve a breach of the rules as well as the statute, particularly since many unions reflect the requirements of the statute in their rule books, this section would seem to preclude the courts from exercising jurisdiction over any such breach. It is true that the member's complaint would technically be a breach of contract rather than a breach of the requirements imposed by the statute, and therefore strictly the court would be considering a complaint on grounds which are different from those which could be made the subject of a complaint to the Certification Officer. It would, however, defeat the intention of the Act to draw this fine distinction. Under the Act, a member has six weeks to complain,[88] and after that period it is not desirable that the merger should continue to be under threat of legal action for the three-year contract limitation period. The sensible interpretation would therefore be to interpret the provision widely so that the phrase 'any ground' in the section should refer to the substance of a complaint to the Certification Officer, rather than to its legal form. Likewise in relation to the 1913 Act, an infringement of the rules made in pursuance of that Act can be made the subject of a complaint to the Certification Officer.[89] But obviously if there is a breach of the rules, it is also *prima facie* a breach of contract. Could members choose to take their actions to the courts for breach of contract rather than to the Certification Officer under the statute? In *Forster* v. *National Amalgamated Union of Shop Assistants, Warehousemen, and Clerks*[90] Eve J left the point open, though he expressed the view that an action cannot be taken in the courts once it has already been made the subject of a complaint to what is now the Certification Officer.[91] The better view would seem to be that the Certification Officer's jurisdiction is exclusive.[92] He will presumably have developed some expertise in this area, and on policy grounds it makes sense to give him exclusive jurisdiction.

The Parties to the Contract

The second question which arises in the area of enforcement is this: once it is determined that the rule is one which may be enforced by the member, against whom should the action be brought? Before the Industrial Relations Act, unregistered unions were not legal persons and were therefore incapable of contracting in their own right, while the judges were divided about whether registered unions had sufficient corporate status to contract or not. In *Bonsor* v. *Musicians' Union*[93] two of their Lordships were firmly of the opinion that they had,[94] but the majority thought otherwise.[95] They considered the contract of membership to be a contract between members *inter se* rather than between the member and the union. A question which arose was how on this basis could a member bring an action against the union for breach of contract, if the union is not even a party to that contract? The traditional answer would be that there can be no action against the union as such and instead the member has to bring a representative action whereby certain named members can be sued as representing the other members in the organization. However, this is fraught with difficulties. For example, it is necessary to establish the personal liability of each member represented. This means that the plaintiff must exclude individuals who could have no personal contractual liability, such as members who joined after the act complained of, or those who were in law infants at that time. For an organization of any significant size, therefore, this procedure is useless because identifying such people becomes impossible.

In *Bonsor's* case the majority, who had of course rejected the view that the union could be liable directly as the other contracting party, nevertheless managed to sidestep these complications. They held that it was possible to take action against a registered union in its registered name as an anomalous but simpler procedural alternative to the representative action. Any damages awarded could be recovered only from the union funds and not from individual members. This was a difficult conclusion to sustain since in a proper representative action the individuals sued remain personally liable. Lord MacDermott's rather unconvincing justification for limiting liability to the union funds was that where the registered name procedure was used, there was no procedure for levying execution against individual members.[96] The effect of this approach was to treat the union precisely as if it were a corporate body which had contracted separately with each member. The members as a collective body were recognized as a separate entity; the registered name was used to denote the collective embodiment of all the members who were parties to the membership contract. In short, the majority of their Lordships in the *Bonsor* case was simply not prepared to follow the logic of treating the union as an unincorporated body to its inevitable conclusion. They were not willing to accept the lack of effective accountability which the analysis of the union as a voluntary, unincorporated body would produce if traditional legal principles were followed.

The Industrial Relations Act 1971 provided that registered unions were incorporated bodies and so could contract.[97] In contrast, unregistered unions were given a status stimilar to that enjoyed by registered unions before the Act[98] so, at least on the majority view in *Bonsor*, they continued to have no contractual capacity. With the repeal of that Act, all unions can contract, whether listed or not.[99] There are, however, still nice theoretical problems. First, it does not necessarily follow that because the union has the power to contract that the contract of membership will be with the union rather than the members *inter se*. No doubt it will be easy to argue that members who have joined the union since the capacity to contract was granted will have entered into such a contractual relationship, probably in addition to being in contractual relations with all their fellow members. This was the view of Donaldson LJ in the *Cheall* case.[100] But this ultimately depends upon the intention of the parties, for as Lord Somervell pointed out in *Bonsor's* case, even if the union has the capacity to contract, 'it would still . . . be open to the members so to draft the rules as to constitute a contract inter se only and not a contract with the union'.[101] Secondly, some members will have had contracts *inter se* (having joined before 1974), whereas

48 *Trade Union Democracy, Members' Rights and the Law*

others will have direct contracts with the union (having joined since 1974). Theoretically, therefore, the position could be extremely complicated. In practice, however, it would be clearly unsatisfactory to draw a distinction of this kind between the legal position of different members, however much it may be dictated by the logic of the law. Consequently the courts may be tempted to adopt the view that every member is contractually bound to the union, unless there is a clear intention to the contrary.[102] In order to reach this conclusion it would have to be agreed that not only were unions granted the capacity to contract, but in addition they have in fact exercised that power with those who were members when the capacity to contract was granted. However, even if the courts do not take this approach, *Bonsor* shows that the member will have no difficulty in enforcing the contract — even if it is with the members *inter se*.

Union contractual liability for acts of officials

The union then can be sued irrespective of whether it is a party to the membership contract or not where there has been a breach of the rules. But for whose acts can it be sued? Obviously it will be liable for the acts of officials who are acting within the scope of their authority.[103] Generally the scope of that authority is determined by an examination of the union rules but, in addition to this express authority, the official or officials may also have certain implied authority to bind the union. This will be the case where action is taken by those committees and bodies which represent the 'directing mind and will' of the union.[104] Generally these will be the governing bodies of the union, the national executive committee and annual conference. They represent the union: their actions are those of the union. But generally a breach of the membership contract will involve action taken in breach of the rules and will involve the official or committee concerned exceeding the scope of their authority. How can the union be made liable for such unauthorized acts? Surprisingly there has been remarkably little discussion of this problem in the courts, no doubt because the union generally accepts responsibility for the action and the relevant question to be determined is merely whether the action was lawful or not. However, there would seem to be three possible bases of liability in these circumstances, two resting upon contractual principles and one upon an agency analysis.

The strictest approach is that adopted by Lord Morton in *Bonsor* v. *Musicians' Union*:

> When Mr Bonsor applied to join the respondent union, and his application was accepted, a contract came into existence between

Mr Bonsor and the respondent union, whereby Mr Bonsor agreed to abide by the rules of the defendant union, and the union impliedly agreed that Mr Bonsor would not be excluded by the union or its officers otherwise than in accordance with the rules.[105]

The implied term envisaged by Lord Morton is that the union effectively *guarantees* that officials will not exceed their powers under the rules in a manner which adversely affects the member. If they do, the union is automatically liable for their wrongful acts, and any subsequent attempt to rectify the error will not strictly alter the basic contractual liability, though obviously it will affect any damages that may be recovered. On this basis, the union may be liable even though its governing body is wholly unaware of the action which is being challenged. The difficulty with accepting this basis of liability is that to imply a term of this stringency seems to involve a distortion of the principles usually employed for implying terms into contracts. Trade unions rely upon a vast number of voluntary officials to run their affairs, and many will exercise powers affecting the rights of members. Yet however honestly and carefully those officials act, it is likely that they will sometimes commit a technical breach of the law. The flexibility of the concept of natural justice makes it difficult enough even for lawyers to determine precisely what safeguards may be necessary in any particular situation. In these circumstances the layman can hardly be criticized for falling foul of the law, and infringements of the membership contract are inevitable. Yet Lord Morton's judgment would make unions automatically liable for unlawful acts of this nature. It can hardly be supposed that it would be the intention of the union to accept such liability in these circumstances; nor is its imposition necessary to give business efficacy to the contract.

A more logical solution to the problem is to recognize that the union undertakes a less onerous duty to take all reasonably practicable steps to correct any unauthorized act and to remedy any adverse consequences flowing from it. There seems to be no authority supporting this approach, but it is submitted that it is acceptable on policy grounds and can, moreover, be realistically implied into the contract of membership. Provided that the governing body of the union takes these steps, then no liability will attach to the union itself, even though the officials concerned continue to act in defiance of that body's instructions. If the officials do this, they will then be personally liable for their own actions, as in *Huntley* v. *Thornton*[106] where a group of union officials were held liable for civil conspiracy when they continued to treat the plaintiff as an expelled member even though this directly contravened instructions issued by the union's executive committee. This less stringent con-

tractual duty effectively gives the full-time officials, who will usually
have more experience and knowledge both of the rules and the law, an
opportunity to review the acts of local officials, and perhaps take legal
advice before the union itself is committed. This approach is in fact not
unlike the third which rests on agency principles. It asserts that the
union may become liable for the unauthorized act if it ratifies it. This
approach was adopted by Lords Keith and MacDermott in *Bonsor*. In
that case the appellant in the House of Lords had been wrongfully
excluded from the union by the branch secretary for non-payment of his
dues. The secretary had no authority to take such action. In fact, the
executive committee had argued that the expulsion was lawful and
thereby effectively adopted the act as its own. But Lord Keith indicated
how liability might sometimes be avoided in the circumstances:

> There may be cases where a trade union disclaims the action of an
> official or officials and in which, accordingly, the conduct com-
> plained of cannot be said to be the act of that trade union. But in
> such a case the member would be speedily restored to his status as a
> union member and would, presumably, in the matter of any claim
> of damages, have to proceed against the individual or individuals
> concerned.[107]

Likewise, Lord MacDermott suggested that the union could escape
liability if there was some form of disavowal.[108]

Wedderburn has argued that ratification probably does not involve a
duty to disclaim the action, merely a duty not positively to ratify it.[109]
Admittedly in many circumstances silence cannot amount to ratification, but it must be doubtful whether this is so in this context. Could a
union wash its hands of purported expulsions at local level even though
the effect was that for all practical purposes the members were excluded
from the union, perhaps even resulting in the loss of their jobs? This
would hardly be satisfactory. Once the matter is brought to the attention
of the relevant union committee, it is surely not unreasonable to treat its
inactivity, or the turning of a blind eye, as sufficient acquiescence to
amount to ratification. If this is so — and it seems consistent with the
views expressed by Lords Keith and MacDermott — then the onus rests
on the union to disavow and probably to take such steps as it can to
minimize any adverse consequences stemming from the unauthorized
act. This would mean that there is thus little practical difference between
the more lenient contractual approach and the agency solution, at least if
the latter is interpreted as requiring a positive duty to disavow. On the
agency view, the union is liable for adopting the agent's act as its own,
whereas on the contractual view it is liable for a breach of its own

independent contractual obligation, but in effect they are simply two separate ways of explaining the same duty. Nevertheless, the contractual approach would seem to provide a sounder juridical basis. This is because the agency approach assumes that the governing body — or possibly some other group within the union — will have the authority to ratify unauthorized acts, albeit by its inaction. But where does it derive that authority? Obviously such a power is never expressly found in union constitutions, yet to treat it as an implied power which the members have conceded to the governing body seems highly artificial. The implied term which needs to be invoked on the contractual basis would seem to be far less open to objection in this respect, and to more accurately reflect the way in which the members of the union would see the situation.

However, whether agency or the implication of the less rigorous contractual duty is adopted as the basis of liability, it will not be possible to impose liability upon the union unless the 'directing mind and will' of the union has knowledge of the unauthorized action and an opportunity to remedy it. This potentially raises an interesting argument which does not yet seem to have been put forward in the courts. If the governing body must have knowledge of the unauthorized act, could it not claim that, at least where the facts are in dispute, an inquiry is necessary to enable it to determine whether the action was in fact unauthorized or not? It seems unreasonable to assume that the governing body is bound either to adopt the member's view of events and immediately disavow the action, or else to face liability for ratifying the action when it has had no opportunity to investigate the matter at all. If this argument is accepted, then the member's refusal to participate in any such investigation would seem to preclude the union as an entity from being held liable. Indeed, it could be argued that, in some circumstances at least, the member's duty to co-operate should involve an appeal to any appellate body created by the union constitution, at least in circumstances where the status quo operates pending the inquiry. The union could be seen to be delegating its task of investigation to that body. If this contention were to be accepted, it would mean that a duty to pursue internal procedures could be necessary not in order to enable the union to redress a wrong which it has committed, but rather because until that stage is reached it cannot be established that the union is responsible for the wrongful act at all. This argument cannot be sustained, though, if the contractual obligation is held to involve a guarantee by the union that its officials will not act contrary to their authority, because in that situation union liability arises immediately the unlawful action is taken.

REMEDIES FOR BREACH OF CONTRACT

The final question which we consider in this chapter is the remedies which may be awarded against a trade union. In the past this is a question which has given rise to great legal difficulty and no end of controversy. The legal position is now much more straight-forward — particularly after the enactment of TULRA, section 2, but recent decisions of the courts make the issue no less controversial. The early legal problems arose under the Trade Union Act 1871, with its attempt to oust the jurisdiction of the courts from internal affairs, and with its lack of clarity about the legal status of trade unions. As we have seen in Chapter 1, however, section 4 of the 1871 Act proved ineffective to exclude the courts which were ready to intervene by way of declaration and injunction to prevent the misapplication of funds, and to prevent the discipline or expulsion of members in breach of the rules. The pretext for such intervention was that such conduct did not constitute the direct enforcement of any agreement for the application of the funds of a trade union. But while the courts were willing to grant declarations and injunctions in appropriate cases, from a relatively early stage in the life of the 1871 Act, the question of damages remained much more difficult. The courts were expressly prohibited from awarding damages for breach of any agreement to which section 4 applied, but this would not disable them in principle from awarding damages for wrongful expulsion. Nevertheless in *Kelly* v. *National Society of Operative Printers*,[110] the Court of Appeal held that damages were not available in an action by a member for breach of the rules. The plaintiff failed 'because the agent of the society who had done him wrong was agent for himself as well as the other members, since the persons sued were an unincorporated body of which he was one. Looked at from this angle he was suing his own agent and therefore suing himself, a thing he could not do.'[111] In fact it was not until the House of Lords in *Bonsor* v. *Musicians' Union*[112] reversed this decision that damages were available. Some of their Lordships held that a trade union was a form of quasi-corporation which in certain respects has an existence apart from its members, and so could be sued by its members for breach of contract. Other members of the House of Lords held that a trade union did not have a legal status independent of its members. They also held that although a trade union was in fact a voluntary association, a member could nevertheless sue the union in its registered name for breach of contract. The provisions of section 2 of TULRA fortunately make it unnecessary to examine any further the complexities of *Bonsor*, a decision which generated a large but erudite literature.[113] It is true that section 2 provides that a trade union is not and shall not be treated as if it were a body corporate. However, it then provides that a trade union shall be capable of making contracts and that 'it shall be capable of suing and being sued in its own name, whether in proceedings relating to property or founded on contract or tort or any other cause of action whatsoever'.[114] So TULRA overcomes the difficulties facing their Lordships in *Bonsor*[115] by enacting that despite the absence of corporate status, a trade union may be sued in contract as if it were a corporate body. We now consider the remedies which are available in actions against trade unions. Essentially there are three: declarations, injunctions and damages. Increasingly, however, there are statutory remedies for failure to comply with statutory duties, such as those imposed by the Trade Union Act 1913,[116] the Employment Act 1980,[117] and the Trade Union Act 1984.[118] We deal with the statutory remedies in Chapters 3, 5 and 6.

Declaration and Injunction

Before the miners' strike there was little to say about the declaration as a remedy in trade union cases. It was open to litigants to seek a declaration of rights in the normal way, though in practice a declaration, it seems, was combined with an injunction. There was nothing in any of the reported cases to suggest any issues or problems. An interesting development did occur, however, in *Clarke* v. *Chadburn (No. 2)*[119]. At the beginning of the miners' strike the National Union had no authority in its rules to expel members, though its constituent unions did. Steps were taken by the National Union to introduce a new rule (rule 51) to remedy this defect at an Extraordinary Annual Conference on July 12, 1984. The new rule was introduced, however, in violation of an order of the court. Because of an occupation of the offices of the Nottinghamshire Area of the union, the Area Council had been unable to meet in order to mandate its delegates as to how they should vote on the proposed rule changes on July 12. At the initiative of 17 members of the Nottinghamshire Area, Sir Robert Megarry granted an *ex parte* order restraining the National Union from 'putting proposing allowing to be put or proposed or discussed or voted upon or passing' any resolution to alter the NUM rules. Despite the order, however, the union decided to hold the meeting and in fact the conference voted to change the rules, with a resolution to this effect obtaining the two-thirds majority required by the rules. The new rule 51 provided for the establishment of a National Disciplinary Committee, with power to expel or suspend from membership any member who 'has done any act (which includes any omission) which may be detrimental to the interests of the Union'.

In *Clarke* v. *Chadburn (No. 2)*, rule 51 was held by Sir Robert Megarry to be void for illegality. Wilful disobedience of a court order is unlawful as a contempt of court, and 'those who defy a prohibition ought not to be able to claim that the fruits of their defiance are good, and not tainted by the illegality which produced them'.[120] So the rule was invalid because it was passed in defiance of the court. An interesting feature of the case, however, was the remedy sought in what were interlocutory proceedings. The plaintiffs were not satisfied with an injunction against enforcing the new rule about discipline 'because that would require application to the court to enforce it'.[121] So the plaintiffs sought a declaration, despite the fact that in modern practice an interim declaration seems unknown. However, the plaintiffs relied on an *obiter dictum* of Upjohn LJ in a case in 1962 where the concept of an interim declaration was rejected, with the qualification that exceptionally it might be possible for such a remedy to exist, particularly in cases where the declaration would finally determine the point, and would not operate only for the interim.[122] Sir Robert Megarry endorsed this dictum and held that the present case was one in which a declaration should be made, taking the view that what was at issue in the motion was 'a matter of such public concern to so many people that it seems to . . . fall within the category of infrequent cases in which the sparing exercise of this jurisdiction is fully justified. If the defendants had wished to contend to the contrary, they could have attended or asked for an adjournment.'[123] The declaration was reinforced by an injunction to restrain the defendants from acting upon the rule which had been declared void. This was done because although in 'many cases in which declarations are granted, there is a justifiable expectation that the declaration will be honoured and observed', there was 'no such expectation here'.[124]

Interim declarations are as novel as interlocutory injunctions in labour law are controversial. But again there is no difficulty in principle with the injunction as a remedy, but there is some difficulty in practice relating to the use of the remedy in interlocutory proceedings. The source of much of the trouble is the decision of the House of Lords in *American Cyanamid Ltd* v. *Ethicon Co Ltd*[125] which changed the basis by which interlocutory injunctions might be granted. Previously applicants had to show a *prima facie* case and that the balance of convenience lay in favour of granting the injunction. Since *American Cyanamid*, however, the applicant need only show that there is a serious question of law or fact to be considered and that the balance of convenience lies with him or her. This is particularly important in labour law. The courts tend always to conclude that the balance of convenience lies with the plaintiff (whether it be an employer or a trade union member) in actions against trade unions. The case thus facilitated the grant of injunctions by reducing the substantive barrier over which the plaintiff must cross. In industrial conflict cases the threat was met swiftly by an amendment in 1975 to section 17 of TULRA.[126] This provides that in any case where the defence of acting in contemplation or furtherance of a trade dispute is claimed, the court must have regard to the likelihood of its succeeding at the trial of the action. It has been held in the House of Lords that an injunction should not normally be granted where it is more likely than not that the statutory defence will succeed at the trial of the action.[127] There is, however, no equivalent measure operating in cases brought by members for breach of contract. The 1975 amendment applies only to tort-based actions. As a result, trade unions are left exposed in interlocutory proceedings to members wishing to restrain allegedly unlawful conduct.[128] This may include the calling of a strike, the expenditure of money on a strike, and the discipline of members who fail to participate in a strike. We consider this issue more fully in Chapter 6.

Damages

As already pointed out, damages have been available in rulebook disputes since *Bonsor*, and the 1974 Act removes any possible doubts about the availability of the remedy. There are very few reported cases dealing with this question, and it is clear that the leading case is still *Edwards* v. *SOGAT*[129] in the sense that it offers the fullest guidance as to the principles by which the measure of the damages should be assessed. The plaintiff was employed by Hugh Stevenson Ltd as a skilled craftsman in a grade I post in the printing trade. He was employed as an auto platen operator, a 'relatively rare post'.[130] Stevensons was a closed shop and Edwards had been admitted as a temporary member of SOGAT under the rules of which a temporary membership would automatically terminate if the member became six weeks in arrears. In 1965 the plaintiff was held by the union to be six weeks in arrears, 'despite the fact that it was the union itself which by its own muddle had failed to collect [the] dues from the employers and credit [the plaintiff] with them'.[131] Following pressure from the union, Mr Edwards was eventually dismissed, after seven and a half years' service with the company. For reasons which will recur throughout the book and which do not need to be rehearsed here, it was held that the expulsion was unlawful. The main issue in the case in fact was not liability in damages, but the measure of the damages. Before considering the judgments on this point, it is relevant to note also that between his dismissal and the trial, the plaintiff obtained employment for a short period with a company called Boxmakers, a job which he lost when he failed to comply with an instruction from the employer which was outside the scope of the contract of employment. It is also to be noted that after the action commenced the union admitted that it had made a mistake and made the plaintiff offers of various printing jobs. But these were all unskilled labouring jobs, inferior to the grade I post which the plaintiff had held at Stevensons. As a result, the plaintiff either did not apply for nor accept any of the positions in question.

In measuring damages, the starting point is Lord Denning's remark that they:

> are to be ascertained by putting the plaintiff in as good a position, so far as money can do it, as if he had never been excluded from the union, taking into account, of course, all contingencies which might have led him to losing his employment anyway: and remembering, too, that it was his duty to do what was reasonable to mitigate the damage.[132]

The assessment was divided into two parts, the first relating to the loss suffered between the dismissal and the hearing, and the second relating to future loss. So far as the actual loss suffered was concerned, this was based on the wages the plaintiff would have earned with Stevensons, less his earnings with Boxmakers, unemployment benefit and wages in lieu of notice. Important issues of mitigation were raised unsuccessfully by the union. Thus it was argued that the plaintiff was under a duty to accept the jobs which he had been offered; he should have retrained in some different skill; or he should have moved to another part of the country where he might have stood a better chance of being recruited to a SOGAT branch and consequently of obtaining suitable employment. As might be expected, these arguments were rightly rejected. As to the first, it was said:

> The authorities I think establish that where someone has lost employment as the result of a breach of contract or tort on the part of another, and is under an obligation to mitigate his damage, he will only be required to mitigate his damage by accepting other employment if that employment is of a kind which he can reasonably be expected to accept, having regard to his standing, his experience and his personal history.[133]

In this case, it was not reasonable to expect the plaintiff to accept work as a labourer, although there was evidence that skilled men in the trade would rather do this than accept unemployment. The second and third points were met tersely by Sachs LJ in the following terms:

> . . . Coming from a defendant whose wrongful act caused the situation, who could and should have taken all possible steps to end

it, and who took the opposite course, I confess this submission was viewed by me with repugnance and I reject it. It lies particularly ill in the mouth of this trade union defendant to say it can in effect dictate the whole way of life to be pursued by the plaintiff.[134]

So far as the future loss was concerned, Buckley J at first instance applied by way of analogy the principles that are applied in cases of personal injury where 'having ascertained the loss of earning capacity of the person injured, the court has then to try to make an estimate of his probable earning life, and then, discounting that, to multiply one year's loss of earning capacity by a suitable number of years to arrive at a lump sum in damages'.[135] He then calculated future loss by deducting projected annual income as a labourer from what the plaintiff's annual income would have been had he remained at Stevensons. He then multiplied that figure by ten, giving a total award of £7,971 with costs. The Court of Appeal rejected this approach, apparently as being too extravagant, with Lord Denning expressing the view that 'There is a great difference between permanent incapacity due to personal injury (which cannot be overcome) and loss of membership due to expulsion from a trade union (which can be overcome by learning another skill or by being reinstated, and so forth)'.[136] In this case the union had in fact given the plaintiff a full membership since the trial. Yet although the court rejected an approach based on personal injury claims, it is by no means clear with what principles these were displaced. Indeed, the reader of the judgment is left with the impression that in this area it is an even bigger lottery, with the judges plucking figures at random. Thus, Lord Denning said that 'damages in such a case as this are so difficult to assess' that he would be induced 'to view them somewhat broadly'.[137] He would start with the loss of earnings which the plaintiff might reasonably be expected to have suffered over two years from his expulsion, taking his cue on this point from a recommendation of the Donovan Commission which had reported a few years earlier.[138] He would 'then work upwards or downwards from that figure', according to the circumstances of the case'.[139] In this case he would award damages at the reduced figure of £3,500, a conclusion supported by Sachs and Megaw LJJ.

NOTES

1. The 1871 Trade Union Act was passed on the assumption that there was a contract between the members of the trade union *inter se* (s. 4(1)). Furthermore, in *Rigby* v. *Connol* (1880) 14 Ch. D. 482, the case which established the proprietary basis of jurisdiction, the existence of a contractual relationship was fully recognized. Jessel MR referred to 'contracts entered into by the members' (p. 490).

2. E.g. *Osborne* v. *Amalgamated Society of Railway Servants* [1911] 1 Ch. 540; *Amalgamated Society of Carpenters and Joiners* v. *Braithwaite* [1922] 2 AC 440.

3. (1880) 14 Ch. D. 482.

4. He argued that the action was barred by section 4 of the Trade Union Act 1871. This reasoning was later rejected. See generally Grunfeld, pp. 73–8.

5. At p. 487.

6. The proprietary basis was established by Lord Eldon in *Gee* v. *Pritchard* (1818) 2 Swans. 402.

7. See Pound, 'Equitable Relief against Defamation and Injuries to Personality' (1916) 29 Harvard L Rev. 640 at pp. 678–9.

8. See e.g. Chafee, 'The Internal Affairs of Associations Not for Profit' (1930) 43 Harvard L Rev. 993.

9. In *Chapman* v. *Michaelson* [1909] 1 Ch. 238 it was held that the declaration was not equitable relief, and in *Gray* v. *Spyer* [1921] 2 Ch. 549 Younger LJ (for Astbury J) observed that 'In truth these abstract declarations, whatever else they may be, are neither law nor equity' (p. 557). These cases were of course decided after *Rigby*'s case, but they seem to decide that the equitable origins of the declaration were lost following the Judicature Act 1873. (See generally, Zamir, *The Declaratory Judgment* (1962), pp. 187–91.)

10. Apart from *Rigby*'s case, property has only proved a bar to jurisdiction in one other union case: *Drennan* v. *Associated Ironmoulders of Scotland* 1921 SC 151. Even then it was only one of the grounds precluding jurisdiction (the other being s. 4 of the Trade Union Act 1871). (Strictly the court was concerned to establish a patrimonial rather than a proprietary loss.) Lack of property has, however, precluded jurisdiction in other non-union cases, e.g. *Baird* v. *Wells* (1890) LR 44 Ch. D. 661; and *Cookson* v. *Harewood* [1932] 2 KB 478.

11. The lack of property might, for example, have precluded jurisdiction in *Burn* v. *National Amalgamated Labourers' Union* [1920] 2 Ch. 364, or *Watson* v. *Smith* [1941] 2 All ER 725, but in fact the issue was not raised.

12. *Osborne* v. *Amalgamated Society of Railway Servants* [1911] 1 Ch. 540 at p. 554 (per Cozens-Hardy MR) and p. 567 (per Buckley LJ, relying on the company law case of *Pender* v. *Lushington* (1887) 6 Ch. D. 771).

13. It seems that Jessel MR himself considered this to be a sufficiently substantial proprietary basis: see *Rigby*'s case (1880) 14 Ch. D. 482 at p. 483.

14. Grodin, *Union Government and the Law* (1961) at p. 55.

15. It was not even as if the courts themselves were convinced by their own fiction. See e.g. *Fisher* v. *Keane* (1879) 11 Ch. D. 353, where Jessel MR recognized that the real concern with wrongful expulsion from a club was the adverse effect on the member's reputation. See too *Baird* v. *Wells* (1890) 44 Ch. D. 661 where, as Pound points out, the court surreptitiously protected the plaintiff's reputation by first holding the expulsion to be irregular before considering the issue of jurisdiction (Pound, *op. cit.*, p. 679).

16. [1952] 2 QB 329.

17. *Ibid*, at pp. 341–2. However, the germ of the contract approach appears in the judgment of Fletcher-Moulton LJ in *Osborne* v. *Amalgamated Society of Railway Servants* [1911] 1 Ch. 540 at p. 562, and was also adopted by Denning LJ (as he then was) in *Abbott* v. *Sullivan* [1952] 1 KB 189.

18. See too *Nagle* v. *Feilden* [1966] 2 QB 633 and *Edwards* v. *SOGAT* [1971] Ch. 354. In practice, this is of little importance since the member will almost certainly be able to show some kind of proprietary interest in membership itself.

19. [1940] Ch. 326.

20. [1941] 2 All ER 725. See also *Burn* v. *National Amalgamated Labourers' Union* [1920] 2 Ch. 364 where an injunction was granted to prevent the wrongful exclusion from office of the plaintiff. If the office had been paid, then a clear proprietary right would have been infringed; but in fact the courts seems to have attached no significance to the question of whether it was paid or not.

21. [1972] 1 WLR 130. But the possible argument that no injunction should have been granted because there was no proprietary right was not raised. See also *Cohen* v. *NUTGW, The Times*, January 13, 1962.

22. Injunctions have been available to protect rights other than property rights, but only in rare cases, e.g. defamation. More recently, however, the courts have firmly recognized that injunctions will be granted to prevent a breach of confidence, regardless of any proprietary rights. See *Argyll* v. *Argyll* [1967] Ch. 302 and *Fraser* v. *Evans* [1969] 1 QB 349 at p. 361.

23. *Law, Society and Industrial Justice* (1969), p. 53.

24. TULRA 1974, s. 11(4).

25. [1982] IRLR 362.

26. On the power of the 'platform' at union conferences, see Clegg, *The Changing System of Industrial Relations in Great Britain* (1979), p. 203.

27. See also Roberts, *Trade Union Government and Administration in Great Britain* (1956), p. 209.

28. This right was firmly established in *Lee* v. *Showmen's Guild of Great Britain* [1952] 2 QB 329, where the Court of Appeal held that, although a union tribunal could determine questions of fact, it could not determine issues of law. Even express clauses which purport to leave matters to the opinion of a union committee cannot oust the jurisdiction of the courts. The case has frequently been followed. See *Leigh* v. *NUR* [1970] Ch. 326.

29. [1972] ICR 308.

30. *Ibid.*, at p. 393. And see *Bourne* v. *Colodense Ltd* [1985] IRLR 339.

31. *British Actors' Equity Association* v. *Goring* [1977] ICR 393 at p. 397.

32. *Ibid.*, at p. 402.

33. [1978] ICR 791.

34. *Ibid.*, at pp. 794–5.

35. See 1871 Act, s. 14, and Schedule 1.

36. 1971 Act, Schedule 4(14) and (16).

37. 1971 Act, Schedule 4(7).

38. See Weekes, Mellish, Dickens and Lloyd, *Industrial Relations and the Limits of Law* (1975), pp. 94–119.

39. As was said in *Bourne* v. *Colodense Ltd* [1985] IRLR 339 it is not to be assumed that 'all terms of the agreement between the members and the Union are to be found in the rule-book' (at p. 342). For a discussion and strong criticism of this case, see Wedderburn of Charlton, *The Worker and the Law* (3rd edn, 1986), pp. 746–7.

40. [1956] 1 WLR 585.

41. [1970] Ch. 326.

42. [1972] ICR 484.

43. Industrial Relations Review and Report, *Legal Information Bulletin*, July 23, 1985, p. 14.

44. [1972] ICR 308 at p. 394, approving para. 99 of the said TUC Handbook.

45. *The Times*, November 25, 1953.

46. The case is not fully reported, and this part of the judgment is taken from a report in the Annual Report of the Chief Registrar of Friendly Societies, 1953, Part IV, p. 6.

47. See Treitel, p. 154.

48. *Ibid.* In borderline cases, the difference is 'one of emphasis'. *Ibid.*

49. [1950] 2 All ER 1064.

50. *The Times*, June 12, 1975.

51. [1976] ICR 147.

52. *Ibid.*, at pp. 161–2.

53. *Amalgamated Society of Railway Servants* v. *Osborne* [1910] AC 87.

54. Trade Union (Amendment) Act 1876, s. 16.

55. See *Bonsor* v. *Musicians' Union* [1954] Ch. 479 at p. 485, and see *Breen* v. *AEU* [1971] 2 QB 175 at p. 190.

56. [1898] 2 QB 91.

57. [1954] Ch. 479 at p. 485.

58. [1977] ICR 393 at pp. 396–7

59. [1982] IRLR 362 at p. 367.

60. [1964] AC 925 at pp. 943 and 947. See also *Cheall* v. *APEX* [1983] ICR 398.

61. *Op. cit.*

62. [1963] 2 QB 527 at pp. 540–2.

63. [1964] AC 925.

64. *Ibid.*, at p. 943.

65. [1971] Ch. 354 at p. 382.

66. An attempt to draw a similar distinction to avoid s. 2(5) was also made in *Goring* v. *British Actors' Equity Association* (1986 Unreported). It was argued that s. 2(5) did not protect an 'instruction' given by a union to members, because this was neither a purpose nor a rule of the union. The argument was rejected, with Browne-Wilkinson VC noting that if the argument was

correct 'the effect would be to deprive all trade unions of a statutory defence in relation to instructions to members to withdraw their labour'.

67. [1952] 2 QB 329. See also *Abbott* v. *Sullivan* [1952] 1 KB 189 at p. 204.
68. [1966] 2 QB 633.
69. See Rideout, 'Upon Training an Unruly Horse' (1966) 29 MLR 424 at p. 427.
70. [1971] Ch. 354.
71. *McInnes* v. *Onslow-Fane* [1978] 1 WLR 1520 at p. 1528.
72. *Op. cit.*, at p. 383.
73. *Op. cit.*, at p. 653.
74. It is to be noted that in *British Actors' Equity Association* v. *Goring* (1986 Unreported) it was held that an instruction not to work in South Africa was not an infringement of the right to work, by restricting the plaintiff's ability to earn his living. According to the Vice-Chancellor, the principle has no application to a case where the plaintiff is a member of the union exercising the monopoly power. In such a case the plaintiff's remedies lie in contract, under the rules.
75. [1898] 2 QB 91.
76. *McInnes* v. *Onslow-Fane, op. cit.*, at p. 1530.
77. [1971] 2 QB 175.
78. *Ibid.*, at p. 190. It is to be noted, however, that in *Hamlet* v. *GMBATU* [1986] IRLR 293, Harman J suggested that the *Wednesbury* principles had no application to trade union machinery for resolving disputes. Compare, however, *British Actors' Equity Association* v. *Goring* (1986 Unreported) where the Vice-Chancellor said that the rules of the union 'include expressly or implicitly an obligation not to act capriciously or arbitrarily'.
79. [1978] 1 WLR 1520.
80. *Ibid.*, at p. 1533.
81. *Ibid.*, at p. 1527.
82. [1898] 2 QB 91 at pp. 99–100.
83. [1982] IRLR 362 at p. 371.
84. Gower, pp. 317–19.
85. 1951 SC 350.
86. 1965 SLT 319.
87. 1964 Act, s. 4(7).
88. 1964 Act, s. 4(2).
89. 1913 Act, s. 3(2).
90. [1927] 1 Ch. 539.
91. At that time complaints were made to the Chief Registrar of Friendly Societies.
92. See Ewing, *Trade Unions, the Labour Party and the Law* (1982), p. 134.
93. [1956] AC 104.
94. Lords Morton and Porter.
95. Lords MacDermott, Keith and Somervell.
96. At p. 146.
97. 1971 Act, s. 74.
98. 1971 Act, s. 154.
99. TULRA 1974, s. 2.
100. [1982] IRLR 362 at p. 370.
101. [1956] AC 104 at p. 157.
102. Admittedly the position is complicated further by the Employment Act 1982, s. 15(7) where trade union rules are defined as meaning provisions 'forming part of the contract between a member and the other members'.
103. See Kidner, *Trade Union Law* (2nd edn, 1983), pp. 33–4.
104. See Gower, p. 211.
105. [1956] AC 104 at p. 127.
106. [1957] 1 WLR 321.
107. [1956] AC 104 at p. 153.
108. *Ibid.*, at p. 147.
109. 'The Bonsor Affair: A Postscript' (1957) 20 MLR 105.
110. (1915) 84 LJ KB 2236.
111. *Bonsor* v. *Musicians' Union* [1956] AC 104 at p. 131 (Lord Porter).
112. [1956] AC 104.

113. See Lloyd, 'Damages for Wrongful Expulsion from a Trade Union' (1956) 19 MLR 121; Thomas, 'Trade Unions and their Members' [1956] CLJ 67; Wedderburn, 'The Bonsor Affair: A Postscript' (1957) 20 MLR 105.

114. TULRA 1974, s. 2(1)(c).

115. *Bonsor* v. *Musicians' Union* [1956] AC 104.

116. 1913 Act, s. 3.

117. 1980 Act, ss. 4, 5.

118. 1984 Act, esp. ss. 1–9.

119. [1984] IRLR 350.

120. *Ibid.*, at p. 352.

121. *Ibid.*

122. *International General Electric Co. of New York Ltd.* v. *Commissioners of Customs and Excise* [1962] Ch. 784.

123. *Op. cit.*, at p. 352.

124. *Ibid.*

125. [1975] AC 326.

126. Employment Protection Act 1975, Schedule 6, Part IV, para. 6, inserting a new TULRA 1974, s. 17(2).

127. *NWL Ltd.* v. *Woods* [1979] ICR 867.

128. Cf *Cayne* v. *Global Natural Resources plc* [1984] 1 All ER 225 where it was held in a company law context that the court should have regard to the merits of the case if the interlocutory injunction will in practice finally dispose of the matter. See also *News Group Newspapers Ltd* v. *DSOGAT'82* [1986] IRLR 337.

129. [1971] Ch. 354.

130. Sachs LJ, at p. 378.

131. *Ibid.*

132. *Ibid.*, at p. 377.

133. *Ibid.*, at p. 363 (Buckley J).

134. *Ibid.*, at p. 383.

135. *Ibid.*, at p. 365.

136. *Ibid.*, at p. 378.

137. *Ibid.*

138. Royal Commission on Trade Unions and Employers' Associations 1965–68. *Report.* Cmnd. 3623, para. 661.

139. [1971] Ch. 354 at p. 378.

3

Admissions and the Closed Shop

Unions will rarely refuse to admit applicants for membership who have relevant qualifications under the union rules. After all, membership is their life blood. There are no comprehensive statistics on the proportion of rejected applications but in a survey of affiliated unions the TUC found that the number was very small.[1] They are likely to be more common in certain 'closed' unions, particularly those organizations which are keen to emphasize the status or professionalism of their members. For example, in their evidence to the Donovan Commission, the Showmen's Guild stated that about one in ten applicants is rejected.[2] Obviously the consequences can be very significant. If the closed shop operates, the person's livelihood will be affected; but, as will be argued, a rejection is still important apart from this because it prevents individuals from participating in an institution which can fundamentally affect their working lives. Legally, a distinction must be made between those situations where applicants are simply ineligible for membership and those where, despite being eligible, they are nevertheless considered unsuitable. In the former case it will be *ultra vires* the union to admit them into membership, provided the eligibility rules are valid and so there will be no discretion to admit; in the latter, the union is obviously empowered to admit if it so wishes. Before dealing with the different legal problems which arise in these areas, we refer to the procedure for admission operated by trade unions and consider the means available for resolving disputes about either eligibility or exclusion. The account which follows draws heavily on information provided in the report of a study conducted in 1982 by the *Industrial Relations Review and Report* (hereafter referred to as the 1982 study).[3]

ADMISSION PROCEDURES

Union Eligibility Rules

The 1982 study discovered that in terms of eligibility requirements, unions fall into four categories. The first are craft unions which usually set out admission requirements in great detail. The now amalgamated Boilermakers' Society, for example, outlined 53 separate occupational groups eligible for membership. Another common feature of craft unions is their insistence on a period of apprenticeship or similar training as a condition of full membership. APAC, for example, required either a three-year apprenticeship or four years' skilled work in the trade. An interesting feature of the study, however, is the evidence that the restrictive conditions of craft unions are being replaced by more flexible eligibility rules, 'enabling them to adapt to changing occupational structures, and in particular the long term decline of traditional craft trades'.[4] The report of the survey continues by explaining that the purpose of this development 'is partly to maintain membership levels and partly to protect the interests of their traditional memberships by gaining influence in the growth areas of employment that threaten to undermine their position'.[5] An example is provided by the NGA which, although composed mainly of printers, may now accept 'such other members whom the National Council shall consider it in the interests of the membership to admit'.[6]

The second category of unions is 'grade unions' which recruit from particular grades of employees. Examples include the FDA (senior civil servants) and STE (executive personnel at British Telecom). This type of union is particularly common in the public sector and it appears that membership is confined to people working in the grades in question. The third category is 'industrial and professional unions', with membership 'open to all, or at least a very wide range of, employees within a particular industry', as in the case of the NUR, or a particular profession, as in the case of the NUT or the NUJ.[7] The final category of unions is 'open unions'. It is true that the only entirely open union was the NUGMW (now GMBATU) where eligibility was extended to 'all persons engaged in any kind of industry or service'. There are, however, a number of unions — including ASTMS and APEX — which are open to a wide range of white-collar employees. There are also unions, such as the TGWU, which in general recruit from a wide range of employees, while many other unions can, at the discretion of their executive committee, recruit workers other than those expressly qualified.[8] It appears, however, that 'such discretionary powers are intended to allow the union to expand into new areas of employment in the future rather than to admit particular individuals'.[9]

Applications for Admission

The 1982 study revealed that although union admission procedures vary widely, applications are usually handled at branch level, though in some cases admissions must be approved by the national executive committee of the unions concerned. Where the latter practice is adopted, individuals will usually apply to the branch which will then make a recommendation for ratification by the executive committee. It appears in practice that 'the executive would only use its powers and vary the decision of the branch in unusual circumstances'.[10] Obviously, applicants may be rejected if they are ineligible for membership under the rules. But most unions have the power to reject applicants for other reasons, though it is not common for these to be expressly stated.[11] Those which are include previous expulsion for misconduct; previous dismissal from employment for misconduct; a criminal record; bad health; and lack of 'steady habits and good moral character'. It is common also for unions to restrict transfers from other unions, typically by requiring transferring workers to be in good financial standing with the union they have left. In addition, the NUGMW (now GMBATU) uniquely required that all admissions should be in accordance with the Bridlington principles.[12]

The 1982 study disclosed that only half the unions covered gave excluded applicants a right of appeal against exclusion.[13] The unions which did provide an appeal tended to fall into three categories: they were large (such as TGWU and ASTMS); they operated practices where exclusion would have a serious effect on the individual concerned (such as the NUJ); or they operated in the public sector or in banking where it was 'important for their image to be seen to be fair'.[14] It is to be noted, however, that a number of unions which had a large number of members working in closed shops — including AUEW, NUPE and APEX — did not provide a right of appeal for rejected applicants. Where there is an appeal, it will normally be to a higher body in the union: applicants rejected by a branch will be able to appeal to the national executive; those rejected by the national executive may appeal to a specially appointed appeals committee in the case of the NUT or the annual conference in the case of the NUR. Rules normally provide for rejected applicants to be given notice of their right of appeal and of the reason for their rejection. In some unions the appeal is less detailed than that which applies in the case of discipline of existing members: in some unions the appeal is in writing only. In contrast, a small minority of unions provide very extensive procedures, comparable to the disciplinary arrangements. So occasionally there will be a right to be heard in person, to produce written documents and to call witnesses. And, in addition to the right of appeal expressly provided in the rule book, there may also be a right of appeal to the TUC Independent Review Committee.

TUC Independent Review Committee

In 1976 Parliament repealed TULRA, section 5. This had enabled individuals to complain to an industrial tribunal for unreasonable exclusion or expulsion from union membership. Some opposition was expressed about the weakening of individual rights, and the TUC responded by establishing its own Independent Review Committee to consider certain cases of exclusion and expulsion. The Committee (Professor Lord Wedderburn, Lord McCarthy and Mr George Doughty) was appointed after consultations with the Secretary of State for Employment and the Chairman of ACAS. Unlike earlier statutory regulation in this area, the jurisdiction of the Committee does not extend to all internal union conflict or, indeed, to all complaints of arbitrary or unreasonable exclusion or expulsion. Rather, the IRC is seen specifically as a safeguard in the context of the closed shop, and its terms of reference are thus 'to consider appeals from individuals who have been dismissed, or given notice of dismissal, from their jobs as a result of being expelled from, or having been refused admission to, a union in a situation where trade union membership is a condition of employment'.[15] The requirement that a complainant must be dismissed, or have been given notice of dismissal, places an important constraint on the jurisdiction of the IRC; it means that the Committee has no authority to intervene in pre-entry closed shop cases where the complainant is seeking access to a trade or industry. Nevertheless, with the gradual extension of closed shops between 1976 and 1980 the Committee clearly had an important role to play in protecting workers from the arbitrary exercise of power by trade unions.

The Committee operates in a flexible and informal way, combining the functions of adjudication and conciliation. In a review of the Committee's work, it has been pointed out that in its approach to adjudication the IRC takes into account four issues.[16] These are whether the union has failed to act in accordance with its rules, whether it failed to comply with the requirements of natural justice, whether it has exceeded its powers under the rules, and whether it failed to act reasonably in all the circumstances, even where the power to expel or exclude did exist and where the terms of the rules were followed. The importance of this last consideration is illustrated by *Mayhew-Smith and ACTT*[17] where the applicant was told by a union official that if he successfully applied for a job in television he would be given union membership. The official even drew the applicant's attention to a job for which he successfully applied. However, following a ballot of the members he was refused admission to the union, principally because the union had a large number of unemployed members, many of whom were suitable for this post. Nevertheless the IRC determined to make a decision favourable to Mayhew-Smith, partly because of the unsatisfactory way the ballot was conducted and partly because of the conduct of the union official. A solution was made difficult, however, because the appellant could not immediately be made a full member without the union acting in breach of its rules, though the Committee did not explain why the union would be in breach of its rules by admitting the applicant. These difficulties were surmounted, however, with the Committee proposing and the parties agreeing that the union should provide the appellant with a document stating that 'in any application for suitable employment within the industry, he is to be treated as though he were a full member of the union in good standing, and on obtaining suitable employment, he will be admitted to membership of the union on reasonable terms'.

As already suggested, the Committee has eschewed traditional adjudicatory methods, attaching great importance to the role of conciliation in its work. Not only is an attempt made to conciliate in complaints, before they come to a formal hearing, but even in cases which do come to a full hearing, the Committee may engage in a process of post-hearing conciliation. This is never done without the agreement of both parties, and is undertaken in order 'to explore further the possibility of finding an agreed solution to the dispute'.[18] It has been explained that:

> The Committee tries, in most cases in which it engages in post-hearing conciliation, to ensure that the complainant does not remain unemployed if he is at the time of the hearing and to ascertain whether the union or unions involved are willing to assist in any way to this end, and if so, on what terms. The Committee believes that this approach is often more valuable than merely stating an 'award' or 'decision' and leaving the parties to go away and solve their difficulties unaided by the goodwill which frequently emerges at the hearing.[19]

Post-hearing conciliation was in fact attempted in all but three of the first 20 cases which went to full hearing. In some cases it was conducted without any formal decision on the merits, in cases where an agreed solution seemed possible. In other cases it was attempted despite decisions which upheld the unions in question. An example of this is *Buxton and TGWU*[20] where the complainant lost his job when a branch of the

TGWU refused to accept him into membership, following the introduction of a union membership agreement. In its evidence the union said that Buxton had once crossed a picket line at the plant and was regarded as anti-social and unco-operative by his workmates by whom he was resented. On the basis of these and other considerations, the Committee felt that the union had reasonable grounds to reject Buxton and said that it was unable to recommend his admission to the union as that 'would clearly create a very grave industrial relations problem in the plant'. Yet the Committee did seek to conciliate between the parties in order to arrive at an agreed solution. However, this broke down when Buxton refused to accept an offer by the union to find him suitable alternative employment, provided he promised to join the union should these attempts prove successful.

In view of the fact that the Committee does not have the power to award compensation, 'it is especially important that [its] approach to dispute settlement and its aim to preserve the employment of complainants should be effective'.[21] It has been claimed, however, that the IRC has been 'only partially successful in providing effective remedies for complainants. It has been extremely successful in getting complainants admitted or re-admitted into membership where it has recommended such a step [but] it has been singularly ineffective in securing re-engagement or alternative employment for complainants.'[22] It would have been possible to deal with this problem by unions agreeing to suspend any decision to expel pending a decision of the IRC. Alternatively, it could have been provided in union membership agreements that the dismissal of an excluded or expelled worker would not take place until the Committee had dealt with a complaint. It is true that some union membership agreements did in fact make provision for appeals to the Committee, and that following decisions of the EAT dismissals for non-membership will be unfair unless such procedural requirements are exhausted.[23] It is true also that several unions had pointed out that 'they would not carry out a decision to expel until the IRC had deliberated'.[24] But such arrangements were far from universal with the result that 'there is considerable scope for improvement'[25] in union practices on this issue. The matter has, however, become largely academic in view of the fact that the work of the Committee has been taken over to a large extent by the industrial tribunals following the statutory right introduced by sections 4 and 5 of the Employment Act 1980. Although the IRC has a number of advantages over the tribunals (relating mainly to informality), it has to be said that the statutory jurisdiction is not without its virtues for rejected applicants. This is a point to which we return.

ADMISSIONS AND ELIGIBILITY

A difficult problem which has occasionally arisen in the context of union membership occurs where persons are admitted into the union but it is later claimed that the admissions are invalid, on the ground that he or she is ineligible for membership. One such case, *Boulting* v. *ACTT*,[26] involved a claim by union members that they were never lawfully members because it was contrary to public policy that they should have been admitted. The others have involved claims by the union that the members were never validly members at all because they were not properly admitted, either because they did not comply with the eligibility rules of the union concerned, or because they did not comply with the procedures for admission. It is important to note that if the union can establish that the 'member' was never validly admitted, it may evade all the safeguards which would normally apply where membership is forfeited — notably by expulsion. They are able to discontinue treating the individuals as members without any need for a formal expulsion since they are deemed never to have had a valid contract, and as a consequence are left without any effective common law redress.

Public Policy

The *Boulting* case raised a very important issue of public policy. The plaintiffs were managing directors of a film company, and as such they exercised both managerial and technical functions. They had at one time joined the union, but later, by agreement with a local union official, their membership was suspended after they had contended that their position as managing directors was incompatible with their status as union members. However, several years later the union again required them to be full members, indicating that industrial action might be taken if they refused. The plaintiffs then sought protection in the courts, claiming a declaration that they were ineligible for membership, and an injunction to prevent the union from taking any action designed to compel them to hold current membership cards. The union eligibility rule stated:

> The association shall consist of all employees engaged on the technical side of film production . . . including film directors, employee producers, associate producers, script-writers, and all employees of the cine-camera . . . departments.

The plaintiffs argued that they were ineligible on two counts. First, they claimed that they were employers and not employees, so that on the construction of the union rules themselves they were ineligible. But a majority of the Court of Appeal rejected this contention. They held that, as managing directors, the plaintiffs were employees of their company and so fell within the purview of the rule, Upjohn LJ asserting that 'a rule dealing with eligibility should be broadly construed and not narrowly'.[27] Any success on this score would, in any event, have proved a pyrrhic victory for the plaintiffs since the union rules were subsequently altered to make it clear that employers were eligible for membership. The second contention of the plaintiffs was that even if they were *prima facie* eligible for membership, their fiduciary duties to their company would render any membership unlawful or *ultra vires*, because their obligations as union members would inevitably bring them into conflict with this duty. This argument, too, was rejected by the majority. They were not convinced that a genuine conflict of duty and interest would inevitably arise, particularly since other persons in a position comparable to the plaintiffs were union members.[28]

Lord Denning gave a powerful dissenting judgment.[29] He thought it contrary to public policy for the union to have a rule which would require its members to act inconsistently with a fiduciary duty which they had undertaken. Unlike the majority, he was in no doubt that the conflict was inevitable. The majority did not, however, leave the plaintiffs totally defenceless. They left open the possibility that the contract of membership might have been avoided at the company's option. Logically though, this would seem to be possible only if the conflict was inevitable, and the majority was not prepared to say that it was. If it is not inevitable, then the company can intervene only if and when the union actually seeks to induce the members to breach their fiduciary duties to the company: a potential conflict is not enough. Indeed, the courts have not even been willing to restrain a person from holding directorships in rival companies — though admittedly there are hints that they might now be willing to do so, and yet the probability of conflict would seem to be far greater in that situation.[30] It appears then that the company could not, at common law, argue that its directors are infringing their fiduciary duties *merely* by belonging to the union. Even if they could, the common law has now been overtaken by statute. Parliament has given a right to all employees to belong to independent trade unions and take part in their activities at the appropriate time.[31] No exception is made for executive directors or employees of senior managerial rank and therefore they would seem to be able to assert, as against their company, the right to belong. They could, however, be restrained from furthering the interests of the union at the expense of the company and in breach of their fiduciary obligations. But then it would be particular activities which could be attacked by the company rather than membership *per se*.

Invalid Admissions

There have been a few cases where the union has claimed that a person who has been exercising all the rights of membership and been subject to the duties of membership was never in law a member at all. The argument is that people who have failed to comply with the qualifications for membership under the rules are not, and never can be, eligible for membership. Consequently it is *ultra vires* for the union to accept them, and even if they purport to do so, this apparent membership can never be valid. In *Martin* v. *Scottish Transport and General Workers' Union*,[32] the pursuer had been admitted in wartime to the union, but only on special conditions which enabled the executive committee to terminate his membership once hostilities ceased. He was, however, assured that this would not happen. After the war the executive purported to exercise this power. The pursuer claimed, *inter alia*, a declarator that he was a member of the union as the condition affecting the duration of his membership was *ultra vires*. The House of Lords dismissed his appeal. The rules made no provision for a temporary class of membership, and in attempting to create such a category without any proper amendment of the union rules, the executive committee had exceeded its powers. The court held that the original act of admission had been invalid so that the plaintiff had never been a member at all. Nor were their Lordships dissuaded from reaching that decision by the difficulty involved in working out an equitable adjustment of rights between the pursuer and the union.[33]

In *Faramus* v. *Film Artistes' Association*[34] the plaintiff claimed to be a member of the defendant union which operated a pre-entry closed shop policy. One of the union rules was designed to prevent dishonest persons from joining the union. In principle such a rule was desirable, for 'it might create trouble between member and managers or between member and member if such dishonest persons could roam the changing rooms as of right'.[35] But, unfortunately, the rule was drawn too widely and rendered ineligible, for instance, persons convicted of riding a pedal cycle without lights. It stated: 'No person who has been convicted in a court of law of a criminal offence (other than a motoring offence not punishable by imprisonment) shall be eligible for, or retain membership of, the association.' On application for membership the plaintiff denied that he had been convicted of any offences, whereas he had in fact been twice convicted of rather trivial offences in Jersey. After he had been an active member for several years, the union discovered this fact and, for reasons that are not clear, they challenged his membership, claiming that he was not and never had been a member since he was never eligible for membership. The plaintiff sought a declaration that he was a member and an injunction to prevent the union from excluding him from membership. The House of Lords refused both claims, declining to treat the particular rule as invalid either because it was unreasonable or because in the context of the closed shop it operated in restraint of trade.

The union was saved from the latter invalidity by section 3 of the Trade Union Act 1871 which made such agreements lawful.[36] As we have seen, this aspect of the decision has now been cast into some doubt by the development of the concept of the right to work and the duty to act fairly with the result that some eligibility rules will now be treated as invalid at common law, and possibly even this particular rule. Clearly, however, where the rule is deemed valid, then at common law the union is in no position to admit an ineligible applicant, even if it desires to do so. Such an action is *ultra vires* the union and so cannot be ratified even by the members collectively. But not every wrongful admission will be *ultra vires* the union. Where the applicant is eligible for admission but the procedures are irregular, then different considerations apply. Here the admission is within the powers of the union and it is only the method employed which is irregular. Consequently, the membership of a person admitted in this way would not automatically be void. This conclusion is supported by *Clarke* v. *NUFTO*.[37] The plaintiff signed an application form but it was lost. However, he paid his dues and even became a shop steward. At a later point he was in dispute with the union and they purported then to reject his application. Upjohn J concluded that this was tantamount to an expulsion because 'there was no doubt that Clarke was a member'. Again in *Rothwell* v. *APEX*[38] Foster J held that individuals could become union members by conduct alone providing they were qualified for membership.

The *Faramus* and *Martin* decisions both give rise to some disquiet;[39] neither case does the unions concerned much credit. It is, however, arguable that a union should not be obliged to retain in membership people they were induced to admit as a result of a misrepresentation about their credentials. Indeed, under the Misrepresentation Act 1967 the union would be entitled to rescind the contract of membership whether such misrepresentation was innocent or fraudulent. However, they would have to do so within a reasonable time, otherwise they would be deemed to have affirmed the contract.[40] The unsatisfactory feature about *Faramus* is that it apparently permits the union to take advantage of the member's ineligibility at any time notwithstanding that it has been fully aware of the facts. The risk of ineligibility at any time hovers like the sword of Damocles above the member's head, perhaps to strike only if the member become unpopular or opposes official decisions. The union may thus be able to take advantage of the *ultra vires* principle well beyond the time when it could rescind for misrepresentation. It is not even open to the member to rely on estoppel. In *Faramus* such a plea was rejected on the ground that the plaintiff could not rely on his own misrepresentation 'to create any sort of estoppel in his own favour'.[41] This is perfectly consistent with principle: it is well established that the doctrine of estoppel cannot operate to extend an organization's powers. The Donovan Commission recommended that a member's admission should not be open to question after a period of two years had elapsed.[42] But this has never been implemented.

EXCLUSION FROM MEMBERSHIP

The classic common law position was that union membership is a privilege and not a right, and that unions could exercise a wide and virtually untrammelled decision as to whom they would admit. It was thought that there were no grounds upon which the courts could intervene. An applicant for membership has no rights in the union itself, nor will he or she have any contractual relationship with it. Because they have no legally recognized right, they have no remedy. Admittedly, in *Weinberger* v. *Inglis*[43] the House of Lords asserted that refusal to re-admit a member to the Stock Exchange might be actionable if it were made in bad faith, but their Lordships did not make clear how that duty to act in good faith could be enforced. The traditional view, illustrating the defenceless position of the rejected applicant, was succinctly stated by Budd J in the Irish case, *Tierney* v. *Amalgamated Society of Woodworkers*:

> But what right of property or of contract or what existing right of any sort, one must ask, is a person who is not a member of a trade union, deprived of by not being permitted to join such union? He is certainly not deprived of any right of property, nor is he deprived of any other right, be it work or otherwise, which he had before. He is, at most, only deprived of acquiring a right.[44]

However, a close analysis of this dictum suggests that it may overstate the question in principle, though in practice the analysis is no doubt sound. There are three possible areas for intervention by the common law.

Declaration of Eligibility

It is now well established in English law that the court may grant a declaration even though the plaintiff has no cause of action recognized in law. In *Guaranty Trust Co. of New York* v. *Hannay and Co.*,[45] Pickford LJ stated that the effect of the rule of the Supreme Court relating to declarations[46] was 'to give a general power to make a declaration whether there be a cause of action or not, and at the instance of any party who is interested in the subject matter of the declaration'.[47] The courts have been very flexible in their use of the remedy and, as Megarry J has remarked, the tendency towards width and flexibility has in recent years been accentuated.[48] The decisions in particular would lend support to the view that the courts would be willing to grant at least a declaration of eligibility to a rejected applicant. In *Boulting* v. *ACTT*[49] the plaintiffs sought a declaration that they were not eligible for union membership, and the Court of Appeal accepted that it was in principle the kind of situation where a declaration could be granted, while refusing one in this particular case. Lord Denning expressly stated that the courts have jurisdiction to grant a declaration of right 'whenever the interest of the plaintiff is sufficient to justify it';[50] and Upjohn LJ also indicated that a declaration could be granted even in the absence of any contractual link. In *Eastham* v. *Newcastle United Football Club Ltd.*,[51] Wilberforce J followed these opinions and granted the plaintiff a declaration that the rules of the Football League and Football Association were in unreasonable restraint of trade. Furthermore, he considered it no bar to such a remedy that the plaintiff had no contract with either of these bodies. This approach was also followed by Slade J in *Greig* v. *Insole*.[52]

In the light of this liberal approach to the declaration, it is possible that a court would be willing to grant a declaration as to the eligibility of a rejected applicant. This does not secure membership, but it is at least a step in that direction. Furthermore, in the context of a rejection based on Bridlington, a court might well be prepared to hold that an award of the Disputes Committee was *ultra vires* and therefore not binding on the accepting union; or that the union itself had wrongly interpreted Bridlington in rejecting the applicant. However, this is far less valuable to a rejected applicant than it would be to an expelled member. For whereas any purported rejection will certainly be unlawful if it is to implement an *ultra vires* award of the Disputes Committee, a finding of *ultra vires* in an admissions context will not necessarily secure admission into the union at all. This is because subject to possible constraints imposed by the doctrines of the right to work and the duty to act fairly, which are discussed below, the union can reject a member for any reason it wishes, and therefore whether it is relying upon an *ultra vires* or *intra vires* award, or even no award at all, would seem to be irrelevant. However, this does not make such a declaration wholly pointless. The union concerned may well have complied with reluctance with the Disputes Committee award, and may be delighted to treat the declaration as an excuse to ignore the award and take the individual concerned into membership. Furthermore, the TUC could no doubt be prevented by an injunction from imposing any sanctions upon a union acting in breach of an *ultra vires* award.

Tortious Remedies

Secondly, in exceptional cases a rejected applicant may be able to frame an action in tort, relying upon one or more of the economic torts. Had English law accepted the view that any unjustifiable interference with a person's trade was unlawful, this would have provided the obvious remedy for a rejected applicant arbitrarily refused admission. But in *Allen* v. *Flood*[53] the House of Lords held that there was no such wrong in English law. Consequently other more specific torts must be relied upon. The most likely relevant tort in this context is conspiracy to injure. This requires action by two or more persons, but since most applicants are rejected by committees, this will generally be the case. An action for conspiracy can take two forms. In its narrow form, it consists of any combination to do an act by unlawful means; in its wider form, it consists of any combination intended to injure another by means not necessarily unlawful in themselves.

The narrow form of conspiracy is however, unlikely to prove relevant in the case of a rejected applicant. The only unlawful act union officials would be likely to commit would be to break certain statutes regulating union admissions, such as the Sex Discrimination Act or the Race Relations Act which would probably be considered unlawful means for the purposes of conspiracy. But in any event, if those Acts are breached they will provide their own remedies, and the conspiracy action will be rarely invoked, though considerations of time limits and remedies could make them attractive in certain circumstances. However, in neither form of conspiracy is there liability unless the plaintiff can show that the defendants are acting without justification. This requirement has long been necessary to establish the wider form of conspiracy, and surprisingly it has now been applied to the narrow form also by the House of Lords in *Lonrho Ltd.* v. *Shell Petroleum Co. Ltd.*[54] In law the question of whether the action of the defendants is justifiable or not depends upon their motives. If they act honestly and with the intention of furthering their own interests, then they will not be liable for any damage inflicted on the plaintiff providing the courts consider their interests to be proper ones. If, on the other hand, they act dishonestly or in bad faith or in pursuit of improper objectives, then they may be liable. This does not mean that the defendants are required to have a malicious intent to injure personally, as is made clear by the speech of Lord Maugham in *Crofter Hand Woven Harris Tweed Company* v. *Veitch*:

> It seems to me, therefore, . . . a mistake to hold that combinations to do acts which necessarily result in injury to the business or interference with the means of subsistence of a third person are not actionable provided only that the true or predominant motive was not to injure the plaintiff and that no unlawful means are used. For instance, the object of the combination may be a dislike of the religious views or the politics or the race or the colour of the plaintiff, or a mere demonstration of power by busybodies . . . There is, I think, no authority to be found which justifies the view that a combination of such a character, causing damage to the plaintiff, would be lawful.[55]

The significance of this dictum is that it indicates that an action for conspiracy can possibly lie where the defendants are pursuing wholly unreasonable objectives. No personal spite or malice need be involved. But ultimately the judges will determine whether the purpose of a combination which inflicts damage is one which the law will protect. There are a number of difficulties in pursuing this action. First, it is possible that in the present state of the law there is no obligation on the union to give reasons for its decision. Yet without reasons, it is difficult to determine the defendants' motives. Secondly, the conspiracy action can be brought only where interests of the plaintiff are adversely affected. It is essential to establish damage. Where the closed shop operates, so that job opportunities are affected, this will be relatively easy, but outside that context it will be far more difficult. Plaintiffs need to establish that loss of union membership *per se* is sufficient damage: that is, that the loss of an opportunity to influence the institution which can significantly affect their terms and conditions of employment is itself enough. It must remain doubtful whether the courts would be inclined to recognize this damage as actionable at the present time. If not, then the conspiracy action would be limited to the closed shop context, in which case it would in any event prove to be practically redundant if a claim based on the right to work (to which return) were accepted by the courts, because the latter does not rest on motive and is thus far easier to establish.

Action Based on Contract

It is readily assumed that contract can have no role to play in the regulation of union admission. Mere publication of union rules will not usually be construed as giving rise to a contractual offer of any kind, though it was thought at one stage that it might. In *Davies* v. *Carew-Pole*,[56] Pilcher J concluded that a contract could arise where people submitted themselves to the jurisdiction of a domestic tribunal, and that its terms would be to oblige the body to comply with its rules and natural justice. Harman J also accepted this possibility in *Byrne* v. *Kinematograph Renters' Society*.[57] This situation is analogous in some respects to that which arises when an application is made for union membership. Hence it was thought that a union might similarly be bound by some contractual obligation towards an applicant for membership, if only an obligation to give reasonable consideration to the application.

However, in *Nagle* v. *Fielden*[58] the Court of Appeal emphatically rejected this argument. In that case, it will be recalled, the Jockey Club had refused Mrs Nagle a licence because she was a woman. She argued, *inter alia*, that the rules of the Club constituted an offer that applications for a licence would be reasonably considered and not rejected on arbitrary or capricious grounds. The relevant rule stated: 'The Stewards of the Jockey Club have power at their discretion . . . to grant and withdraw licences'. Lord Denning thought that to spell any contractual obligation from the rules could only be achieved by inventing a fictitious contract,[59] and Salmon LJ agreed. At most, the rule was an invitation to treat. No doubt it would have been a perversion of the ordinary principles of contract to have inferred any contractual intention from the rule in question. The same can be said of union rules which constitute a mere statement of qualifications for membership. But ultimately it all depends upon the particular rules under consideration. It is misleading to make assumptions about union rules as though they were all alike. In practice, they all display wide diversity both in form and content, and in assessing the degree of potential regulation much is likely to depend upon the particular language used. In *Nagle's* case, Salmon LJ held that 'It is impossible *as a matter of construction* to spell any offer such as the plaintiff suggests' (emphasis added).[60]

It is true that Salmon LJ carefully refrained from saying that it should never be possible to spell any offer from the construction of a union's rule, but it is only in very exceptional circumstances — if at all — that the way in which union rules are framed could be held to constitute an offer of membership. It might arise, however, by unions specifying that applicants who qualify under the rules should be entitled to admission, or that they will admit persons who fulfil the conditions of eligibility. This might well be construed as an offer, indicating a willingness to be bound by any person meeting the conditions. Another possible contractual situation could arise from a rule which provides an applicant with 'provisional membership', pending a decision about full membership.

In such cases a court might now assert that since a form of membership has been obtained, the union must comply with the rules of natural justice before it can reject the applicant, the latter having a legitimate expectation of full membership.[61] Finally, it is possible that the court might treat a person re-applying for membership differently from an original applicant. In *Weinberger* v. *Inglis*[62] the plaintiff re-applied for his annual membership of the Stock Exchange but his application was rejected. The House of Lords held that the only duty of the committee of the Stock Exchange was to act honestly and in good faith. In the Court of Appeal, Bankes LJ said that he thought there was 'considerable force' in the argument that the plaintiff had a 'contractual right to have his application for re-election considered and dealt with by the committee in accordance with the rules and regulations of the Stock Exchange for the time being in force',[63] and this received some support from Lord Birkenhead LC in the House of Lords.[64]

This contractual right, if it exists, must therefore arise as an implied term in the original contract of membership. However, in the Stock Exchange members were re-elected annually, and it would be easier to justify an implied term of this kind in those circumstances than it would in a union where membership is of indefinite duration. Moreover, union rules often deal specifically with re-election in terms which would be inconsistent with any such implied term. Particularly where the original membership was terminated through lapsing or expulsion, the terms of re-admission will be stricter than those of admission, and there will be no grounds for construing any implied obligation on the union. However, exceptionally it might be possible to argue that the position of members who 'honourably' left the union, that is amicably and after settling their dues, is different. Thus, the rules of the Scottish Typographical Association stated that 'such members shall ordinarily be granted provisional cards and admitted free'.[65] The NGA states that, where a member has lawfully resigned, re-admission *shall* be granted him 'provided his conduct towards the trade has been honourable'.[66] In these rare cases it might be possible for applicants to argue, on the basis of the slender dicta in *Weinberger's* case, that they have a continuing contractual right at least to have their applications fairly considered in accordance with the rules and perhaps, in the case of the NGA at least, a right of admission if the conditions in the proviso have been met.

THE RIGHT TO WORK AND THE DUTY TO ACT FAIRLY

It is clear so far that the rejected applicants have little scope to challenge their exclusion from membership, even in closed shop cases. Union autonomy is, however, under threat, first by the potential which may yet be fulfilled by embryonic common law developments, and more immediately by statute. So far as common law developments are concerned, the possibility that the right to work or the closely related doctrine of the duty to act fairly might found a basis for providing a remedy to a rejected applicant has already been considered. In *Nagle's* case it was accepted that it was at least arguable that the right to work could provide a cause of action recognized by English law, and the decision in *Edwards* v. *SOGAT*[67] adds a little weight to that contention. Although the latter case was primarily concerned with expulsion from the union and the doctrine of the right to work was employed to invalidate a union rule, there had also been a refusal to re-admit the member after his expulsion. Lord Denning treated the matter thus:

> Once [the plaintiff] was excluded, the union treated his readmission as a matter for their discretion. He applied twice and each time he was refused. Such a refusal may sometimes be justified, as when the trade is oversupplied with labour. But it will not be justified if it is exercised in an arbitrary or capricious manner or with unfair discrimination.[68]

Sachs LJ was content to leave open the question of whether a refusal to admit or re-admit was 'so destructive of the "right to work", in the sense of "right of equal opportunity to obtain work", that it is invalid as being contrary to public policy for the reasons discussed in *Nagle* v. *Fielden*'.[69] This doctrine would at the time of writing enable the courts to intervene in those unions operating the closed shop, though it probably would not permit them to challenge other exclusions.

As we have also argued, however, the duty to act fairly might give a rejected applicant a cause of action even where no closed shop operates. However, while the duty to act fairly could possibly extend to provide a more extensive coverage than the action based upon the right to work, the substance of the protection would seem to be the same in both cases. Both are concerned with preventing arbitrary or capricious decisions. Moreover, although these doctrines were discussed in Chapter 2 in the context of considering how far they might be utilized to enable the courts to exercise control over the substantive decisions taken by the union, they are also capable of imposing basic procedural obligations, at least in a suitable case. As Jackson has argued:

> Once it is conceded that the courts will control the grounds on which bodies such as the Jockey Club may refuse to grant licences it surely follows that the procedure for the consideration of applications is subject to legal control. Without a hearing how can the facts be established? To decide without a hearing of important matters is, in itself, arbitrary and unreasonable.[70]

If this is intended to imply that there should always be a hearing involving written notice of any considerations which are likely to be adverse to the plaintiff's application, coupled with an opportunity for him or her to make representations, it is plainly overstating the case. This might create an unduly onerous burden on the organization; but at the same time, procedural considerations are clearly relevant when determining whether the union had handled an application fairly.

The Scope of the Doctrines

What then is the scope of these doctrines, either on substantive or procedural grounds? The indications are that they will be limited though, as was pointed out in Chapter 2, they could undermine the union's cohesiveness if widely construed. In particular, there are uncertainties about how the concepts will be applied to rejections made in accordance with the Bridlington principles, or where admission is refused because the trade is oversupplied with labour. At a substantive level, both concepts will clearly cover the more obvious discriminatory rules, though unions which formerly discriminated on grounds of sex or nationality will in any event be acting unlawfully to continue to do so because such discrimination is contrary to the Sex Discrimination and Race Relations Acts.[71] But in practice the problems are likely to arise not because of discriminatory rules as such; these will be extremely rare. Far more likely will be the possibility of an arbitrary or unreasonable rejection being concealed behind the exercise of a discretion given by the rules, such as where personality clashes, favouritism, or perhaps a dislike of political views will lead to a person's exclusion. This is particularly likely to occur in unions which have a decentralized admissions procedure and where local conflicts may be bitter. However, the difficulties facing a rejected applicant in these cases lie not so much in the substantive principles, as vague as these are, but rather in the problem of proof.

This leads on to a consideration of procedures, and in particular the question of whether reasons need be given for a refusal. If there is no such obligation it becomes extremely difficult indeed to challenge effectively the exercise of a discretion to reject. The only significant discussion of the procedural safeguards which are likely to be required in the case of a refusal to admit is in the decision of Sir Robert Megarry in *McInnes* v. *Onslow-Fane*.[72] It gives little comfort to rejected applicants. Sir Robert held that the content of the duty to act fairly would vary depending upon the particular matter in issue, and he distinguished three broad categories of situations. First there are the forfeiture cases, such as expulsion from a union, where the principles of natural justice will apply in a detailed and vigorous way. Second there are the pure application cases where the only question for the committee is the general suitability of the applicant. Here there is an obligation not to act capriciously or arbitrarily, but there are no procedural obligations as such, neither an opportunity to give a hearing nor the duty to give reasons. In arriving at this conclusion that no reasons need be given, Sir Robert was following the traditional common law view which the House of Lords had accepted in *Weinberger* v. *Inglis* and which had been more recently confirmed by Salmon LJ in *Nagle* v. *Fielden*. But this does not mean that procedural obligations will never arise, for Sir Robert distinguished a third intermediate category which he discussed as the 'legitimate expectation' cases. These arise where applicants may have an expectation that they will be granted a licence or membership of an organization, but this is refused to them.

Could admissions into the union ever be brought within this intermediate category? And, if so, what procedural safeguards will then apply? Arguably some admissions could, particularly since the phrase 'legitimate expectation' is a vague one which leaves the courts much room for manoeuvre. Effectively it means no more than those expectations which the judges think ought to be given some protection in law. So, if an admission is normally a formality as it is in many of the 'open' unions, then it might be argued that applicants have a legitimate expectation, particularly since a rejection may involve a slur on their character or integrity. Again, where a closed shop is introduced into a company the court might be taken to conclude that existing employees have a legitimate expectation of membership and that certain procedural safeguards should apply to them, even though they cannot be fairly dismissed by their employer on the ground of their exclusion from the union. Nevertheless, it must be admitted that even if the applicants can bring themselves into this category, the procedural requirements are still likely to be considered to be highly exiguous. A consideration of these safeguards arose in *Breen* v. *AEU*[73] which, while not an application case, was classified by the court as a 'legitimate expectation' case. The plaintiff had been elected as a shop steward but the district committee had refused to confirm his election. Although it was held that the committee was under a duty to act fairly, the majority in the Court of Appeal thought that this would not necessarily involve any procedural obligations at all. Generally, there was no duty to inform the plaintiff of the considerations which were likely to weigh with the committee, nor to give the plaintiff a hearing, nor to give reasons.

Lord Denning, dissenting, would, in contrast, have imposed fuller procedural obligations:

> If . . . a man . . . has some right or interest, or some legitimate expectation, of which it would not be fair to deprive him without a hearing, or reasons given, then these should be afforded him, according as the case may demand.[74]

But the law may yet be developed to protect the applicant. In the Closed Shop Code of Practice it is provided that union procedures on exclusion as well as on expulsion should comply with the principles of natural justice.[75] It is specifically stated that these include a notice of the complaint and a reasonable opportunity of being heard. The potential impact of its provisions is considered in more detail below when the statutory action for unreasonable exclusion is considered. However, it should be emphasized that the Code has to be taken into account not merely in tribunals but also in the courts.[76] And while it is not law, it is likely to be influential in moulding the development of procedural standards at common law. It must be distinctly possible in the light of the Code that Lord Denning's dissenting judgment in *Breen* will in future be taken to represent the state of English law on the question of procedural safeguards for applicants to membership, at least where the applicant is seeking work in employment regulated by the closed shop. Independently of the Code, there are two other principles which the courts could employ to aid the rejected applicant. First, even if the courts continue to reject the proposition that there is a duty to give reasons, they may be willing to say that if none are given adverse inferences may be drawn from that fact. In *Padfield* v. *Minister of Agriculture, Fisheries and Food*,[77] the House of Lords indicated that they would be willing to draw such inferences where a Minister refused to give reasons, so this would be a far from revolutionary development. Furthermore, in *Breen's* case Lord Denning considered that this would apply to trade union committees.[78] Secondly, now that statute has provided a right of appeal for a person unreasonably refused membership of the union,[79] it might be contended — as it has been in the field of unfair dismissal — that the union is under an obligation to give reasons in order to make that right effective. But this would apply only where the applicant is affected by the closed shop.

The Remedy

One important question is what remedy rejected applicants could claim if they could establish that there had been an infringement of their 'right to work' or of the 'duty to act fairly'. In *Nagle* v. *Fielden* the plaintiff sought, *inter alia*, a *mandatory* injunction ordering the stewards to grant her a licence, and Lord Denning commented that if the facts were proved 'she may have a good case to ask for a declaration and injunction';[80] though he did not specify that this could be a mandatory one.[81] To grant a mandatory injunction could be to compel a party to contract and it is most unlikely that the courts would be willing to do this. Nor should they: the gist of the wrong in *Nagle's* case was not that Mrs Nagle was refused her licence but that she was refused it for an arbitrary reason. And this would be precisely the nature of the complaint of someone arbitrarily excluded from a union. Hence the injunction can only be justified in order to prohibit the union from refusing admission for that arbitrary reason, not for refusing it at all. Admittedly, in practice this will often be sufficient to enable the applicant to secure the membership he or she is seeking. So would the courts be willing to grant a negative injunction? It seems highly likely that they would, particularly since they will give an injunction to protect a property right, and Lord Denning has frequently asserted that the 'right to work' is equally as important as any proprietary right, if not more so.[82] There is no evidence, however, that damages will be available. The right to work is an independent cause of action falling outside the traditional categories of contract and tort. Apart from the fact that damages are not available, this has other important consequences. If the right to work is not a tort, any restoration of trade union immunity in tort, by the repeal of section 15 of the Employment Act 1982, would not prevent the doctrine from being relied upon.

STATUTORY REGULATION

Statutory regulation of trade union admission has traditionally been of marginal importance only. The Trade Union Act 1913 provided that unions could not lawfully refuse admission to applicants who indicated that they would be unwilling to contribute to the political fund. Unions are required to have a rule to that effect,[83] though Parliament failed to provide any means by which such a rule might be enforced.[84] The Sex Discrimination Act 1975[85] and the Race Relations Act 1976[86] both apply to trade unions, making it unlawful for unions to discriminate on grounds of sex or race in the terms by which they are prepared to admit people into membership, or by refusing or deliberately omitting to accept applications for membership. Regulation of this kind has proved uncontroversial, though it has been necessary to invoke it against trade unions from time to time, despite the fact that trade unions are one of the driving forces behind attempts to remove discriminatory practices from the workplace. These discrimination provisions are supplemented by EEC Regulation 1612/68 which provides by Article 8 that 'A worker who is a national of a Member State and who is employed in the territory of another Member State shall enjoy equality of treatment as regards membership of trade unions and the exercise of rights attaching thereto . . .' But so far as this applies to admissions, it appears now to be well covered by domestic law for under the 1976 Act discrimination on racial grounds is defined to mean discrimination on the ground of colour, race, *nationality*, or ethnic or national origins.[87]

Much more controversial, however, is the more general regulation of union admission procedures. Potentially, this gives the courts a considerable power to usurp the autonomy of union rules and their administration — a particularly significant power in the context of the pre-entry closed shop. A degree of regulation of union admission procedures was proposed by the Donovan Commission which recommended some independent legal scrutiny of 'alleged arbitrary rejection of an application for admission to a trade union, or a particular section of a trade union'.[88] Control of this kind has also been high on the Conservative Party's shopping list, having been introduced in the Industrial Relations Act 1971[89] and the Trade Union and Labour Relations Act 1974,[90] at the insistence of Conservative peers. In the latter case the measures in question were repealed in 1976,[91] but controls were re-introduced by the Thatcher administration's Employment Act 1980. Like the TUC Independent Review Committee, this is a remedy confined to areas where the closed shop operates, though the new statutory jurisdiction is wider in crucial respects than the voluntary jurisdiction of the Independent Review Committee. Section 4 of the 1980 Act applies 'to employment by an employer with respect to which it is the practice, in accordance with a union membership agreement, for the employee to belong to a specified trade union or one of a number of specified trade unions'.[92] In such circumstances any person who is, or who is seeking to be, in such employment has the right not to be unreasonably refused admission to a trade union (or unreasonably expelled — a point to which we will return in Chapter 6).

The Scope of Section 4

Unlike the Independent Review Committee, the statute applies to both pre-entry and post-entry closed shops: applicants need not identify a specific job which they have lost as a result of their exclusion. This was confirmed by *Clark* v. *NATSOPA*[93] where the EAT held that section 4(1) plainly contemplates someone who is seeking engagement in a particular field of industry, and that it would strain the statutory language 'to attribute to Parliament the intention that every complainant should be able to point to a particular job that it is open to him to accept but which he cannot accept because he has been denied membership of a union operating in the closed shop where that job exists'. The Appeal Tribunal continued by saying that such an interpretation would not only involve an artificial view of the statutory language, it 'would lead to injustice in its application in everyday industrial life'.[94] And they concluded on this question:

> That would be particularly true of an industry like the printing industry where the union with which we are currently concerned has achieved a remarkable degree of success in establishing a closed shop policy. Such success is reflected by the fact that many job vacancies are not advertised to the world at large but are only notified to the union, so that a printer who is not a member may never even learn of them. Much of the mischief at which the 1980 Act was directed would be eroded if it were to be construed so narrowly as to required each complainant to show that he had been denied a specific job opportunity as a result of his refusal of membership — when the harsh facts of industrial life would have supplied him with no means of ever discovering what the job opportunities were.[95]

So Section 4 applies to any exclusion from membership of a specified trade union where a closed shop exists. For this purpose, a trade union is widely defined by section 4(10) to include a branch or section of a trade union. In *NATSOPA* v. *Kirkham*,[96] however, that provision was rather narrowly construed in a way which may significantly restrict the operation of the section in the printing industry.

The *Kirkham* case concerned an application by Mr Kirkham that he had been refused membership of a particular section of the appellate union. He was a union member but had been placed in a particular category by the union, namely class 3 casual worker, and as a result was unable to get regular employment because the union determined how work should be allotted and would not give regular work to persons in that category. In order to be able to obtain regular employment, he had to be transferred out of the category allotted to him. He applied for a transfer on various occasions but each time he was refused entry into another category. Furthermore, he was denied the right to appeal to the Executive Council notwithstanding that the union rules purported to confer that right upon him. On the face of it, exclusions of this kind would seem to be precisely the kind of mischief which the provision was designed to remedy. But the EAT found that nonetheless section 4 was drafted too narrowly to cover this situation, taking the view that it meant that applicants had to show that they had been rejected from membership of a trade union specified in the union membership agreement itself. But in this case Mr Kirkham had not been so rejected: he was in the specified union (NATSOPA being specified in the relevant union membership agreement). The problem was that he was not in the relevant category to gain permanent employment.

So could Mr Kirkham go further? Could he invoke section 4(10) and successfully allege that even though he was in the specified union there was still an unlawful exclusion since he had been unreasonably denied access to the relevant category of the union from which permanent employees were drawn? Section 4(10) of the Act seemed to suggest that he could since it expressly states that reference to a trade union includes 'a reference to a branch or section of a trade union'. But the EAT found against him on this argument also, for two separate reasons. First, it said that the term 'branch or section' referred to an organizational unit within the union. It did not in the EAT's opinion describe the situation in which Mr Kirkham found himself. Although he was in a category which had rights different from those of other members, this did not constitute a *distinct* organizational unit.[97] Secondly, it held that since under section 4(1) the employee had to be a member 'in accordance with a union membership agreement', this meant that it was necessary for the relevant branch or section to be specified in the union membership agreement itself.[98] The EAT reached these conclusions reluctantly, recognizing that as a result unions could be able readily to evade the clutches of section 4. All a union will need to do is specify in a formal union membership agreement that membership of the union is a condition of employment while in practice imposing a stiffer condition and permitting certain members only to be employed, namely those falling within a particular category of membership which does not constitute an independent organizational unit. Although few unions are likely to seek to avoid section 4 in this way, a number of cases have already shown how important a decision this is in the printing industry where arrangements of the kind in *Kirkham* are not uncommon.

A different, less formal, approach is in fact evident in the decision of the EAT in *Howard* v. *NGA (No. 3)*,[99] Browne-Wilkinson J also presiding, though the value of this case is undermined slightly by the fact that the only evidence available was that provided by the respondent. His evidence was that he had been a member of the Liverpool Typographical Association which in time became part of the NGA. In 1966, he took a managerial position and became ineligible for membership of the Association. In such circumstances he could, however, become a 'country member' of the Association, paying no subscriptions but being kept on a supernumerary list. His evidence was that if at a later date a country member wished to become a full member again 'he could simply do so and start paying his dues again without any problem'.[100] Howard remained in managerial positions until 1981 when he found non-managerial work at a firm called Rudham and Rowley which was offered subject to his union membership being in order. The respondent was assured by a branch secretary that there would be no difficulty in his becoming a full member again and his application was submitted accordingly. In anticipation of being accepted, Howard began work but was suspended pending his union membership being confirmed. In the event, however, the branch committee decided not to admit him for reasons which will be discussed in the next section. One of the issues which arose in the appeal was that there was no case under section 4 because Howard had not been excluded from membership of the Association; he was already a country member and was merely refused full membership; there was no refusal of membership of a branch or section of the union. However, this was rejected on the ground that 'he was being refused membership of the kind required under the union membership agreement between the employers and the union',[101] and *Kirkham* was distinguished unconvincingly as 'dealing with a wholly different factual situation'. The contrast in approach is profound: *Kirkham* limited section 4 to membership of an organizational unit; *Howard* extended it to membership of a kind required in order to obtain or retain employment. If this approach had been adopted in *Kirkham*, both of the arguments presented by the EAT for its decision would have been unsustainable: Kirkham was excluded from membership of the kind necessary for the employment which he sought. It remains to be seen which of these approaches is subsequently followed. Although the EAT in *Goodfellow* v. *NATSOPA*[102] (Bristow J presiding) appeared to accept *Kirkham* as authoritative on this point, *Howard (No. 3)* was not cited and the matter must thus remain open.

Unreasonable Exclusion

The Act applies in the event of an 'unreasonable' exclusion from membership. The question of reasonableness is tested 'in accordance with equity and the substantial merits of the case', thereby mirroring the reasonableness test in unfair dismissal. The Act specifically provides that compliance with the rules does not of itself establish that the union has acted reasonably, nor does a breach of the rules automatically demonstrate unreasonableness. This is the same as the position with the contract of employment in unfair dismissal cases. No other guidance is given in the Act, though the matter is dealt with in the Code of Practice on Closed Shop Agreements and Arrangements. Although the Code is not directly enforceable, section 3(8) of the Employment Act 1980 provides that it is admissible in evidence and that it shall be taken into account where it appears to be relevant to the proceedings. While it is true that the application of the Code is confined to exclusions and expulsions in closed shop cases, it is also true that it may be taken into consideration not just before an industrial tribunal in the statutory jurisdiction under discussion, but also in actions brought at common law, where for example the plaintiffs are seeking to enforce their right to work.[103]

The Code makes it clear that reasonableness embraces both procedural and substantive requirements. So far as procedural requirements are concerned, the Code provides in paragraph 56 that in handling admissions, 'unions should adopt and apply clear and fair rules' which cover:

(a) who is qualified for membership;
(b) who has power to consider and decide upon applications;
(c) what reasons will justify rejecting an application;
(d) the appeals procedure open to a rejected applicant;
(e) the power to admit applicants where an appeal is upheld.

The 1982 study by IRRR discovered that the degree of union compliance with the Code was patchy. Then 'most rulebooks state very clearly which body within the union has the power to accept or reject applicants for membership'.[104] Similarly, 'union rules are reasonably clear on which types of workers are qualified for membership'.[105] On the other hand, generally unions 'do not state in detail the other grounds on which an applicant might be rejected. A great deal is left to the absolute discretion of the body within the union making the decision.'[106] Similarly, only half of the unions reviewed comply with the Code of Practice by giving excluded applicants a right of appeal, and where there is an appeal this is generally separate from and much less detailed than those applying to members on a disciplinary charge. Yet the Code proposes in paragraph 58 that union procedures on exclusion, as well as expulsion, should 'comply with the rules of natural justice. These include giving the individual member fair notice of the complaint against him, a reasonable opportunity of being heard, a fair hearing and an impartial decision.' However, although admission appeal procedures tend to fall short of disciplinary procedures, it does not follow that these procedures (where they are provided) fall short of the requirements of natural justice. As was pointed out in *McInnes* v. *Onslow-Fane*[107] natural justice is a flexible concept which applies differently in different contexts. In particular, the standards demanded of an admissions procedure are likely to be much less rigorous than those demanded of a disciplinary or expulsion procedure.

Failure to comply with these procedural requirements could well render an exclusion unlawful, even though the union had good cause to reject a particular application. As a result, the Code may yet have some influence on the content of union rules. So far as substantive considerations are concerned, the Code provides by paragraph 56 that when determining whom they might accept into membership, unions should have regard to the following three factors:

(a) whether the person applying for membership has the appropriate qualifications for the type of work done by members of the union or section thereof;

(b) whether because of the nature of the work concerned the number of applicants or potential applicants has long been and is likely to continue to be so great as to pose a serious threat of undermining negotiated terms and conditions of employment. The Code expressly refers to 'acting' as the type of work which it has in mind, but to nothing else;

(c) whether the TUC's principles and procedures governing relations between unions or any finding of a TUC Dispute Committee are relevant. This is a rather tepid recognition of the Bridlington principles. It's to be noted that these are only 'relevant', and that the union may not necessarily be in the clear if it excludes someone in accordance with these principles. They are 'relevant', not conclusive.

One final point in this context is that TUC-affiliated unions are instructed to bear in mind its guidance on matters of exclusion and expulsion. It is not clear to what guidance this refers. Indeed, it appears that the last time the TUC took any serious initiative in this area was in 1969, in response to the Donovan Report.[108]

At the time of writing there is only one reported case which deals with what is meant by 'an unreasonable exclusion', and the value of this is limited slightly by the fact that the union did not appear at the initial hearing before the industrial tribunal. In *Howard* v. *NGA (No. 3)*[109] a case to which we return again in the next section, the evidence before the industrial tribunal was that the complainant had been refused full membership of the NGA on the ground that he had been expelled for arrears of £6.18.9d. (£6.94) in July 1966, the branch committee also taking into account the considerable number of unemployed members that they had in the branch. The industrial tribunal, in upholding the complaint, rejected the claim that there were in fact any arrears, accepting Mr Howard's uncontradicted evidence on the point. But even if there had been arrears, the tribunal held further that this would not be a reasonable ground for refusing admission, whatever the terms of the union's rules as then constituted. On the question of the existing levels of unemployment in the branch, the tribunal could not see this as a justifiable reason for excluding Howard from membership and thus prevent him from taking a job which he had been offered. They continued, embracing the underlying values of the legislation, uncritically and without equivocation, 'It appears to be a gross interference with the natural liberties of the subject to do something of that nature, whatever the respondent's rules may say . . .'[110] In so holding, the tribunal appeared to disregard the rules completely, having regard only to considerations of reasonableness. On appeal the EAT substantially qualified the holdings on both the relevance of the union's rules and on the question of unemployment. So far as the first of these issues is concerned, the appeal tribunal held that union rules were not irrelevant in determining unreasonableness, but that they are not decisive. Thus it concluded that the industrial tribunal had erred in law to the extent that they held that the matter did not have to be decided on the basis of the rules which each individual union may have. This is a crucially important holding of the *Howard* litigation, which not only restores some autonomy to trade unions, but may ensure that reasonableness is determined in the context of each particular union, rather than in accordance with some general judicially imposed concept of reasonableness.

On the question of unemployment, the EAT drew attention to the Code of Practice. Although the Code did not directly cover the facts of the *Howard* case, 'it does indicate that the state of unemployment or otherwise amongst members of the union in a particular industry can be taken into account as a factor in deciding whether or not a union's refusal to admit further applicants is, or is not, reasonable'.[111] Consequently the appeal tribunal held that the industrial tribunal had made a second error of law, to the extent that it had said that 'the state of employment amongst members of the union was irrelevant'.[112] Again this is crucially important and safeguards at least one of the functions of the pre-entry closed shop. But the union won a pyrrhic victory on these counts, for the EAT then went on to uphold the decision of the industrial tribunal. The major problem facing the union was the evidential one. The union had boycotted the tribunal proceedings and, having lost, appealed against the decision, wishing to admit evidence at the appeal of a kind which they would have led had they appeared before the industrial tribunal in the first place. On a preliminary point, however, both the EAT and the Court of Appeal held that the former body was empowered to exclude evidence from the appeal where the evidence was reasonably available at the time of the industrial tribunal hearing. So, in dealing with the appeal from the industrial tribunal's decision, the EAT was led to conclude, despite the errors of law in the reasoning of the IT:

> . . . the Industrial Tribunal had before it only evidence from Mr. Howard and none from the Association. The facts, as the Tribunal found them on the basis of that evidence, were that Mr. Howard had been a country member; he was not in arrears with his dues; as a country member he was entitled, more or less as a right, again to become a full member; he had been assured that there would be no trouble about it; he had taken a job on that basis, and the Association had then refused him membership. All those facts, if correct (as we are bound to assume that they are), would show a very strong case of unreasonable conduct by the Association in refusing to give him membership. All that would come into the balance on the other side would be such evidence as there was before the Tribunal as to the rules of the Association and as to the unemployment position amongst members of the Association. There was no such evidence before the Tribunal. Therefore, even if the Industrial Tribunal had weighed them, the factors that they could have taken into account would have been very limited and could not possibly have, in our judgment, altered the decision on fairness and reasonableness in this case.[113]

Remedies

A union cannot be compelled to take an individual into membership. The sanctions merely seek to encourage the union to admit (or re-admit), but ultimately it can refuse to do so and 'buy off' a dissentient member, in much the same way as an employer can finally refuse to re-engage or reinstate a dismissed worker. However, even if the union refuses to take him or her, any dismissal by the employer will be automatically unfair once a tribunal has established unreasonable exclusion or expulsion. Initially, people wishing to make a complaint will take their case to an industrial tribunal. This must be done within 6 months of the alleged unreasonable act.[114] In the case of exclusion, it is provided that if the union drags its feet and simply fails to make any decision on a person's application, it will be deemed to have refused it at the end of a period within which it might reasonably have been expected to have granted admission.[115] Before the case is heard, conciliation officers will seek to settle the matter, just as they do in other employment cases, and a settlement so reached will be legally binding. However, if they fail, and the tribunal upholds the complaint, it may initially award only a declaration to that effect.[116]

No doubt many applicants would be admitted or reinstated following the declaration, and some will choose to take no further action. However, a claim for compensation can be made at any time after four weeks from the date when the declaration has been made,[117] though the procedure for so doing, and the potential sums which may be awarded, vary depending upon whether the union has admitted or re-admitted the member before the case is presented.[118] If it has, the claim for compensation lies to a tribunal which may award compensation up to the maximum which can be awarded in unfair dismissal cases where there has been no order of re-engagement or reinstatement.[119] If there has been no admission or re-admission in that period, the claim lies to the EAT and there is a higher maximum payment — this time the maximum sum that can be awarded in an unfair dismissal case when there has been a refusal to re-engage or reinstate.[120] The measure of compensation is also different in the two claims. In the tribunal application the purpose is simply to compensate the applicant for the loss sustained by the exclusion or expulsion.[121] In the EAT proceedings it is to award what it considers 'just and equitable',[122] which suggests a broader basis of assessment. In *Howard* v. *NGA (No. 5)*,[123] account was taken not only of loss of earnings but also non-pecuniary loss, including injury to feelings and upset in the applicant's personal life suffered as a result of the refusal of membership.[124] It would not have been open to an industrial tribunal to take into account this non-pecuniary loss, though it is taken into account by them in unfair dismissal proceedings. A disturbing feature of the judgment in *Howard (No. 5)* is the failure of the EAT to attribute a particular figure to any of the different heads of damage (four in that case) identified by it.[125]

There are several significant features of the statutory jurisdiction which arise in the context. First, when hearing section 4 cases the industrial tribunal and the EAT will continue to adopt their usual form of a lawyer, employer representative and union representative. This contrasts with the proposal of the Donovan Commission, which had suggested the creation of a statutory review body to hear complaints of arbitrary exclusion from membership.[126] The view of Donovan, however, was that there should be two union representatives sitting with the lawyer, on the ground that the employer is not really a party to these problems. An attempt to introduce such an arrangement into the 1980 Act failed when the government rejected an amendment to this effect, taking the view that it would unnecessarily fragment the unity of the tribunal system. It is a matter of regret that this amendment was not accepted. It would have given unions greater confidence in the ability of the tribunals to give adequate consideration to the unions' collective interests in cases of this kind. A second significant feature of the jurisdiction is that although the Code of Practice requires unions to have an appeals procedure open to rejected applicants, they are not required to exhaust such remedies before making a complaint to an industrial tribunal. A union rule to this effect appears to be expressly prohibited by section 4(11) which declares void an agreement purporting to exclude or limit the operation of the section, or purporting to preclude any person from making a complaint. Any discretion which the tribunals might have in this regard appears to be eliminated by the Code which, although agreeing that voluntary procedures are generally to be preferred to legal action, nevertheless states at paragraph 60 that 'since an individual may face considerable economic loss or adverse social consequences as a result of exclusion or expulsion from a union it would be unreasonable to expect him to defer his application to a tribunal'.

A third point to note is that on the initial question of whether the union has acted unreasonably, there is right of appeal for either party both on fact and law to the EAT, thereby providing the only case where there can be an appeal on a point of fact from a tribunal.[127] This was justified on the ground that in principle all tribunal decisions should be subject to appeal on fact and law, but the volume of unfair dismissal cases precludes this possibility. It is envisaged that the number of internal union cases will be small, and that appeals on fact and law can readily be brought. If such appeals were treated as a complete rehearing, such as where decisions of magistrates are appealed to the Crown Court, it could add considerably to the cost of an appeal, such as the extra time in rehearing all the witnesses, particularly since the hearings will normally be in London and perhaps a long way from the locality where the dispute arose and where the tribunal heard the original case. However, in *NATSOPA* v. *Kirkham*[128] the EAT held that complete rehearings were not what section 4 required.[129] Browne-Wilkinson J (presiding) said that the appeals were similar to those made to the Court of Appeal from the High

Court: the evidence was to be found in the transcript or notes of evidence before the industrial tribunal, and further evidence could be admitted only in exceptional cases. Although this severely limits the ability of an appellant to re-open matters of fact, this approach was nevertheless endorsed by the Court of Appeal in *Howard* v. *NGA (No. 4)*.[130] It is to be noted that appeal from an industrial tribunal on the level of compensation is on a point of law only.

NOTES

1. TUC Annual Report 1969, p. 142.

2. Royal Commission on Trade Unions and Employers' Associations 1965–1968, Written Evidence 208.

3. 'Union Procedures on the Admission and Expulsion of Members — A Survey of Current Practice', *Industrial Relations Review and Report*, No. 272, May 1982, pp. 2–7.

4. *Ibid.*, at p. 3.

5. *Ibid.*

6. *Ibid.*

7. *Ibid.*, at p. 4.

8. *Ibid.*

9. *Ibid.*

10. *Ibid.*, at p. 3.

11. *Ibid.*

12. *Ibid.*, at p. 4.

13. *Ibid.*

14. *Ibid.*

15. TUC Annual Report 1976, p. 94.

16. Ewing and Rees, 'The TUC Independent Review Committee and the Closed Shop' (1981) 10 ILJ 84, on which this account draws heavily.

17. TUC Annual Report 1979, p. 385, noted by Ewing (1979) 8 ILJ 184.

18. TUC Annual Report 1978, p. 391.

19. *Ibid.*

20. TUC Annual Report 1977, p. 341.

21. Ewing and Rees, *op. cit.*, pp. 95–6.

22. 'The Independent Review Committee: The Success of Voluntarism', *Industrial Relations Review and Report*, No. 208, September 1979, p. 2 at p. 5.

23. *Jeffrey* v. *Laurence Scott Electromotors Ltd.* [1977] IRLR 466; and *Curry* v. *Harlow DC* [1979] ICR 769.

24. Ewing and Rees, *op. cit.*, p. 98.

25. *Ibid.*

26. [1963] 2 QB 606.

27. *Ibid.*, at p. 634. As Grunfeld states, this illustrates a tendency, often not found in other areas of trade union affairs, to treat the union as a voluntary association to run its affairs and determine its membership as it sees fit (p. 18).

28. *Ibid.*, at pp. 636–40 and 647–9.

29. Lord Denning relied heavily on *The Roundabout Ltd.* v. *Beirne* [1959] IR 423 where it was held that the directors of a company were not employees. However, he ignored decisions to the contrary, e.g. *Lee* v. *Lee's Air Farming* [1961] AC 12. For a criticism of this aspect of his judgment, see Rideout, 'Liberty of a Trade Union to Compel Breach of a Legal Duty' (1963) 26 MLR 565 at pp. 566–8.

30. See Gower, pp. 599–604.

31. See 1978 Act, ss. 23 and 58.
32. 1952 SC(HL) 1.
33. *Ibid.*, at p. 8.
34. [1964] AC 925.
35. *Ibid.*, per Lord Pearce at p. 946.
36. See now TULRA, s. 2(5).
37. *The Times*, October 18, 1957.
38. [1976] ICR 211.
39. See Rideout, 'Trade Union Membership, the 1890 Style' (1963) 26 MLR 436 at p. 438.
40. Misrepresentation Act 1967, s. 1. See Treitel, pp. 294–6.
41. *Op. cit.*, at p. 948.
42. Royal Commission on Trade Unions and Employers' Associations 1965–1968. *Report.* Cmnd. 3623, para. 617.
43. [1919] AC 606.
44. [1959] IR 254 at p. 258.
45. [1915] 2 KB 536.
46. RSC, Ord. 15, r. 16.
47. *Op. cit.*, at p. 562.
48. *Thorne RDC* v. *Bunting* [1972] 1 All ER 439 at p. 442.
49. *Op. cit.*
50. *Ibid.*, at p. 629.
51. [1964] Ch. 413.
52. [1978] 1 WLR 302.
53. [1898] AC 1.
54. [1981] 2 All ER 456.
55. [1942] AC 435 at p. 451.
56. [1956] 1 WLR 833.
57. [1958] 2 All ER 579.
58. [1966] 2 QB 633.
59. *Ibid.*, at p. 646.
60. *Ibid.*, at p. 652.
61. See *infra*, pp. 78–82.
62. [1919] AC 606.
63. [1918] 1 Ch. 517 at p. 547.
64. [1919] AC 606 at p. 616.
65. STA Rules (1968), r. 32(1).
66. NGA Rules (1979), r. 19(2).
67. [1971] Ch. 354.
68. *Ibid.*, at p. 377.
69. *Ibid.*, at p. 383.
70. Jackson, *Natural Justice* (1973), pp. 51–2. See also Jackson, *Natural Justice* (2nd edn., 1979), p. 121.
71. Sex Discrimination Act 1975, s. 12, and Race Relations Act 1976, s. 11.
72. [1978] 1 WLR 1520.
73. [1971] 2 QB 175.
74. *Ibid.*, at p. 191.
75. Code of Practice on Closed Shop Agreements and Arrangements (1983), para. 58.
76. Employment Act 1980, s. 3(8).
77. [1968] AC 997.
78. *Op. cit.*, at p. 191.
79. Employment Act 1980, s. 4.
80. [1966] 2 QB 633 at p. 647.
81. See Weir, 'Discrimination in Private Law' [1966] CLJ 165.
82. See *Lee* v. *Showmen's Guild of Great Britain* [1952] 2 QB 329 at p. 343, and *Edwards* v. *SOGAT*, *op. cit.*, at p. 376.
83. Trade Union Act 1913, s. 3(1)(b).
84. Ewing, *Trade Unions, the Labour Party and the Law* (1982), pp. 133–4.
85. Sex Discrimination Act 1975, s. 12.

86. Race Relations Act 1976, s. 11.

87. Emphasis added. The word in parenthesis was added to the definition following the decision of the House of Lords in *Ealing LBC* v. *Race Relations Board* [1972] AC 342 that the term 'national origins' in the Race Relations Act 1968 did not extend to present nationality.

88. *Op. cit.*, para. 659.

89. 1971 Act, s. 65.

90. TULRA 1974, s. 5.

91. TULR(Am.) A 1976, s. 1.

92. 1980 Act, s. 4(1).

93. [1985] IRLR 494 (noted by Kidner (1986) 15 ILJ 129).

94. *Ibid.*, at p. 498.

95. *Ibid.*

96. [1983] IRLR 70.

97. *Ibid.*, at p. 76.

98. *Ibid.*

99. [1983] IRLR 445.

100. *Ibid.*, at p. 446.

101. *Ibid.*, at p. 447.

102. [1985] IRLR 3.

103. Employment Act 1980, s. 3(8).

104. *Op. cit.*, p. 3.

105. *Ibid.*

106. *Ibid.*

107. *Op. cit.*

108. This point is considered in detail in Chapter 8.

109. *Op. cit.*

110. EMP 4490/82. Discussed by the EAT, *ibid.*, at p. 446.

111. *Ibid.*, at p. 448.

112. *Ibid.*

113. *Ibid.*

114. Employment Act 1980, s. 4(6).

115. 1980 Act, s. 4(9).

116. 1980 Act, s. 4(7).

117. 1980 Act, s. 5(3).

118. 1980 Act, s. 5.

119. 1980 Act, s. 5(7). The maximum award of compensation is governed EPCA 1978, s. 75(1).

120. 1980 Act, s. 5(7).

121. 1980 Act, s. 5(4)(a).

122. 1980 Act, s. 5(4)(b).

123. [1984] IRLR 489.

124. See also *Day* v. *SOGAT 82*, IDS Brief 327 (1986).

125. Cf, however, the subsequent cases, *Saunders* v. *Bakers, Food and Allied Workers' Union* [1986] IRLR 16 and *Day* v. *SOGAT 82, op. cit.*, where clear breakdowns were made. It is to be noted also that in *Saunders* a 20 per cent deduction was made for contributory conduct and in *Day* a deduction of half of state benefits received was also made.

126. *Op. cit.*, para. 658.

127. s. 4(8)

128. *Op. cit.*

129. *Ibid.*, at p. 77.

130. [1984] IRLR 250, upholding the EAT in *Howard* v. *NGA (No. 2)* [1983] IRLR 442.

4

Trade Union Government and The Courts

Trade unions must be governed in accordance with the constitution laid down in their rules. This is subject to any overriding statutory requirements, such as those introduced by the Trade Union Act 1984, which we consider in Chapter 5. If the union does not act in accordance with its constitution, it will be open to any member to challenge the validity of the action in the courts on the ground that it is a breach of contract. This is subject to certain ill-defined limitations which together operate occasionally (but very rarely) to prevent the member from restraining every constitutional irregularity. In this chapter we consider the power which the constitution gives the courts as an instrument to control trade union government, and we look specifically at the miners' strike of 1984/85 as an illustration of the nature of that control and the power which it confers upon the judges.

Control of the powers of union officials through the contract of membership is supplemented by fiduciary constraints. Curiously the precise application of these fiduciary principles to trade unions is uncertain. Not only is there a dearth of authority defining the nature and scope of the fiduciary obligation of union officers, there is scarcely any recognition that such duties exist. This is in sharp contrast to company law where the nature of the fiduciary duties which directors owe to their companies has been exhaustively analysed. In part, this is because of the different interests at stake. A shareholder's financial interests may well be adversely affected by a breach of fiduciary duty — especially since this breach frequently takes the form of directors benefiting themselves at the expense of the company — whereas union membership does not confer similar material benefits which will be threatened by the exercise of powers by union officials. Consequently there may be a greater reluctance to get involved in the expense of litigation. Perhaps an additional reason lies in the fact that the different origins of unions and companies have resulted in an emphasis on different techniques of legal control.

Because of their unincorporated origins, contract has provided so dominant a mechanism for controlling internal union affairs that even where issues might have been decided on equitable principles, lawyers have tended to ignore these and have argued instead on the basis of contractual principles only. As a result, in this chapter we concentrate our attention on the contractual remedies, though equitable considerations will be considered where appropriate.

THE *ULTRA VIRES* RULE

Some of the most important cases in trade union law have involved a union member obtaining an injunction to prevent the union exceeding its powers. These powers are to be found within the constitution. As we have seen, in the celebrated *Osborne*[1] case the House of Lords went further and imposed a concept of statutory *ultra vires* upon the unions, treating the unions' powers as being derived from statute. However, with the reversal of that decision by the Trade Union Act 1913 unions can do what their constitutions permit, and the concept of *ultra vires* is contractual rather than statutory. Even so, it provides a significant basis for judicial intervention. A House of Lords decision in the early years of this century provides a vivid illustration. In *Yorkshire Miners' Association* v. *Howden*[2] a member was able to restrain the payment of strike pay. The union rules permitted strike benefit to be paid for strikes which were taken with the sanction of the association. However, in the particular case the sanction was obtained after the industrial action had commenced. Their Lordships held that on a proper construction of the rule the payments were unlawful even for the period subsequent to the sanction being given, and furthermore they refused to imply any power to grant such benefits. It was completely irrelevant that the activity had been acquiesced in by the vast majority of the members. If the union lacks the capacity to pursue the act in question, then it will remain unlawful for it to do so until the necessary rule book alteration, made in accordance with the rule-amending procedures stipulated in the constitution, is effected.

On the surface the restraining of unconstitutional action simply involves the courts in their normal functions of interpreting the constitution and implying terms into the contract of membership. Both are involved in establishing the scope of the union's power. The union's capacity will be determined primarily by examining its rule book. From the Trade Union Act 1871 up until the repeal of the Industrial Relations Act in 1974 it was always obligatory for registered unions to specify all of their objects in their constitution, and although this is not now strictly

necessary[3] — indeed, not even listed unions need have a formal constitution at all — in practice the vast majority still do so. The rules usually
set out the objects or purposes of the union and the powers or methods
which it employs to pursue them. But whatever the apparent scope of its
powers, the union cannot of course be authorized to take action which
will involve it in various unlawful activities or will otherwise be contrary
to public policy, though the precise scope of this category is not always
certain. So in two early cases it was held to be unlawful for a union to
give financial support to officers who had incurred legal costs in prosecu-
ting civil actions, even though the action directly benefited the union, on
the grounds that such payments amounted to the now abolished tort of
maintenance.[4] Problems of illegality still occasionally arise. In *Drake* v.
Morgan[5] a member of the NUJ sought to restrain the union from paying
the fines of certain of its members who had been convicted of unlawful
picketing. Boreham J held that a resolution authorizing the payment of
fines for crimes already committed was not unlawful. However, he
added that it would be illegal to indemnify members in advance for fines
incurred in committing future crimes, and that if the union were to make
a practice of indemnifying for crimes already committed, thereby
creating an expectation among the membership that they would be able
to rely upon the union for payment, this would likewise be unlawful.

Implying Powers

For most purposes the distinction between objects and powers is
unimportant, and many union constitutions tend to use the terms inter-
changeably. However, occasionally the distinction is highly important
in law, for whereas it is possible to imply powers where they are reasonably necessary for the attainment of the union's objects, it is not possible
to imply fresh objects themselves.[6] In practice, powers will readily be
implied in the administrative sphere. For example, there will inevitably
be powers to appoint employees, acquire property, invest funds and
generally carry out those administrative functions which any organization needs to be able to do, irrespective of whether any such power can
be found in the rule book. But outside this area, implication will be rare:
there is virtually no room for implying powers to discipline, for example.
Furthermore, a power will not be implied merely because this will
benefit the union. So in *Oram* v. *Hutt*,[7] Lord Parker declined to hold that
the payment by the union of legal costs incurred by union officers who
had successfully sued a member for slander should be treated as implicitly
authorized by the union constitution, even though he conceded that the
union had been adversely affected by the slander.

Nevertheless there is some scope for implication, though inevitably judicial perceptions of the way in which the union ought to function will influence the way in which the discretion to imply fresh powers is exercised. This influence was clearly seen in *NUM (Kent Area)* v. *Gormley*.[8] The union's national executive committee proposed to hold a secret ballot of the whole membership on the question of whether the union should enter into a national productivity incentive scheme agreed with the National Coal Board. Its acceptance would divert a likely confrontation between the miners and the then Labour Government over incomes policy. Certain members of the NEC, representing particular areas, were strongly opposed to the scheme and sought an interim injunction, ex parte, to prevent the ballot taking place. One of the arguments advanced was that proposals for the scheme and the calling of the ballot were inconsistent with conference resolutions. This is further discussed below. The other was that there was no power in the constitution to permit a ballot to be called by the executive since there were express provisions in the rules permitting ballots to be called by the union conference in certain circumstances, and it was urged that these should be considered exhaustive. The Court of Appeal rejected this on the grounds that the NEC was entrusted with wide powers and duties and so this power to take a ballot could readily be implied. It was particularly willing to do so since the result was that the membership would have the opportunity to comment directly on the proposals, and the court clearly considered this to be desirable. Lord Denning said that:

> the ballot was a sensible and reasonable proposal by the NEC to take the views by the democratic method of a secret ballot of all the workers affected. It was a far more satisfactory and democratic method than leaving it to the delegates of a conference who might not be truly representative in their individual capacities of the views of the various men they represented.[9]

Interpreting the Constitution

The tests for implying powers are vague, but questions of interpretation often give the judges even wider discretionary powers over the manner of trade union government. An interesting illustration of this is *Bennett* v. *National Amalgamated Society of Operative House and Ship Painters and Decorators*[10] This case also demonstrates the importance of distinguishing between transactions which are wholly outside the union's power and those which, while within its powers, have been exercised in an unlawful manner. The general council of the union instructed the union trustees to buy shares in a company which had been formed for the purpose of publishing a newspaper to support and promote the policies of the Labour Party. One of the objects of the union was 'to aid other societies having for their objects the promotion of the interests of workmen'. The rules of the union did not specifically provide for investment in commercial concerns, but the court seems to have accepted that such a power could be implied, being reasonably incidental to the union's objects. A member sought a declaration that the payment was *ultra vires*, an order requiring the trustees to repay the money wrongly invested, and an injunction to restrain any such expenditure in the future. Warrington J upheld the member's contentions. The expenditure did not, in his Lordship's view, fall within the specific power to aid other societies promoting the interests of workmen; and his Lordship further expressed the opinion that even if investing in commercial concerns had been expressly provided for, this particular expenditure would have been an *ultra vires* transaction since its purpose was not simply to make an investment but rather to make a contribution towards the expenses of publishing a newspaper.

Yet the issue was by no means clear, and the opposite result could readily have been reached in relation to both conclusions. First, the company would no doubt have been seen by the union as a society whose objects were to promote the interests of workmen, albeit in an indirect way, and it would not have been unreasonable for his Lordship to have interpreted the rule accordingly. Instead, he held that it only permitted support for societies which, like the defendant society, were established primarily to promote the interests of workmen. Secondly, it could be argued that in holding that this expenditure was not an investment, his Lordship was confusing two separate questions. One is whether the payment was *ultra vires* the union, and the other is the different issue of whether the general council were acting properly in exercising their power to invest in the way in which they did. Once it is conceded that there is a power to invest in trading concerns it is difficult to see how that activity can become *ultra vires* because of the motive with which it is done. No doubt it would have been possible to argue that the general council, and through them the trustees, had acted in breach of their fiduciary obligations when they sought to make this payment since there was evidence to suggest that they were exercising their power to benefit a third party rather than the union. But as the judge himself seemed inclined to accept, it would not then have been open to an individual member to complain of that breach of duty since it was not owed to him. The 'proper plaintiff' aspect of the rule in *Foss* v. *Harbottle*[11] would have prevented the member from taking action on his own account. Only the union itself could have complained since only its rights would have been infringed. However, once the expenditure was held to be *ultra vires*, it was open to individual members to restrain it. The classification of the unlawful act was all-important.

In *Bennett's*[12] case the union trustees were held liable to repay the money unlawfully distributed. This case was followed in *Carter* v. *United Society of Boilermakers*[13] where the facts were almost identical, but in that case the action was taken against the union and the members of the Executive Council and it was they, rather than the union trustees, who had to make good the expenditure. Younger J commented that 'it is from those within their own union who supported their action that they must look for relief, and not from the funds contributed in part by members who disapproved of the whole transaction from the beginning'.[14] It is not possible to say how far the courts in these two cases were influenced by the particular political stance which the respective unions adopted, although it is difficult to believe that this was a wholly irrelevant factor. What these cases do demonstrate is that where the rules of the union are expressed in sufficiently broad terms, judicial policies and attitudes are given a relatively free play in the process of construction. An interesting case contrasting with *Bennett* and *Carter* on the question of interpretation is the decision of the Court of Appeal in *Cotter* v. *NUS*[15] The union passed a resolution to make a long-term loan to support the miners' non-political movement. This was shortly after the general strike. The loan was challenged on a number of grounds including on the basis that the payment was *ultra vires*. The union sought to justify it as falling within the scope of an objective 'to promote and to provide funds to extend the adoption of trade union principles', and this was accepted by the Court of Appeal. Yet it might easily have been persuaded by the arguments of the plaintiff that the primary purpose was to foster non-political activity rather than extend trade union principles[16] In that case the loan would either have been *ultra vires*, or at least an *intra vires* loan for an unlawful purpose.

Evading an *ultra vires* Challenge

Because of the courts' reluctance to imply powers, unions sometimes seek to include in the rule book not only a statement of specific detailed powers but also a general residual power. The form in which this is expressed varies, but the rule in NUFLAT is fairly typical. It stipulates a power 'generally to improve the conditions and promote the interests of members of the union and to do all such things as are conducive to the attainment of the above objects and which a trade union may lawfully do'.[17] Interpreted literally, a provision of this kind will make an *ultra vires* challenge very different. In *Kelly* v. *Wyld*[18] the Civil Service Clerical Association had as one of its objects the aim to protect and promote the interests of its members, and it was provided that the association could take any lawful action it might choose in pursuance of its objects. The Executive Committee approved a small charitable grant to a fund set up to relieve the distress, caused by the Spanish Civil War, of women and children in Spain. The plaintiff alleged that this payment was *ultra vires*, but Luxmoore J rejected this contention. The objects were, he said, of a wide and elastic character, and the court could not determine what was in the interests of members of the association. Consequently the expenditure was *intra vires*.

However, it should not be assumed that the courts will always adopt such a favourable construction of rules of this kind. It is true that in the area of company law they will have been willing to interpret general subjective powers very widely,[19] but the principles of construction which the courts will adopt in that context are not necessarily the same as those which they will adopt in relation to unions. In the former, the questions of *ultra vires* generally arise in disputes between a company and third parties, whereas in the latter they typically involve the union and its members. The policy reasons for wishing to narrow the scope of the *ultra vires* rules in the company cases, notably a desire to uphold commercial arrangements entered into in good faith, do not similarly apply to unions. There the policy is more likely to be to curb the power of officers and ensure that they have a clear authority for the activities they undertake. This will lead to a restrictive rather than an expansive interpretation of the constitution. So *Kelly's* case should be treated with caution. The clause in that case could be read as a statement indicating how specific discretions given by the rules should be exercised rather than as a separate, broad power. Some evidence of a reluctance to read apparently wide powers literally is afforded by *Jordan* v. *UCATT*.[20] The High Court refused to accept that a power given to the Executive Committee 'to determine anything whereon the rules are silent' enabled the committee to impose conditions of eligibility for union office in addition to those specified in the rules. In the light of that decision, it is inconceivable that the courts would be willing to interpret such a rule as enabling a union committee to have *carte blanche* to extend the union's specific powers in any way, though the broader construction of that rule would permit this.

INTRA VIRES BREACHES

There are relatively few cases falling into this category. This is hardly surprising since the cost of bringing an action is not inconsiderable, and most members will be reluctant to take proceedings, at least unless their personal rights or interests are directly at stake. This unwillingness to litigate is reinforced by the fact that there are certain restrictions limiting the member's right to enforce compliance with the constitution where *intra vires* breaches are concerned. However, despite the paucity of cases, it is useful to analyse the authorities into three categories. This is partly because it helps to clarify the various kinds of complaints that tend to be made, and partly because it brings into relief situations where the restrictions on enforcement are likely to operate. The first category includes those cases where action is taken by the right body which is improperly constituted; the second is where action is taken by the body which has power under the constitution to make the relevant decision, but that decision is made in breach of procedural or substantive limitations imposed by the constitution or the general law; and the third is where the action is taken by the wrong body.

Action by the Right Body Wrongly Constituted

The defects under this first category arise where members of the particular committee or other body within the union making the decisions have not been properly elected or appointed in accordance with the rules. The allegation is not that the body concerned is acting outside its powers; rather, it is that it never had any lawful powers to exercise because it was not properly constituted. A few examples will illustrate the problem. In *Cotter* v. *NUS*,[21] another ground upon which it was claimed that the loan to the miners' organization was unlawful was that the meeting of Conference which determined to grant the loan had been irregularly constituted, the delegates at the meeting having been elected by the branches instead of the districts as the rules required. The court held that even if true, these defects were technical and procedural infringements only, and could be ratified by the majority. Hence they applied the majority rule principle in *Foss* v. *Harbottle*. This aspect of the decision is further discussed below. A similar approach was adopted in *Chapple* v. *ETU*[22] where the court refused to grant an injunction restraining the holding of a rules revision conference where up to four of the fifty delegates had been irregularly elected. Pennycuick J observed that such irregularities would not render the whole of the proceedings invalid, particularly since there was no evidence that the conference was so evenly balanced that these delegates could tip the scales; nor was there evidence of bad faith. He did advise the particular delegates not to participate in the proceedings, however.

It does not follow that minor infringements will always be overlooked in this way. In a disciplinary context, even the most apparently insignificant procedural defect is likely to render any disciplinary action invalid. *Kimberley* v. *Showmen's Guild of Great Britain*[23] suggests that a similar approach will be adopted in other situations where members allege that their right to membership has been directly affected by a decision of a body constituted in breach of the rules. In that case the Guild wished to exclude fish and chip van owners from membership and interpreted its qualification rules accordingly. Thereupon the plaintiff initiated legal proceedings, but while they were pending the defendant organization purported to alter its rules so as to make the exclusion beyond doubt. However, representatives at that meeting had not been authorized as the rules required. Consequently the rule-amending body was not legally constituted and the resolution purporting to alter the rule was declared invalid. Similarly, if disciplinary proceedings are conducted by a committee which has persons not entitled to sit with it participating in its deliberations, any decision it reaches will be invalid. Questions relating to discipline and disciplinary procedures are discussed in Chapter 6.

Action by the Proper Body in Excess of Power

A second category of *intra vires* breaches is where action is taken by the right body, properly constituted, but where certain limitations imposed by the constitution or the general law are not observed. These limitations may be procedural or substantive. As we have seen, the general law may impose substantive constraints upon the exercise of power through the fiduciary principle. But, in addition, the union constitution itself might limit the scope of authority of a particular organ within the union. Here we are concerned not with a body purporting to assume an authority it never had, as in the category discussed below, but rather with the situation where the range of decisions it can make has been limited by the decision of another union body which is subsequently ignored.

PROCEDURAL LIMITATIONS

There are numerous cases where it is claimed that decisions have been taken in breach of certain procedural obligations, such as a failure to call a meeting properly because of inadequate notice, or insufficient details of the meeting were given. *Cotter's*[24] case also illustrates this. A further ground for challenging the loan from the seamen to the miners' non-political movement was that the notice convening the meeting was defective. The Court of Appeal again applied the majority rule aspect of the *Foss* v. *Harbottle*[25] principle and held that this was not a defect which an individual could challenge. But certain procedural infringements have been considered in other contexts. They are more likely to invalidate a decision where individual rights are affected, though even then not inevitably. In *Cotter's* case one of the resolutions complained of had confirmed the suspension, admittedly on full pay, of certain union officials from office, but it was nevertheless held valid. However, procedural defects will often invalidate union action. For example, in *Brodie* v. *Bevan*[26] it was necessary to conduct a national ballot of the membership before any general levy could be imposed. This was done, but the votes were not all checked by independent scrutineers as the rules required. Neville J accordingly held that the ballot was invalid and that the plaintiffs were justified in withholding their contributions to the levy. But, of course, material individual interests were directly affected in this case. Procedural requirements can be imposed by the general law as well as by express rule-book terms. An important decision in this connection is *MacLelland* v. *NUJ*[27] where Whitford J held that where a mandatory meeting was called, reasonable notice of it should be given to the members required to attend. Other procedural requirements stemming from the general law of meetings include an obligation to furnish adequate particulars of the business to be discussed on the agenda of the meeting — though this does not prevent amendments being accepted and passed at the meeting itself; and a duty to inform all those eligible to attend the meeting, except perhaps if it is known to be impossible for them to attend.

SUBSTANTIVE LIMITATIONS

The cases which have come before the courts in this area all involve situations where the Executive Council is obliged to act consistently with decisions of Conference, and where it is alleged that the Council has failed to do so. Since Conference resolutions sometimes tend to be framed in a general and vague way, the limits they set on the powers of the Council are not always clear. The result is that there may be much scope for policy considerations to weigh with the courts when they are resolving conflicts of this nature. The case involving the *NUM*[28] graphically demonstrates this point. It has already been mentioned that the Court of Appeal there held that the Executive had an implied power to hold a ballot on productivity bargaining. But counsel for the appellants contended that even if such a power could in principle be implied, it could not be exercised in the particular circumstances since Conference had passed a number of resolutions which indicated that it was specifically opposed to a move towards productivity deals. In one of the resolutions, Conference had affirmed the result of a previous ballot of the membership when proposals for a productivity incentive scheme had been rejected; and in another, a resolution calling for an incentive scheme was rejected. Nevertheless the Court of Appeal, affirming the decision of Sir Robert Megarry, inexplicably refused to accept that the ballot which the Executive was proposing to hold could be said to be 'contrary to or in defiance of any resolution of Conference' within the terms of the rules. On this approach, Conference would have to trumpet its precise intentions very loud and clear before the powers of the Executive would be treated as fettered.

The sequel to this decision was that a ballot of the membership was held and it rejected a proposal for national incentive schemes. However, the Executive Committee remained undaunted and authorized its constituent areas to enter into local incentive or productivity schemes. The Kent area, supported this time by the Yorkshire and South Wales miners, returned to the courts for a second time seeking an interlocutory injunction to restrain such schemes from being negotiated or concluded.[29] Again the argument was that such schemes were inconsistent with the policy of the union as expressed by Conference, but again the claim was rejected, this time by Watkins J, who specifically relied upon the reasoning of Lord Denning in the Court of Appeal in the case relating to the legality of the ballot. It was accepted that the result of the ballot did not, under the particular rules, bind the Executive Committee, but was persuasive only. So these legal actions confirmed that the Executive was empowered to try and mobilize the membership to express opposition to the decisions of Conference, while at the same time being free to pursue a modification of their own policies when their original proposals were rejected by the membership as a whole. It is interesting to speculate whether the interpretation of the resolution would have been the same had the Executive and not Conference been adopting the more militant posture.

In contrast with the approach in these cases are the decisions adopted in *Hodgson* v. *NALGO*[30] and *McNamee* v. *Cooper*.[31] In the first, Conference passed a resolution stating that it was opposed to Britain's entry into the European Community unless it could be shown to be 'in the long-term interests of both Britain and the Community'. Subsequently the Executive Council resolved that a sub-committee should examine the question of Britain's entry into the Community, and that sub-committee narrowly passed a resolution favouring Britain's accession. The Executive then adopted this position and instructed its delegates to the TUC Annual Conference to vote in support of accession. Three members of the union successfully sought a declaration that these instructions contravened the union constitution, and a mandatory injunction directing the delegates to oppose Britain's entry. Goulding J held that the Executive had 'arrogated to themselves a power to determine the policy of the union instead of merely managing the affairs of the union and acting in an executive capacity to carry out policy'.[32] It was not for them to determine whether the conditions attached to the resolution had been met. It must be emphasized, though, that the court could have refused relief because of the rule in *Foss* v. *Harbottle* had not the particular circumstances in that case precluded its application. It was the application of this rule which denied the plaintiff a remedy in *McNamee* v. *Cooper*. He had brought an action seeking to restrain union delegates at the TUC Conference voting in favour of the government's prices and incomes policy, contrary to a resolution of the union conference, but the court refused to intervene on his behalf.

Action by the Wrong Body

The powers of any body or committee constituted within the union are derived from the rules and from custom and practice. If the wrong body makes a decision, then the courts will readily permit any member to challenge that decision, even though it is *intra vires*. As we shall see, there are numerous illustrations of this in the context of union discipline. The principle applies equally to any other action taken by the union. A clear example of this principle in operation was *Edwards* v. *Halliwell*[33] where the plaintiffs were able to restrain the union from imposing an increase in subscriptions when the decision to increase resulted from a resolution of a delegate conference rather than a two-thirds majority in a membership ballot as the rules required. In most cases in this category there is no dispute about the fact that the wrong body has made the decision but occasionally the matter is more complex and involves determining the relationship between different organs within the union itself. These cases are of crucial importance because they raise fundamental questions about the distribution of functions between the various bodies within the union. More particularly, they involve the inter-relationship between the conference, the executive, and the membership as a whole.

Ultimately the relationship between these various organs depends entirely upon the particular union constitution. In practice, though, most unions adopt a similar constitutional system. The executive committee administers the union between delegate conferences and it is given a free rein to pursue the objectives of the union in any way it thinks desirable, providing it does nothing inconsistent with the rules of the union or the general policy as determined by the conference. But although the rules may, and usually do, leave matters of policy ultimately in the hands of the conference, it is a mistake to assume that conference is in any sense superior to the executive or can interfere with its functions. The point was succinctly made by the Lord President in *Paterson* v. *NALGO*,[34] a case heard in the Inner House of the Court of Session. The issue arose out of a dispute between the union and certain of its members over a resolution of the Special Conference of the Association which sought to instruct its members in Scotland to participate in a one-day strike against public expenditure cuts. This resolution involved an alteration of a previous resolution of the union's Emergency Committee which had merely authorized, but not instructed, such action. The rules of the Association placed the initiation of industrial action in the hands of the Emergency Committee and the Executive Council, and the petitioners claimed that there was no residual power left in the hands of the Conference to issue this instruction. The Association denied this on two grounds.

First, it considered that the consitution specifically empowered Conference to direct general policy, and that this was wide enough to permit it to take any course of action it thought was advantageous or expedient. Secondly, it argued that Conference was ultimately the sovereign power in the union and retained the right to do whatever the Council could do as long as no entrenched right of a member was infringed. The Inner House unanimously rejected both contentions. As to the first, they were of the view that general policy could not extend to making decisions or acting on matters expressly confined to Council; and nor, according to Lord Johnston, was the phrase 'general policy' appropriate to cover a specific instruction of this kind. The second contention was likewise unanimously and emphatically rejected. The Lord President put the matter thus:

> Underlying [the second] submission was the concept that 'Conference' should be equiparated with a general meeting of all members of an unincorporated association for all members are represented there. This is at the root of the proposition that Conference is sovereign and supreme in all matters. In my opinion, however, the analogy is imperfect. This Association, which consists of all the individual members, has by its constitution provided for the government and management of its affairs and has set up two bodies for that purpose. One is 'Conference' and the other is the 'National Executive Council'. In no sense is the Council to be regarded as the Committee of Conference with powers delegated by conference. Both are independent creatures of the Constitution and it is to the rules of the Consitution that one must look to discover the function and powers of each . . . Nowhere in the rule defining the scope of the authority of Conference or in the rules prescribing the functions and powers of the Council, is there any express reservation of a

concurrent jurisdiction in matters expressly confided to the Council and where concurrent jurisdiction is intended the Constitution expressly so provides.[35]

Consequently the action of Conference was unconstitutional, and the Inner House upheld the interdict granted by Lord Cameron in the Outer House, thereby preventing the union from putting the instruction in force.

This view of the relationship between Conference and the Executive emphasizes that ultimately everything depends upon the particular constitution under scrutiny. If Conference is to be supreme, this must be made abundantly clear in the union rules: it will not be assumed that this is the intention. Lord Denning's judgment in *NUM (Kent Area)* v. *Gormley* also follows this line and emphasizes that relationships found in other spheres, such as that between Parliament and Cabinet, or the board of directors and the general meeting in a limited liability company, are not necessarily analogous to those found within a union. Again, it cannot be assumed that the membership as a body has ultimate power. Even a decision of the members in a referendum will not necessarily be binding in law upon other constitutional organs, as was recognized in the *NUM*[36] case when the Court of Appeal accepted that constitutionally the result of any referendum could be persuasive only. However, as that case shows, there may be a tendency for the courts to be particularly willing to imply a term when it leads to the members having the right to comment on a particular proposal. Similarly, where the courts are interpreting contentious union rules, it seems that they will be keen to construe the constitution so as to promote the right of members collectively to determine union policy, even if this is inconsistent with the decision of Conference.

This is supported by the House of Lords' decision in *British Actors' Equity Association* v. *Goring*,[37] where a problem of interpretation arose because of the ambiguous inter-relationship between two union rules. Rule 43 of the appellant's constitution provided that alteration of the rules could be effected by a two-thirds majority of those members present and voting at an annual general meeting. Rule 34 provided that the union's council had power to conduct a vote of the entire association, on any question or resolution passed at a general meeting. The question which arose for decision was whether rule 34 applied to resolutions passed under rule 43. Could the council seek to overturn resolutions either approving of, or rejecting, rule amendments by appealing over the heads of the general meeting to the membership as a whole in a referendum? And could a group of dissident members likewise seek to challenge resolutions which had altered the rules? A left-wing faction in the union argued not, but their Lordships disagreed and said that they could, in both cases. Viscount Dilhorne, who gave the leading judgment, and whose decision was concurred in by Lords Pearson, Salmon and Scarman, was clearly influenced by the notion that members ought to be given the opportunity to express their views in this way. He said:

> . . . one would expect the rules to enable a vote of the entire membership to be taken on a matter of vital importance . . . [otherwise] it would mean that an important rule could be altered and a new rule made by a minority of the members . . . contrary to the wishes of the council and of the majority of the members.[38]

This assumption is perhaps more questionable than the extract suggests. Ought a decision of the members obtained by a referendum always be accorded priority over a resolution passed at a meeting where those voting do so after a debate about the relative merits of the proposal? Is direct democracy, where there is no discussion, obviously more desirable than representative democracy, where there is? The point is highly debatable, and particularly so where, as in the *British Actors' Equity* case itself, all of the members, and not merely elected delegates, were eligible to attend the meeting and vote. In effect, the House of Lords' judgment was showing a preference for one form of direct democracy over another.

THE LIMITS TO ENFORCEMENT

The cases discussed above provide illustrations of situations where the courts have been asked to intervene at the behest of a member or groups of members to prevent the union from adopting a particular course of action. However, as we have seen, the courts will sometimes refuse to give a remedy even though infringements of the constitution have occurred. So what are the limits of a member's rights to enforce the constitution? Essentially the answer depends upon the judges' views about how to accommodate two conflicting principles. On the one hand, there is the contractual right of the member to have the constitution obeyed; on the other, the principle of majority rule which is coupled with a reluctance of the courts to oversee the detailed administration of every union in the country. First, there is what might be termed the principle of insubstantial irregularity, such as was applied in *Chapple* v. *ETU*.[39] This is similar to but varies slightly from the principle of substantial compliance adopted in *Brown* v. *AUEW*.[40] Finally, there is the majority rule principle enunciated in *Foss* v. *Harbottle*[41] itself. This reflects the view that there are certain breaches of the constitution which can be remedied only by the majority, though it is often far from clear which breaches fall into the category.

Insubstantial Irregularities

In *Chapple* v. *ETU*[42] the rule infringements were ignored but in circumstances where it appeared that they had made no difference to the outcome. This is effectively looking at the infringements in the light of the result. If compliance with the rules would have made no difference, breaches may be ignored. Furthermore, it would seem that what constitutes a technical irregularity may well depend not merely on an examination of the particular rule or rules in question, but also on the circumstances in which the breach or breaches occur. For example, where, as in *Kimberley* v. *Showmen's Guild of Great Britain*,[43] a resolution has the effect of excluding a member, the courts will not readily listen to the argument that the rules were broken in a technical way only, and that the result would have been the same even if the constitution had been strictly followed. In disciplinary situations in particular, the breach of procedure is likely to invalidate a decision or resolution, however minor, and whether it affects the outcome or not. But greater tolerance will be displayed where an administrative decision is under scrutiny.

Substantial Compliance

Under the substantial compliance principle, the detailed rules relating to resolutions and elections are seen essentially as subsidiary to the main purpose of achieving a fair result. Consequently if these rules have been substantially complied with, then the fact that there have been particular rule infringements — even an infringement of the right to vote — will not invalidate that result. In *Brown* v. *AUEW*[44] a postal ballot was held for the office of union divisional organizer and the plaintiff was held duly elected by a majority of 180 votes in a poll of a little under 7,000 members. However, there were a number of rule infringements in the conduct of the election, notably in that certain members received ballot papers late while others received none at all. Altogether about 600 members were involved so obviously the result could have been affected. Subsequently, after much internal wrangling, another election was held and this time a different candidate was elected, and the union's final appeal court upheld his claim that he should replace the plaintiff as divisional organizer. The plaintiff sought an interlocutory injunction to restrain the union from acting on this decision. Walton J granted the injunction: he held that on the proper construction of the rules it was not possible for a second ballot to be ordered once the result had been declared unless the first ballot was so utterly chaotic as to be completely void as an election. However, it would not be void if it had been conducted 'substantially in accordance with the procedure laid down in the rules and otherwise in accordance with the directions of the executive council'.[45] Since this election had been so conducted, the mere fact that a considerable number of members did not receive a ballot paper was not of itself sufficient to invalidate the election, even though the result might have been different had the constitution been strictly followed.

The Majority Rule Aspect of *Foss* v. *Harbottle*

The principle in *Chapple's* case is in turn similar to the majority rule principle in *Foss* v. *Harbottle*. This rests on the basis that there are certain breaches of the constitution which can be challenged only by the majority, and the individual member has no standing to complain about them. It differs from the principle of insubstantial irregularity insofar as the latter suggests that not even the majority can complain of the particular infringements, whereas the *Foss* v. *Harbottle* rule rests on the assumption that although the individual cannot take action, the majority could authorize that action if it so wished. In almost all the cases where the courts have refused to intervene to enforce the details of the constitution, it is on the basis of this principle. The rule in *Foss* v. *Harbottle* is a doctrine developed in company law yet with its roots in partnership. There are two separate but closely interwoven strands to the rule, one procedural and one substantive. The procedural or 'proper plaintiff' principle stems from the *Foss* case itself, which asserts that where the directors have broken their duties of loyalty, care and skill to the company, so that the wrong is to the company itself, then only the company can complain. It alone is the proper plaintiff because in law it alone has suffered the wrong. Legal proceedings can be instituted only on behalf of the company if supported by a majority of members in a general meeting. We return to this aspect below.

The other principle is the substantive or majority rule principle. It has its origins in earlier partnership cases and requires that where any internal irregularity occurs in the operation of a company then, if it can be ratified by a majority of members in a general meeting, the court will not intervene, even though the irregularity might involve a breach of the articles of the company. The advantages of this principle, according to the judges, are that it prevents multiplicity of suits by individuals — a flimsy advantage since it could have been just as effectively achieved by the power of the courts to stay and consolidate actions — and that it would in any event be futile for the court to interfere on behalf of the minority if the general meeting could ultimately ratify the act and in effect reverse the judgment of the court.[46] The majority rule principle operates to limit the member's right to enforce the contract of membership. The proper plaintiff aspect, on the other hand, is principally concerned with the fiduciary duties owed by union officers rather than the members' constitutional rights.

A preliminary problem which arises from the application of the majority rule principle is that very few unions hold general meetings of members in the same way as companies have meetings of shareholders. Usually, as we have seen, the members' wishes are made known through delegates at a conference. Strictly, therefore, the majority never have the opportunity to express their views at all. In *Cotter's* case the court decisively rejected the contention that this distinction should preclude the operation of the rule. Russell LJ noted that it was 'only a question of the machinery by which, under the constitution of the particular union, the views and desires of the union are to be ascertained'.[47] This is a sensible approach, and one which is entirely consistent with the rationale of the rule. Yet if on the other hand the courts were stringently to apply the majority rule principle to trade unions, it would mock the very concept of the contract of membership and the rights which such a contract entails. But they have not done so. The rule is subject to five separate so-called exceptions which drastically reduce its impact. Indeed, as Grunfeld argues, it is misleading to call these exceptions to the rule.[48] The rule itself is no more than an initial proposition and the exceptions are modifications of that proposition which are so comprehensive that little of the original principle remains. Consequently, very few contractual irregularities will escape the scrutiny of the courts under the *Foss* v. *Harbottle* rule.

The exceptions to the rule embracing both the 'proper plaintiff' and 'majority rule' aspects provide that proceedings may be instituted by the members without first obtaining the support of the general meeting in five circumstances:

(1) Where the action is *ultra vires* the union. This exception is firmly established and will apply even where the rule can be amended by a simple majority of the members.
(2) Where the act complained of is *intra vires* but requires something more than a majority vote, such as a special or extraordinary resolution, before it can be lawfully implemented. This exception was one of the grounds relied upon by the court in *Edwards* v. *Halliwell*[49] for refusing to apply the rule. In that case the union

rules required a two-thirds majority vote of the members before the subscription could be raised, but the union purported to increase it by the decision of a delegate conference.

(3) Where those controlling the union are perpetrating a fraud on the minority. This exception has not so far been applied to trade unions, but the authorities in company law supporting it are plentiful.[50] It is concerned with the 'proper plaintiff' aspect rather than the 'majority rule' principle, and so will not be further considered here.

(4) Where personal rights of the member have been infringed.[51] This is the most difficult exception to analyse because the scope of personal rights is so uncertain. Obviously direct proprietary rights would fall into this category, but beyond that it is still an open question how far the concept of personal rights extends.

(5) Where the constitutional machinery cannot operate in time to be of practical effect. This exception was developed specifically in the trade union context. It was propounded by Goulding J in *Hodgson* v. *NALGO*,[52] the facts of which have already been discussed. One of the reasons why the rule in *Foss* v. *Harbottle* was not applied was that the judge thought it inapplicable where there was no opportunity to call a meeting to have the matter ratified. This provides an exception which is far more significant to trade unions than to companies. In the latter case, extraordinary general meetings can usually be called relatively quickly, but summoning a special delegate conference is a far more complicated and longwinded affair. It will frequently be necessary for the branches to appoint the delegates before the meeting can be organized. Furthermore, there may exceptionally be no power to summon a special delegate conference at all, in which case it will be necessary to carry out a referendum, if the rules permit, or to wait until the next conference. The mere theoretical possibility that the decision may be ratified is no longer, as was once thought, sufficient to invoke the rule.

The Majority Rule Principle in Practice

The majority rule principle has been successfully relied upon directly in only five trade union cases. The first is *Steele* v. *South Wales Miners' Federation*[53] where one of the objects of the defendant union under its rules was to provide funds to pay the expenses of returning and retaining representatives to Parliament. The rules did not, however, provide any procedure whereby levies could be imposed for this purpose, but a levy was imposed on the members after a resolution was passed by delegates at the annual conference. The levy was challenged on a number of grounds, principally because political action fell outside the purposes for which a trade union could lawfully exist. Although this argument failed, it nevertheless did succeed several years later, being the basis of the *Osborne* judgment.[54] However, it was also argued in *Steele* that even if political objects were not illegal, the plaintiff was entitled to an injunction to restrain the levy on the ground that there was no machinery in the rules whereby it might be imposed. But this argument also failed, with Darling J holding:

> the application for an injunction here is a request to the Court to interfere in what is a mere matter of internal administration of the society, and as such is covered by the decision of the Court of Appeal in *Macdougall* v. *Gardiner*. The proposed levies may be irregular in the sense that the manner in which they are to be made is not expressly provided for, but, being for purposes authorized by the rules, they are not in any way illegal, and the majority of the members of the federation have assented to the levies being made.[55]

and with Phillimore J concluding in similar terms:

> There are limits to the extent to which a Court will interfere with the internal administration of an association. If the Court is satisfied that a clear majority of the members, with an unpacked meeting and a regular vote, have arrived at some conclusion as to the management of the association, which is within the scope of the memorandum of association of the company or the purposes of the trade union, as the case may be, it will not interfere merely because some formal step was omitted which ought to have been taken to make the act of the association regular and complete.[56]

The second successful application of *Foss* v. *Harbottle* was *Goodfellow* v. *London and Provincial Union of Licensed Vehicle Workers*[57] where the plaintiff alleged that certain resolutions passed at a special delegate meeting of the union were *ultra vires* and illegal as no notice of them had been included on the agenda of the meeting. Although Peterson J accepted that the rules of the union had not been complied with, he refused to interfere since 'it was at most an irregular proceeding which might be made regular by subsequent resolutions'. It was a matter of the internal management of the union, and the individual member could not sue. In the third case, *Cox* v. *National Union of Foundry Workers of Great Britain and Ireland*,[58] the plaintiff sought a declaration that resolutions by the national executive council altering rules of the union were *ultra vires*, and injunctions to restrain the union from acting on these resolutions. The effect of the resolutions was to reduce the plaintiff's weekly super- annuation payment from 7/6d. to 5/-, a measure taken because of the financial difficulties facing the union. The court denied the relief sought, with Astbury J in a rare moment of judicial abstention com- menting that 'the Court had no right to interfere with the internal arrangements of the union'.[59] This is despite the fact that the rules could be altered only with the consent of five-sixths of the members in a vote, and despite the fact that the case must surely have fallen into the private right exception to the rule in *Foss* v. *Harbottle*. It is submitted that the decision can be explained on the basis of its wholly exceptional facts and it would almost certainly not be followed. According to Astbury J, 'The resolutions were temporary while the finances of the union did not admit of payment in full'; 'Matters in the foundry trade were very bad'; 'the union was in a serious financial position'; and it was 'better for the plaintiff to receive 5s. a week than nothing at all'.

The only occasion when *Foss* v. *Harbottle* was applied by the Court of Appeal was in *Cotter* v. *NUS*[60] where it was held that neither the grounds of inadequate notice of a meeting, nor the fact that certain delegates to the meeting were improperly elected under the rules, were grounds justifying action by the individual member. In giving judgment, Lawrence LJ said that these were 'irregularities in matters affecting the internal management of the union, which could be regularized by the majority of the members assembled in a properly convened general meeting of the union'.[61] And he continued:

> Bearing in mind the nature of such a union as this, the position in life of the members, the fact that the rules are obviously framed without legal assistance, and the fact that the persons who manage the affairs of the union, convene meetings and arrange for the elec- tion of delegates are not lawyers, I think that it would be lamentable if a technical breach of the rules were held to entitle a dissentient member or minority to obtain an injunction to restrain the carrying out of a resolution of the union.[62]

The remarkable feature about *Cotter* is that it was decided in 1929. This means that in only one subsequent case has a union successfully relied upon *Foss* v. *Harbottle*, a fact which tends to suggest that it genuinely discourages litigation or that it is effectively ignored by the courts. The only relatively modern case then is *McNamee* v. *Cooper*[63] where the plain- tiff sought to restrain his union's delegation to the TUC from voting in favour of an incomes policy. He claimed that to do so would be in breach of a conference resolution which had been overwhelmingly carried. It was accepted by Goff J that under the rules, decisions of conference bound the union. Nevertheless he refused to grant the remedy sought, holding:

> What was happening was that the general council was allegedly about to act contrary to the policy of the union laid down by the congress. It was said that that was an *ultra vires* act. As the general council was only acting, if what the plaintiff alleged was right, contrary to the composite motion and not outside the scope of the rules of the union it was in breach of the rules. Its acts could not be regarded as *ultra vires*.

A Desirable Rule?

So the majority rule principle has rarely been applied to trade union affairs. This is not only because the courts are reluctant to apply it, but also because until recently there were relatively few cases where union action was challenged. It is impossible to know how frequently minor infringements are ignored because members think it not worth complaining, or are advised that they would get no redress in the courts. However, is it desirable that the majority rule principle should be applied to trade unions at all? There is a good case for saying that it is inappropriate to apply it not merely to trade unions, but to other organizations also. The theory behind the principle is that in certain circumstances the majority is entitled, if it so wishes, to take proceedings to have the constitution strictly enforced whereas the individual member is not. There is, according to the theory, a certain vague and ill-defined category of constitutional breaches which lies beyond the realm of the contract of membership and which the member therefore has no contractual right to enforce. This is an unsatisfactory doctrine. First, it is impossible to predict confidently which rules the member can enforce personally and which only the majority can enforce. Secondly, although the principle is that the majority can enforce the rules, in reality it is a myth to believe that it will do so, particularly since it will be virtually impossible for dissenting members to mobilize the membership and establish that they have the majority with them.

In any event, it may be questioned whether the courts would have given a remedy to the majority in those cases where the *Foss* rule has been applied. Generally the doctrine has been employed in circumstances where there are relatively minor procedural breaches of union rules which do not affect the individual complainant any more than any other member. Admittedly it would indeed be damaging to internal union government if a member could readily seize upon insignificant breaches of this nature and thereby invalidate union action. But a court might even refuse relief to a majority which was seeking to use the courts for this purpose. Moreover, it does not follow that the removal of the majority rule principle would result in unions being harried and pressed by individual members. The cost of bringing the action would of itself inhibit most members. But apart from that, even if the courts were to accept that there was no majority rule principle and that individuals could enforce the terms of the constitution, it still would not enable them to frustrate union actions by latching on to minor irregularities. This is because the remedy that the member is seeking in these cases is an injunction, not damages (which in any event would be nominal in circumstances where the member has suffered no significant personal detriment). But the injunction is, of course, an equitable remedy, and it is perfectly proper for the court to consider the nature of the breach when deciding whether to grant it. Minor procedural infringements that do not adversely affect the complainant any more than any other member would in general constitute insufficiently serious contractual breaches to warrant an injunction being granted. The member has suffered no real injustice. It is submitted that it would in principle be preferable to accept that the members have the right to enforce all aspects of the constitution, but that in certain circumstances they cannot obtain injunctive relief, rather than to say that in these cases they have no right to enforce the constitution at all, but that the majority have.

It is true that in one sense it matters not whether the court refuses relief to the members by denying that they have the right or by refusing them the remedy: in either case they will not obtain the injunction they are seeking. Nevertheless there are two advantages in explaining the reluctance to intervene by focusing on the remedy. First, it is more satisfactory because it accords better with the theory that all of the rule book constitutes the terms of the contract between the union and the member or the members *inter se*. Secondly, once it is recognized that the reluctance to intervene is to be explained on the basis of the discretionary nature of injunctive relief, then since the agreed principle is that a plaintiff is entitled to an injunction if his or her right is infringed, it will be recognized that the court should depart from this principle only where the member has clearly suffered no injustice. This will be the position where minor procedural breaches arise, for the court can then often state with some confidence that compliance would have made no difference to that eventual decision. But clearly this does not apply where certain substantial limitations are ignored, such as in *McNamee* v. *Cooper*[64] or *Hodgson* v. *NALGO*.[65] In these cases the *Foss* rule was applied (or, in the latter case, could have been applied but for other considerations) in circumstances where it was clearly inappropriate because there had been a significant interference with the member's right to have the union governed according to its own constitution. Effectively the decision of the body constitutionally entitled to make that decision was ignored. The application of the majority rule principle in these cases was misconceived. However, if a judge starts from the premise that the rule should apply unless the members can establish that they fall into one of the exceptions, his approach will inevitably be different than if he starts with the assumption that the member has a contractual right to enforce the constitution, but then sometimes an injunction will not be a suitable remedy. Yet despite its unsound foundations, the rule survives. As a result, the courts have in many cases a device by which to justify intervention or restraint. The way in which that choice is exercised can have enormous consequences for the trade union government.

THE *ULTRA VIRES* RULE AND THE MINERS' STRIKE

The significance and importance of the *ultra vires* rule was highlighted forcefully by the events in the miners' strike of 1984–5. The origins of the mining dispute lie in the fear that the government and the National Coal Board proposed to reduce capacity in the industry by closing pits which were regarded as being uneconomic. The immediate cause of the strike was the announcement by the Board of the proposed closure of the Cortonwood Colliery in South Yorkshire. This led to a meeting of the Yorkshire Area Council of the NUM resolving to call on all members to strike as from March 8, 1984 'to stop the action of the NCB to butcher our pits and jobs'. Under the rules of the NUM, rule 41 provides that no strike is to take place in any area of the union without the sanction of the national executive committee. Also on March 8, 1984, the NEC met and approved the action in Yorkshire, as well as similar action which had been proposed by the Scottish Area where Polmaise Colliery was faced ' with closure. Significantly in the March 8 resolution, the NEC took the additional step of endorsing or approving any action which any other area might wish to take. So by this resolution the NEC 'gave a nationwide, blanket sanction to all areas, in advance'.[66]

The other rule of the national union which is significant is rule 43. This provided that in the event of national action being proposed by the union, 'a national strike shall only be entered upon as the result of a ballot vote of the members taken in pursuance of a resolution of

Conference, and a strike shall not be declared unless 55 per cent of those voting in the ballot vote in favour of such a strike'. Although no national ballot was held, a number of other areas called upon their members to join the strike, while several, most notably Nottinghamshire, voted to remain at work. A special delegate conference of the union held on April 19 resolved (by 69 votes to 54) that the NUM should call on all areas to join the 80 per cent of miners already on strike and thereby ensure maximum unity in the union; and that in order to secure as much unity as possible the strike should be co-ordinated by the national office of the union. This was followed by the publication of *The Miner* on April 30 which carried a statement that 'the miners' strike is now a fully official national stoppage'. The statement continued: 'The key resolution instructed all miners throughout Britain to join nearly 90 per cent already on strike'.[67]

An Unlawful Strike

The legal position of the strike was tested in a number of cases. After the NEC statement of March 8, the Derbyshire Area balloted its members on March 16 for authority to call out the area to support the strike. The rules of the area union required a 55 per cent vote in favour of industrial action by those members voting in the ballot before a strike could be called and before rule 41 of the national rules could be invoked. Although the Derbyshire ballot in fact resulted in a slender majority voting against industrial action, the Area Executive nevertheless called upon its members to join the strike, and followed this by suspending from membership of the union individuals who continued to work. In *Taylor* v. *NUM (Derbyshire Area) (No. 1)*[68] one of the grounds for the relief sought by the plaintiffs was that the strike was in contravention of the rules and constitutions of both the area and the national unions. In granting a declaration on this effect, Nicholls J said that it was 'plain as a pikestaff'[69] that the strike in Derbyshire was unlawful. There had been no national ballot under national rule 43, so the strike call could not stand as a lawful call for a national strike. There had been a majority against the strike in the ballot held in Derbyshire, so the strike call could not stand as a lawful strike of the area union. More significantly, perhaps, Nicholls J also granted relief against the national union, holding that it had also acted unlawfully. It was arguable perhaps that there was no need to ballot under rule 43 because this was a series of area disputes, not a 'national strike', and that no strike had been 'declared', with members merely having been 'called upon' to take action. This argument was rejected by Nicholls J:

A national call to strike by the NUM conference, coupled with the organization of 'official' picket lines on a national basis and with threats to officers who encourage miners to cross such picket lines, seems to me in practice to place a miner deciding whether or not to work in a position not substantially different from that existing where there is a formal declaration of a national strike or an instruction to strike. A national call coupled with threats and the need to cross a so-called 'official' picket line to get to work in my judgment is entering upon a national strike.[70]

So the strike was unlawful, first because it was in breach of the area's rules and secondly because it was in reality a national strike called in breach of the rules of the national union.[71] The latter ground would presumably mean that any other area which pulled its members out would also be acting unlawfully. In fact, as was later pointed out, most of these areas were acting unlawfully because like Derbyshire the strike was called in breach of the rules of the area unions concerned.[72] But what about the two areas which were already on strike before March 8? Was the strike lawful in Yorkshire and Scotland? Under the rules of the Yorkshire union, a ballot must be held before a strike is called, and 55 per cent of those voting must support the strike. In the case of the Yorkshire Area, there had in fact been a ballot, but this had been conducted in 1981, with 85.6 per cent of those voting approving a resolution giving the area authority to take various forms of industrial action to stop pit closures. In *Taylor* v. *NUM (Yorkshire Area)*,[73] Nicholls J accepted that it was arguable that although the area strike had begun before the call for national action, what the Yorkshire union and the NUM had entered into was, and was alone, national action. In view of the fact that there was no national ballot under rule 43, the action was in breach of the rules. But he also accepted as highly arguable the submission that even if this was only an area strike and not a national strike, the obligation to ballot under the area rules had not been satisfied. The 1981 ballot was too remote in time, there having been too much change in the branch membership of the area since then for that ballot to be capable of justifying a call to strike action some two and a half years later.

So the Yorkshire action was unlawful first because it was in fact part of a national strike and secondly because in any event the area rules had not been complied with. In Scotland the area union is not required by its rules to ballot before calling area action. However, following the arguments accepted by Nicholls J, the strike there might have been unlawful anyway, if the Scottish Area and the NUM had in fact entered into national action. In *Fettes* v. *NUM (Scottish Area)* it was argued (as reported in the press)[74] by three working miners that the union had acted unlaw-

fully by calling a strike without a ballot, that the call by the special delegate conference on April 19 was tantamount to national action, and that
'it would be a curious situation if a Scottish court was to reach a different
decision from the . . . cases in England where the strike had been
declared illegal'. But Lord Jauncey rejected this and other arguments,
and refused to grant the interim interdict. It was not disputed that the
Scottish Area strike had complied with the rule 41 procedure which had
been properly carried out. The only question was whether the resolution
of April 19 converted the Scottish strike from being an area stoppage to
being a national one. In answering this question in the negative, Lord
Jauncey was not prepared to say that an area and a national stoppage
could not run in parallel. An area strike might already be in existence
when a national strike was called, and the area strike could continue
after the national strike had ended, if the latter was settled first.
Although he accepted that the April 19 resolution constituted a national
strike call, this meant that a national strike was entered into only by
those who went on strike from that date. The resolution did not affect the
areas already on strike, and it did not necessarily follow from the resolution that 'the Scottish Area members exchanged their Area bonnets for
national hats'.[75]

The Effect of the Breach of the Rules

In view of the decision in the Scottish case, all attention focuses on events
south of the border. Having established that the strike was unlawful,
what were the consequences of this? First, it exposed the unions to
injunctions restraining them from calling upon their members to support the strike and not to cross picket-lines. In *Taylor* v. *NUM (Derbyshire
Area) (No. 1)*,[76] Nicholls J held that the fact that the strike call was in
breach of the rules meant that the unions could not properly issue
instructions and directions to the membership to strike, not to work, or
not to cross picket-lines. Any such action would be unofficial, entitling
the plaintiffs to disregard the call to strike and to cross the lines. The
plaintiffs were granted a declaration to this effect and in the Yorkshire
Area[77] case an interlocutory injunction was granted to restrain the
unions from instructing members not to work, to strike, or not to cross
any picket-line. In the same case, an injunction was granted to restrain
the defendants from describing or treating the strike or any picket-line as
official. In no case, however, was an injunction granted to have the
strike called off, though in the Yorkshire Area case an attempt was made
to compel the national union to hold a ballot under rule 43. But this
failed, with Nicholls J holding that he was unable:

to spell out of rule 43 by implication any such positive obligation entitling a member to compel the NUM to hold a ballot. The member's right under the Rules is confined to being able to insist that a national strike cannot lawfully be held without a national ballot; but he has no greater right than that in respect of a national ballot.[78]

A second consequence of the holding that the action was outside the rules was the risk that the use of union funds to support the strike might also be restrained. The use of funds in this way was one of the issues in *Taylor* v. *NUM (Derbyshire Area) (No. 3)*.[79] A problem for the plaintiffs, however, was the rule in *Foss* v. *Harbottle*,[80] which Vinelott J held still applied to trade unions following the enactment of TULRA, section 2. This he interpreted as being designed 'to restore the law as it was under the 1871 Act', and *Foss* v. *Harbottle* clearly operated until the repeal of that Act, having been applied in *Cotter* v. *NUS*.[81] A well-established exception to the rule, however, is 'cases where the act complained of is wholly *ultra vires* the company or association'.[82] The issue which arose in *Taylor (No. 3)* then was whether it was *ultra vires* to make payments from union funds to meet the expenses of picketing and to relieve the hardship suffered by union members and their families. One of the objects of the union, as provided by its rules, is to provide 'in accordance with these rules a weekly allowance for the support of the members and of their families when the member is . . . on strike . . .' Rule 66 provides that members on strike by the authority of the National Executive Committee shall be paid an amount specified in the rule. It was held, following *Durham Miners' Association*[83] and *Yorkshire Miners' Association* v. *Howden*,[84] that if the rules of a union provide expressly for allowances to be made for what Vinelott J called an official strike (one called within the rules), it is impossible to imply consistently with that a power for officers to make a similar allowance to members on unofficial strike (that is one called in breach of the rules). Although 'today a more liberal approach to the construction of the rules of a union is appropriate', it was also held that 'Every member of the union, as he has an interest in preserving the funds of the union, is entitled to prevent the funds of the union from being used' to support a strike called in breach of the rules.

So the plaintiffs were granted an injunction to restrain any other expenditure from the funds of the Derbyshire union to promote the strike. Their other claim related to the £1.7 million which had already been spent. Apart from the injunction, the plaintiffs sought damages against the secretary and the treasurer of the union for breach of contract and/or breach of trust. In dealing with this point, Vinelott J found himself driven to the 'uncomfortable conclusion' that the defendants, having made or sanctioned payments which were beyond the powers of the union, were 'liable to reimburse the union'.[85] He also held, however, that he should not make the order sought by the plaintiffs on the ground that although the misapplication of the funds could not be ratified by a majority of the members of the union, 'it is open to a majority of the members, if they think it is right in the interests of the [union] to do so, to resolve that no action should be taken to remedy the wrong done to the [union] and such a resolution, if made in good faith and for the benefit of the [union], will bind the minority'. In this case, however, the members had not met to pass the necessary resolution. Nevertheless, Vinelott J refused summary judgment for the plaintiff. First, because there was substantial support for the strike, even though a majority had voted against the ballot. Secondly, because the payments were made in the honest belief that there was power to make them, and were not made for the personal and private benefit of the defendants. In these 'wholly exceptional circumstances' it was thought unsafe 'to rule out entirely the possibility that a majority of members may in the future be able, properly and lawfully, to take the view that it would not be in the interests of the union that the individual defendants should be made personally liable'. The court was also influenced by the fact that the defendants did not have any substantial resources and that the benefit to the union of recovering everything that could be extracted from them was likely to prove 'wholly insignificant' in contrast with the sum of money in issue.[86]

Contempt of Court

So, the fact that the strike was unlawful had several consequences. Instructions to strike were unlawful; union funds could be restrained from supporting the strike; and members could not be disciplined for failing to join the action. However, although declarations and injunctions were granted, the orders of the courts were not always obeyed. On October 10 both the National Union of Mineworkers and Mr Scargill were fined for contempt of court, the union being given 14 days to pay and Mr Scargill being given 28 days.[87] The fines were imposed by Nicholls J for failure to comply with the injunctions granted in *Taylor* v. *NUM (Yorkshire Area)* whereby the union was enjoined from referring to the strike as an official dispute and forbidden from urging its members not to cross picket-lines. In imposing the fines of £200,000 and £1,000 respectively, Nicholls J is reported to have said: 'A great and powerful union with a large membership has decided to regard itself as above the law . . . if orders of the court are set at nought in this way — openly and repeatedly defied by such a body with impunity — where is the rule of law?'[88] Rather predictably, however, the union refused to pay the fine and repeated its contempt of court, steps which led to an application for sequestration by Mr Taylor and his colleague in these proceedings, Mr Ken Foulstone.[89] Sequestration proceedings are provided for by RSC Order 45, rule 5, which applies where a person required by a judgment or order to do an act within a specified time refuses or neglects to do so within the time. In such circumstances the judgment or order may be enforced by a writ of sequestration against the property of that person. Although the order does not refer expressly to sequestration proceedings against trade unions, by virtue of section 2(1) of TULRA, judgments orders or awards are to be enforced against a trade union as if the union was a body corporate.

The sequestration of trade union funds is not now an unfamiliar feature of industrial disputes in Britain. The tactic was deployed under the Industrial Relations Act 1971[90] and was used to enforce the fines for contempt of court which were imposed on the NGA in the Stockport Messenger dispute.[91] The distinguishing feature in the miners' case was the use of this procedure by union members ultimately for failure by the union to act in accordance with its own rules. A more significant development, however, was the appointment of a receiver in a separate application.[92] Also by virtue of section 2(1) of TULRA, all property belonging to a trade union is vested in trustees in trust for the union. The trustees of the NUM included three leading officials, namely, Mr Scargill, Mr Michael McGahey and Mr Peter Heathfield. The leading text, *Kerr on Receivers*, states that the court will upon a proper case being made out dispossess a trustee of the trust estate, 'but it will not do so on slight grounds'.[93] The editor continues, however, by stating that 'If any misconduct, waste, or improper disposition of the assets can be shown, or if it appears that the trust property has been improperly managed, or is in danger of being lost . . . or if it can be satisfactorily established that the parties in a fiduciary position have been in a breach of duty, there is sufficient foundation for the appointment of a receiver'.[94] But even though union officials might act in breach of trust, it was unclear whether or to what extent a receiver could be appointed to manage the affairs of a trade union before the repeal of the Trade Union Act 1871. By section 4, this precluded the courts from entertaining any legal proceedings instituted with the object of directly enforcing any agreement for the application of the funds of a trade union. The view of *Kerr* is that this section prevented a receiver from being appointed over the general funds of a trade union or over funds collected for a special purpose, a view supported by *Sansom* v. *London and Provincial Union of Licensed Vehicle-Workers*.[95] However, the repeal of the 1871 Act and the enactment of TULRA, absent an equivalent to section 4, opened up the possibility of receivers being appointed, though there is no evidence of this having been done before 1984.

The order for sequestration was made on October 25, following an application by Taylor and Foulstone. Although the reasons for the sequestration are not altogether clear from the published information, it does appear that it was not just for non-payment of the fine, but that it was a response to the continuing failure of the union to comply with the orders of the court. The effect of the sequestration was to deny the NUM and its officers any legal control over the union funds, premises and other assets, with control being vested in the hands of the sequestration commissioners who in this case were partners in a City firm of chartered accountants. By November 29, however, the sequestrators had been able to locate only £8,174 of the union's estimated funds of £10.6 million, with the bulk of the money having already been transferred by the union to banks in Luxembourg, Switzerland and Ireland.[96] Partly in order to expedite the return of this money, a receiver was appointed following another application by working miners. The appointment was made by Mervyn-Davies J on November 30 on the ground that the union's trustees were 'not fit and proper people to be in charge of other people's money'.[97] One reason for this it seems was that the actions of the trustees had been 'to continue serious and deliberate contempts of orders which place the funds that they hold for the union in jeopardy'.[98] The order was upheld by the Court of Appeal on December 1, leave to appeal having been refused.[99] The appointment proved successful, for after 'lengthy, difficult and complicated negotiations' the receiver was able to recover over £4 million from Luxembourg with which he paid the contempt fine of £200,000.[100] And following the decision of a Swiss court, announced on April 4, 1985, he was able to recover £217,000 lodged in a Swiss bank account, it having been accepted by the court in Zurich that he was the lawful representative of the NUM.[101] The appointment was at first only partially successful, however, in the sense that £2.75 million remained locked in an Irish bank, frozen by an injunction with the Irish High Court holding that the fund was to be preserved until permanent trustees of the union's property were appointed in accordance with the provisions of English law.[102] In the end, however, the funds were released two weeks after the Irish judgment, following the consent of the union, the sequestrators and the receiver.[103]

Sequestration and Financial Support

The sequestration of the assets of the NUM did not simply prevent the union from having access to these funds, it also affected the financial support which it might expect from trade unions and others. This support ran into a number of problems, the first being whether the donations were lawful on the part of the bodies which made them, a difficulty which was confronted by student unions in particular. The Polytechnic of North London, for example, was restrained from giving money to the miners following an application to the High Court by the Attorney General, Sir Michael Havers. The injunction restrained the union's officers from

> Causing or permitting (whether by themselves or by any person authorised or purporting to be authorised by them) any payments to be made out of the funds of the Polytechnic of North London Students' Union (whether out of capital or income) for the purpose of giving assistance in any manner howsoever to persons being dependants of employees of the National Coal Board, not being students of the polytechnic, or for any other purpose than the advancement of the education or the fostering of the wellbeing of the body of members of the said students' union as students of the said polytechnic.[104]

So far as trade unions are concerned, the only reported case is *Hopkins* v. *NUS*[105] where the executive council of the union approved payments of £5,000 and £10,000 which had been made to the NUM out of the seamen's general fund. The executive council also resolved to introduce a by-law giving itself power to raise funds by way of a levy on union members. The council then proceeded to exercise the power which it had thereby conferred upon itself and resolved to impose a weekly levy on union members to help the members of the NUM in their dispute with the Coal Board. The plaintiff challenged both of these steps and did so successfully with regard to the levy of the members on the ground that under the rules of the NUS the power to raise a levy was expressly conferred on the biennial general meeting or on a special general meeting. The executive council had no authority under the rules to impose a levy and an injunction was granted to restrain the use of funds raised by the levy. So far as the transfer of money from the general funds of the union was concerned, the plaintiff's claim failed. Under the rules of the union the executive committee was empowered to authorize expenditure of the general fund for all or any of the objects of the union. Among the objects of the union are 'To promote and to provide funds to extend the adoption of trade union principles', and 'To improve the conditions and protect the interests of all members of the union'. It was accepted by the plaintiff that it was within the powers of the executive committee to make a payment from general funds to another trade union engaged in an industrial dispute. It was argued, however, that the payment to the NUM to assist the conduct of an unlawful or illegal strike was not within the powers of the committee.

In a welcome decision this argument was rejected, with Scott J contending that if the strike is in pursuit of objectives which will further the objects of the NUS, it was capable of support from the funds of the NUS under the rules of that union irrespective of whether it was unlawful in the sense that it was unofficial. Thus although the NUM itself could not use its own funds to finance the strike, this did not prevent other unions from using their funds. There was, however, a second point in the *Hopkins* case, namely, that if the funds of the NUS were to be transferred to the NUM they were liable to be seized by the sequestrators. In these circumstances it appears to have been accepted in *Hopkins* that a payment to the NUM could not be a payment in pursuit of the objects of the NUS. But it was also accepted as being within the powers of the executive committee to make payments for the more limited and specific purpose of alleviating hardship and distress among the families of striking miners. Such a payment, impressed with a trust for the relief of distress, would not be liable to be seized by the sequestrators. So the sequestration of the NUM's assets would prevent direct financial assistance to the union, but it did not disable other trade unions from taking steps to relieve the distress of miners and their families by making donations to independent funds for the alleviation of hardship. The only qualification is that the unions making gifts must have been authorized to do so by their rules. In *Hopkins*, Scott J held that if the executive committee of the NUS 'takes the view that payments made to alleviate hardship and distress among the families of striking miners will tend to promote trades union principles of solidarity, I am not prepared to say that such payments would be *ultra vires* the executive council.'

Ultra vires and Trade Unions

The litigation in the miners' strike engendered great bitterness, not to say considerable misery for miners and their families. The key which ultimately unlocked the door to contempt and receivership was the holding that the calling of the strike and the financing of the action was *ultra vires*. Yet it has been argued by Lord Wedderburn of Charlton[106] that the *ultra vires* rule does not apply to trade unions because of the operation of TULRA, section 2. This provides that a trade union shall not be, or be treated as if it were, a body corporate. The section then qualifies this by extending to trade unions some of the incidents of incorporation. As *ultra vires* is not one of the features of incorporation so extended, it is 'not now relevant'[107] to trade unions. It thus appears to be the intention of Parliament that trade unions shall be treated as voluntary associations, and in the case of 'a voluntary association of individuals, the doctrine of *ultra vires* has no place'.[108] Wedderburn does not deny that the individual may sue in some cases. He or she can do so 'for breach of contract' to protect his or her individual right, 'but not for those breaches of rule which the majority of the association can put right'. Indeed, he goes further and argues that the members may not enforce 'propriety in the use of the funds, even if they allege breach of trust . . . and even if the rule expresses an ''object'' '. There is now no *ultra vires* doctrine to prevent ratification by the majority.[109]

At first sight, this ingenious argument suggests that the jurisdiction of the courts in internal affairs has been struck a 'fatal blow'.[110] Further examination may tend to suggest, however, that the matter is more equivocal. In the first place, it must be right that the doctrine of *ultra vires* has no application to trade unions — for the reasons given by Wedderburn. But this is not the end of the matter, for although the doctrine of *ultra vires* does not apply, the 'rules form part of the contract between the members' and may be enforced as such.[111] Consequently any action in breach of the rules may be restrained by injunction.[112] But the matter does not end there either, for it appears that despite the absence of corporate status, the rule in *Foss* v. *Harbottle* still applies to trade unions. Authority for this slightly anomalous position is provided by *Cotter* v. *NUS*[113] and *Hodgson* v. *NALGO*[114] where it is made clear that the condition precedent to the operation of *Foss* v. *Harbottle* is not legal status, but the capacity to be sued:

> The principle, as I understand it, does not depend upon the existence of a corporation. The reasoning of it surely applies to any legal entity which is capable of suing in its own name and which is composed of individuals bound together by rules which give the majority of them the power to bind the minority.[115]

In *Cotter* the rule applied because a registered trade union could sue and be sued in its own name, whereas in *Hodgson* it did not apply on the ground that an unregistered union could not. The position now, however, is governed by TULRA 1974, which has no concept of registration and which provides by section 2 that trade unions, although not corporations, have the capacity to sue and be sued.

So the position would seem to be that the member may sue to restrain a breach of contract, but that the majority rule principle in *Foss* v. *Harbottle* could operate to prevent the action succeeding. As we have seen, however, there are five circumstances in which the rule may be displaced. One of these is *ultra vires* but, as has been shown, this has no operation in the area of trade union law. The question which arises then is whether *Foss* v. *Harbottle* can operate to prevent all actions in breach of the rules unless covered by one of the other four so-called exceptions. It must be at least arguable that it does not. According to Gower, 'all these exceptions could be reduced to one by saying that an individual share-holder can always sue, notwithstanding the rule in *Foss* v. *Harbottle*, when what he complains of could not be validly effected or ratified by an ordinary resolution'.[116] Yet it is not clear that to call a strike in breach of the rules can be ratified by a majority. So in *Harington* v. *Sendall*, Joyce J said:

> Indeed, so far as there can be said to be authority upon the subject, and, as I think, upon principle, there is no more inherent authority in the members of the club by a majority in general meeting to alter the rules against the wishes of a minority than there is in the members of any other society or association the constitution of which depends upon and is [sic] matter of contract — there being as there is here a written contract expressing the terms upon which the members associate together. In my opinion, there is no power in the majority of the members to alter those terms and the consti-tution of the club as they may think fit, when such a power forms no part of the written contract by which the members are bound.[117]

And in *Institution of Mechanical Engineers* v. *Cane*, Lord Denning expressed very similar views when he said:

> The purposes of . . . a [voluntary] society can be changed after its original institution, by the mutual assent of the members, without any record in the formal documents. If the society, without such assent, does in fact pursue a new or additional purpose, not fairly incidental to its original purposes, any member can object and take proceedings to stop it: but no one else can.[118]

One answer, of course, is to say that a strike in breach of the rules is not a new or additional purpose, but a means of doing irregularly that which may be done regularly.[119] The difficulty with this, however, are cases such as *Durham Miners' Association* where the headnote reads as follows:

> The rules of a trade union, the management of which was vested in a council, under whom an executive committee acted, provided that no lodge was to give notice of a strike until its case had been

laid before a council or committee meeting for their approval; and that any lodge or member, or number of men in a lodge, ceasing work without the approval of either the committee or council should forfeit all claims on the union. A number of men in a lodge ceased work on account of a dispute with their employer without having laid their case before the council or the committee for their approval. The executive committee refused to grant strike pay, but the council on appeal allowed it. *Held*: that the resolution of the council was *ultra vires*.[120]

It is true that this decision was based on the operation of the *ultra vires* rule. But, even if the rule does not apply, it would no doubt be open to the court to hold consistently with these cases that the existing purpose on strikes includes the procedure and that a strike by another procedure is a new and additional purpose. Clearly, such an interpretation of the rulebook is completely unreasonable and is no doubt contrary to how company lawyers would expect company government to be treated by the courts. For all practical purposes, the calling of a strike in breach of the rules is doing improperly that which may be done properly. Yet even if the judges were to approach the construction of the rules in a sensible manner, that would not deal with the problem in all cases. In many unions (including the NUM) a special procedure must be invoked before a strike is called. Sometimes this will involve a special majority of the members voting in a ballot. As we have seen, one of the exceptions to *Foss* v. *Harbottle* is where a special resolution is required. So even if *ultra vires* is out, and even if the court adopted a sensible approach to construction, in many cases the court could still avoid *Foss* v. *Harbottle* where a procedure is laid down in the rules whereby something more than a simple majority is necessary to call the strike.

What then are the implications of all of this? The first is that it seems that the *ultra vires* rule now has no application to trade unions and that it is being applied wrongly by the courts. The second point, however, is that this does not give unions complete autonomy from the law. Members may still sue for breach of the rules where there is a breach of contract. The third point then is that although *Foss* v. *Harbottle* still applies to trade unions, potentially to restrict the members' right of action, it is unlikely to have any great impact. Although the *ultra vires* exception does not apply, much of the conduct which is now improperly and before 1974 properly so characterized is incapable of ratification and so may be restrained as a result. In many cases the union conduct will in any event involve the invasion of personal rights, and may indeed require a special resolution. In other words, the fact that the *ultra vires* is out may not have major implications in practice. It may invite a conceptual shift, but it is difficult to see how it will limit access to the courts. It would indeed be unacceptable if trade union members were left without a remedy where the union is acting in breach of the rules,[121] particularly where there is impropriety in the use of funds. This is not to say that the judges always get it right, or indeed that it is in the interests of trade unions or the judiciary for legal issues in bitter trade disputes to be resolved by the High Court. But the solution to these problems lies not in denying the member a right to enforce the rule book. Rather, it invites consideration about an alternative system of adjudication of internal disputes, which enjoys the confidence of both trade unions and their members, in relation to which the courts play at best a supervisory role, being involved as an instrument of last rather than first resort.

NOTES

1. *Amalgamated Society of Railway Servants* v. *Osborne* [1910] AC 87.
2. [1905] AC 256.
3. See Trade Union Act 1871, s. 14(1) and Industrial Relations Act 1971, ss. 75, 76.
4. *Grieg* v. *National Amalgamated Union of Shop Assistants* (1906) 22 TLR 274, *Oram* v. *Hutt* [1913] 1 Ch. 259; [1914] 1 Ch. 98.
5. [1978] ICR 56. See also *Thomas* v. *NUM (South Wales Area)* [1985] 2 All ER 1.
6. The distinction is well established in company law. See Gower, pp. 180. *et seq.*
7. [1914] 1 Ch. 98.
8. *The Times*, October 20, 1977.
9. *Ibid.*
10. (1916) 85 LJ Ch. 298.
11. (1843) 2 Hare 461.
12. (1916) 85 LJ Ch. 298.
13. (1916) 85 LJ Ch. 289.
14. *Ibid.*, at p. 297.
15. [1929] 2 Ch. 58.
16. As in *Goring* v. *British Actors' Equity Association* (1986 Unreported). In that case the preamble to the objects' clause of the union referred to Equity as a non-party political and non-sectarian union. The union members voted in a ballot to boycott South Africa, and the Council of the union then issued an instruction to members not to work in South Africa. One of the objects of the union was to promote the professional interest of its members. As a result, it was held that the union could take political action for professional purposes. It was also held, however, that the instruction was unlawful because, on the evidence, it has been issued exclusively or primarily for a sectarian purpose.
17. NUFLAT Rules (1979), r. 4(p).
18. (1937) 81 Sol. Jo. 179.
19. See Gower, pp. 165–8.
20. Unreported.
21. [1929] 2 Ch. 58.
22. *The Times*, November 22, 1961.
23. *The Times*, November 25, 1953.
24. *Cotter* v. *NUS* [1929] 2 Ch. 58.
25. (1843) 2 Hare 461.
26. [1922] 1 Ch. 276.
27. [1975] ICR 116.

28. *NUM (Kent Area)* v. *Gormley, The Times*, October 20, 1977.
29. *The Times*, October 21, 1977.
30. [1972] 1 WLR 130.
31. *The Times*, September 8, 1966.
32. [1972] 1 WLR 130 at p. 136.
33. [1950] 2 All ER 1064.
34. 1977 SC 345.
35. *Ibid.*, at p. 357.
36. *The Times*, October 20, 1977.
37. [1978] ICR 791.
38. *Ibid.*, at p. 796.
39. *The Times*, November 22, 1961.
40. [1976] ICR 147.
41. (1843) 2 Hare 461.
42. *The Times*, November 22, 1961.
43. *The Times*, November 25, 1953.
44. [1976] ICR 147.
45. *Ibid.*, at p. 157.
46. This aspect of the rule is most clearly enunciated in *MacDougall* v. *Gardiner* (1975) 1 Ch. D. 13.
47. [1929] 2 Ch. 58 at p. 111.
48. p. 103.
49. [1950] 2 All ER 1064.
50. See Gower, pp. 616–30.
51. Gower, pp. 653–6.
52. [1972] 1 WLR 130.
53. [1907] 1 KB 361.
54. *Amalgamted Society of Railway Servants* v. *Osborne* [1910] AC 87.
55. [1907] 1 KB 361 at p. 368.
56. *Ibid.*, at p. 370.
57. *The Times*, May 22 and June 5, 1919.
58. (1928) 44 TLR 345.
59. *Ibid.*, at p. 346.
60. [1929] 2 Ch. 58.
61. *Ibid.*, at p. 107.
62. *Ibid.*
63. *The Times*, September 8, 1966.
64. *Ibid.*
65. [1972] 1 WLR 130.
66. *Taylor* v. *NUM (Yorkshire Area)* [1985] IRLR 445 at p. 448.
67. This account of the key developments of the strike is taken from the very informative judgment in *Clarke* v. *Chadburn (No. 1)* (Unreported, May 25, 1984); *Taylor* v. *NUM (Derbyshire Area) (No. 1)* [1985] IRLR 440; and *Taylor* v. *NUM (Yorkshire Area) op. cit.*, see also (1984) 22 BJIR 275–7 and 411–13; and (1985) 23 BJIR 153–8. A particularly valuable and thorough account of the legal developments is to be found in Wedderburn of Charlton, *The Worker and The Law* (3rd edn., 1986), esp. Chapter 9.
68. [1985] IRLR 440.
69. At p. 444.
70. *Ibid.*
71. A similar conclusion about the status of the national action was reached earlier by Sir Robert Megarry in *Clarke* v. *Chadburn (No. 1), op. cit.*, which was an action brought by at least 638 members of the Nottinghamshire Area against both area officials and national officials.
72. In *Taylor* v. *NUM (Yorkshire Area),op. cit.*, Nicholls J said at p. 449: 'No ballot was held in the Yorkshire Area, but ballots were held in Nottingham, Midlands, North Wales, Derbyshire, Northumberland, Group No. 1, Cumberland, North Western, Leicestershire and South Derbyshire. Of these 10 areas, the majority vote in nine was against strike action, and the only one where the majority was in favour (Northumberland) the majority in favour (52 per cent) fell short

of the 55 per cent required by that area's rules for strike action in that area. Nonetheless by May 10 the NUM had given or purported to give its sanction under rule 41 in accordance with the NEC resolution of March 8 to official action in 13 areas, including six of the areas where the ballot was against a strike action or fell short of the majority required for strike action.' An order was made declaring the strike unlawful in Lancashire (*The Times*, 27 June, 1984). An injunction was also granted to prevent the NUM from treating the Midlands Area strike as having been officially sanctioned (*The Times*, April 23, 1984). For details of still further actions, see Wedderburn of Charlton, *The Worker and The Law* (3rd edn., 1986), p. 732.

73. *Op. cit.*

74. The following account is based upon reports of the case in *The Scotsman* September 25, 1984 and November 3, 1984; *The Edinburgh Evening News*, November 6, 1984; and a News Agency Report ('United News from High Court') of November 6, 1984.

75. 'United News from High Court', *op. cit.*

76. *Op. cit.*

77. *Op. cit.*

78. *Ibid.*, at p. 451.

79. [1985] IRLR 99.

80. (1843) 2 Hare 461.

81. [1929] 2 Ch. 58.

82. *Edwards* v. *Halliwell* [1950] 2 All ER 1064 at p. 1067 (Jenkins LJ).

83. (1900) 17 TLR 39.

84. [1905] AC 256, aff. [1903] 1 KB 309.

85. In so holding, Vinelott J followed and applied *Bennett* v. *National Amalgamated Society of Operative House and Ship Painters and Decorators* (1916) 85 LJ Ch. 298 and *Carter* v. *United Society of Boilermakers* (1916) 85 LJ Ch. 289. In each case the court ordered 'restoration of funds of a union applied in breach of the rules of the union and for purposes not authorised by its constitution' (per Vinelott J at p. 103).

86. For an important critique of this *Taylor* case, see Wedderburn of Charlton (1985) 14 ILJ 127. But see *infra*, pp. 128–32.

87. *The Times*, October 11, 1984.

88. *Ibid.*

89. *Financial Times*, October, 25 and 26 1984.

90. See e.g., *Con-Mech (Engineering) Ltd.* v. *AUEW (No. 3)* [1974] ICR 464.

91. For an analysis of contempt of court in labour law in recent years, see the valuable Research Note by S. Evans, 'The Use of Injunctions in Industrial Disputes' (1983) 23 BJIR 133. See also Wedderburn of Charlton, *The Worker and The Law* (3rd edn., 1986), pp. 705–17.

92. *The Times*, December 1, 1984.

93. *Kerr on Receivers* (16th edn., 1983, by R. Walton), p. 12.

94. *Ibid.*, at pp. 13–14. Footnotes omitted.

95. (1920) 36 TLR 666.

96. *Financial Times*, November 29, 1984.

97. *The Times*, December 1, 1984. See further *Clarke* v. *Heathfield* (No. 2) [1985] ICR 606.

98. *Ibid.*

99. *Clarke* v. *Heathfield (No. 1)* [1985] ICR 203.

100. *Financial Times*, January 31, 1985.

101. *Financial Times*, April 4, 1985.

102. *Financial Times*, June 19, 1985.

103. Wedderburn of Charlton, *The Worker and The Law* (3rd edn., 1986), p. 739.

104. *The Irish Times*, June 19, 1985.

105. [1985] IRLR 157.

106. (1985) 14 ILJ 127.

107. *Ibid.*, at p. 129.

108. *Institution of Mechanical Engineers* v. *Cane* [1961] 696 at p. 724 per Lord Denning.

109. *Op. cit.*, at p. 129.

110. Ewing, 'The Strike, the Courts and the Rule-Books' (1985) 14 ILJ 160 at p. 175.

111. *Williams* v. *Hursey* (1960) 103 CLR 30 at p. 66 per Fullager J.

112. See e.g., *Harington* v. *Sendall* [1903] 1 Ch. 921.

113. [1929] 2 Ch. 58.

114. [1972] 1 WLR 130.

115. *Cotter* v. *NUS* [1929] 2 Ch. 58 at p. 71, per Romer J.

116. Gower, p. 645.

117. [1903] 1 Ch. 921 at p. 926.

118. [1961] AC 696 at p. 724.

119. *MacDougall* v. *Gardiner* (1875) 1 Ch. D. 13.

120. (1900) 17 TLR 39. See also *Yorkshire Miners' Association* v. *Howden* [1905] AC 256, aff. [1903] 1 KB 309.

121. See Wedderburn of Charlton, *The Worker and The Law* (3rd edn., 1986): 'Upholding the rules is a central article of faith in a trade union' (p. 730).

5

Statutory Regulation of Trade Union Government

As we saw in Chapter 1, statute has traditionally played a residual part in regulating trade union government. Indeed, the first statutory intervention — the Trade Union Act 1871, section 4 — was designed to avoid rather than increase legal control over the internal affairs of trade unions. Parliament's original position was thus to confer complete autonomy upon trade unions in matters of internal government. As we also saw in Chapter 1, however, section 4 proved an inefficient means of excluding the courts, so that in practice complete autonomy gave way to constitutional autonomy. Nevertheless, the unions had a wide measure of freedom in drafting their rules, the only real constraint being that the courts could intervene to interpret the rule book and exceptionally to control its terms. But significantly, Parliament had not sought to control the substance of the rules or the form of government.

This framework of constitutional autonomy survived for exactly 100 years, the 1871 Act being repealed by the Industrial Relations Act 1971. This marked the beginning of a period of detailed regulation of union government and a rejection of the notion of the sanctity of the rules. The 1971 Act did not simply repeal section 4, it sought to impose direct statutory controls on the conduct of internal affairs. This experiment survived for only three years, to be replaced by a return to constitutional autonomy as a result of TULRA 1974. This was qualified slightly, principally to the extent only that unions could not discriminate against members on the grounds of race or sex.[1] But the pendulum swung again, though this time the state has intruded more gradually but much more significantly into the heart of trade union government. First, by the Employment Act 1980 public money was made available to encourage unions to hold postal ballots on a range of issues — including elections to executive committees and strikes.[2] Secondly, in the Trade Union Act 1984, Parliament has imposed a duty for unions to hold ballots in a prescribed form in three crucial areas: the election of executive committees;[3] to authorize official industrial action;[4] and to test support for the continued operation of political funds.[5]

Under section 1 of the 1980 Act the Secretary of State was empowered, by regulations, to draw up a scheme for subsidizing trade union ballots. Only independent trade unions can benefit from the scheme, and only secret ballots are included. The ballots which may qualify for a subsidy are: strike ballots (whether decisive or consultatory, and whether about calling or calling off such action); elections under the union's rules; elections of workplace representatives; ballots on amendments of union rules; merger ballots under the Trade Union (Amalgamations, etc.) Act 1964; and other purposes specified by the Secretary of State. In fact, one other purpose has so far been specified, namely ballots on an employer's proposals about terms and conditions of employment.[6] It is to be noted that the scheme now in operation does not in fact include all the potential ballots which are specified in the Act itself. In particular, ballots for workplace representatives have not been included, and the election of only some officers is included. The scheme — which applies only to postal ballots — sets out certain kinds of expenditure only which then qualifies for the subsidy.[7] These include second-class postage and reasonable stationery and printing costs for ballot papers and various explanatory leaflets.

The facility is operated by the Certification Officer who may not reimburse expenditure on any ballot unless it satisfies certain basic criteria. For example, it must be free and fair, with every voter having a full opportunity to vote; the election must be properly conducted under the rules (though breaches will be ignored if they have no significant effect); and in strike ballots, all participants or likely participants must be entitled to vote. The Certification Officer may hear objections from any person that these conditions have not been complied with, and there will be at least a six-week delay between the application for funds and any subsequent payment which will give an individual time to lodge objections. In addition to the subsidy, by section 2 the 1980 Act provided unions with the right to use employers' premises for workplace ballots. This applies to independent recognized trade unions in all but the smallest firms, that is those with no more than twenty workers. To qualify, the ballot must be secret and it must be on a question which is covered by the state subsidy scheme. If the employer refuses to permit a ballot when it was reasonably practicable to do so, the union may make a complaint to an industrial tribunal and may ultimately be awarded compensation which is to be calculated by taking into account the seriousness of the employer's default and the additional expense caused to the union.

ELECTION OF OFFICIALS

Although it is sometimes argued to the contrary,[8] it is important to recognize that sections 1 and 2 of the 1980 Act do not interfere with union autonomy. It is perfectly consistent with the voluntarist approach to trade unions: the measure did not compel unions to hold ballots on the matters covered by these provisions, but if they chose to do so they could take advantage of their rights to public financing or to use the employer's premises for a workplace ballot. The same cannot be said, however, of the 1984 Act. Firm proposals for the election of union officials were made by the government in the Green Paper, *Democracy in Trade Unions*,[9] which stated the standards for electoral arrangements which the government sought to apply: (i) voting should be in secret; (ii) all eligible to vote should have the chance to do so under a system providing the best opportunity of 'reasonable turnout'; (iii) votes should be counted fairly; and (iv) those at the highest levels taking decisions should be 'properly representative, of and accountable, to' the membership as a whole.[10] The authors claimed that there is 'widespread concern' about current electoral arrangements in trade unions, first because of the low turn-out at union elections which diminished the credibility of those elected.[11] A second factor for this concern was trade union rules which, in quoting from the Donovan Royal Commission, the Green Paper claimed were 'confused, self-contradictory and obscure' and 'generally fall far short of reaching a satisfactory standard'.[12] The Paper noted that union rules differ widely on election procedures and that some are quite unspecific on the subject. This, it was claimed, opened up the possibility 'of a union's governing body having power under the rules to draw up its own preferred method of election procedure and then selecting one best suited to securing its own re-election'.[13] The third factor which it was claimed causes concern about union electoral arrangements are the allegations of 'forgery, ballot-rigging and other corrupt practices' which are made from 'time to time'.[14]

The case for legislation was based on three different considerations. First, trade union members are 'entitled to expect that their unions are democratic institutions responsive to their wishes'.[15] But this of course begs two questions: it presupposes that unions ought to be democratic and it assumes that democracy can be secured only by a prescribed statutory formula. Secondly, it was argued that 'given the immunities and privileges enjoyed by trade unions and the power they can exert in disrupting or stopping the manufacture of goods and the provision of services, there is an evident wider public interest in seeking to ensure that they are truly representative'.[16] This rather startling argument is evidently the government's principal justification for it is a point to which they returned time and time again. For example, in Standing Committee, Mr Gummer said:

> The direct election of those who finally control a union is a mini-
> mum requirement if that union is to have the immunities that I
> consider indispensible if trade unionism is to operate. Those
> immunities are given to the trade unions as a body of people, and
> they are to protect the rights of every individual within the unions.
> Therefore, it is not unreasonable that all members should have an
> equal opportunity to direct the union through those whom they
> elect, and they should be able to elect them directly.[17]

The third argument in favour of reform was that although voluntary 'reform' was the most desirable means, it was evident that with a few notable exceptions 'trade unions have made few or painfully slow attempts to reform their internal affairs and electoral practices in ways which can attract general public confidence in them'.[18] This was no doubt an allusion to the failure of the Employment Act 1980, section 1, which had sought to encourage unions to extend postal balloting by making state funding available to meet the costs. The initiative failed, however, because the TUC boycotted the facility.

So far as the content of legislation was concerned, the Green Paper claimed that 'The Government is conscious that any legislation must take into account the wide variety and complexity of existing electoral arrangements. These reflect in part the diversity in the history, nature and size of trade unions.'[19] But all this appeared to mean, however, was that there would be no compulsory ballots for all elected positions in trade unions from shop stewards upwards. Rather, 'the desirable aim should be to achieve full secret ballots in elections to the union's govern-ing body'[20] and that eventually it should be possible to introduce fully postal ballots for this purpose. Indeed, it was 'hard not to believe that what is lacking in unions who have not [adopted these procedures] is the will to adopt more democratic and fairer voting procedures'.[21] Moreover, the government's respect for union autonomy was not enough to prevent it from interfering with the system of election to the extent of suggesting direct elections only, despite the fact that a number of unions (including GMBATU and TGWU) elected their executive committees by a system of indirect elections. The Green Paper accepted that indirect elections are deep-rooted in some trade unions and that the system reflects the basis on which different organizations came together to form the present-day unions and that, given the diversity of occupa-tional and other groups within many unions, it may be a fairer method than direct elections of ensuring a representative outcome.[22] However, the government appeared to be unpersuaded by these arguments, for the Green Paper continues:

> On the other hand it may be thought that the system is often an important cause of *unrepresentative* leadership and influence in the union. If members are unable to vote directly for candidates, the actual degree of support of the members for each of the successful candidates cannot be determined. Direct election by the members, particularly to the governing body, is likely to secure a more democratic outcome.[23]

The government's proposals were supported by CTU,[24] by the Institute of Directors,[25] Aims of Industry,[26] the CBI[27] and the EEF.[28] There was general agreement that ballots should be confined to the principal executive committees, though the IOD proposed that general secretaries should be subject to periodic re-election by the NEC while Aims of Industry argued that general secretaries should have to stand for re-election by the members. There was, however, some concern expressed about the possible effects of the proposals by the employers' organizations. The EEF, for example, found it necessary 'to stress the need to reach a solution which so far as possible promotes a measure of continuity in the character and composition of the governing bodies of unions: violent periodic changes would almost certainly have adverse consequences for the stable conduct of industrial relations with the union concerned'.[29] Similarly, the CBI was anxious to point out that 'it should not be assumed that employees are always more moderate than those who represent them, nor that legislating for trade union elections will necessarily lead to more responsible and less militant behaviour'.[30] This conclusion was subsequently fully confirmed by the research of Undy and Martin.[31] As might be expected, the TUC on the other hand opposed the government's proposals as 'a politically motivated encroachment into unions' internal affairs',[32] asserting that:

> The Green Paper's discussion of unions' internal mechanisms fails to understand the democratic basis of trade union organisation. Far from being monolithic organisations, many unions tend to be highly decentralised. Unions' election procedures do vary considerably, but, whether elected or appointed, union officials by the nature of their role are continuously accountable to the membership's wishes. The Government's proposals, however, are based on the simplistic assumptions that 'unrepresentative militants' occupy positions of power within unions, and that different electoral arrangements would result in more 'moderate' union leaderships being chosen.[33]

The Scope of the Act

The 1984 Act applies to 'every person who is a voting member of the principal executive committee' of a trade union.[34] It thus excludes general secretaries and presidents unless they have a vote. Unions are under a duty to ensure that voting members are in fact elected to office.[35] No person is to hold office for more than five years without securing re-election.[36] But it is not enough that unions should hold periodic elections. Controversially, the Act also imposes a uniform system of election, despite the respect for union autonomy which appeared — albeit briefly — in the Green Paper. The effect of the Act is that elections must be conducted by direct elections,[37] with the result that indirect elections and branch block-elections are unlawful.[38] The former practice was followed by a number of unions, including APEX, GMBATU and NALGO. In the case of NALGO, the union has refused to change its arrangements, on the ground that to do so would make its NEC less rather than more democratic. NALGO's executive committee is elected mainly by direct elections, but there are positions which are filled by indirect election 'by service or industry via district and national service conditions committees'.[39] There are eight members elected by this latter method, on an annual basis, with the seats being allocated to the services and industries 'by a formula designed to give fair representation to the minority membership groups in NALGO'.[40] The union's argument is that a system of direct election for all places would make the union less representative, in view of the domination of local government members within the organization. As it is, 85 per cent of the 60 directly elected NEC places are filled by local government officers, though they account for only 71 per cent of the union's membership. The reserved places by indirect election are seen as a way of ensuring proper representation by members working in health, gas, electricity, universities and water. Although it might be possible in principle for NALGO to operate a federal system of direct elections from each service or industry, for practical reasons this is objected to as something which the union has always opposed on the ground that it would create divisiveness. It must be doubted anyway whether the 1984 Act could cope with such an arrangement. The Act permits unions to reserve places only for members of trade or occupational groups and to confine voting to members of these groups. There are other possibilities for reserved places, but these are not directly relevant here. The problem for NALGO is that the service and industry groups cut across trades and occupations. As a result, it would not be possible to confine voting to members of the services and industries alone.

Nevertheless, a complaint has been made against NALGO to the

Certification Officer on the ground that its system of combined direct and indirect elections fails to comply with the Act. A complaint has also been made against the NUR on the ground that its system of branch block voting is inconsistent with the Act. In the NUR, a proportion of the executive committee is elected each year. The members are chosen by the branches which means that there is a show of hands at a branch meeting. The branch's preference is then submitted, with all the members of the branch being taken to have supported the preferred candidate. In other words, 'the view of the majority of those who voted in each branch became the branch view and was passed forward to be counted as if it had been the unanimous view of the entire membership of the branch'.[41] In *Stemp* v. *NUR*[42] — the first decision under Part I — the Certification Officer declared that the union had failed to comply with the provisions of Part I, for several reasons, but principally because it had failed 'to conduct the ballot so as to ensure that the election was determined solely by counting the number of votes cast directly for each candidate at the election by those voting'.[43] Under the Act, the Certification Officer is required, when he makes a declaration, to specify any steps which have been taken or which a union has agreed to take, with a view to remedying the declared failure or to securing that a failure of the same, or any similar kind, does not arise.[44] In this case the President and the General Secretary of the union assured the Certification Officer that 'urgent and serious consideration'[45] would be given to the necessary rule changes required to ensure that all future executive committee elections complied with the requirements of Part I. The other point which arose was that the officers who had been elected were entitled under the rules to hold office for three years, and the view of the Certification Officer was that it would not be right for the nine representatives in this position to run the full period. Under the rules, some executive positions were released every year so that there were elections every year. In this case, after some discussion the President and General Secretary of the union indicated that, from a practical point of view, the 1985 election could be re-run at the same time as the election due in the autumn of 1986 for a further group of seats on the executive committee. The Certification Officer concluded by observing that he regarded the steps which the union undertook to adopt to be 'a not unreasonable response to the complaints'[46] which he upheld.

The Conduct of Elections

The Act regulates in some detail the members who may be given the opportunity to vote, and the procedure which must be followed in the conduct of the elections. Section 2(1) provides that entitlement to vote must be extended equally to all members of the union in question. This is, however, subject to three important qualifications. First, entitlement may be excluded to four different classes of members, provided that all of the members of the class in question are excluded by the rules from voting at the election.[47] These are respectively unemployed members, members in arrears, members who are apprentices, trainees or students, and members who are 'new members of the union'. Secondly, entitlement to vote may be restricted to members who fall within:

(a) a trade or occupational class;
(b) a class determined by a geographical area;
(c) a class which is by the rules treated as a separate section of the union;
(d) or a class which is determined by any combination of the above.[48]

This means in effect that a union may still reserve places on its executive committee for particular trade groups or particular regions. It also means that a union such as the NUM may leave its federal structure undisturbed and permit only the members of each constituent union to vote in the election of their representative on the NEC. The third qualification of the wide franchise is that a union which has overseas members may choose whether or not to accord any of these members entitlement to vote at the election.[49] An overseas member is defined in turn to mean a member of the union who is outside Great Britain throughout the period during which votes may be cast.[50] This thus excludes not only members who may be resident in Northern Ireland and the Irish Republic, but also those who may be absent on holiday. It is expressly provided, however, that an overseas member does not include merchant seamen or offshore workers. There is consequently the strange anomaly that while BALPA may exclude members on foreign trips, the NUS may not, even though members of the latter are likely to be absent for longer periods at any one time.

As originally drafted, the Bill had little to say about the way in which ballots were to be held. It did provide that they are to be conducted by the marking of a voting paper — thereby making it clear that a show of hands at a mass meeting will not suffice.[51] It also provided that those entitled to vote should be allowed to do so without interference or constraint from the union, its officials, members or employees.[52] And those entitled to vote were, so far as reasonably practicable, to be enabled to do so without incurring any direct cost to themselves.[53] The public subsidy scheme was amended, however, to ensure that it applied to ballots held under the 1984 Act. As it stood before the enactment of this measure, the

1980 Act applied, *inter alia*, to ballots for 'carrying out an election provided for by the rules of a trade union'.[54] Although some unions have altered their rules to embrace the requirements of the Act and so would have qualified under the original subsidy scheme, others have not, though as we shall see they are complying with the Act despite their rules. Such unions would have had no claim on the subsidy, but section 20 of the 1984 Act has amended the 1980 Act by extending the purposes for which money may be paid to include ballots in relation to which section 2 of the 1984 Act is required to be satisfied. At the time of writing the matter is, it is true, largely academic in view of the TUC's boycott of the state subsidy. As a result, the requirements of the 1984 Act on cost to the members means that in practice the financial burden of the ballots must fall directly on the union, though presumably there is nothing which could be done to prevent the union from recouping the money indirectly by raising the subscriptions to the extent required. But although these measures were all built into the Bill as introduced, there was one crucial omission. The government had nothing to say on the way in which the ballot was conducted — provided it was done by the marking of a voting paper. In particular, there was no requirement that ballots should be conducted by post or at the workplace.

Regulation of this kind was in fact not introduced until the Report stage in the Lords when the government bowed to pressure from within its own ranks.[55] A government amendment has established the principle that postal ballots must be held unless departure from the norm can be justified. Thus section 2(7) provides that so far as is reasonably practicable every person who is entitled to vote at the election must have sent to him or her at his or her proper address and by post a voting paper and a list of candidates.[56] The members should also be given a convenient opportunity to vote by post. Section 3 then permits the principle to be modified where the union is satisfied 'that there are no reasonable grounds for believing' that the requirements of section 2 would not be satisfied if the alternative arrangements in section 3 were to replace section 2(7). It is to be noted that this alternative method may be adopted at the discretion of the union, the government having rejected an amendment which would have permitted a departure from full postal ballots only if the union could satisfy the Certification Officer that the requirements of what is now section 2(7) are inappropriate in the particular circumstances of the case.[57] The alternative system of balloting permitted is confined to workplace ballots, with section 3 providing that electors should have made available to them a ballot paper and a list of candidates at their places of work (or at a place more convenient to them). This should be done immediately before, immediately after, or during working hours. Where this system is adopted, electors must also be given a convenient opportunity to vote by post, to vote at the work-place, or as alternatives to be given both of these opportunities.[58] One of the reasons why a union might have been able to satisfy itself that postal ballots might be departed from is the absence of a full and accurate record of members and their addresses. Under the Act, however, this ought not to be possible, with section 4 imposing a duty on every trade union to compile and maintain a register of the names and proper addresses of its members. There is, however, no duty on the part of members to provide this information.

Candidates for Office

In the Green Paper it was pointed out that electoral arrangements such as 'qualifications of candidates . . . differ widely between trade unions',[59] and that 'it might be impracticable and undesirable to lay down detailed requirements on such matters'.[60] The Act does nevertheless regulate this question. First, it provides that no member of a trade union shall be unreasonably excluded from standing as a candidate at an election to which the Act applies.[61] If this had been all that was enacted, it would have had particularly far-reaching implications in the sense that it would have enabled the courts to roam all over trade union rules restricting eligibility for office — rules which, for example, impose an age limit; a requirement of so many years' membership; or a written examination. That power is denied the courts, however, by section 2(11) which provides that members shall not be taken to have been unreasonably excluded from standing as a candidate if they have been excluded on the ground that they are members of a class, all the members of which are excluded by the rules of the union. The effect of this is that rules which automatically exclude a class of members may not be challenged. Apart from the fact that it protects eligibility rules of the kind already dis-cussed, it also protects the anti-communist rule of the EETPU, a point not lost on the Minister in Standing Committee.[62]

What then are the courts empowered to do? The answer it seems is that although they may not challenge clear and specific exclusion rules, they do nevertheless have not inconsiderable power to control the way in which discretionary powers are exercised. Some consideration was given in Standing Committee to the type of rules which might come under scrutiny.[63] Mr Tony Blair referred generally to rules which authorize unions to exclude people who are not fit and proper to hold office, and specifically to the following rule of the TGWU:

> Membership of an organisation which in the opinion of the General Executive Council is contrary, detrimental, inconsistent or injurious to the policy and purpose of the Union will render the member liable to be declared ineligible to hold any office within the Union.

Some speculation was made also in Committee as to the type of exclusion which might be unreasonable.[64] It was accepted for the government that it is highly unlikely that people excluded for misappropriation of union funds or some benefit fraud 'would ever get near a court to test reasonableness there'.[65] But no similarly re-assuring speeches were made about the exclusion of members who had failed to obey a strike call, or who were members of the National Front, though this is precisely the type of issue the courts may be called upon to consider. Yet how are they to determine whether such exclusions are reasonable or not: what criteria will they apply? The statute simply extends to the courts an invitation to intervene or abstain as they wish.

Although the Act does not challenge union rules on candidacy, and although it does not give any guidance on what would be an unreasonable exclusion, both of these points are subject to an important qualification. This is the terms of section 2(10) which provides that 'No candidate at the election shall be required, whether directly or indirectly, to be a member of a political party'. Note that it does not strike out rules or practices prohibiting members of a political party (such as the Communist) from standing. The function of this subsection is clearly to strike at union rules requiring leading officials to be members of the Labour Party either by making this an express term of office (as in the case of the NUR) or indirectly by requiring attendance at the Labour Party's annual conference. Since 1962 the Standing Orders of the Party have required delegates to conference to be individual members of the Party.[66] The effect then is that a rule or a practice requiring candidates to attend conference will be unlawful under section 2(10). In some respects this is a rather strange provision for the Thatcher government to have proposed. Although it is true that a number of unions have rules of one or other of these kinds, they exist in many cases to exclude Communists from office. Under the rules of the Labour Party, membership of another political party is not permitted. The effect then is to open up eligibility rules to people on the left who previously might have been excluded. This is despite the support for the EETPU's express ban on Communists in defence of which Mr Selwyn Gummer said:

> A major trade union has found that arrangement (i.e. the Communist ban) necessary for its own protection. Therefore, unless

there is any strong reason to the contrary, I feel that we should resist the amendments and keep the clause as it is.[67]

The amendment in question proposed that it should be unlawful to exclude people on the ground that they were members of a particular political party.[68]

Remedies

As originally drafted, the Bill proposed that any member of a trade union could make a complaint of a failure to comply with the terms of the Act to the High Court. In the Lords, however, this was amended to give trade unionists the option of proceeding either in the High Court or before the Certification Officer.[69] In the words of the Earl of Gowrie, this was done for reasons of 'informality, flexibility and lack of cost'.[70] The enforcement machinery is, nevertheless, one of considerable confusion and complexity. If the member proceeds before the Certification Officer, the officer may make a declaration if the complaint is upheld.[71] In dealing with applications, the Certification Officer is empowered to make such inquiries as he thinks fit, and where he considers it appropriate, to give the applicant and the trade union the opportunity to be heard.[72] Although this gives a wide discretion to the officer in the conduct of the proceedings, the discretion will of course have to be exercised reasonably[73] and it seems unlikely that the Certification Officer could waive the obligations of natural justice,[74] save in exceptional circumstances — as, for example, where the complaint is clearly frivolous or vexatious.[75]

The existence of a dual remedy is perhaps peculiar. But so too are some of the details. The Certification Officer is required to give reasons for his decision, which may be accompanied 'by written observations on any matter arising from, or connected with, the proceedings'.[76] It is not altogether clear what is the purpose of this power. Lord Wedderburn raised the following questions in the Lords:

> What do the Government imagine that the Certification Officer is going to talk about except the reasons for his decisions and the findings of fact which he has made? What are these 'observations' going to be? Are they going to be on the desirability of union policies, or on matters connected with officers of the union?[77]

If these powers do exist to encourage the Certification Officer to intervene in internal affairs more fully than the Act permits, then there is clearly a danger that such work will be deeply resented by trade unions and that respect for one of the most successful institutions of British labour law will be seriously undermined.[78] Yet this is not the only odd feature of the arrangements. Section 6(3) provides that the making of an application to the Certification Officer is not to be taken to prevent the applicant, or any other person, from making a subsequent application to a court 'in respect of the same matter'. So if the individual fails before the inexpensive, accessible body, he or she may proceed to have the same issue reviewed by the High Court. And it is important to note that the whole question may be re-examined for as was pointed out in Parliament,[79] the court is not bound by the Certification Officer's findings of fact.

Apart from the fact that this arrangement contravenes 'a fundamental principle of any system of jurisprudence that no party should be put in double jeopardy',[80] it curiously fails to provide a remedy for the trade union which wishes to challenge a decision of the Certification Officer. Although there is a lot to be said for giving exclusive jurisdiction to specialist tribunals such as this, there is nevertheless little to be said for giving one but not the other party to the proceedings the right to take the matter further if he or she is dissatisfied with the original outcome. The intention of the government it seems was even to exclude judicial review from unions, with the Minister saying in the Lords that if the union was aggrieved by a decision of the Certification Officer it could simply ignore the decision, in view of the fact that declarations of the Certification Officer have no normative effect.[81] The onus would then be on the individual to seek a declaration from the High Court, together with an enforcement order. At this stage, the union would have the opportunity to put its objections to the Certification Officer's decision. However, this really is not good enough. In the first place it is astonishing that a government committed to the rule of law (particularly in industrial relations) should now find it appropriate to encourage unions to ignore rulings of quasi-judicial bodies, merely because it has become expedient to do so. Secondly, although decisions of the Certification Officer have no normative effect, they may nevertheless have important social consequences. As Kidner has argued, the solution proposed by the Minister 'places the union in the awkward position of having to justify to the public its refusal to comply with the declaration'.[82] And to borrow from the language of Lord Denning in a rather different context, the decision of the Certification Officer 'may have wide repercussions'.[83] He may 'make findings of fact which are very damaging to those whom they name; [he] may accuse some; [he] may condemn others; [he] may ruin reputations or careers. [His] report may lead to judicial proceedings.'[84] Thirdly, although it is true (despite the apparent expression of a contrary view by the Minister)[85] that judicial review will be available, there is a big difference between judicial review (the only remedy available to the union) and the right to institute proceedings *de novo* in another forum (the remedy available to the litigious member).

As already pointed out, the Certification Officer has no jurisdiction to make a legally binding order. This contrasts, for example, with his jurisdiction in political fund disputes.[86] The High Court, in contrast, may make a declaration in which case it may also make an enforcement order unless it considers that to do so would be inappropriate.[87] An enforcement order is defined as meaning an order which imposes on the trade union one or more of the following requirements:

(a) to secure the holding of an election;
(b) to take any other specified steps to remedy a failure to comply with the Act;
(c) to abstain from specified acts.[88]

Where the enforcement order requires the union to hold a fresh election, the Act requires the order to contain directions as to the conduct of the election which must also include the direction that it should be conducted by postal ballot (if appropriate).[89] It is to be noted, however, that in no case is an enforcement order mandatory even where a declaration is granted. It need not be made if the court deems it inappropriate to do so.[90] This gives the courts a very wide discretion not only as to the terms of their intervention, but whether to intervene at all. Several attempts were made in Parliament to constrain this discretion. In the Lords, for example, Lord Wedderburn unsuccessfully moved the following amendment:

> Where the court makes such a declaration but the failure to comply consists only of a procedural irregularity which has had, or, as the case may be, is likely to have, no substantial effect in regard to the result of the election, the court shall make a finding to that effect and shall not make an enforcement order.[91]

However, supported by Lord Denning,[92] the government argued that measures of this kind were unnecessary and that the judges could be trusted not to make an enforcement order in cases of trivial breaches which do not affect the result.[93] In any event, it would be wrong 'to restrict the court's ability to weigh the issues involved in the light of all relevant circumstances'.[94]

Implications

Having thus examined the requirements imposed by the 1984 Act, the question which now arises is what effect it will have in practice? In other words, to what degree will trade unions be required to modify their arrangements for the selection of their national executive committees? Evidence provided by Undy and Martin suggests that the implications may be considerable. In their authoritative study, *Ballots and Trade Union Democracy*, the authors pointed out that executive committees are 'that part of a union's national hierarchy which is most frequently directly accountable to the membership through election, and most likely to be elected by postal ballots'.[95] Nevertheless, there are a number of unions which are required to revise their arrangements drastically in order to conform to the new standards. In a survey of 103 unions affiliated to the TUC, 65 chose their executive committees by an election of the whole membership. The others were chosen by conference delegates (22), by another national committee (3), by local committee (12) or by a combination of methods (7).[95a] The 65 unions using the membership vote 'accounted in 1980 for 61 per cent of the TUC's membership'.[96] It is not clear, however, whether the system of election includes both direct and indirect elections by the membership.

It is evident that a number of unions will be required to change the system of election, either because they do not select their executives by membership vote or because they do so but only by means of an indirect election. The unions in question include GMBATU, TGWU and NUR. It is clear also, moreover, that many of those unions which elected their executive committees by membership vote were required to change their electoral practices to comply with the Act. Undy and Martin showed that of the 65 unions electing their executive committees by means of a membership election, only 9 used full postal ballots and that only 6 used half postal ballots. Of the remainder, 13 used a ballot at branch meetings, 4 used a show of hands at branch meetings, 1 used a ballot in general meeting, and 15 used some other balloting methods which of course include workplace ballots, though in fact the authors referred to only two unions (CPSA and NUM) which adopted this method.[97] The remaining 17 either had a discretion in the balloting method or failed to specify the method of election. Although some change is thus required in the method of election, there is little change needed in the tenure of office. Undy and Martin point out that 'almost 50 per cent of unions give their executive committees only one year's tenure before they face re-election, and 72 per cent hold office for two years or less'.[98] In fact, only one union was found to exceed the five-year period, and then only by one year.

At the time of writing, it is too early meaningfully to assess the impact of the legislation. Nevertheless, it is clear that where it has been necessary to do so, many unions in fact have taken steps to avoid any clash with the Act or have brought their arrangements into line with it. As to the first approach, the NUM removed the vote on its executive from Mr Arthur Scargill to prevent him from having to stand for re-election every five years. As to the second approach, a number of unions have overhauled their systems of selection and election. These include ASTMS and UCATT, the latter having already held some executive elections under its new system, which also gives members a postal ballot. Two other major casualties of the legislation are the TGWU and the NUR. The former was 'forced . . . to change its method of electing indirectly its . . . executive members representing [trade] groups' following 'a media campaign'.[99] The latter was the subject of the first declaration by the Certification Officer who, as we have seen, held that the union's system of branch block-voting was in breach of the Act.[100] An interesting feature of the response by some of the unions is that changes have been made without any alteration to the rule book. Thus the civil service union SCPS and the telecom unions NCU and STE 'have taken the novel course of leaving their rule books unchanged, but issuing supplementary regulations that elections must be carried out under the Act'.[101] This is done, apparently, in the hope that the unions will be able to return quickly to their old ways if the Act is repealed. At a practical level, it also restricts the remedies available to members. If the terms of the Act are incorporated into the rule book, members acquire the right to contractual remedies (including injunctions and interlocutory injunctions) in addition to the statutory remedies.

There is little doubt that the unions have good cause to be anxious about the prospect of crippling litigation. As was pointed out in Standing Committee, there are some people associated with well-known right-wing organizations who appear to make a sport out of suing trade unions.[102] The point is the more serious for the fact that as was also pointed out in Committee, the scope for litigation under the Act is considerable.[103] Several attempts to control access to the courts were made in amendments proposed by Labour members. Thus it was suggested first that a case could be heard only if the applicant was supported by at least 10 per cent of the members entitled to vote at the disputed election;[104] secondly, that applicants should be estopped if the union's failure to comply was caused by the applicants or by a class of members of which they were members;[105] and thirdly, that a time limit should be imposed on applications — perhaps 6 weeks,[106] 13 weeks,[107] or 26 weeks.[108] The only concession which the government was prepared to make was to impose a time limit of 52 weeks from the date on which the

result of the election is announced by the union.[109] The reason for
adopting this very generous time limit is that the government sought to
encourage disputes to be resolved by voluntary procedures and that
these take some time.[110] It is to be noted that the government also sought
to encourage the use of voluntary procedures in expulsion cases where
section 4 of the 1980 Act applies. There, however, the government was
willing to extend the normal three-month time limit for applications to
six months.[111] 52 weeks does seem extraordinarily long and the ready
access to the courts which this and the generally unrestrained provisions
of section 5 permit are difficult to defend. As long ago as 1968 the
Donovan Commission warned that if legislation was introduced to regulate trade union government:

> Some check would be required to prevent misuse of the procedure
> by vexatious litigants. It might be provided that no such second or
> subsequent application by the same persons should be heard with-
> out the leave of the review body: and additionally that on the
> hearing of any such successive application all previous awards of
> compensation should be taken into account to the extent that the
> review body thought proper.[112]

More recently, in a submission on the Green Paper, the British Institute
of Management wrote:

> The question remained of who should be able to apply for an order
> to enforce compliance with legislation on union elections. The
> answers here clearly indicated that this was a matter that should be
> in the hands of union members themselves. A very strong majority
> thought that the application for a court order should come from a
> member or members of the union; most of those respondents
> thought that the support of a minimum proportion of the member-
> ship should be required.[113]

BALLOTS BEFORE INDUSTRIAL ACTION

A significant factor for the introduction of the directly elected governing
body is the assumption, arguably misconceived, that it will result in a
more moderate union leadership and less industrial conflict. This
assumption that the members are more moderate than the active union
participants is also reflected in the provision which seeks more directly to
restrict industrial action — the mandatory strike ballots. This is not

new. There was extensive discussion of the possibility of introducing similar legislation shortly before and soon after the general strike, and most of the arguments employed since were used then. The idea of compulsory strike ballots was also considered but rejected by the Donovan Commission. First, the Commission claimed that:

> there is little justification in the available evidence for the view that workers are less likely to vote for strike action than their leaders; and findings from our workshop relations survey . . . confirm this.[114]

A second objection raised by Donovan was that strike ballots would damage rather than promote good industrial relations. One anticipated problem is that the ballot would create rigidity in the possible responses of negotiators, who would cease to be representatives of their members but would become their mandates. In the words of the Donovan Report:

> Once a vote has been taken and has gone in favour of strike action, the resulting stoppage may delay a settlement by restricting union leaders' freedom of action.[115]

This caution was thought to have been vindicated by experience under the Industrial Relations Act 1971 — the only other occasion when mandatory ballots were introduced into English law. Under the Act the Secretary of State could, in a dispute which threatened the national interest, apply to the National Industrial Relations Court for an order requiring a ballot to be held where he considered that there were doubts about whether the workers concerned supported the action.[116] This provision was used in the railway workers' dispute in 1972. A postal ballot was conducted of 175,000 British Rail employees, of whom 85 per cent voted: 129,441 employees voted in favour of continued industrial action while only 23,181 voted against. Following this embarrassment, the emergency procedures were never used again.[117]

Despite this experience, the government again raised the question of strike ballots in the Green Paper. It argued that strikes inflict inconvenience and hardship on the public and that society has a right to expect that the strike weapon will be used 'sparingly, responsibly and democratically'.[118] The authors continued by claiming that the methods trade unions had used to consult their members were often totally inadequate. A particular concern was:

> the spectacle of strike decisions being taken by a show of hands at stage-managed mass meetings to which outsiders may be admitted and where dissenters may be intimidated.[119]

However, despite this concern, the government was not proposing ballots before all strikes. It ruled out unofficial action and industrial action short of a strike on the ground that a ballot in such cases would be unenforceable. The government's proposals were thus more limited, the Green Paper raising two possibilities. The first was 'strike ballots imposed by the State in specific, defined circumstances; and ballots "triggered" by a proportion of trade union members or by the employers directly concerned'.[120] This latter proposal was not new. It had been raised but rejected in Mr Prior's earlier Green Paper, *Trade Union Immunities*.[121] A number of potential difficulties — some weightier than others — were anticipated. First, how would it be determined whether the required threshold had been achieved? Secondly, where there was uncertainty (for example about the scope of the electorate, or whether a sufficient number of members were calling the ballot), who would resolve these difficulties and how long would this take? Thirdly, in the meantime, would there be immunity for the action or not? Fourthly, it might be necessary to involve an outside supervisory agency with some of these problems in which case one advantage of triggered ballots — that it did not involve state intervention in union affairs — would be lost. Finally, would triggered ballots apply to unofficial action? On this question, the authors of the 1981 Green Paper wrote:

> If a compulsory ballot provision did not apply to unofficial action, which already constitutes the overwhelming majority of industrial action, such action would continue to enjoy immunity in which case a premium would be placed on irresponsible behaviour. On the other hand, if a compulsory ballot provision applied equally to unofficial action, it might be possible for unofficial strike leaders to use the ballot procedure to secure respectability and recognition.[122]

Yet the government did in fact decide to adopt a system of triggered ballots — triggered by the employer in the sense of requiring a ballot as a condition of immunity from liability in tort. This is despite the fact that the two main employers' organizations were lukewarm in their support of strike ballots. The farthest the CBI was prepared to go was to note that support had been expressed for employee-triggered ballots in the limited area of national strikes, that is to say 'strikes serious enough to endanger the public interest', 'especially those in public utilities'.[123] Similarly, in its response to the Green Paper, the Engineering Employers' Federation was concerned to point out that it did not consider that it is 'practicable to contemplate any universal system of compulsory ballots before strike action. The technical difficulties . . . would render any such system inoperable.' The Federation continued by arguing that 'the . . .

obligation to hold a ballot could be misused to "legitimise" unconstitutional strike action and to pressure employers during the course of negotiations'.[124] All the EEF was prepared to support at that time was the idea of ballots triggered by union members in major strikes only, that is to say, strikes involving more than 5,000 employees. Unlike the CBI, the EEF also expressed some support for the government to be empowered to compel a union to hold a ballot in the case of strikes causing a serious threat to the economy or the public interest. But otherwise the position of these two employers' organizations was broadly similar: no ballots in every case; and certainly no employer responsibility for ensuring that ballots were held. Yet the latter is precisely what has happened. If the employer chooses not to take action when faced with a strike without a ballot, the member cannot compel the employer to sue, and the members themselves cannot directly enforce the duty in the courts. This is not to say that a failure to ballot will not affect the legal relationship between the union and its members. The closed shop Code of Practice provides in some circumstances that a union may not discipline a member for failing to take part in such action. Moreover, any damages incurred as a result of such a strike may be recoverable from the officials who ordered it, for reasons discussed in the previous chapter.

To which Trade Unions?

The first issue which arises under Part II is to determine to which trade unions it applies. What is meant by a trade union? The matter was considered in *Shipping Company Uniform Inc.* v *ITF*[125] where the plaintiffs owned a vessel called *Uniform Star* which was loading cargo at Tilbury for carriage to Japan. Most of the crew were Indonesian, and all members of the crew had been asked to sign two contracts, the first at ITF rates and the other stating a rate of pay agreed with the crews' union in Indonesia. This was less favourable than the ITF rates but was in fact the contract which governed the terms and conditions of the crew. This subterfuge did not deceive the ITF for long and it demanded that the owners should pay to the crew the outstanding wages due under the ITF contract. The Federation issued a writ on behalf of the crew for recovery of the money and the owners applied for a *quia timet* injunction because they feared that the ITF would engage in unlawful industrial action to obtain a settlement of the dispute. There are good practical reasons why the ITF might wish to adopt such a course: the legal action would not be resolved before the ship set sail and 'experience shows that foreign crew members often are persuaded to change their minds, once they leave the comfort and safety of these shores'.[126]

In this case no threat had in fact been made by the ITF: the owners merely feared that the union might act unlawfully. However, 'it is not sufficient ground for granting an injunction that, if there is no such intention, the injunction will do the defendant no harm'.[127] And in this case, Staughton J accepted that the defendants had no intention of engaging in unlawful conduct. Yet he proceeded nevertheless to rule on whether the conduct the owners claimed was threatened would be unlawful, though he stood over the question of whether the owners had made out a case for a *quia timet* injunction, presumably in view of the absence of evidence as to the intentions of the defendants. In determining whether the alleged threatened action would be unlawful, it was assumed that the ITF would have blacked the vessel as a result of which tug crews, linesmen, pilots and lockgate-keepers would be induced to break their contracts of employment. This would clearly be tortious; immunity would be provided by TULRA, section 13; but liability would be restored by the Employment Act 1980, section 17, on the ground that the secondary action would not directly disrupt the supply of goods or services between the party to the trade dispute (the owners) and the party to the secondary action (the employer of the tug crews etc.).[128] This is because the latter party did not contract with the owners but with the charterers.

A second, and for present purposes, a more interesting ground for the decision was that the action would be unlawful because it was not supported by a ballot. The case raised a hitherto unforeseen problem with sections 10 and 11. What section 10 appears to do in fact is to withdraw the immunity from action not supported by a ballot. Section 10(3) then reinstates the immunity, but only in the case of some ballots. So the immunity may be lost because the ballot fails to meet the requirement of the Act; but it may also be lost because the action is such that a ballot cannot possibly be held. The present case is a good example of the latter limitation, with Staughton J concluding:

> So the position is that ITF cannot, under its present rules, hold a ballot which complies with the Act. Mr Jarvis submits that accordingly the Act does not apply to ITF. I do not reach that conclusion. I do not suppose that Parliament, when enacting the principle that industrial action should be supported by a majority vote, intended to exempt federated unions. It seems to me that if they cannot and do not hold a ballot, then the action is taken without the support of a ballot and is unlawful. The remedy is for their rules to be amended.[129]

The reason why the ITF cannot hold a ballot is simply because it has no individual members who may be balloted.

Removing the Immunities

The idea that the duty to ballot should be a condition precedent to the operation of the statutory immunities is one which was made briefly in the Green Paper.[130] The proposal was also made by the Institute of Directors in its response to the document, though it was tied in with the additional proposal that the obligation to ballot would arise only where a ballot had been requisitioned by a group of the members. In other words, the immunities were conditional on the union holding a ballot where this was requested by a specified minority of members. It was recognized that such an arrangement would not be free from difficulty:

> The Institute believes that the sanction for refusal to hold a ballot, or for organising strike action in contravention of a ballot result should be loss of immunity. This is because the issues are intrinsically connected to the conduct of a trade dispute which legislation currently seeks to regulate by the ultimate sanction of loss of immunity. Although not mentioned in the Green Paper, it has been suggested that it would be unreasonable to expect trade union members to trigger a ballot if they knew that any subsequent refusal by the relevant union officials to cooperate would result in loss of immunity and therefore vulnerability to actions for damages amounting to thousands of pounds. The Institute accepts that such a prospect might limit the incidence of trigger ballots to those occasions where union members felt particularly strongly. However, it would not inhibit such ballots altogether, since in many cases individual union members are able to balance against the potential financial damage to the union their own keen awareness of the financial damage which both they and their employers will suffer. Anonymity in such cases could be ensured by requiring individuals to lodge requisitions for a ballot with the Certification Officer or other independent body.[131]

In the end the government adopted the proposal that the immunities should be conditional on a ballot being held but decided that it should be a condition of immunity for tortious action taken by a union regardless of whether or not a ballot has in fact been requested. The government thus took a more far-rearching position than had been proposed by any of its friends in the business community.

Section 10(1) of the 1984 Act provides that 'Nothing in section 13 of [TULRA] shall prevent an act done by a trade union without the support of a ballot from being actionable in tort (whether or not against the trade union) on the ground that it induced a person to break his contract of employment or to interfere with its performance'. Section 10(2) then removes the immunity for procuring breach (or interference with the performance of) a commercial contract by unlawful means where the unlawful means consist of action by the union which induces another person to break his contract of employment or interfere with its performance. The balloting requirements do not of course cover all torts which might be committed in the course of a trade dispute. They are confined to those which require workers to break or to interfere with the performance of their contracts. This is not to deny, however, that the scope of the balloting requirement is extremely wide. In *Metropolitan Borough of Solihull* v. *NUT*[132] the union had issued 'Action Guidelines' in pursuit of its 1985 Salaries Campaign. This called upon members not to cover for absent colleagues; not to supervise pupils during the lunch hour; not to undertake administrative duties with regard to school meals; not to attend meetings outside school hours; and to refuse to take part in sporting and dramatic events. The plaintiffs sought an injunction on the ground that the union had induced its members to break their contracts of employment and that TULRA, section 13 did not apply because there had not been a ballot. For its part the union argued that it did not induce a breach of contract: it was not calling on its members to refuse to perform contractual obligations, but only obligations which had been voluntarily assumed by them. An important point which the case emphasizes, however, is that the duty to ballot does not depend on there being an inducement to break a contract. Rather, following *American Cyanamid Ltd* v. *Ethicon Co Ltd,*[133] it depends on whether there is a serious issue to be tried that that in fact is what happened. What this means is that if there is a genuine dispute about the terms of the contract, the court will conclude, as it did in this case, that there is a serious issue to be tried. And as is well known, once this step is taken, the courts will always conclude, as Warner J did in this case, that the balance of convenience lies in favour of granting the relief sought by the employer.

It is true that section 17(2) of the Employment Protection Act 1975 provides that in granting an interlocutory injunction, a court must have regard to the likelihood of the defence of statutory immunity succeeding at the trial of the action. But section 10(1) of the 1984 Act makes it clear that the statutory immunity will not apply to acts done by a union where there has not been a ballot. So the only way to retain the immunity for tortious acts is to hold a ballot. But perhaps more importantly, there is also in practice a duty to hold a ballot in respect of action which is perhaps lawful but allegedly tortious. So in effect the duty is extended by the generosity to employers of English procedural law. And there is a second factor which may extend the duty further still. This is the fact that it applies not only where workers are induced to break their contracts, but also where they are induced to interfere with the performance of their contracts. This could take the form, for example, of an overtime ban in circumstances where overtime is clearly and unequivocally not a contractual requirement.[134] Such a result depends, it is true, on the scope of the tort of interfering with the performance of contract. In *Torquay Hotels Co. Ltd. v. Cousins*,[135] Lord Denning said that tortious conduct included 'deliberate and direct interference with the execution of a contract without that causing any breach'. In *Merkur Island Shipping Corporation v. Laughton*, while Lord Diplock endorsed some of Lord Denning's remarks in *Torquay Hotel*,[136] he did not endorse this wide statement of principle. Indeed, insofar as he acknowledged the existence of this tort, Lord Diplock did so only in its narrow form (interference not causing breach because there is a force majeure clause) and not in the Denning form (all direct interference actionable). The scope of the tort is thus unclear and the government rejected opposition amendments which would have ensured that for the purposes of section 10 it operated only in the narrow form.[137] As a result, unions will be well advised to ballot in the case of all industrial action. Remarkably, this means that there would be a duty to ballot even where there was an express term in the contract of employment that a strike, boycotting, or any other form of industrial action is not a breach.

Acts by a Trade Union

The ballot requirement before industrial action applies only to an act done by a trade union. In determining what amounts to an act done by a trade union, it is necessary to refer to the Employment Act 1982, section 15. This provides that where proceedings in tort are brought against a trade union on one of the grounds in TULRA, section 13, or for conspiracy to commit any tort, the 'act shall be taken to have been done by the union if, but only if, it was authorised or endorsed by a responsible person'.[138] It is then provided that an act shall not be taken to have been authorized or endorsed by a responsible person unless it was done by one of the following:

(a) the principal executive committee;
(b) any other person who is empowered by the rules to authorize or endorse acts of the kind in question;
(c) the president or general secretary;
(d) any other official who is an employed official;
(e) any committee of the union to which an employed official regularly reports.

In effect, this means that the duty to ballot applies only to action which is official action in the sense that it has the support of the union establishment. It does not apply to unofficial disputes, deliberately so, the government acknowledging the wisdom of the Donovan Commission that 'a law forbidding strike action before the holding of a secret ballot could not be enforced in the case of small-scale unofficial stoppages, which make up the overwhelming majority of the total number of strikes'.[139] So in *Austin Rover* v. *AUEW (Engineering Section)*[140] the plaintiffs failed to obtain an injunction to restrain a strike at Longbridge, because at no time had the strike been sanctioned by the union's 'responsible' authorities which, according to the Court of Appeal, had opposed the action from the beginning.

The question of what constitutes an authorization or endorsement has not been widely considered. It might have been reasonable to expect that the statute presumes some formal process and that it would be insufficient for the purpose of activating liability that a responsible person knew of the action, turned a blind eye, and did nothing to stop it. In *Express and Star Ltd.* v. *NGA (1982)*[141] it was held by Skinner J on the one hand that it is enough that the action is 'authorised by nods, winks, turning of blind eyes and similar clandestine methods of approval',[142] but on the other hand that it is not enough to constitute authorization or endorsement that an official failed to dissuade members from taking industrial action.[143] It is also to be noted, however, at least in the case of the fourth and fifth of the five categories of responsible person outlined above, that the Act qualifies union liability in the sense that a union will not be liable for the acts of those people if either the person concerned was prevented by the rules from authorizing or endorsing acts of the kind in question, or the act has been repudiated by the union.[144] The first escape route means that a union will not be liable for the acts of officers (other than the president or the general secretary) where the rules expressly exclude such officers from authorizing the action. An example of this would be divisional officers in NUR. It might have been thought also that where the rules confer exclusive authority on a particular body within the union, the union will not be liable where the action has been authorized by someone else. There are many examples of union rules which confer exclusive authority on the NEC (or similar body) to call industrial action. So the term 'prohibited' in this context would apply to those officers expressly prohibited as well as those impliedly prohibited. It remains to be seen, however, whether the courts will favour the unions in this way. A dictum of Skinner J in the NGA case suggests that they may not:

> Mr Goudie also submitted, on the basis of the rules, that the union could escape liability by virtue of s.15(4)(a). He argued that none

of the acts complained of was authorised by the rules of the union; but that is not the question under (4)(a). None of the officials in question was prevented by the rules from authorising or endorsing the acts in question.[145]

This may be taken as suggesting that the first escape route will apply only where the official is prohibited by the rules from authorizing the action in question.

In order to take advantage of the second escape route (that of repudiation), the union must first repudiate the act as soon as reasonably practicable after it has come to its knowledge; secondly, notify in writing the person who purported to authorize or endorse the action that it has been repudiated; and thirdly, refrain from behaving in a manner which is inconsistent with repudiation.[146] This last measure is clearly intended to prevent a union from repudiating a strike but continuing nevertheless to pay strike pay. The only authority at the time of writing on what constitutes a repudiation is the *Express and Star* case where the employer had introduced new technology without the agreement of the union. A strike was called and blacking instructions were issued. This was done without holding a ballot and as a result the employer was granted an injunction to restrain the union from inducing its members at the *Express and Star* to break their contracts of employment other than pursuant to a ballot under sections 10 and 11. The present action related to complaints that the terms of the injunction had been broken, one of the complaints being that a branch secretary (Lowe) and a national official of the union (Harris) had persuaded three men by blandishments and threats to break their contracts of employment. The three men had left their employment on April 17, 1985, the day of a meeting with the union officials in a hotel. It was held that the officials were employed officials of the union who had authorized the breaches complained of. A second question which arose, however, at least in relation to Harris, was whether the union had repudiated his conduct. Harris had received a letter from the general secretary of the union which referred to the hotel meeting of April 17. The letter continued:

> . . . support of their colleagues at the Express and Star. If, in your support, you infringed an order of the court, this was contrary to the National Council's decisions. The rules of the Association prevent you from taking such action in any event and I must make it clear to you that I have now repudiated your support of Tom (Lowe) and any authorisation or endorsements you may allegedly have given to Tom's action.[147]

It was held that this was not a repudiation:

> The union had known of the allegations against Mr Harris since
> early in May. There is no indication in the letter that it had
> enquired of Mr Harris whether or not they were admitted. Mr
> Lowe, in his affidavit sworn on 17 May, virtually accepts them to
> be true. . . . Mr Dubbins' letter therefore amounts to a conditional
> and half-hearted reprimand and no more. I agree with Mr Lee that
> a repudiation involves an open disavowal and disowning of the acts
> of the official concerned which must, at the very least, be commu-
> nicated to the victims of the tort in question. The first and only
> attempt to do this is in Mr Dubbins' affidavit of 20 May in these
> proceedings, and that plainly was not as soon as practicable after
> Mr Harris's acts had come to his knowledge. A true repudiation
> would also have involved a disowning of Mr Harris to all the
> members of the union who attended the meeting on 17 April.[148]

The Ballot Requirements

In circumstances where the duty to ballot arises, the Act lays down
detailed requirements which must be satisfied. First, the union must
have held a ballot in respect of the strike or other industrial action in the
course of which the tortious conduct took place (section 10(3)(a)). This
means that a ballot for one strike cannot be used to authorize the calling
of a second unrelated strike by the same group of workers. Secondly, the
majority of those voting in the ballot must have voted in favour of the
action (section 10(3)(b)). As first drafted, the Bill contained no requirement of a majority vote: it merely required a ballot to be held with the
result that a union could technically call a strike even though only a
minority of members voted in favour. In introducing this measure in
Committee in the Lords, the Earl of Gowrie said that 'When the provisions of this Bill were originally framed, it seemed scarcely credible that
any trade union leader would call a strike after a ballot in which a
majority of those voting had voted against such action'.[149] He continued
by claiming, however, that the miners' strike had shown otherwise and
that 'the scarcely credible can sometimes happen'.[150] He claimed in
particular that 'Nottinghamshire miners voted 3 to 1 against strike
action. At least five other areas voted the same way. Yet the leaders of
those areas, which are constitutionally trade unions in their own right,
instructed the members not to cross picket lines'.[151] It is to be noted,
however, that although a majority vote in a ballot will protect a union
from actions in tort by an employer, it will not necessarily protect it from

liability in contract to its members. In some cases the rules of the union may require a larger vote than a simple majority. In such cases it would still be open to a member to seek an injunction to restrain action in breach of the rules.

The third requirement of a valid ballot is that the first authorization or endorsement of the tortious act must have taken place after, but within four weeks of the ballot (section 10(3)(c)). Where the ballot is held on more than one day, the date of the ballot is treated as being the last of those days (section 10(5)). In the case of activity which is authorized by the union, the tortious act itself must be called within four weeks of the ballot. So if a union wishes to organize strike action, it must authorize the action and actually commit the tortious acts within four weeks. The purpose of this measure is clear: a ballot falls after four weeks unless it has been activated. In other words, a union cannot conduct a ballot and sit on it forever as a possible basis for industrial action at some indeterminate time in the future.[152] But if the ballot is activated it will operate to protect the action for as long as it lasts, there being no need for review ballots of the workforce on a periodic basis in the case, say, of a particularly long dispute. A point of some controversy, however, is the fact that the union has only four weeks from the date of the ballot, a period regarded by Labour members in both the Commons and the Lords as being too short and too rigid, leading to amendments proposing that it should be extended to 16 weeks.[153] Mr Gummer defended the government's position in the following terms:

> The Government's intention is that the ballot and the strike, if there is one, should be closely connected. We do not intend that a strike unconnected with a ballot, held in different circumstances and long afterwards, could be held to be covered by that ballot. That would not be sensible, so we start from the assumption that the period between the ballot and the strike, if it is to be held, should be short.[154]

In reply, a number of interesting points about the inflexibility of the measure were made, including the following by Mr Tony Blair:

> . . . let us suppose that negotiations are taking place between union and employer. Negotiations can easily go on for more than four weeks. The union has held a ballot, because as soon as it sees an advantage, it wants, rightly, to call for industrial action. Towards the end of these four weeks, it may be forced into authorising industrial action, although both employer and union may wish to let the negotiations continue.[155]

He continued in a similar vein by pointing out that although both sides
'may be very close to agreement, and although neither union nor
employer wants the union to have to make a decision about authorisa-
tion, it will be prodded by the [Act] into making such a decision'.[156]

The fourth requirement of a valid ballot is that it must comply with
the very detailed requirements of section 11 (section 10(3)(d)). This
begins by specifying the franchise. Entitlement to vote must be given
equally to all those members of the union who it is reasonable at the time
of the ballot for the union to believe will be called upon in the strike or
other action to break their contracts of employment, or interfere with
their performance (section 11(1)(a)). And entitlement must be given
only to those people (section 11(1)(b)). This means that everyone who
will be called upon to take the action must have the opportunity to
vote.[157] The union may not restrict entitlement. Equally it may not
extend the franchise to include people whom it knows will not be pulled
out. Conceivably this might be done in order to increase the chances of a
favourable result. So the franchise must be neither too narrow nor too
wide. The section also deals with the manner of voting which must be by
the marking of a ballot paper (section 11(3)); a show of hands at a branch
meeting is not enough. Moreover, by section 11(4) the ballot paper must
include one of the following notorious intimidation questions:

(a) a question (however framed) which requires the voter to say,
    by answering 'Yes' or 'No', whether he is prepared to take
    part, or as the case may be to continue to take part, in a strike
    involving him in a breach of his contract of employment;

(b) a question (however framed) which requires the voter to say,
    by answering 'Yes' or 'No', whether he is prepared to take
    part, or as the case may be to continue to take part, in indus-
    trial action falling short of a strike but involving him in a
    breach of his contract of employment.

Also on the manner of the ballot, the Act provides that ballot papers
must be distributed at the workplace or at a place more convenient to the
member. In addition, the member must be given the opportunity to vote
by post at the workplace or at a place more convenient to him or her
(section 11(6)). Unlike the ballots under Part I, however, there is no
preference in the statute for full postal ballots. There is in fact no obligation to send ballot papers by post, and a union has a choice as to the
method by which the papers are returned. As with Part I ballots, however, the union must secure so far as reasonably practicable that voting
may be conducted in secret (section 11(7)) and that those who vote may
do so without incurring any direct cost to themselves (section 11(5)).

Members must also be allowed to vote without interference or constraint from the union (section 11(5)). At the time of writing, these rather onerous requirements have invalidated several ballot results. In *Brinks-Mat* v. *APEX* an injunction was granted because the ballot papers had accidentally failed to include the intimidation question, and an injunction was granted to the Treasury to restrain action by the CPSA where the ballot had been conducted by way of a show of hands at a branch meeting.[158]

Implications

Although the duty to ballot applies only to official disputes, it is nevertheless potentially far-reaching in its implications for trade unions. It could, of course, have had a marginal impact only if employers chose not to use the facility. This has not been the case, however, with Hutton pointing out in a very valuable note that in the first year of Part II, there had been twelve reported instances in which employers had either sought or obtained injunctions on the ground that a union failed to ballot in accordance with the Act.[159] As Hutton also points out, 'This usage must be contrasted with a much slower take-up by employers of earlier Government legislation in the areas of secondary picketing and secondary action'.[160] Details of the first twelve cases are shown in Table 1. Employer enthusiasm for sections 10 and 11 shows no sign of abating. These provisions proved to be a very important weapon in the Wapping dispute, with News International obtaining injunctions against the NGA, SOGAT and the TGWU to lift blacking instructions which had been imposed without a ballot of the members affected.[161] Although much of this conduct constituted unlawful secondary action, it is nevertheless clear that many of the injunctions were granted partly or wholly because there had been a failure to ballot.

Given this employer enthusiasm, what are the implications of sections 10 and 11 for trade union government? The first point is that the Act will require fairly fundamental changes in a large number of unions if they are successfully to avoid litigation. Undy and Martin considered where power to call industrial action was located in unions. They found that in the case of national action, in 53 out of 77 unions the authority lay with the executive.[162] What they also found, however, was that the executive 'may or may not consult the union membership before undertaking strike action'.[163] Indeed, in most unions there is no duty to consult the members, whether the power to authorize the action is vested in the executive or any other organ or body within the union. Indeed, out of 103 rule books examined, 78 made no specific provision for a ballot to be held

TABLE 1.   *Litigation under Part II of the Trade Union Act 1984*

Employer	Trade union	Result
Brinks-Mat	Association of Professional Executive, Clerical and Computer Staff	Injunction granted — fresh ballot held
News International	National Graphical Association SOGAT 82	Injunction granted. Industrial action suspended
Treasury	Civil and Public Services' Association	Writ served — fresh ballot held
Wolverhampton Express and Star	National Graphical Association	Injunction granted — fresh ballot held
Solihull Borough Council	National Union of Teachers	Injunction granted — ballot held
Stephenson Clarke	National Union of Seamen	Outcome unknown
Austin Rover	TGWU, AUEW and others	Injunction granted — TGWU fined for contempt for refusing to comply. Other unions obey injunction
Safeway	GMBATU	Injunction granted
Ilford (CIBA-Geigy)	GMBATU	Injunction granted — fresh ballot
Shipping Company Uniform	International Transport Federation	Injunction granted
Post Office	Union of Communication Workers	Injunction granted — ballot held
London Regional Transport	National Union of Railwaymen	Injunction granted — union defied court order

Source: J. Hutton, 'Ballots before Industrial Action' (1985) 14 ILJ 255 at p. 256

before national industrial action is called, though a total of 41 unions did confer a discretion to conduct a ballot before taking strike action.[164] Nevertheless, it has been suggested that although the 'number of unions requiring ballots before calling industrial action is thus small . . . the requirement is more important than the number of unions suggests, since larger unions were more likely to be required to ballot their members than smaller unions'.[165] There is not, however, a great deal which can be made of this in the present context. First, in terms of the number of unions affected, it is very clear that many changes will have to be made. Secondly, although larger unions did ballot, this was true of only 7 out of 25 with 100,000 or more members. That means that there were still 18 large unions without mandatory ballots. Finally, in some of the cases the mandatory balloting rules were not as sweeping as the statutory requirements. In the TGWU, for example, the duty applied only to national action involving more than one trade group.

The second point which arises from Part II is that unions which did ballot their members will also be required to make changes in order to bring their ballot procedures into line with the requirements of the Act. As we have seen, the Act permits full postal ballots (papers distributed *and* returned by post), half postal ballots (papers distributed at the workplace and returned by post) and workplace ballots (papers distributed at the workplace and returned there).[166] Undy and Martin found that 25 unions provided for mandatory consulting of the members before national industrial action is called, but of these 25 only two — BIFU and NUS — specifically provided for full postal ballots.[167] But even here some change of practice may be called for. Although the rules of BIFU thus provide for a postal ballot, they also provide that members who have not been balloted may take part in action in support of those on strike if authorized to do so by the General Secretary. The effect of section 10 is that in many cases these people will also have to be balloted before being called out. Of the remaining 23 unions, only one provided for a half postal ballot (SLADE) while three provided for a ballot at a branch meeting and another three for a show of hands at a branch meeting. None of these methods is acceptable: both would be unlawful under section 11(6), while the latter category would be unlawful additionally under section 11(3) which provides that the method of voting must be by the marking of a voting paper by the person voting. And, of course, it is highly unlikely that any union would contain the section 11(4) intimidation question in its voting paper and, as the *Brinks-Mat* case shows, a ballot may be invalidated for this omission alone. In the case of the 41 unions which had a discretion to hold a ballot, it is clear that here too changes will have to be made before the discretion becomes mandatory. Only five of the 41 specified that the ballot must be a full postal one

(BALPA, AUEW (Engineering Section), EETPU, Equity and HVA) and only six expressly provided for a half postal ballot (AUT, Bakers' Union, NACO, NALHM, NALGO and the Rossendale Union of Boot, Shoe and Slipper Operatives).

POLITICAL FUND BALLOTS

From the early days, the flow of money from the unions for political purposes has been closely controlled by law. In 1908, W. V. Osborne, the Secretary of the Walthamstow branch of the railwaymen's union, sought a declaration that the compulsory political levy of his union was unlawful and an injunction to restrain the union from raising and distributing money for political purposes. The case turned mainly on the Trade Union Acts 1871–6 — organized labour's charter of freedom — which for the first time conferred a legal status upon the unions and brought them within the law. For the purposes of this legislation, trade unions were defined as meaning any combination for the regulation of relations between masters and men or for the imposition of restrictive conditions on any trade or employment.[168] Both the Court of Appeal[169] and the House of Lords[170] held that because the definition did not make any reference to political action, this was not contemplated by Parliament as being a lawful object of trade unionism, and therefore was beyond the powers of a union registered under the Acts. This was clearly a great threat to the future of the Labour Party, with injunctions being imposed subsequently on a considerable number of other unions.[171] If this process had continued, the Party would have been slowly starved to death. However, the Liberal government of the day responded in two different ways. First, in 1911 public money was made available to provide salaries for the hitherto unpaid Members of Parliament. This at least provided Labour MPs with a guaranteed source of income and relieved the Party of what had been a substantial burden. Secondly, the government introduced a Bill to remove the legal restraints on trade union political spending, it being readily accepted that trade unions had a right to seek the realization of their goals by representation in Parliament and that they should not be disabled from so doing by economic and legal barriers.[172]

However, the Liberal government was unwilling to reverse *Osborne* completely, largely because of the closed shop whereby unions could in effect require workers to make a political contribution as a condition of obtaining or retaining a particular employment.[173] The Trade Union Act 1913 imposed a number of preconditions with which unions must comply before they could lawfully incur expenditure on the activity to which the Act applies. Unions are required to ballot their members on a resolution for the adoption of political objects.[174] If a majority of the members voting in the ballot approve, the union may adopt rules to establish a separate political fund which alone can be used for the purpose of financing the political objects. The rules must provide that every member has a right to be exempt from the obligation to contribute to the fund,[175] a measure which is reinforced by the additional requirement that individuals exercising this right must not be denied any of the benefits of the union, or exposed to any disability or disadvantage (except in relation to the control and management of the political fund) for so doing.[176] Breach of any of the political fund rules may be enforced by an aggrieved member making a complaint to the government-appointed Certification Officer who inherited this jurisdiction from the Chief Registrar of Friendly Societies.[177] If, after a hearing, the CO concludes that a breach of the political fund rules has been committed, he may make such an order for remedying the breach as he thinks just under the circumstances.[178] An appeal lies on a point of law from a decision of the Certification Officer to the EAT,[179] from there to the Court of Appeal and ultimately to the House of Lords.[180]

The balance struck by the 1913 Act between the collective and individual interest was generally much more favourable to the individual than that struck by the law of many other western democracies on this particular issue. In Sweden and in the federal laws of Australia and Canada, trade unionists have no legally enforceable right to claim exemption from the obligation to finance the political activities of their respective unions. Yet the 1913 Act has never been fully accepted as striking a fair balance and its terms have since been revised on two occasions. The first revision was made by the Trade Disputes and Trade Unions Act 1927, passed in the wake of the general strike, which altered the arrangements for paying the levy from a system of contracting out to one of contracting in, whereby union members were presumed unwilling to pay unless they had positively agreed to do so. The 1913 settlement was restored by the post-war Labour government in 1946,[181] and a subsequent attempt to re-introduce the 1927 arrangements was considered but rejected by the Donovan Commission.[182] The second major revision of the 1913 Act was by the Trade Union Act 1984, Part III of which implemented proposals raised in the Green Paper, *Democracy in Trade Unions*[183] in which trade union political activity was subjected to a wide-ranging examination. The major change introduced by the 1984 Act is the requirement that unions periodically ballot their members for approval to continue to pursue political objects. However, although this is the principal change, it is not the only one. The Act redefines and extends the definition of political objects; it limits the potential sources of financing of trade union political funds; and it prohibits the practice where, because of the operation of the check-off, a political levy is deducted from the wages of contracted-out members.

Redefining Political Objects

The statutory controls on trade union political expenditure apply only to that in furtherance of the political objects listed in section 3(3) of the 1913 Act. If the expenditure falls outside the scope of section 3(3) it may be financed by general funds, and may be incurred by unions which have no political objects.[184] In the Green Paper[185] the government argued that there was a need to bring section 3(3) up to date, and this was done in section 17 of the 1984 Act which substitutes a new subsection for the existing definition.[186] Paragraphs (a) and (b) of the new section 3(3) relate to payments to political parties. So the political objects now expressly include contributions to the funds of a political party; the payment of any expenses incurred directly or indirectly by a political party; and the provision of any service or property for use by or on behalf of any political party. A contribution is defined to include affiliation fees and loans[187] and would also cover payments to Labour's election fund. Expenses incurred by a party would catch matters such as salaries, rents and administration. And in addition to buildings, 'property in this context could include equipment such as computers and printing presses. Services that unions might provide could include the provision of staff as, say, research assistants or facilities such as transport . . . mailing services and data processing.'[188] This introduces no new principle to the law. It was always assumed that affiliation fees to the Labour Party were caught by the 1913 Act. Indeed, the old definition was wide enough to require the unions to use their political funds to finance the provision of new headquarters for the Labour Party. However, it does not follow from these examples that all the expenditures now clearly within the scope of the legislation would have been caught by the old definition.

Paragraph (c) relates to electoral matters and covers expenditure in connection with the registration of electors, the selection of any candidate for political office, and the candidature itself. In addition, paragraph (d) applies to expenditure incurred in the maintenance of any holder of a political office. A candidate is defined as meaning a candidate for election to a political office and includes a prospective candidate.[189] This is broadly similar to the provisions contained initially in section 3(3). There are, however, two profoundly important differences. These arise from the definition of political office which means not only the office of Member of Parliament or membership of a local authority, but also membership of the European Assembly, and any position within a political party.[190] This last provision would cover any expenditure incurred in the election of a Labour Party leader or deputy leader, an inclusion which is ensured by the fact that paragraph (c) applies also to the holding of a ballot by the union in connection with any election to political office. Under the old definition of political objects, no express provision was made for European Assembly elections or for internal party elections. It is true that some of the expenditure could potentially have been covered as falling within section 3(3)(e) of the old definition. However, in *Coleman* v *POEU*[191] the Certification Officer cut down the scope of the paragraph by holding that it was 'aimed at expenditure on literature or meetings held by a party which has or seeks to have members in Parliament, or directly and expressly in support of such a party'.[192] This could be interpreted to exclude meetings held not by a party but by groups within it. And although the paragraph arguably could have been construed to cover meetings and literature expenses of candidates for the European Assembly, it would not have caught all the expenditure of such candidates, nor would it have applied to any maintenance payments to members of that Assembly.

Paragraph (e) of the new definition applies to expenditure on the holding of any conference or meeting by or on behalf of a political party, or of any other meeting the main purpose of which is the transaction of business in connection with a political party. It is expressly provided that expenditure incurred by delegates or participants (but apparently not observers) in connection with their attendance shall be treated as expenditure incurred on the holding of the conference or meeting.[193] Again, much of this expenditure would have been caught by the original definition of political objects, with paragraph (e) applying to the holding of political meetings. Although this was qualified in the sense that it would not cover expenditure on the holding of meetings where the main purpose was the furtherance of statutory objects, this qualification was cut down significantly in *Richards* v. *NUM*[194] in such a way that it is difficult to see how support for a meeting held by a political party would not have been covered. *Richards'* case is important also for making clear that the cost of sending delegates or participants was already covered as being expenditure on the holding of a meeting.[195] It appears then that the new paragraph (e) may not significantly extend the definition of political objects, though as originally drafted it was written in much wider terms and applied to any meetings at which the business of a political party was transacted. If enacted, this would have required the entire cost of a meeting to be financed from the political fund, even though only a small part of it related to political fund business.[196] However, the government withdrew from this bizarre outcome after not inconsiderable prompting from the Opposition by introducing the 'main purpose' qualification.

Paragraph (f) of the new political objects definition is perhaps the most controversial. This is expenditure on the production, publication or distribution of any literature, document, film, sound recording or advertisement the main purpose of which is to persuade any person to vote or not to vote for a political party or candidate. This measure clears up some of the anomalies of the corresponding measure of the old definition which were identified by the Green Paper. Although this extended political objects to include the cost of distributing literature, it did not apply to the cost of printing and preparation. Also, the original definition pre-dated the use of radio, television, film and video for political purposes and it was unclear to what extent the existing definition applied to such publicity. However, by enacting the new paragraph (f) the government had much larger targets in its sights, the measure being aimed principally at the electoral expenditure of public sector unions concerned to protect their members' interests in the face of privatization and cuts. In Standing Committee, the £1 million campaign against the cuts conducted by NALGO in 1983 was singled out as a clear example of tendentious political advertising which would be unlawful unless financed from a political fund. The view of the Opposition was that this amounts 'to political censorship by the Government of those who criticise them',[197] while Mr Clark for the government claimed that 'the advertisement is already caught by the 1913 Act'.[198] There may be substance to each of these views, though the latter is possibly more controversial. Indeed, if the government was so confident it is difficult to see the need to change the statutory formula.

Mr Clark's assertion about the NALGO expenditure does not appear to be supported by the views expressed by the Certification Officer in *Coleman's* case.[199] In order to have been caught by the old definition it would have had to be shown that the expenditure fell within paragraph (e) as being the distribution of political literature. But in *Coleman* the Certification Officer held that for this purpose the expenditure would have to be directly and expressly in support of a party. In the Minister's favour is the Certification Officer's own admission that his narrow interpretation 'may invite scepticism in the world of today',[200] and the fact that any challenge to expenditure such as that by NALGO would be in the High Court where the union in question could expect a much less sympathetic audience that before the Certification Officer.[201] But although most election campaigning is now clearly covered, some concern has been expressed that paragraph (f) has a much wider impact, the Opposition fearing that it would prevent all publicity campaigning by unions to mobilize support against government policies.[202] However, the government always denied that this was their intention, and some substance was added to the claim by their acceptance of a main purpose amendment here also. As originally drafted, the paragraph would have applied to any expenditure which sought to persuade people to vote in a particular way — even if this intention was secondary and remote.[203] This amendment does make a very considerable difference, if only to protect public-sector unions from the gauntlet of harassing litigation (financed perhaps by organizations which have complete freedom to promote cuts and privatization) every time they mount a campaign. Nevertheless, paragraph (f) ensures that such unions have no right to promote such campaigns at a time when they might be most effective.

Periodic Review

Section 12 of the 1984 Act gives effect to the government's concern that trade union members are not formally consulted on a regular basis about the operation of their unions' political funds,[204] by providing that a political fund resolution will automatically cease to have effect (if it has not been previously rescinded) ten years from the date of the ballot on which it was passed.[205] So if a union is to retain an unbroken authority to devote funds for political objects, it must ballot its members before the ten-year period lapses. Where a ballot is held before the expiry of the ten-year period and the motion for a new resolution is passed, the old resolution is rescinded on the passing of the new one.[206] This means, for the purposes of the next ballot, that the ten-year period runs from the date of the new resolution. Where the ballot is held while an existing resolution is in force and the motion for a new one is lost, the existing resolution expires two weeks from the date of the ballot.[207] The two-week period of grace is designed 'to allow for counting the votes, putting things into proper form and arranging for the practice to cease'.[208] Although the government was criticized on the ground that a longer period than two weeks was necessary to minimize disruption and to allow all relationships and arrangements to be neatly terminated, Mr Alan Clark (then Under Secretary of State for Employment) replied by saying that it was exactly right, but only after conceding that 'Perhaps the piece of paper with two weeks written on it was the only piece that landed face upwards . . .'[209]

However, although unions are thus required to ballot their members every decade for authority to continue to operate their respective political funds, this did not give them ten years from the commencement date in which to hold the first ballots. For section 12(3) provides that if a political fund resolution was approved more than nine years before the commencement date, it shall be deemed to have been passed nine years before that date. This means that resolutions passed more than nine years before March 31, 1985[210] expired one year thereafter. Most unions with political funds were in fact in this position. In the case of a union which is the product of an amalgamation, section 5 of the Trade Union (Amalgamations, etc.) Act 1964 provides that where the amalgamation is between two unions with political objects, the new union is treated for the purposes of the 1913 Act as having passed a resolution immediately after the amalgamation. However, a union which is the product of a recent amalgamation (such as GMBATU) could not wait for ten years from the date of the amalgamation before it balloted its members. Section 12(5) provides that for the purposes of periodic review, it is necessary to look at the dates when the amalgamating unions passed their respective resolutions. To illustrate, let us suppose that the Workers' Union passed a resolution in 1920, that the Transport Union passed a resolution in 1980, and that the two unions amalgamated in 1982. For the purposes of the 1964 Act, the resolution would be treated as having been made in 1982, but for the purposes of the 1984 Act it would be treated as having been made in 1920.[211] As a result the amalgamated union would be required to ballot by March 31, 1986.

The arrangements for the political fund ballots are governed by section 13 which provides that where it is proposed to hold a ballot, section 4(1) of the 1913 Act shall have effect.[212] This enacts that the ballot is to be conducted in accordance with rules which are to be approved by the Certification Officer. The 1984 Act provides that the rules must be approved on the occasion of each ballot: an approval of rules for a ballot held some time in the past is not enough.[213] However, for the purposes of a first review (that is, one held within a year of the commencement date),[214] the Certification Officer could accept rules which had been approved by the principal executive committee of the union concerned, even though the union's own procedures for the making of new rules had not been complied with.[215] This is because the time-scale for the introduction of Part III would have made it difficult, if not impossible, for some unions to make the necessary arrangements in accordance with their rules. So far as the content of ballot rules is concerned, section 4(1) of the 1913 Act gave the unions considerable discretion as to how they would conduct their ballots, with the Certification Officer being required to ensure only that every member had an equal right and, if reasonably possible, a fair opportunity of voting, and that the secrecy of the ballot was properly secured. However, this provision has been amended in response to government fears that unions would hold the ballots at branch offices.[216] The government was also concerned to ensure that the arrangements for ballots under Part III were the same as those under Part I.[217] It is to be noted that the new rules — which replace the original terms of section 4(1) — apply to all political fund ballots — that is to say, to those held when a resolution is in force and to those held when there is no such resolution.

Unions must now adopt rules, to be approved by the Certification Officer, which meet conditions similar to those required for ballots under Part I, the details of which are considered above. But despite the government's desire for parallel treatment, there are several differences. First, as with section 2, entitlement to vote must be accorded equally to all members of the union but, unlike section 2, there is no exception for members who are unemployed, in arrears or apprenticed.[218] The only qualification of the wide franchise lies in section 13(7)(a) which provides that where ballot rules are drawn up before a resolution expires, overseas members (a category which includes Northern Ireland) may lawfully be excluded. Secondly, there is no statutory preference for postal ballots as there is in section 2(7). The provisions for the distribution of ballot papers and voting are almost identical to the alternative arrangements in section 3, which provides for distribution of ballot papers at the work-place or at a place more convenient to the member, and which provides for voting at the workplace or by post. But as with Part I, the Act does not impose any direct obligation on employers to co-operate with the holding of political fund ballots. There is not even an obligation on employers to permit union officials access to the workplace to deliver ballot papers. There are, however, the more general rights of unions and their members arising under the 1978 and 1980 Acts. So, for example, ballot papers could be distributed by lay officials at the workplace with-out the employer's consent if this is done before or after working hours or during breaks.[219] This is unless the employer would be exposed to 'substantial inconvenience'[220] as a result, a qualification which may enable him to prohibit 'disruptive' campaigning. Employers could also be required to provide facilities for the ballot on their premises, though problems may be encountered by the fact that this obligation applies only to employers who recognize the union in question.

Political Fund Assets and Liabilities

As originally enacted, the 1913 Act required unions to use only their political funds for political purposes, but apart from the members' right of exemption it did not restrict the sources for financing the fund. Section 14, however, introduces three important controls which relate to the financing of political funds and political activities. The first provides that at any time when there is a resolution in force, no property shall be added to a union's political fund other than contributions to it by members of the union or any other person, and property which accrues to the fund in the course of administering its assets.[221] So far as the Green Paper is any guide, it appears that the main concern of the government was with the practice whereby a number of unions added to their political funds income which was yielded by the investment of other funds.[222] However, unions may also be disabled by this measure from borrowing money to finance their political action. This may not be insignificant: the Certification Officer's 1983 Annual Report shows that at the end of 1982 (the year before a general election) four unions had a political fund deficit.[223] In the case of at least one of these unions, the deficit was financed by an unsecured overdraft, the interest on which was charged to the political fund. Although this practice was upheld by the EAT as not violating the requirements of the 1913 Act and the rules made thereunder,[224] such a practice may now be unlawful on the ground that an overdraft involves the addition of money to the political fund which is neither a contribution nor income arising from the investments of the fund.[225]

The second restraint on the financing of the political fund is designed to ensure that unions do not continue to raise funds for political purposes after a resolution has ceased to have effect.[226] So unions cannot require members to contribute to the fund[227] and no property may be added to the fund.[228] This last restriction is subject to two qualifications. The first relates to property which accrues in the course of administering the assets of the fund[229] such as income that will come from the building society or wherever the funds are lodged. The other qualification relates to contributions paid before the expiry of the resolution but not yet deposited in the political fund.[230] This would cover the situation where the employer has deducted contributions by way of the check-off but not yet handed them over, and also the practice whereby unions deposit all income into general funds before distributing the assets to the respective funds at the end of each quarter, or other period. Otherwise a union may not add to its political fund after a resolution has expired. So, for example, it seems that a union may not take action to recover any unpaid contributions. Nor, indeed, may they be added to the fund if the members concerned should make good their arrears.

The third control on trade union political funding applies both where a resolution is in force and to cases where there is no resolution. Section 14(3) enacts that no liability of a political fund shall be discharged out of any other fund of the union, regardless of whether an asset of that other fund has been charged in connection with the liability. Quite simply, this means that a creditor will not be able to secure payment of a political fund debt out of the general fund of a union, or out of the assets of that fund. It is not altogether clear that this measure introduces any change to the law, though section 14(4) suggests that it does by enacting that it 'shall not have effect in relation to any liability incurred before the passing of [the] Act'.[231] But although section 14(4) has the virtue of clarity, it is nevertheless not free from controversy. The position could easily arise whereby a union with a low balance holds a ballot to renew political objects, the resolution is lost, and the union has a number of debts which exceed the balance in its funds, with no income to meet these debts. Concern on this count was raised in Standing Committee, particularly on behalf of small businesses, but Mr Clark pointed out that any debts were likely to be miniscule, that creditors well know what the law is, and that if 'such debts were to be settled out of the general fund [that is unlawfully in breach of section 14(3)] . . . it would be unlikely that any consequences would follow'.[232]

When a political fund resolution expires, several issues will arise. Decisions will have to be made about what to do with the assets in the political fund. As a result of the Act, a union may have three options. First, it may freeze the fund in the hope that the members will approve a new resolution some time in the future.[233] Secondly, it may transfer the money to other funds. Express provision is made for this in section 14(2)(c), a measure attacked by Labour members as a law-breaking provision in view of the fact that it permits transfers to other funds notwithstanding any rules of the union in question or any trusts on which the political fund is held.[234] Thirdly, in certain circumstances the union may continue to spend from the fund for political purposes. Section 15(1) provides that where a ballot is held before the expiry of a resolution, and the adoption of a fresh resolution is not approved, the union may continue to use its funds for political purposes for up to six months beginning with the date of the ballot.[235] But otherwise, political funds cannot be spent for political purposes after the expiry of a resolution. This is the effect of section 3(1) of the 1913 Act which prohibits the use of any union funds for political purposes unless there is a resolution for the time being in force.

A second issue which arises on the expiry of a resolution is that practical steps must be taken to implement the decision of the membership. Section 15(3)(a) is important in this context, and provides that on a resolution ceasing to have effect the union shall take such steps as are necessary to ensure that the collection of political fund contributions is discontinued as soon as reasonably practicable. This will involve giving notice to employers to modify check-off arrangements. However, because check-off agreements require varying periods of notice before any change can be made, the decision of the members of the union in question may not be implemented immediately. However, where money does continue to be collected after the expiry of the resolution, any member may apply for a refund of any contribution.[236] Otherwise the money in question must be put into the general funds of the union concerned.[237] The duty imposed by section 15(3)(a) is reinforced by section 16 which provides that a union member may apply to the High Court, or to the Court of Session in Scotland. Where the member's claim is upheld, the court is empowered to grant a declaration (even in Scotland) and, if it considers it appropriate, to make an order requiring the union to take steps necessary to secure that the collection of contributions is discontinued.[238] It is to be noted that any member of a union may apply under these provisions, including those who may not be directly affected in the sense that the union is not collecting contributions from them.[239] Section 16 also provides that where an order is made, it may be enforced by any member, as if he had made the original application.[240]

A third issue which arises on the expiry of a resolution relates to the position of the union's political fund rules. Section 15(6) provides that these shall cease to have effect six months from the expiry of the ballot in cases where the ballot was held while an existing resolution was in force. In all other cases the political fund rules cease to have effect on the revocation of the resolution. However, section 15(6) is subject to two qualifications. First, it does not prevent the union adopting rules for the administration of its fund in accordance with the Act during the period when no resolution is in force.[241] And secondly, the automatic revocation of the rules does not affect the right of a member to bring a complaint to the Certification Officer under these rules about an alleged breach which occurred while the resolution was in force.[242] One final point here is that section 15(8) extends the protection for exempt members which is contained in section 3(2) of the 1913 Act. After the expiry of a resolution, a member of the union who had contracted out when the resolution was in force may not be excluded from any benefits of the union or exposed to any disability or disadvantage (except in relation to the control or management of the political fund). But unlike section 3(2) of the 1913 Act which is incorporated in the political fund rules, enforcement of subsection 8 is by the High Court, and not by the Certification Officer and the EAT.

The Right of Exemption

Section 14 of the 1984 Act now makes clear that trade union political funds may be financed only by the contributions of members or any other person; or by money which accrues from the administration of the assets of the fund. By section 3(1)(a) of the 1913 Act, a union's political fund rules must permit the exemption of any member of the union from any obligation to contribute to the fund. A union is required to notify its members of their right of exemption following the passing of a political fund resolution.[243] The notice, which is to be given in accordance with rules to be approved by the CO, should also advise members that any exemption form may be obtained from the head office or branch office of the union, or from the CO.[244] However, it is not necessary to use the form provided by the union and it is sufficient to use one similar to that prescribed by the statute. It has been held that the members may write out their own forms and hand them to the appropriate union officials[245] and it has been suggested that there may be circumstances where an oral notification will suffice.[246] The effect of a notice of exemption depends on when it was delivered to the union. If it is given within 28 days of receiving a notification of the right of exemption following the passing for the first time of a political objects' resolution, it has immediate effect.[247] In all other cases, however, it does not become effective until January 1 immediately following the date of delivery.[248] It is to be noted that after a periodic review ballot, a union is required to notify its members of their right of exemption.[249] However, any exemption delivered thereafter becomes effective only from the following January.[250]

A question which has given rise to considerable difficulty relates to the use of the check-off as a method of collecting the political levy. In practice, some employers have been willing to grant check-off facilities only if the dues paid by union members are fixed and regular. This has meant that the employers in question have been reluctant to deduct a smaller trade union subscription of employees who are exempt from paying the political levy from their respective unions. Consequently, many unions benefiting from check-off facilities required exempt members to pay the political levy and then claim a rebate from the union periodically. This proved to be a controversial practice which gave rise to two quite different legal problems. The first point, which was never resolved, is whether this practice amounted to a breach of the now repealed Truck Acts 1831–1940.[251] These Acts — which generally applied only to manual workers — required that wages due must be paid to the worker concerned in the current coin of the realm. In *Hewlett* v. *Allen*,[252] however, the House of Lords held that there was no violation of their terms if money was withheld from the wage packet by the employer and transferred to a third party at the request of the employee. The third party might be a trade union, which means that in principle the operation of the check-off did not run foul of the Truck Acts.[253] It has never been decided, however, whether it was lawful for an employer to check-off a full trade union contribution where the employee has assented to only a portion of it being deducted. The matter was raised before the EAT in *Reeves* v. *TGWU*[254] but not decided because the Tribunal lacked jurisdiction.

The litigation which has taken place has related exclusively to the second issue, namely whether the operation of the practice of rebates constituted a breach by the unions concerned of their political fund rules. By section 6 of the 1913 Act, a union may adopt one of two methods for the collection of the political levy. First, it may impose a separate levy of the members. In that case it was held by the CO in *Elliott* v. *SOGAT 1975*[255] that 'if the same deduction is made from the pay of both exempt and non-exempt members a separate levy of non-exempt members is not being made',[256] even though contracted-out members were reimbursed and even though their money never reached the political fund. Alternatively, unions may adopt a system which relieves exempt members of the whole or any part of any periodical contribution payable to the union, in which case relief is to be given '*as far as possible* to all members who are exempt on the occasion of the same periodical payment'. In *Reeves* v. *TGWU*[257] the EAT construed the words in parenthesis to mean that if it is not possible, because of the operation of the check-off, to relieve exempt members when dues are actually paid, there is no breach of the rules if the union adopts a system of rebating the political contribution to exempt members. The EAT added, however, that the rebates should be paid in advance where possible, yet accepted that there would be sufficient compliance if in the circumstances rebates in advance were not possible, and the union paid the rebate in arrears at a time as soon as reasonably possible after the date when collection was made by the employer. But the EAT concluded by making clear that, for the purposes of its decision, it presumed that the rebates would be made automatically without the need for the exempt member to make a claim. If the complainant in a future case was required to claim a rebate, 'that might wholly change the position'.[258]

In practice, most unions adopted the second method for exempting their members and so were governed by *Reeves*. Although the decision seemed to strike a reasonable balance between the interests of the unions in the effective operation of the check-off on the one hand, and the interests of exempt members on the other, it did not satisfy the government. Section 18 of the 1984 Act now makes it unlawful for employers to deduct a political levy where they have been notified in writing by employees either that the employee in question is exempt from the obligation to contribute to the political fund or that the employee has notified the union in writing of an objection to contributing to the fund. The employer must give effect to this new obligation as soon as reasonably practicable, and may not do so by refusing to operate the check-off in respect of contracted-out members. Clearly, this will put an end to the system of rebates, for quite simply an amount in respect of the levy is not to be deducted at source regardless of whether a refund has been paid. If employers refuse to deal with differential contributions, they will either have to suspend the operation of the check-off or simply deduct a flat-rate general contribution from all members and leave the unions to collect the political levy by separate manual procedures. Because the obligations under these new provisions are owed by the employer, enforcement is not by way of complaint to the CO but to the county court, or to the sheriff if in Scotland.[259] If the court finds the employer in breach of the section, it may make a declaration and may also make an order requiring the employer to take whatever steps the court may specify to ensure that the breach is not repeated.[260]

Implications

Part III thus introduces new restrictions on trade union political activity, at a time when unions are already subject to quite exceptional legal controls,[261] and at a time when the closed shop — the principal justification for these controls — is in retreat.[262] By far the most important of these measures is periodic review, for it did seem likely that a number of unions would be required to discontinue the operation of their political funds. Those most at risk appeared to be the ten unions in which at the end of 1982 less than 50 per cent of the members paid the levy. These included ACTT (7 per cent contributing); the Blastfurnacemen (48 per cent); NGA (42 per cent); SOGAT (44 per cent); and ASTMS (30 per cent).[263] Yet Part III is not the only threat to political action with which the unions must now contend. Following its 'agreement' with the government, the TUC issued a Statement of Guidance in response to the criticisms that some unions with political funds do not take adequate steps to inform their members that they may claim exemption, and that in some cases the practical arrangements for contracting out are of doubtful efficiency.[264] The Statement encourages unions to ensure that no obstacles are placed in the way of members wishing to contract out, and that exemption procedures operate promptly and efficiently.[265] These measures are designed to guarantee that trade unionists have 'a free and effective right of choice',[266] and the Employment Secretary stated that additional steps would be taken if the agreement failed to realize this goal.[267] By this he appeared to mean the introduction of 'contracting in' which, by shifting the burden of apathy,[268] is calculated to lead to a fall in the number of contributors to political funds. Although he was evasive about how the success or failure of the agreement would be determined, rather ominously Mr King did say that he would be 'staggered' if 'the free and effective right of choice'[269] resulted in a situation whereby 98 per cent of the members of the TGWU paid the levy, as was the case in 1982.

There was thus a distinct possibility that the combined effects of the Act and the agreement would be that fewer people would end up paying the levy in what could well have been a smaller number of trade unions. And, indeed, the democratic rhetoric of the government in the Green Paper barely disguised the fact that this was their intention. As *The Times* pointed out in a revealing leader, the reason for the concern about trade union political activity was 'the political one of quickening the decline of the Labour Party, and perhaps also assisting the realignment of the Left'.[270] Later the same newspaper was to write that:

> Mr Norman Tebbit, when he was Employment Secretary privately made no bones about his hope that by ballots on the levy (which we shall have) and individual contracting in (which we shall not) the demise of the Labour Party could be hastened, and its possible replacement by the SDP (alternating with the Conservatives like Democrats and Republicans in America) could be stimulated. That ambition arose from something more than a politician's wish to do down his opponents; it touched on the need to recreate a basic political consensus which is impossible unless the Labour Party changes.[271]

In this purpose, the government has been outflanked for the staggering reality is that all trade unions with political funds and which were required to ballot returned a majority in favour of retention. During the balloting period, a total of 7 million ballot papers were issued, of which 3.6 million were returned, this constituting a 51 per cent turn-out. Of those voting, 83 per cent voted in favour of retention, with 16.7 per cent voting against. The union with the highest percentage poll was ASLEF with 93 per cent in favour on a turn-out of 85 per cent. The union with the lowest percentage poll was ACTT with 59 per cent in favour on a 49 per cent turn-out. What is more, a number of unions which did not have political funds took advantage of the momentum created by the run of successful ballots to set up their own political funds for the first time. These included the Hosiery Workers, which had held several unsuccessful ballots in the past and, to the government's dismay, the Inland Revenue Staff Federation. For the first time since 1927 a civil service union (with the exception of the post office unions — the post office being a government department until 1969) has now authority to engage in political campaigns unrelated to employment matters.[272]

As might be expected, trade unions generally are much less pessimistic about the impact of Part III. It remains to be seen, however, whether a Labour government would choose to retain the measure. In the first place, the confidence generated by the ballots may yet be tempered by the reality that these results might not be repeated in ten years' time. If Labour is in government, and is unpopular in government, trade union members may be rather less willing to support the links with the Party. If the ballots had been held in 1978/79 the outcomes might well have been much different. Secondly, it is in any event difficult to see the justification for the ballots given the rights of members already provided in the Trade Union Act 1913. Individual trade unionists are not required to pay a political contribution; they may contract out, and are protected from discriminatory treatment should they do so. Indeed, given the constraints on the closed shop, they may contract out of membership in many circumstances, should they feel strongly enough on the point. This is not to deny that there might have been a case for periodic review if the 1913 Act had failed adequately to guarantee the right of exemption in practice. But the government failed to produce any evidence to demonstrate that, despite the formal right of exemption, trade unionists were systematically compelled to pay the levy against their will. In fact, all the credible and reliable evidence points in the other direction. The Donovan Commission[273] found no evidence (despite having sought it) that the procedures of the 1913 Act 'are ineffective, and that the protection conferred by the Act . . . is illusory'. More recently, the EEF alleged that the Labour Party was 'significantly dependent upon the unwilling or unconscious contributions of a probably large number of union members'.[274] Yet in the course of examination by the Commons Select Committee on Employment, the EEF was unable to produce evidence to support its allegation.[275] It would in fact be highly surprising if anything other than isolated examples of abuse were to be found. There are now some 1.3 million trade unionists who do not pay the levy in those unions with a political fund.[276] As Grunfeld[277] has written, 'it is most ingenuous to allege that other individuals are not perfectly free to do the same when so large a company stands as an example before them'.[278]

NOTES

1. Sex Discrimination Act 1975, s. 12; Race Relations Act 1976, s. 11.
2. Employment Act 1980, s. 1.

3. 1984 Act, Part I.

4. 1984 Act, Part II.

5. 1984 Act, Part III.

6. Funds for Trade Union Ballots Order 1982, SI 953/1982.

7. Funds for Trade Union Ballots Regulations 1980, SI 1252/1980.

8. Lewis and Simpson, *Striking a Balance? Employment Law after the 1980 Act* (1981), p. 131.

9. Cmnd. 8778 (1983), paras. 5–55.

10. *Ibid.*, para. 5.

11. *Ibid.*, para. 7.

12. Royal Commission on Trade Unions and Employers' Associations 1965–1968. *Report*, Cmnd. 3623, para. 625.

13. Democracy in Trade Unions, *op. cit.*, para. 10.

14. *Ibid.*, para. 12.

15. *Ibid.*, para. 13.

16. *Ibid.*

17. Official Report, Standing Committee F, col. 53 (November 24, 1983).

18. Democracy in Trade Unions, *op. cit.*, para. 13.

19. *Ibid.*, para. 18.

20. *Ibid.*, para. 37.

21. *Ibid.*

22. *Ibid.*, paras. 39–40.

23. *Ibid.*, para. 39.

24. CTU, 'Working Party Report on Consensus of Opinions Sought on the Green Paper "Democracy in Trade Unions" ' (1983).

25. IOD, 'Democracy and Competitiveness — Further Steps Towards Trade Union Reform' (1983), paras. 5–18.

26. Aims of Industry, 'Recommendations on the Green Paper "Democracy in the Trade Unions" ' (*sic*) (1983).

27. CBI, 'Green Paper on Democracy in Trade Unions' (1983), paras. 7–9.

28. EEF, 'Response to Green Paper "Democracy in Trade Unions" ' (1983), paras. 3–6.

29. *Ibid.*, para. 5.

30. *Op. cit.*, para. 7.

31. Undy and Martin, *Ballots and Trade Union Democracy* (1984), p. 84.

32. HC 243 – i (1982–83), p. 2.

33. *Ibid.*

34. 1984 Act, s. 1(1)(a).

35. *Ibid.*

36. 1984 Act, s. 1(1)(b).

37. 1984 Act, s. 2(8)(b).

38. The prohibition on indirect elections proved to be particularly controversial. See Official Report, Standing Committee F, cols. 6–12 (November 22, 1983).

39. *Public Service*, Vol. 60, No. 5 (April 1986), pp. 8–9.

40. *Ibid.*

41. *Stemp* v. *NUR*, March 10, 1986, para. 3.

42. March 10, 1986.

43. *Ibid.*

44. 1984 Act, s. 6(1).

45. *Stemp* v. *NUR*, March 10, 1986, para. 6.

46. *Ibid.*, para. 8.

47. 1984 Act, s. 2(2).

48. 1984 Act, s. 2(3).

49. 1984 Act, s. 2(13).

50. 1984 Act, s. 9.

51. Now s. 2(5).

52. Now s. 2(6)(a). It has been held by the CO, however, that this measure is not violated by a telephone call to a union member from a union official, asking the member to vote for a particular candidate. In the view of the CO, 'the right to allow a person to vote without interference or

constraint is intended to exclude such conduct as would intimidate or put a member in fear of voting, or amount to physical interference'. The words spoken in this case did not amount to that. *Rey* v. *Film Artistes' Association*, April 11, 1986.

53. Now s. 2(6)(b).

54. 1980 Act, s. 1(3)(b).

55. 454 HL Debs 1073-1079 (July 12, 1984).

56. On this, see *Liley* v. *TGWU*, April 21, 1986, and *Wills* v. *TGWU*, May 22, 1986.

57. *Op. cit.*, col. 1079.

58. An important case on this is *Noakes* v. *TGWU*, June 24, 1986 where a workplace ballot was held for executive elections in the TGWU. The union publicized the election with notices at the workplace and provided both fixed and roving ballot boxes daily throughout the ballot period. In the view of the CO, 'because Mr Noakes was at work throughout that period and, according to his own evidence, remained in the workplace during breaks, I cannot see that more could reasonably have been expected of the union as regards making a ballot paper available to Mr Noakes and providing him with an opportunity to vote in the manner required by section 3(1) . . .' The CO also pointed out that 'This case shows that even "best efforts" will not necessarily ensure that every union member realises that opportunities are available for him to vote in a ballot'.

59. *Democracy in Trade Unions.* Cmnd. 8778 (1983), para. 44.

60. *Ibid.*

61. 1984 Act, s. 2(9).

62. Official Report, Standing Committee F, col. 681 (January 24, 1984).

63. Official Report, Standing Committee F, col. 615 *et seq.* (January 19, 24, 1984).

64. *Ibid.*, col. 668.

65. *Ibid.*, col. 657 (Mr Alan Clark).

66. See Ewing, *Trade Unions, the Labour Party and the Law* (1982), p. 120.

67. Official Report, Standing Committee F, col. 681 (January 24, 1984).

68. Official Report, Standing Committee F, col. 673 (January 24, 1984).

69. 1984 Act, s. 5. See 454, HL Debs 1074 (July 12, 1984).

70. *Ibid.*, col. 1078.

71. 1984 Act, s. 5(1).

72. 1984 Act, s. 6(5).

73. In the *Wednesbury* sense. See *Associated Provincial Picture Houses Ltd.* v. *Wednesbury Corporation* [1948] 1 KB 223.

74. See Lord Wedderburn of Charlton, 454 HL Debs 1109 (July 12, 1984).

75. There is a line of cases which suggests that natural justice may be dispensed with if the provision of a hearing would not affect the outcome. See *Cinnamond* v. *British Airways Authority* [1980] 1 WLR 582. In the trade union context, see *Cheall* v. *APEX* [1983] ICR 398.

76. 1984 Act, s. 6(2).

77. 454 HL Debs 1110 (July 12, 1984).

78. *Ibid.*, col. 1084.

79. *Ibid.*, col. 1111.

80. *Ibid.*, col. 1110.

81. *Ibid.*, col. 1118.

82. Kidner, 'Trade Union Democracy: Election of Trade Union Officers' (1984) 13 ILJ 193 at p. 209.

83. *In re Pergamon Press Ltd.* [1971] Ch. 388 at p. 399.

84. *Ibid.*

85. 454 HL Debs 1114 (July 12, 1984) (Earl of Gowrie). The same view is expressed by Lord Denning, *ibid.*, col. 1519.

86. Trade Union Act 1913, s. 3(2).

87. 1984 Act, s. 5(5).

88. 1984 Act, s. 5(7).

89. 1984 Act, s. 5(8).

90. 1984 Act, s. 5(5).

91. 453 HL Debs 672 (June 25, 1984).

92. *Ibid.*, col. 674.

93. *Ibid.* (Earl of Gowrie).

94. *Ibid.*
95. Undy and Martin, *Ballots and Trade Union Democracy* (1984), p. 58.
95a. Some unions appeared twice.
96. *Ibid.*, p. 59.
97. *Ibid.*
98. *Ibid.*, p. 60.
99. *Financial Times*, March 17, 1986.
100. *Stemp* v. *NUR*, March 10, 1986.
101. *Financial Times*, March 17, 1986.
102. Official Report, Standing Committee F, col. 808 (January 26, 1984).
103. *Ibid.*, col. 171 (December 6, 1983).
104. *Ibid.*, col. 807 (January 26, 1984).
105. *Ibid.*, col. 760 (January 26, 1984).
106. *Ibid.*, col. 820 (January 26, 1984).
107. *Ibid.*
108. *Ibid.*
109. *Ibid.*, col. 826.
110. *Ibid.*, col. 827.
111. 1980 Act, s. 5(3).
112. Royal Commission on Trade Unions and Employers' Associations 1965–1968. *Report.* Cmnd. 3623, para. 662.
113. As quoted in Official Report, Standing Committee F, col. 723 (January 24, 1984) (Mr Gordon Brown).
114. Royal Commission on Trade Unions and Employers' Associations 1965–1968. *Report.* Cmnd. 3623, para. 428.
115. *Ibid.*, para. 429.
116. 1971 Act, s. 141.
117. See further, Thomson and Engleman, *The Industrial Relations Act: A Review and Analysis* (1975), pp.113–18.
118. *Democracy in Trade Unions.* Cmnd. 8778 (1983), para. 56.
119. *Ibid.*
120. *Ibid.*, para. 61.
121. *Trade Union Immunities.* Cmnd. 8128 (1981).
122. *Ibid.*, para. 260.
123. CBI, 'Green Paper on Democracy in Trade Unions' (1983), para. 14.
124. EEF, 'Response to Green Paper "Democracy in Trade Unions" ' (1983), paras. 7–14.
125. [1985] IRLR 71.
126. *Ibid.*, at p. 73.
127. *Halsbury's Laws of England* (4th edn), Vol. 24, para. 932.
128. See further *Marina Shipping Ltd.* v. *Laughton* [1982] IRLR 20 and *Merkur Island Corporation* v. *Laughton* [1983] IRLR 218.
129. *Op. cit.*, at p. 76.
130. *Democracy in Trade Unions, op. cit.*, para. 65.
131. IOD, *op. cit.*, at p. 10.
132. [1985] IRLR 211.
133. [1975] AC 396.
134. See *Power Packing Casemakers Ltd.* v. *Faust* [1983] QB 471.
135. [1969] 2 Ch. 106 at p. 138.
136. *Op. cit.*, at p. 222.
137. Official Report, Standing Committee F, col. 1044 (February 9, 1984) and 453 HL Debs 750 (June 25, 1984).
138. 1982 Act. s. 15(3).
139. Royal Commission on Trade Unions, etc., *op. cit.*, para. 427.
140. Unreported, See Hutton, 'Ballots before Industrial Action' (1985) 14 ILJ 255.
141. [1985] IRLR 455. See now [1986] IRLR 222.
142. *Ibid.*, at p. 459.
143. *Ibid.*, at p. 457.
144. 1982 Act, s. 15(4).

145. [1985] IRLR 455 at p. 459.

146. 1982 Act, s. 15(5).

147. [1985] IRLR 455 at pp. 458-9.

148. *Ibid.*, at p. 459.

149. 453 HL Debs 700 (June 25, 1984).

150. *Ibid.*

151. *Ibid.*, col. 706.

152. Where, however, a ballot is held and action taken, there is no need to conduct a fresh ballot to resume the action which has been suspended for the purpose of negotiations: *Monsanto plc* v. *TGWU* [1986] IRLR 406.

153. Official Report, Standing Committee F, col. 1012 (February 7, 1984) and 453 HL Debs 721 (June 25, 1984).

154. Official Report, Standing Committee F, col. 1013 (February 7, 1984).

155. *Ibid.*, cols. 1014-15.

156. *Ibid.*, col. 1015.

157. The 1984 Act expressly provides that if a member has been denied entitlement to vote and is nevertheless pulled out in breach of contract or in interference with its performance, section 11 'shall be taken not to have been satisfied in relation to that ballot' (s. 11(2)).

158. These cases are unreported but are discussed by Hutton, *op. cit.*

159. 'Ballots before Industrial Action', *op. cit.*

160. *Ibid.*, p. 256.

161. See Ewing and Napier, 'The Wapping Dispute and Labour Law' [1986] 45 CLJ 285.

162. *Ballots and Trade Union Democracy* (1984), pp. 120-5.

163. *Ibid.*, at p. 120.

164. *Ibid.*, at p. 121.

165. *Ibid.*, at pp. 121-2.

166. 1984 Act, s. 11(6).

167. *Op. cit.*, at pp. 122-3.

168. Trade Union (Amendment) Act 1876, s. 16.

169. [1909] Ch. 163.

170. [1910] AC 87.

171. Ewing, *Trade Unions, the Labour Party and the Law* (1982), p. 38.

172. *Ibid.*, p. 41.

173. *Ibid.*, p. 43.

174. 1913 Act, s. 3(1).

175. 1913 Act, s. 3(1)(a).

176. 1913 Act, s. 3(1)(b).

177. Employment Protection Act 1975, s. 7.

178. 1913 Act, s. 3(2).

179. 1913 Act, s. 5A.

180. *Ibid.*

181. Trade Disputes and Trade Unions Act 1946.

182. Royal Commission on Trade Unions, etc., *op. cit.*, para. 924.

183. Cmnd. 8778 (1983).

184. The controls on political objects as defined in s. 3(3) are without prejudice to the furtherance of any other political object — see s. 3(1).

185. Paras. 103-4.

186. Unions were not required formally to change their rules to incorporate the new definition. Section 17(2) of the 1984 Act provided that the new definition would be incorporated into the rule books of unions with political objects at the commencement date.

187. 1913 Act, s. 3(3C), substituted by 1984 Act, s. 17(1).

188. Official Report, Standing Committee F, col. 1316 (February 28, 1984).

189. 1913 Act, s. 3(3C), substituted by 1984 Act, s. 17(1).

190. *Ibid.*

191. [1981] IRLR 427.

192. *Ibid.*, at p. 430.

193. 1913 Act, s. 3(3A), substituted by 1984 Act, s. 17(1).

194. [1981] IRLR 247.
195. *Ibid.*, at p. 253.
196. This would have meant, for example, that trade union annual conferences would have had to have been financed exclusively from the political fund if any political fund business was transacted in any of the sessions
197. Official Report, Standing Committee F, col. 1312 (February 28, 1984).
198. *Ibid.*, col. 1308.
199. [1981] IRLR 427.
200. *Ibid.*, at p. 430.
201. It might be argued that this expenditure would be excluded from the old s. 3(3)(e) because its main purpose was the furtherance of statutory objects — jobs in many cases. But cf. the following dictum of the Certification Officer in *McCarthy* v. *APEX* [1980] 335 at p. 338: 'No doubt the union genuinely believes that the election of a Labour Government is important for the working conditions of its members, and that because of this, material issued in support of the Labour Party is distributed for the main purpose of furthering the statutory objects. I cannot, however, accept that the latter belief is well founded. Although the words "the main purpose . . . of the distribution" imply a test which is primarily subjective, it is to my mind straining the rule to suggest that the main purpose was to further the statutory objects where that purpose could only be indirect and the direct and obviously apparent purpose was to bring about the election of a Labour Government.'
202. Official Report, Standing Committee F, 35th sitting (February 28, 1984).
203. See 453 HL Debs 852 (June 26, 1984).
204. *Democracy in Trade Unions, op. cit.*, paras. 84–5.
205. 1984 Act, s. 12(2)(a).
206. 1984 Act, s. 12(4).
207. 1984 Act, s. 12(2)(b).
208. Official Report, Standing Committee F, col. 1238 (February 23, 1984) (Mr Alan Clark).
209. *Ibid.*
210. The commencement date for Part III (s. 22(5)).
211. This being 'the date of the earliest of the ballots on which the resolutions in force immediately before the amalgamation with respect to the amalgamating unions was passed' — s. 12(5).
212. 1984 Act, s. 13(3).
213. *Ibid.*
214. 1984 Act, s. 13(6).
215. 1984 Act, s. 13(4). This applies only where a resolution was in force with respect to the union at the commencement date — s. 13(5).
216. 453 HL Debs 758 (June 25, 1984).
217. *Ibid.*
218. It is to be noted that the right to vote extends to members who are exempt from paying the levy and to those who may not be eligible to do so under the rules.
219. See EPCA 1978, ss. 23 and 58, as construed by *Zucker* v. *Astrid Jewels Ltd.* [1978] IRLR 385.
220. *Post Office* v. *UPW* [1974] ICR 378 at p. 400.
221. 1984 Act, s. 14(1).
222. *Democracy in Trade Unions, op. cit.*, para. 117.
223. See Annual Report of the Certification Officer for 1983 (1984), Appendix 5.
224. *ASTMS* v. *Parkin* [1983] IRLR 448.
225. The government thus appears to have departed from the view expressed in the Green Paper that 'it would be unreasonably restrictive to seek to prevent a political fund from going into deficit from time to time' (*Democracy in Trade Unions, op. cit.*, para. 118).
226. 1984 Act, s. 14(2).
227. 1984 Act, s. 14(2)(b).
228. 1984 Act, s. 14(2)(a).
229. *Ibid.*
230. 1984 Act, s. 15(5).
231. In the ordinary case a bank has the right to combine the two accounts of a single customer and to discharge the indebtedness on an overdraft account out of the credit balance of the other account. See *Halesowen Presswork and Assemblies Ltd.* v. *Westminster Bank* [1971] 1 QB 1. The only

authority on whether this would have been possible in the present context prior to the enactment of s. 14(3) is the rather inconclusive *ASTMS* v. *Parkin, op. cit.*, in which the EAT appeared to reserve its judgment on what would be the position where a creditor sought to discharge a political fund debt out of the other funds of the union. But given the clear and unequivocal language of the 1913 Act, it is difficult to see how this could have been lawfully done.

232. Official Report, Standing Committee F, cols. 1253–67 (February 28, 1984).

233. But if a successful ballot is subsequently held, this does not retrospectively authorize any collection of political contributions between that date and the expiry of the earlier resolution. Any collection in the interim period will be unlawful. See s. 15(9).

234. Official Report, Standing Committee F, col. 1257 (February 28, 1984).

235. But this does not permit the union to make any payment which would cause the fund to be in deficit, or which would increase the deficit of the fund — 1984 Act, s. 15(2).

236. 1984 Act, s. 15(4).

237. This is the combined effect of ss. 14(2) and 15(3)(b).

238. 1984 Act, s. 16(1)–(2).

239. 1984 Act, s. 16(1).

240. 1984 Act, s. 16(3). However, by s. 16(4) the applicant must have been a member of the union at the time when the order was made.

241. 1984 Act, s. 15(7)(a).

242. 1984 Act, s. 15(7)(b).

243. 1913 Act, s. 5(1).

244. *Ibid.*

245. *Valentine and ETU*, Registrar's Report 1957. See also Royal Commission on Trade Unions and Employers' Associations 1965–1968. *Report.* Cmnd. 3623, para. 926.

246. *Templeman and AUEFW*, Registrar's Report 1969.

247. 1913 Act, s. 5(2).

248. *Ibid.*

249. This is the effect of the 1913 Act, s. 5(1) which requires notification to be made after the passing of a political fund resolution.

250. 1984 Act, s. 13(9).

251. The Truck Acts were repealed by the Wages Act 1986, s. 11. The position is now governed by s. 1(5)(d) of the 1986 Act.

252. [1894] AC 383. See also *Penman* v. *Fife Coal Co. Ltd.* [1936] AC 45.

253. See *Williams* v. *Butlers Ltd.* [1975] ICR 208.

254. [1980] IRLR 307 (noted by Ewing (1981) 44 MLR 219).

255. [1983] IRLR 3.

256. *Ibid.*, at p. 6.

257. [1980] IRLR 307.

258. *Ibid.*, at p. 313.

259. 1984 Act, s. 18(6).

260. 1984 Act, s. 18(4) and (5).

261. Compare the statutory regulation of companies. The Companies Act 1985 merely requires directors to disclose details of political donations in their annual report to members.

262. See Employment Acts 1980–2. On the closed shop provisions, see Elias, 'Closing in on the Closed Shop' (1980) 9 ILJ 201 and Lewis and Simpson, 'Disorganising Industrial Relations: An Analysis of Sections 2–8 and 10–14 of the Employment Act 1982' (1982) 11 ILJ 227.

263. See Annual Report of the Certification Officer for 1983 (1984), Appendix 5.

264. The government's criticisms are to be found in the Green Paper, *Democracy in Trade Unions*, *op. cit.*, paras. 88–98. Cf. Ewing and Rees (1983) 133 NLJ 100.

265. See further Ewing (1984) 13 ILJ 125.

266. 57 HC Debs 755 (April 2, 1984) (Mr King).

267. *Ibid.*

268. In its *Report* (Cmnd. 3623) the Royal Commission on Trade Unions and Employers' Associations (1965–68) acknowledged that fewer people will pay the levy under a system of contracting in, but contended that this is 'due very largely to the innate reluctance of people to take positive steps involving the filling up and despatch of a form when only a very small sum is involved' (para. 924).

269. 57 HC Debs 755 (April 2, 1984) (Mr King).

270. *The Times*, August 13, 1983.

271. *The Times*, February 18, 1984.

272. 'Political Funds — Multiple Victory', *Labour Research*, May 1986, p. 22, as amended by 'Political Fund Errors', *Labour Research*, June 1986, p. 2. See also Steele, Miller and Gennard, 'The Trade Union Act 1984: Political Fund Ballots' (1986) 24 BJIR 443.

273. Royal Commission on Trade Unions, etc., *op. cit.*, para. 924.

274. EEF, 'Response to Green Paper "Democracy in Trade Unions" ' (1983), para. 14.

275. HC 243-i (1982–83), p. 25.

276. Annual Report of the Certification Officer for 1984 (1985), p. 52.

277. p. 296.

278. This paragraph draws from Ewing, 'Trade Unions and Politics' in Lewis (ed.), *Labour Law in Britain* (1986).

6

Discipline and Expulsion

In this chapter we consider the ways in which the courts review the exercise of trade union disciplinary powers. As we shall see, the vast majority of unions have a system of domestic appeals which enable a dispute to be resolved internally by a committee of union members, usually with a further right of appeal to other union bodies. Exceptionally, there may be a form of external review independent of the union. In this chapter we set out to explore the ways in which the courts have asserted jurisdiction to regulate the affairs of these domestic tribunals and the techniques available to control the ways in which disciplinary powers are exercised. There are three such techniques: control through the rule book; control through the principles of natural justice; and now control through statutory standards. Before considering these issues, it is necessary to look briefly at trade union disciplinary procedures.

DISCIPLINARY RULES AND PROCEDURES

As already pointed out, practically all trade unions have their own internal machinery enabling a member to challenge at least some of the decisions made within the union. This is in line with the Code of Practice originally made under the Industrial Relations Act 1971. By paragraph 13, this exhorts unions to 'maintain effective procedures for settling disputes within the union'. It is also in line with advice from the TUC which has encouraged the development of appeals procedures, particularly in the case of exclusion from, or discipline by, a trade union. A survey of current union practice on the expulsion of members was conducted by the *Industrial Relations Review and Report* in 1982,[1] and that survey forms the basis of the following account of union procedures. The survey covered the rules of 35 major unions with over 8 million members.[2]

The survey discloses that '[c]onsiderable variation exists in the degree of detail with which disciplinary offences are defined by unions. But, in addition to particular offences, most union rules contain a generally worded clause permitting the union to take disciplinary action in a wide range of unspecified circumstances', including where the member has 'acted contrary to the interests of the union or its members'. Additionally, many unions specify particular disciplinary offences. In the case of some of the larger unions, these disciplinary rules are 'quite sophisticated in the amount of detail with which particular offences are outlined', with the EEPTU, for example, listing 15 separate offences. According to the survey, the specific disciplinary rules appear to fall into five major categories. The first and most common are those which seek to protect unions from 'the misappropriation of their funds or property', with the rules also stating expressly in some cases that the union in question may take legal action against any member who does act fraudulently. A second category of disciplinary rules are those which authorize penalties to be imposed on members who infringe trade practices. Members of UCATT may be disciplined for breaching customary working rules, and members of the NGA may be disciplined for accepting work from 'unrecognized sources'. Thirdly, it was discovered that white-collar unions such as the NUJ and the NUT are empowered to discipline members for unprofessional misconduct, with the rules of both unions containing 'codes of conduct to provide guidance on how members should behave'. Fourthly, a number of unions use disciplinary rules to regulate the conduct of internal affairs. EEPTU has the power to discipline members for electoral malpractice, the TGWU may discipline members for making false statements about the union, and APEX bans the wearing of para-military uniforms at union meetings. Finally, some unions have specific offences dealing with industrial action. Some unions expressly forbid 'blacklegging' during a strike, while others prohibit strikers from obtaining temporary employment during a strike.

So far as the disciplinary procedure is concerned, the survey discloses that the body normally empowered to take the disciplinary action is the branch meeting. In some unions — usually white collar and craft — the decision may be taken only by the executive committee — though, in the case of the NGA for example, following a branch recommendation. The rules will often impose procedural requirements which must be followed in discipline cases, and they will also normally provide a right of appeal. So far as procedure is concerned, the survey found that disciplinary rules 'usually include written notification of the charges against the individual, a minimum period of notice of the hearing — most commonly seven days — and the right to be heard in person during the hearing'. Some unions also permit the member to call witnesses, to cross-examine witnesses for the other side, to produce written evidence, and to be represented by another union member. Two unions expressly prohibited legal representation. So far as the right to appeal is concerned, there is a tremendous variety in the different kinds of appellate machinery. There are, however, often several stages of appeal, 'finally culminating in appearance before a specially appointed appeals tribunal or the union's annual conference'. Two-thirds of the unions covered by the survey did in fact have a special tribunal, normally composed of long-serving members elected by the annual conference and barred from other office. In some cases, however, the final appeal body is independent in the sense that it is appointed by someone outside the union and consists of people who are not union members. The EETPU, for example, has an appeals committee selected by the general secretary of the TUC. Although this is not dealt with in the survey, both the ISTC and the NCU also have provision for an appeal to an independent body. And as the survey did point out, the GMBATU specifically allows an appeal to the TUC Independent Review Committee.

DOMESTIC PROCEDURES AND THE COURTS

The advantages of utilizing internal procedures are considerable, and they have frequently been canvassed by legal commentators.[3] They benefit the individual in providing a cheap, accessible and relatively informal procedure and disputes may be processed which would have little chance of success in a court of law. The advantages to the union are that using the procedures ensures that some control can be exercised over the decisions of local, and often lay, officers who may unwittingly act in breach of the law; it enables union policies to be uniformly applied throughout the organization; and it may save the unnecessary expense of litigation, which could exceptionally result in a not inconsiderable award of damages. Finally, the private resolution of disputes will also benefit the courts. It reduces the case load of an already overburdened courts system, and even those cases that are not satisfactorily despatched by the domestic procedures will sometimes be clarified, and the issues in the dispute more narrowly defined, than by the initial hearing. There is nevertheless a marked reluctance on the part of the courts to respect union autonomy in the application of disciplinary rules. The courts will assume jurisdiction despite attempts to oust them altogether, and they seem unprepared even to wait until the member has exhausted internal appeals. Indeed, it appears that in some cases the courts may in fact be willing to intervene even before a disciplinary tribunal has dealt with a case.

Ousting the Jurisdiction of the Courts

Attempts to evade the jurisdiction of the common law courts can take two different forms. The first is indicated by those trade unions which purport to oust the jurisdiction of the courts altogether and reserve solely to bodies within the union the power to resolve disputes. It is beyond argument, however, that at common law such a rule is contrary to public policy and void. This head of public policy was established by the House of Lords in *Scott* v. *Avery*[4] and was applied to trade unions by the Court of Appeal in *Lee* v. *Showmen's Guild of Great Britain*.[5] Denning LJ stated the law thus:

> [The parties] can, indeed, make the tribunal the final arbiter on questions of fact, but they cannot make it the final arbiter on questions of law. They cannot prevent its decisions being examined by the courts. If parties should seek, by agreement, to take the law out of the hands of the courts and put it into the hands of a private tribunal, without any recourse at all to the courts in case of error of law, then the agreement is to that extent contrary to public policy and void . . .[6]

As the Court of Appeal made clear in that case, the parties can agree to make the tribunal the final arbiter on questions of fact, but not on questions of law. However, since the interpretation of the rules is a question of law, and to make a finding which cannot be supported by the facts is an error of law, this does not seriously curtail the judges' powers to intervene. Indeed, the distinction between issues of law and fact is so vague that it can be difficult to predict how a court will classify a particular dispute. It is left with much discretion. As de Smith wryly observes in another context:

> where an appellate court has power to review questions of law only, it is apt to hold that a finding or inference was one of law if satisfied that it was wrong but that it was one of fact if satisfied that it was right.[7]

Exhausting Internal Procedures

Although it might be argued that it would be unacceptable if unions were permitted to frame, interpret and enforce their own rules without any external scrutiny, considerations applying to unions seeking to enforce an obligation to exhaust internal procedures are very different. It has already been urged that in the task of finding the delicate balance between union autonomy and the external control of internal union affairs, procedures should be devised which minimize the judicial role. A policy which requires that members should first exhaust internal domestic procedures before having recourse to the courts would seem to provide an obvious cornerstone in the development of any such procedure. The merits of utilizing such procedures have already been summarized and, unlike rules which oust the courts' jurisdiction, an exhaustion doctrine merely delays and does not exclude judicial intervention. Yet despite its obvious advantages, the English courts have shown a marked reluctance to embrace the exhaustion doctrine and in so doing have clearly demonstrated their interventionist attitudes.

DEFECTS IN THE INITIAL HEARING

A preliminary technical question is whether certain defects in the initial hearing render a decision null and void so that in law there is no decision or determination which can be made the subject of an appeal. The argument is precisely analogous to that used by the courts when seeking to circumvent statutory provisions which purport to oust their jurisdiction.[8] Argument abounds as to whether particular defects render a decision voidable and therefore valid until successfully challenged, or void and therefore a complete nullity. Since the question of whether or not exhaustion is required is essentially a matter of policy, such sophisticated distinctions, which would be wholly alien to union members themselves, should surely be ignored. Moreover, to accept this as a justification for excusing a member from an obligation to exhaust is inconsistent with the purposes of the exhaustion doctrine. A primary objective of that doctrine is to give the union an opportunity to correct defects at the initial hearing, mistakes which may well have arisen because of the inexperience of lay officials at a local level, and to save costs. In the light of these considerations, fine distinctions between decisions which exceed the body's jurisdiction on the one hand, and those which are improper but nevertheless within jurisdiction on the other, are wholly out of place in this context. Whatever may be the merits of such an artificial device in contexts where the courts are trying to prevent a statutory exclusion of their jurisdiction, there are none where the issue is essentially whether the exercise of their jurisdiction over a non-statutory body should be postponed.

In *White* v. *Kuzych*[9] the Privy Council refused to accept that there could be no appeal from a void decision. It was claimed that a purported decision made by a union committee was not in fact a decision at all since it was in breach of natural justice, and that consequently a union by-law which required exhaustion of domestic procedures where 'decisions' had been reached was not binding in the circumstances. Their Lordships rejected this argument in the following way:

> The meaning of 'decision' in byelaw 26 must be arrived at by examining the byelaws as a whole. The scheme of them manifestly is that members of the union design to settle disputes between a member and the union in the domestic forum to the exclusion of the law courts, at any rate until the remedies provided by the constitution and byelaws, including the operation of appeal to the federation, are fully exhausted . . . 'Decision' in the byelaw means 'conclusion'. The refinement which lawyers may appreciate between a tribunal's 'decision' and a conclusion pronounced by a tribunal which, though within the tribunal's jurisdiction, may be treated, because of the improper way in which it was reached, as no decision at all and therefore incapable of being subject to appeal, cannot be attributed to the draftsman of these byelaws or to the trade-unionists who adopted them as their domestic code.[10]

Although this was a sensible approach, it is unfortunate that the court reached its decision by interpreting the particular union by-law rather than by canvassing the relevant policy considerations. It suggests that if the constitution is framed in a different way, the argument might succeed. It did so in *Hiles* v. *Amalgamated Society of Woodworkers*[11] in which Stamp J held that where a union executive council had made a decision in a disciplinary case which it was not competent to make, there could be no effective appeal from that decision. A more recent decision of the Privy Council has, however, put the matter more firmly on policy grounds. In *Calvin* v. *Carr*,[12] it was held that it would be 'wholly unreal' to treat the impugned first decision as 'totally void, in the sense of being legally non-existent'.[13] An appeal body may thus take an appeal despite the technical invalidity of the original decision. Their Lordships suggested further that this is a matter of general principle and not a conclusion to be drawn from the construction of particular rules as to the meaning of a 'decision' or 'determination'.

UNION RULES AND PUBLIC POLICY

In *White* v. *Kuzych*[14] the Privy Council held that there was an obligation to exhaust domestic procedures. There, however, the union constitution contained an express requirement to that effect, and subsequent English decisions have explained the case on that basis. Furthermore, that case involved expulsion from a union in Canada, and it is very rare for a British union to have a specific exhaustion provision in its rules, though the Musicians' Union provides an example of one that does. Generally, unions simply set out the procedures without any express mention of an obligation to exhaust at all. In this situation the courts have been unwilling automatically to imply any obligation to exhaust,[15] though in *Leigh* v. *NUR*,[16] Goff J adopted a slightly more liberal approach which indicated that English courts might sometimes require exhaustion even in the absence of an express term:

> I extract from *White* v. *Kuzych* [1951] AC 585, in the Privy Council, and *Lawlor* v. *Union of Post Office Workers* [1965] Ch. 712, in this court, two propositions. The first is that even where there is an express provision in the rules that the plaintiff must first exhaust his domestic remedies, the court is not absolutely bound by that because its jurisdiction cannot be ousted, but the plaintiff will have to show cause why it should interfere with the contractual position. This is consonant with the rule in the case of a submission to arbitration, where the court always has a discretion whether to stay an action but cause must be shown why it should not. The second proposition is largely the converse of the first, namely, that in the absence of such a provision the court can readily, or at all events more readily, grant relief without prior recourse to the domestic remedies, but may require the plaintiff to resort first to those remedies.[17]

There is obvious sense in determining whether or not there is a duty to exhaust on the basis of policy considerations of this kind rather than simply on a construction of the rules. It would, after all, be ridiculous for public policy to make it unlawful for unions to oust the jurisdiction of the courts and yet to permit them to impose upon the member an obligation to use domestic procedures irrespective of how longwinded or unreasonable those might be. These propositions of Goff J were in fact accepted in principle (though not in practice) by Plowman J in *Radford* v. *NATSOPA*.[18] There was no express obligation to exhaust in that case but the union argued that the judge should nevertheless exercise his jurisdiction in favour of exhaustion. Plowman J, however, rejected this contention and he did so on grounds which suggests that the discretion will rarely be exercised in the union's favour, at least in the absence of an express exhaustion requirement. He argued that the issue in that case, involving the expulsion of a union member, was one 'peculiarly appropriate for the court, depending as it does partly on construction and partly on the question of the sufficiency of evidence'.[19] Similarly in *Lawlor* v. *UPW*,[20] Ungoed Thomas J refused to require exhaustion on the ground that the expulsion case before him involved matters of construction and natural justice, and he said that the court was the proper forum for determining these matters. However, in neither case is the argument convincing. The fact that the issue is complex and involves points of law does not of itself constitute a valid reason for refusing to give priority to domestic procedures. The considerations weighing in favour of exhaustion should at least have been put in the balance.

UNSATISFACTORY APPEAL STRUCTURE

Although objections to exhaustion based on the nature of the issue involved should not, it is submitted, carry much force when judicial discretion is being exercised — particularly since there can always be a subsequent challenge in the courts — objections based on the adequacy of the procedures are far more weighty. This is acknowledged in the Report of the Donovan Commission, which favoured an exhaustion policy, yet recognized that exceptions to that doctrine should apply if recourse to the domestic procedures involved hardship or delay.[21] The *Industrial Relations Review and Report* survey pointed out that the AUEW's appeals tribunal sits only once a year, 'and in unions where the appeal is heard by the annual conference there is also the possibility of a considerable gap between initial decision and the hearing of the appeal'.[22] In *Lawlor* v. *UPW* this question of delay in an appeal procedure to conference was in fact one of the factors which influenced Ungoed Thomas J in refusing to require exhaustion.[23] In any event, it is unrealistic to require members to exhaust this final line of appeal, at least in most membership disputes. Where policy matters are at stake, such as where a branch might be in conflict with official union policy, it is perfectly proper and democratic to permit one last opportunity to try and change that policy by pleading the case before conference. For disputes involving rights of members, however, which will usually be justiciable in nature, the democratic process is a wholly unsuitable method of resolution. However honest the conclusions, conference is likely to be a large and unwieldy body and decisions will be ill-informed and taken with little knowledge, background or understanding of the case. Such an appeal will often be more in the nature of a plea for clemency rather than a proper rehearing of the issues. Moreover, the appeal may be particularly futile where it is from the decision of the executive council to an executive-dominated conference. So it is not unreasonable for the courts to give little weight to the availability of this final appellate stage.

The question of delay would be much less significant if the *status quo* was maintained while the appeal was pending. If it was, the member would be very unlikely to suffer adversely from an exhaustion requirement; if not, the damage could be considerable. For example, it would obviously be unreasonable to oblige a member to exhaust procedures in an expulsion case in a closed shop context if, while the appeal was pending, the member was to be treated as expelled and would therefore lose his or her job. As Lord Allanbridge recognized in *Partington* v. *NALGO*,[24] reinstatement in the union might come too late to save the member's employment. Yet the *IRRR* survey found that in practice the position regarding *status quo* arrangements is unclear. The majority of the unions covered in the survey made no reference to the status of members during the appeal. There were, however, some notable exceptions. In some unions, NALGO, NUJ, EETPU, SOGAT, ASLEF, UCW and the FDA, expulsions would take effect from the date of the initial decision. The importance of the *status quo* is stressed by the Code of Practice which provides that 'Unions . . . should not consider taking action likely to lead to an individual losing his job until their own procedures have been fully used and any decision of an external body has been received'. The importance of the *status quo* was also rightly stressed by Stamp J in *Hiles'* case when he distinguished *White* v. *Kuzych*, where exhaustion had been required, partly on the basis that in the latter case the rules had protected the member while his appeal was pending.[25] Surprisingly, however, he even refused to accept an undertaking from the union that they would not force the member out of his job while the procedures were being pursued.

Forestalling the Initial Hearing

In the absence of some statutory provision or guiding principle which establishes a presumption in favour of exhaustion, it is unlikely that the judges will put much emphasis on it. In *Shotton* v. *Hammond*,[26] for example, it was urged that a failure to exhaust ought at least to be taken into account when the judge was exercising his discretion whether or not to grant an injunction, but Oliver J considered it a factor of very little significance. Indeed, in two recent disciplinary cases the courts have further weakened the authority of the unions' domestic procedures, for not only have they rejected an obligation to exhaust, they have even been willing to grant an interlocutory injunction to restrain the union from holding an initial inquiry to determine whether there has been an infringement of the rules.

The first case adopting this approach was *Esterman* v. *NALGO*[27] when Templeman J granted an interlocutory injunction to prevent the union from initiating disciplinary proceedings against the plaintiff which might have led to her expulsion from the union. The judge thought that it would have been impossible to discipline the member under the rules.

Even so, it is difficult to see why the union should not have been permitted the opportunity to come to that decision for itself. There was no pressing urgency, no indication that the delay would have prejudiced the plaintiff in any way, such as by her losing employment. Perhaps this aspect of the case can be explained on the ground that the argument in favour of staying the proceedings does not seem to have been canvassed before the judge. In principle, if there is any doubt about whether disciplinary action could lawfully be taken, the injunction should be refused. This at least narrows the scope of the injunction in these situations, and it was accepted by Slade J in *Porter* v. *NUJ*[28] as an accurate statement of the law. In that case, members of the defendant union sought an interlocutory injunction to prevent disciplinary proceedings being instituted against them for refusing to comply with union instructions to take industrial action. The judge refused the injunction because it could not be said that the case would inevitably be dismissed. He thought that 'the very exceptional circumstances which must be shown before the court can be satisfied in interfering altogether to prevent a domestic tribunal from hearing and adjudicating on a complaint have not been established'.[29]

Unfortunately, this statement to the effect that the court will pre-empt a decision of the union tribunal only in the clearest of circumstances is misleading. This is because of the change effected by the House of Lords in the criteria which should be considered before an interlocutory injunction can be granted. Formerly it was necessary for plaintiffs to prove that they had a *prima facie* case before the court would consider, on the balance of convenience, whether the injunction should be granted or not. But in *American Cyanamid Ltd.* v. *Ethicon Co. Ltd.*[30] the House of Lords held that it is sufficient for the plaintiff to show that there is a serious issue to be tried. If there is, then the court must immediately go on to consider the balance of convenience[31] in determining whether or not to grant the injunction. The *American Cyanamid* principle was in fact applied to an internal union dispute in *Losinka* v. *CPSA*[32] when an interlocutory injunction was granted to restrain the union from debating or passing certain resolutions critical of the plaintiff's conduct. Geoffrey Lane LJ in particular commented that the issue had been made much easier as a result of *Cyanamid*.[33] The application of the principle in this context was in fact confirmed by the House of Lords in *Porter* v. *NUJ*[34] — a case to which we return in Chapter 7 — where an interlocutory injunction was eventually granted to prevent the union from taking disciplinary action against members who had disobeyed a strike call.

In *Porter*, Lord Diplock indicated strongly that in disputes of this kind the balance of convenience will usually be with the plaintiffs rather than the union and the only circumstance where the balance of convenience should not be the decisive factor in determining whether or not to grant an interlocutory injunction is where the meaning of the rule is 'so plain and, on the undisputed facts, so decisive of the lawfulness of the strike order as to leave no serious question to be tried'.[35] So their Lordships have stood on its head Slade J's view that an interlocutory injunction will be granted to prevent the union adjudicating in the complaint only in exceptional circumstances. The courts will readily usurp the union's jurisdiction and will refrain from so doing only where there can be no doubt that the union is acting within its powers. The result will often be that the courts will completely replace the union's own tribunal as the initial arbiter of internal disputes. For if the case goes to full trial, and the individual wins at that stage, the union obviously will not be able to discipline the member at all. It will not even have the opportunity to find in the member's favour. This is a very curious approach for the courts to adopt. The domestic machinery might resolve the matter without it even getting to the court and it could prevent significant costs being imposed on the union. It is perfectly proper and desirable for the courts to protect the position of a union member pending the final resolution of the dispute. It is, however, highly questionable whether this ought to be by usurping the union's jurisdiction altogether.

CONTROL THROUGH THE RULE-BOOK

The basic principle is that the union must have the power under the contract of membership to take the relevant disciplinary action. Moreover, as has already been suggested in the discussion on implied terms, the courts seem unwilling to accept that any conduct of the member can amount to a repudiation of the membership contract unless the union constitution expressly so provides. Consequently, unless the union rules expressly confer the power to take disciplinary action, such action will almost certainly be unlawful. This was the view of Swinfen Eady LJ in *Kelly* v. *National Society of Operative Printers*.[36] He commented that '[a] power to expel would not be implied; it must be found in the rules in plain and unambiguous language'. While this arguably over-states the position, if only because there should be at least an implied power to expel members who refuse to pay their dues, there is no doubt that any scope which does exist for implying disciplinary powers is very limited indeed. This is further illustrated by *Luby* v. *Warwickshire Miners' Association*[37] where a rule providing that disputes between members of the society would be dealt with by the council, whose decision would be final and binding in all cases, was held by Neville J not to cover the expulsion of a member who was in dispute with various union officials, and the judge refused to recognize any inherent power to discipline which the union could employ. It goes without saying that just as there must be authority in the rules to discipline, so the penalty proposed or imposed by the union must be one which is authorised by the rules.[38]

Enforcing Procedures

If the union has the power to discipline, any exercise of that power will be unlawful unless procedural safeguards laid down in the rules are complied with. Procedural infringements can take a variety of forms. An important and basic principle is that disciplinary steps can be taken only by the body properly authorized under the union rules, as *Bonsor's* case demonstrates.[39] And there will be no power to delegate the decision unless such a power is expressly given to the committee concerned or must necessarily be implied from the rules.[40] In addition, in this context the courts will sometimes imply additional obligations even where they are not spelt out in the rules. For example, they have held that each member of a disciplinary committee should be given notice of the rule under which the disciplinary proceedings have been instituted, and also that each should be notified of the relevant committee meeting at which the disciplinary action will be considered even though some may have indicated that they are unwilling or unable to attend.[41] Indeed, unless there is a specific quorum fixed by the rules or by the committee itself, the courts might take the view that each member of the relevant committee is obliged to attend and consider the disciplinary charge. In partly administrative matters the courts will readily imply that the committee can act through a quorum of only a few members even though the rules or the constitution are silent on the point.[42] However, where the proceedings are judicial, they tend to adopt a far stricter approach. Nor are arguments of inconvenience likely to influence the courts in these circumstances. In *Barnard* v. *National Dock Labour Board*[43] a docker was disciplined by a port manager when the relevant statutory provisions stated that he should be disciplined only by the local dock labour board. The disciplinary action was held by the Court of Appeal to be *ultra vires*. It was urged upon the court that it was impracticable for the board to hear all the disciplinary cases, but the court rejected this. Denning LJ commented that the board could fix a quorum so that not all board members would be obliged to be present at all decisions. This suggests that a union committee can form a quorum even though the union rules do not specifically provide for this. But if no quorum is in fact specified by the committee, the courts may not readily imply the necessary power in disciplinary cases.

Procedural breaches do not have to be substantial. The courts will readily seize upon relatively trivial defects in the operation of the union's procedures in order to render the disciplinary action invalid. For example, in *Santer* v. *NGA*[44] the rules required that a member should be informed of his right of appeal when a disciplinary sanction was imposed against him. Because this was not done, the whole disciplinary action was held to be invalid. Melford Stevenson J commented that 'a vital part' of the relevant rule had not been observed. Furthermore, the whole of the disciplinary code must be fully complied with. In *Silvester* v. *National Union of Printing, Bookbinding and Paper Workers*,[45] a union chapel instructed the plaintiff to work overtime. He refused to do so and was subsequently censured by the branch committee for 'acting to the detriment of the interests of the union'. He appealed but was ordered to obey the instructions pending appeal. He failed to do this and was fined on a second charge; and when he again ignored the instructions a third charge was laid against him. At this stage the secretary of the appeal committee withdrew the appeal relating to the first charge from the final appeal court of the union because of the plaintiff's failure to carry out the instructions. However, the secretary had no power under the rules to do this and consequently his action resulted in the plaintiff being deprived of the final stage of his right of appeal. Goff J held that this invalidated the whole of the proceedings relating to the first charge which in turn meant that the other two charges were also invalid since they were inextricably linked to the first. In the course of his judgment, Goff J justified invalidating the first charge in this way:

> In my judgment [the plaintiff] must be entitled to say that he only submitted to be liable to be disciplined on the terms that he should have certain prescribed rights of appeal, and that upon the union refusing him those rights the sentence, albeit only of censure, and the decision that he was bound to obey the chapel committee's instructions in that matter could not stand.[46]

Reviewing the Decision

In considering the substance of union discipline, it is necessary to distinguish between rules which create specific offences and those which create general offences — such as conduct detrimental to the interest of the union. In the case of the former, the rules will be construed strictly in favour of the member. This is illustrated by *MacLelland* v. *NUJ*[47] where it was held that a rule of the defendant union, requiring a member to 'attend' a mandatory meeting, was complied with by his presence, however brief, and did not require the member to remain for the duration of the meeting. It was irrelevant that the union might honestly have construed that rule differently: it is unlawful to act upon rules wrongly interpreted, however reasonable or honest that interpretation may be. In the case of general disciplinary rules, the courts have also contrived to keep a tight rein on union disciplinary powers, though it is true that they have not always been consistent about precisely what principle of review they should adopt. It is possible to distinguish four different approaches from the cases, though they are not always precisely or unambiguously stated.

The first approach does little more than require good faith. Exceptionally, judges have expressed the view that determinations of union tribunals, like those of club committees, should be invalidated only if made in bad faith or in breach of natural justice. This was the view of Maugham J in *MacLean* v. *The Workers' Union*[48] and also of the court at first instance in *Kelly* v. *National Society Operative Printers*.[49] On this basis there is no need for the union to demonstrate that there is any evidence to support its decision though, as Maugham J pointed out, the lack of any evidence on which the decision could be reached might itself constitute evidence of bad faith or dishonesty. This would presumably also explain why, as Maugham J recognized, the courts could intervene if there was a perverse interpretation of an unambiguous rule. The second and more extensive basis for control, which was evident between the wars, emphasized the need for there to be some evidence to justify the tribunal's determination in addition to the decision being reached in good faith. Here the need for evidence is independent of a duty to act in good faith and not merely evidence of bad faith. This seems to have been the test adopted in *Evans* v. *National Union of Printing, Book Binding and Paper Workers*,[50] one of the very few cases in which the union has managed successfully to justify disciplinary action taken under a blanket rule. The plaintiff had refused to comply with union instructions to take certain work and as a result he was expelled under a rule which permitted that sanction for a member who had 'knowingly acted to the detriment of the interests of the union'. Goddard CJ held that on the facts this was a decision which the union could properly reach and he refused to interfere. In another case where the union was successful, *Wolstenholme* v. *Amalgamated Musicians' Union*,[51] the test was similar, though perhaps slightly stricter. The plaintiff had made various improper allegations to the general secretary of the union about certain branch officials. He refused to withdraw these allegations in writing despite having promised to do so and was expelled under a rule which permitted expulsion where a member was 'bringing the union into discredit'. The relevant question to decide, according to Eve J, was whether there was evidence which could satisfactorily justify the union's decision. The judge held that the rule could cover conduct whereby a member brought one part of the union into discredit with other component parts and that on the facts there was ample material supporting the decision to expel.

The second ground for control runs into the third. This requires that there should not merely be some evidence to support the union tribunal's finding, but that the evidence should be reasonably capable of supporting the finding. It was first clearly formulated by Denning LJ in *Lee* v. *Showmen's Guild of Great Britain*:[52]

> The construction of the rules is so bound up with the application of the rules to the facts that no one can tell one from the other. When that happens, the question whether the committee has acted within its jurisdiction depends, in my opinion, on whether the facts adduced before them were reasonably capable of being held to be a breach of the rules. If they were, then the proper inference is that the committee correctly construed the rules and have acted within their jurisdiction. If, however, the facts were not reasonably capable of being held to be a breach, and yet the committee held them to be a breach, then the only inference is that the committee have misconstrued the rules and exceeded their jurisdiction. The proposition is sometimes stated in the form that the court can interfere if there was no evidence to support the finding of the committee; but that only means that the facts were not reasonably capable of supporting the finding.[53]

As the extract makes clear, Denning LJ thought that the 'no evidence' principle and the principle that the facts must be reasonably capable of supporting the finding really express the same test. Logically this cannot be correct. For while it is true that the tests may occasionally be blurred by the judges, and the one may merge into the other, the latter test involves an assessment of the weight of evidence while the former involves merely ascertaining its existence. Essentially, therefore, the distinction between the second and third approaches rests largely in the emphasis given to the weight of evidence as a relevant factor to review. In contrast, the fourth basis of control is much more rigorous. This involves the court intervening if it is of the opinion that the facts found by the union tribunal do not fall within the terms of the disciplinary rule. It is not enough that the facts as found by the tribunal are reasonably capable of constituting a breach of the relevant rule; the court must be satisfied that they do in fact do so. This was the approach of Romer LJ in

Lee v. *Showmen's Guild of Great Britain*.[54] He thought that since the facts in that case were not in dispute, it was entirely for the court to determine whether they gave rise to a breach of the rules. Essentially this approach refuses to distinguish between the specific and the general disciplinary provisions. On this view, the court need no more defer to the domestic tribunal's view of the conduct which falls within the scope of the latter rule than it does in the former.

Of these four different approaches, the courts now clearly favour the test articulated by Denning LJ in *Lee's* case. His formulation of the principles for reviewing the determination of union tribunals has subsequently been followed in numerous cases.[55] It is a more satisfactory basis for control than the fuller regulation which is involved in the analysis of Romer LJ. Whether or not conduct damages the interests of the union obviously depends on how those interests are perceived. Romer LJ's approach makes no concessions to the unions' own views about what they see as disruptive or undesirable conduct, whereas Lord Denning's analysis does, at least in theory, give weight to the union's assessment. On his approach, providing the tribunal's conclusions can be reasonably sustained, the court will not upset them. Yet a student who focuses on what the courts actually do, rather than on the theories they espouse, might be forgiven if she were to conclude that Romer LJ's analysis, involving the substitution of the court's view for that of the union tribunal, has generally held sway. There have been a number of reported cases in which discipline under general rules has come under the scrutiny of the courts, and in all save the two exceptional decisions mentioned above,[56] the courts have held that the union disciplinary action was unlawful. The judges pay lip service to the limited notion of union autonomy inherent in Lord Denning's formulation, but in practice they refuse to recognize it. They seem to be very reluctant to concede that the determination is one which a reasonable tribunal could reach. Several decisions indicate this. In *Lee's* case itself, the Court of Appeal held that certain conduct of the member could not constitute the offence of 'unfair competition' since that required some forms of bribery or undercutting which had not been alleged. In *Radford* v. *NATSOPA*,[57] Plowman J held that the refusal of a member to disclose what had been said in discussions with his solicitor was not capable of constituting 'action against the union'. There was no evidence against the member to warrant this charge being made, and his silence was no substitute for the existence of such evidence. Again in the *Silvester* case referred to above,[58] Goff J held that a member could not be acting 'to the detriment of the interests of the union where he was acting consistently with an express policy of the union'. The member had been disciplined for refusing to work overtime which the union alleged was compulsory; in fact the declared policy of the union was that it should be optional.

However, by far the most important decision in this context is *Esterman* v. *NALGO*[59] which suggests that it might be impossible to contend that members are in breach of any of the general disciplinary rules where they acted in accordance with their consciences. The judge began by taking a restrictive view of his powers and by reiterating the approach developed by Denning LJ in *Lee*. Subsequently, however, he adopted a very different test:

> . . . I emphatically reject the submission that it was the duty of every member blindly to obey the orders of the national executive council in the prevailing circumstances and that he could only disobey the order if he were prepared to take the risk of being expelled from NALGO . . . It must depend on the order and it must depend on the circumstances and, in my judgment, if implicit obedience is to be exacted, those who issue the order must make quite sure that they have power . . . that they are making a proper exercise of the power, and that no reasonable man could conscientiously say to himself that 'this is an order which I have no duty to obey'.[60]

This is a formulation of potentially staggering width. It is no longer asking, as the traditional test does, whether the union tribunal could on the evidence have reasonably concluded that the disciplinary action was justified by the rules: it is not even standing the test on its head and asking whether a reasonable member could have so concluded, itself a very different test which would give the courts a far wider basis for control. Rather, it is asking whether a member might in all conscience feel that the union is mistaken, not merely in construing its powers, but also in deciding to exercise them. If developed, this approach would be tantamount to the writing of a conscience clause in the contract of membership. Providing the member is following his or her conscience, no tribunal could conclude that he or she has acted against the interests of the union. No blanket disciplinary rule could justify the expulsion. Each of the members could effectively decide for themselves what the union interests require. Indeed, it would be possible to go further and to conclude that the member could not be disciplined for breach of even a specific rule. This 'conscience clause' could operate as an implied limitation on the union power to expel under any rule. We return to this case in Chapter 7, and merely add here that the approach evident in *Esterman* is devoid of authority and should not be exaggerated. There is no contractual principle which justifies the incorporation of an overriding conscience clause in this way, nor is there any other juridical basis which would support the development.

Subjectively worded powers: an assessment

The approach of the judges to the interpretation of union rules suggests that Summers' comments on the judicial role in disciplinary cases in the United States apply equally in Britain: 'In large measure, and particularly in the critical cases, the contract is what the judges say it is'.[61] It is clear that even where general vaguely worded disciplinary rules are in issue, the courts are hardly willing to defer at all to the assessment of the tribunal itself as to whether the conduct complained of has infringed the rule. This contrasts sharply with the approach adopted by the judges in cases involving other non-statutory domestic tribunals. For example, the courts have frequently stated that they will not interfere with the findings of a club disciplinary committee provided the body acts in good faith and complies with the principles of natural justice.[62] But in these cases, three factors all militated against intervention. The courts were reluctant on policy grounds to become involved in the legal regulation of purely social relationships; the rules which were the basis of the disciplinary action were generally in subjective terms, so that the decision whether or not the rule had been infringed was a matter of the committee's opinion, and consequently it was easy for the judges to justify deferring to the decision of the committee as a matter of construction of the contract; and finally the conduct enjoined was that which was considered to be detrimental or prejudicial to the club's interests rather than the breach of a specific obligation, and the courts were not prepared to substitute their own view for that of the club on this question. This non-interventionist approach was later adopted in relation to quite different bodies, sometimes even where the three factors did not all point to judicial abstention. For example, in a number of cases the courts displayed a reluctance to interfere with the decisions of professional bodies disciplining a member for breach of professional ethics.[63]

Yet although the degree of control of the unions is clearly more extensive than is the case with most other non-statutory bodies, the judges have only occasionally commented on why this is so. In *Lee's* case, Denning LJ justified the different treatment of unions and other disciplinary professional bodies on the one hand, from clubs on the other, on the ground that decisions of the former could result in a man being deprived of his livelihood.[64] Yet logically this argument supports distinguishing unions and clubs only where union membership is in jeopardy in circumstances where the union is pursuing a closed shop policy. It is only then that livelihood itself is threatened. It does not justify a distinction being drawn between the two institutions in all cases. Another reason for distinguishing the club and union cases was propounded by Romer LJ and Somervell LJ. Both judges commented that the nature of the issue which generally has to be determined in the club cases involves matters of ethics and social behaviour whereas in the union cases it involves a matter of construction of the rule, which is essentially a lawyer's task. The former is not the court's province. The judges are no better equipped than the members of a club committee to decide disputes about ethical behaviour, and they should therefore not seek to substitute their opinion for that of the committee.[65] But why does not the same principle hold for trade unions? It is a gross simplification to make the assumption that union cases involve simply matters of construction. Unambiguous specific disciplinary rules may do so (though even there policy may intrude), but this is not true of the general disciplinary provisions. Inevitably the construction of the latter involves an understanding of union norms of behaviour which are the equivalent of the social and ethical standards expected of the club member. It cannot be seriously asserted that the courts are better able to understand and judge union norms any more than the affairs of a club. Indeed, one of the difficulties of giving the judges power to review union disciplinary decisions is precisely the problem which they have in understanding union values.

Of the three factors outlined above influencing the degree of judicial control in non-trade union cases, neither the nature of the union as an institution nor the particular context of the rules has in practice inhibited the courts from reviewing union determinations made under general disciplinary provisions. But what is the significance of the form which the rule takes? Can the union limit the scope of judicial intervention to simply requiring good faith by adopting a rule which is framed in suitably subjective terms? In *Lee's* case, both Somervell and Romer LJ emphasized that a relevant feature distinguishing the club from the union cases was that in the former virtually all the cases involved general rules subjectively formed, while in the union context the rules were usually phrased objectively.[66] Romer LJ in particular recognized that the power of the court to intervene might well have been more limited in *Lee's* case had the rule prescribed conduct which in the opinion of the relevant committee constituted a breach of the relevant rule. Moreover, one union case at least supports this approach. In *Walton* v. *Yorkshire Miners' Association*[67] a member of the Association who was also a Member of Parliament was expelled under a rule which left a union committee a discretion to expel for conduct detrimental to the union. Although the expulsion was held to be invalid on procedural grounds, Russell J was unwilling to hold that the plaintiff's conduct was not detrimental, saying that he was not at liberty to substitute his discretion for that of the union. But this case was decided before the *Lee* decision, and since then there have been two cases which have simply ignored the distinction between objectively and subjectively worded clauses. In *Mander* v. *Showmen's*

Guild of Great Britain,[68] unfortunately only briefly reported, the plaintiff
was expelled for conduct which in the opinion of the relevant committee
was 'unruly or unseemly'. The Court of Appeal seems to have wholly
ignored the subjective formulation, choosing to interpret the meaning of
the subjective rule itself. Again, in *Esterman* v. *NALGO*,[69] Templeman J
did not defer to the interpretation of the union tribunal where a subjective rule was in issue, and again the distinction was simply ignored
with no reference being made to it.

Yet how can this distinction be rendered irrelevant? Clearly on a
contractual basis it is fundamental. Subjective rules expressly leave the
question of interpretation to the union committee and the member must
be assumed to have contracted on that basis, even if the rule does
virtually entitle the union to determine its own jurisdiction. One possible but artificial approach would be to interpret apparently subjective
phrases objectively so that 'in the opinion of the committee' could be
interpreted as meaning an opinion of a judicial nature based on reasonable evidence. *Lawlor* v. *UPW*[70] gives some support to this approach for
in that case the subjective clause was interpreted in a not dissimilar way.
There a rule permitting the union to expel a member who in the opinion
of the executive council was not a fit and proper person for membership
was held to mean not a wholly subjective opinion but one arrived at
judicially and objectively. Ungoed Thomas J thought this interpretation
particularly appropriate since there was a right of appeal, and his
Lordship held that the decision would have to be capable of being judged
by some objective standards in order for an appeal to be appropriate.
Obviously this very broad construction of a subjective rule, reinterpreting
it in an objective fashion, is likely to be attractive to the judges. But there
are limits to the extent to which the courts can refashion the contractual
obligations in this way. What if the contract approach fails to enable the
courts to determine the jurisdiction of the tribunal — if the contract on
its true construction reserves jurisdiction to the domestic tribunal —
how can the courts then interfere? The answer must be only through
public policy. Two possible interrelated grounds exist, though neither is
clearly applicable. First, the thrust of Lord Denning's judgment in *Lee* v.
Showmen's Guild of Great Britain would suggest that where a person's livelihood is at stake the courts will not permit the union to have rules permitting it to determine its own jurisdiction, even though a strict
contractual approach might lead to that conclusion. This is suggested by
the fact that his Lordship, unlike the other two judges, did not emphasize
the significance of the rule being in objective rather than subjective
language.

An alternative and superficially more attractive view was advanced by
Romer LJ in the same case.[71] He mentioned the possibility that the

courts might treat subjectively worded rules as in effect ousting the jurisdiction of the courts, at least in part, by taking away the courts' power to construe the rule objectively. However, since it does not prevent the court interfering if there is bad faith or a breach of natural justice, it is not wholly ousting jurisdiction. So why can it not be treated as a rule defining the limits of jurisdiction rather than ousting it, just as it is in the club cases? It might be argued in fact that such a rule can be treated as an ouster of jurisdiction only if it is first assumed that the courts have power to interpret the rule irrespective of whether the constitution purports to give that power to the union tribunal by making the decision a matter for its opinion. But on what basis can that assumption be made? Presumably only because there are reasons of public policy which demand that the union should not be entitled to restrict judicial intervention in this way. So in reality an argument denying the validity of subjective rules on the grounds that they oust the courts' jurisdiction simply conceals the real considerations of public policy which are in fact guiding the courts' responses. There are, however, difficulties with a public policy approach. First, as mentioned above, to refuse to permit domestic tribunals to determine their own jurisdiction only where livelihood is at stake could lead to a number of artificial distinctions. For example, it would mean that members subjected to some sanction short of expulsion for breach of a subjective rule would have no grounds for complaint if they thought that the union had misconstrued the rule since their jobs would not then be in jeopardy; in contrast, a person expelled under the same rule in a closed shop context would be able to have the decision more fully reviewed by the courts, and the expulsion declared invalid, if the judges felt that the rule had been wrongly interpreted. A similar anomaly would arise where one person was expelled in a 'closed' shop and another in an 'open' shop even though the same rule was in issue.

However, apart from these unsatisfactory distinctions, there is a more fundamental problem. If a subjective rule is contrary to public policy, then it must surely be void. It cannot be saved by the court effectively reviewing it in objective terms. Indeed, it cannot be made valid even if the union itself chooses to construe the subjective rule objectively. Only if the rule can be interpreted on its proper construction as permitting the court to establish a jurisdiction will it be valid. Consequently, it is difficult to see how in both the *Manders* and *Esterman* cases, the two cases where subjective powers have been construed objectively, the union was able to rely upon the rule at all, unless it is assumed that the courts in both cases accepted that on its true construction the relevant rule would leave the power of interpretation to the courts. But in neither case did the court specifically state that this was the case. The fundamental problems with these subjectively worded rules is that on contractual grounds the wording of the rule simply cannot be ignored, yet on policy grounds there is much to be said for the view that it is highly artificial to distinguish between objective and subjective rules and that they should be treated alike. To differentiate between them will frequently be to place a premium on what will often in reality have been an accident of draftmanship. Furthermore, in the field of administrative law the House of Lords in *Secretary of State for Education and Science* v. *Tameside MBC*[72] has affirmed that it will not be deterred from reviewing statutory powers merely because they are in subjective form. As Lord Wilberforce commented, 'Sections in this form may, no doubt, exclude judicial review on what is or has become a matter of pure judgment. But I do not think that they go further than that.'[73] It is, however, questionable how far this approach is consistent with the notion of sovereignty of Parliament, just as in the trade union sphere the blurring of subjective and objective powers is difficult to equate with the principle of freedom of contract. Nor is the dilemma happily resolved simply by reviewing subjective powers in objective terms by artificial interpretation, for this involves but the barest recognition that the union-member relationship is contractual.

NATURAL JUSTICE

The principles of natural justice have been developed and refined by the courts to a considerable extent, particularly over the past twenty years. But they remain flexible principles, and it is not always easy to predict how they will be applied in particular contexts. However, it is fair to say that they will be applied vigorously in union disciplinary cases and particularly where expulsions are in issue since legal rights are being directly affected. Natural justice encompasses two principles. First, that a person should have an opportunity to state his or her own case before a decision is made which is adverse to him or her (the *audi alteram partem* principle); and secondly that the decision should be made by an unbiased tribunal (the *nemo judex in re sua* principle).

The Right to a Hearing

The right to a hearing encompasses three different aspects. The union must give the members sufficient notice of the case against them; adequate time to prepare their case; and a proper opportunity to present that case. The notice should specify the particular rules under which the member is being charged, preferably in writing. Consequently in *Annamunthodo* v. *Oilfield Workers' Trade Union*[74] the Privy Council held an expulsion to be invalid because the union had notified the member that he would be tried under a rule which merely permitted a fine, but in the event they disciplined him in his absence under a different rule which empowered his expulsion. Counsel for the union contended that the specific formulation of the charges was immaterial and that the substance of the charge lay in the facts which were alleged. He claimed that provided the member had notice of the nature of the alleged misconduct, the particular rule under which it fell was irrelevant. But their Lordships rejected this argument. The union could have resort to other charges only if it first gave appropriate notice to the member. Furthermore, the union should not assume that the charge is so well-known that there is no need formally to notify the member. This also will invalidate the decision, though it is to be noted that there is authority for the view that exceptionally the duty to give notice may be waived. In *Stevenson* v. *URTU*,[75] the Court of Appeal held that this would apply to cases of so uncomplex a character where the issues are so well-known to all the parties that no notification is necessary.

The notice of the charges must be given in sufficient time to enable the members properly to prepare their defence.[76] What is sufficient will depend upon the particular circumstances of the case; obviously where facts are in dispute and witnesses need to be contacted, a longer period will be required than where these factors are absent. Surprisingly there is still some degree of uncertainty about precisely what natural justice requires in relation to the disciplinary hearing itself. For example, it does not necessarily require an oral hearing in all contexts, though in the case of union disciplinary action it almost certainly does, particularly if someone's reputation or livelihood is at stake.[77] In *Bowers* v. *NGA*,[78] however, it was held that written representations were adequate for the purposes of an appeal. However, in that case there had been a right to make oral representations before the branch committee which had taken the original decision, though it is also true that the plaintiff had been expelled. Again, members probably have the right to call and examine witnesses and to cross-examine those who give evidence against them, particularly if they ask to do so.[79] At the very least, if no opportunity to cross-examine is provided, the tribunal should not admit in evidence statements which are adverse to the member and which he or she has challenged.[80] Furthermore, not only should the members be permitted to make representations relating to the disciplinary charge; they should also be allowed to be heard about the penalty to be imposed, at least where the union has a discretion as to the appropriate sanction. Finally, an important question is whether natural justice includes the right to legal representation.

The right to legal representation as a requirement of natural justice was recognized by Lord Denning in *Pett* v. *Greyhound Racing Association (No. 1).*[81] Since then, however, the matter has been reconsidered by the Court of Appeal and the position now appears to be that the right to legal representation may be expressly excluded by the rules of the disciplining authority, in this context a trade union.[82] Where the right is not excluded, then the disciplinary body will have a discretion whether or not to permit representation.[83] That discretion must be exercised properly, and the more serious the consequences the more likely it is that a court would require the discretion to be exercised in favour of permitting legal representation. An illustration of legal representation being required in union affairs is *Walker* v. *AUEFW*,[84] a case which would almost certainly be decided the same way today despite changes in the underlying principles relating to natural justice and legal representation. Walker, an official of the union, was expelled for submitting a fraudulent expenses claim. He appealed against the expulsion and under the rules of that union the matter was referred to an arbiter for decision. Walker wrote to the arbiter saying that at the appeal he intended to be represented by a solicitor and no objection to this proposal was made by the arbiter. The hearing was opened by a union official presenting the union's case, and when the solicitor came to present Walker's case, the arbiter refused to allow him to speak. The Court of Session held in these circumstances that there had been a breach of natural justice. Regardless of whether in principle there is a right to legal representation, the court held that it was inconsistent with fairness that Walker should, at the last moment, be compelled to present his own case when he had been led to suppose that his lawyer would speak for him and when he must have been presumed to have made no preparation for conducting the case himself.

The Rule Against Bias

The second principle of natural justice requires that there should be a hearing by a body which is free from bias. In natural justice cases, generally the courts have wavered as to the test that should be applied in order to determine whether or not bias exists. Occasionally courts use a 'real likelihood' test, i.e. if there is a real likelihood of bias then the decision should be invalidated.[85] However, sometimes they use the more general 'reasonable suspicion' test: if it may reasonably be suspected that the decision may have been biased, then the decision will be invalid.[86] The former concentrates more upon whether there may in fact have been unfairness; the latter upon whether it may appear that there has been unfairness. And the latter is based upon the idea that justice is rooted in confidence and that it is important that justice should not only be done but should manifestly be seen to be done. But the vigour with which the reasonable suspicion test is applied also varies; sometimes it appears to mean the reasonable suspicion of third parties unaware of any of the details of the case, and sometimes the suspicion of a person aware of all the material facts. This latter formulation comes close to the real likelihood test.

The present approach of the courts is to recognize that the tests are not really in conflict. Sometimes the real likelihood test will be more appropriate, as sometimes will be the reasonable suspicion test. The latter is particularly appropriate where the question of the impartiality of the ordinary courts is in issue. It is, for example, of the utmost importance that magistrates should be seen to be free from bias since their decisions affect the whole community. Trade union disciplinary bodies do not impinge in the same way on the public at large, and it cannot be said that confidence in the system of justice generally will be undermined if there are suspicions about the impartiality of trade union bodies. So there is far less justification for imposing the reasonable suspicion test to such bodies. A vigorous application of such a test would in any event mean that virtually every disciplinary action would be invalidated. Where a member is being judged by fellow members, whether it be of a club, trade union or any other domestic body, it is unrealistic to expect what Bowen LJ referred to as 'the icy impartiality of a Rhadamanthus'.[87]

It is possible to disentangle three different kinds of potential prejudice. First there is what might be termed 'establishment bias', the tendency of the disciplinary committee to support union officers and to defend union policies from attack. This in itself will not, however, invalidate a disciplinary decision. As Templeman J realistically remarked in *Roebuck* v. *NUM (Yorkshire Area) (No. 2)*:[88]

> all members of a domestic tribunal where the interests of their own organisation are at stake, have a general inclination to defend the union and its officers against attack from any source; this fact, every trade unionist and every member of a domestic organisation knows and accepts.[89]

The second form of bias is related to the first and may be termed 'ideological' bias. This is the understandable tendency of a committee to be harsher on disciplined members who oppose the dominant ideology of the committee than they would be to members who share that ideology. This again will not of itself render the decision invalid. In *White* v. *Kuzych*[90] a union member was disciplined for publicly opposing the union's closed shop policy. As Viscount Simon pointed out in the Privy Council, the fact that several members of the disciplinary body had expressed the opinion that the closed shop principle was essential to the policy and purpose of the union did not mean that they were so partial as to be incapable of meeting a valid determination.

The third form of bias which is likely to arise is personal bias. This will generally invalidate the decision, though even here the fact that members of the disciplinary body have commented adversely on the particular member on trial will not necessarily render the decision void, as the following advice of the Privy Council in *White* v. *Kuzych* shows:

> What those who considered the charges against the respondent and decided whether he was guilty ought to bring to their task was a will to reach an honest conclusion after hearing what was urged on either side, and a resolve not to make up their minds beforehand on his personal guilt, however firmly they held their conviction as to union policy and however strongly they had shared in previous adverse criticism of the respondent's conduct.[91]

As these cases demonstrate, the courts permit considerable leeway to union disciplinary tribunals when determining whether they are impartial.[92] Although actual bias need not be established, there must clearly be strong grounds for successfully challenging the impartiality of the committee. A successful challenge was mounted in *Roebuck's* case where Arthur Scargill, then leader of the Yorkshire miners, initiated a complaint against two members of the union, sat as chairman of the committee which resolved to charge the members, and then also sat as chairman on the relevant disciplinary and appellate committees. The alleged misconduct consisted of giving evidence in a court of law for a newspaper successfully sued for libel by Mr Scargill. Clearly Mr Scargill did not merely hold strong views about the issue itself; he had been deeply involved as the person who suffered most from the alleged misconduct. As Templeman J pointed out, Mr Scargill acted as 'the complainant, the pleader, the prosecutor, the advocate and the chairman in the union proceedings' with the result that the 'appearance of bias was inevitable; the exercise of bias, conscious or unconscious, was probable'.[93]

The Exclusion of Natural Justice

Are there circumstances where membership of the union can be terminated without the union being obliged to have recourse to the principles of natural justice? The answer depends upon whether the principles of natural justice operate as contractual terms in the contract of membership, or as overriding obligations imposed by public policy. If the obligation is contractual, then of course it can always be excluded by sufficiently clear express terms, but if it stems from public policy, any such exclusion will be ineffective. There are dicta in English law supporting both positions. The roots of the contractual approach can be traced to Maugham J in *MacLean* v. *The Workers' Union*:[94]

> it seems to me reasonably clear that the matter [of whether natural justice is applicable] can only depend on contract express or implied. If, for instance, there was a clearly expressed rule stating that a member might be expelled by a defined body without calling upon the member in question to explain his conduct, I see no reason for supposing that the Courts would interfere with such a rule on the ground of public policy.[95]

This contractual basis of natural justice was also emphasized by the Court of Appeal in *Russell* v. *Duke of Norfolk*,[96] and it has been accepted in subsequent cases, but only because each time the courts were able to justify the application of natural justice on contractual principles alone, and by so doing they were able to evade the more contentious issue of public policy. Indeed, the readiness of the courts to find natural justice applicable, at least since *Russell's* case, demonstrates that even on a contractual view the courts will now virtually automatically imply the principles unless the rule clearly precludes this construction.

Despite the influence of *MacLean's* case, there is another line of authority, pre-dating that decision, which bases the obligation to comply with natural justice firmly on public policy as something independent of contract.[97] There is little doubt that this is the approach which will now be followed by the courts.[98] It has been emphasized by Lord Denning in particular, stating in numerous cases that any attempt to exclude natural justice will be void,[99] and he has received support for this proposition from Plowman J in *Radford* v. *NATSOPA*[100] and Bingham J in *Cheall* v. *APEX*.[101] Moreover, this approach does not merely render invalid a rule specifically excluding natural justice — which will be extremely rare — but also any substantive rules which on their true construction would preclude its application. This means that it embraces automatic forfeiture rules, that is rules which automatically render a member ineligible for membership on the occurrence of a particular event. For example, a rule which stipulated that disobedience to union rules and policies automatically disqualified a member from remaining in the union would fall into this category. If it were a lawful rule, then on the basis of *Faramus* v. *Film Artistes' Association*[102] it could logically be claimed that since it would be *ultra vires* to retain the member in the union, and the breach could not be waived, there would be no room for natural justice at all. However, once it is accepted that natural justice rests on public policy, any such rule is automatically rendered invalid. Moreover, the fact that the rule may actually have been applied in accordance with natural justice will be irrelevant. As Plowman J pointed out in *Radford's* case, once the rule is void it cannot be relied upon irrespective of how fairly it is actually implemented.

In the same case, however, Plowman J indicated that in cases of ambiguity the courts will endeavour to construe the rule so as to be valid rather than void, favouring an interpretation which will imply that there should be a hearing rather than the contrary. So in the particular case, a rule which stated that

> An action taken against the [union] by individual members, or members acting collectively . . . shall be declared a wilful breach of rules, and shall void the membership of the member or members so acting.

was held, on its proper construction, not to exclude natural justice and therefore to be a valid rule. The reason why the rule could be construed as lawful was that some action had to be taken by the appropriate committee, namely to declare the conduct in breach of the rules. Plowman J thought that in view of this one could read the rule consistently with an obligation to comply with natural justice. Had the rule stated that certain conduct 'is hereby declared' a breach of the rules, then there would have been no discretion left to any union committee and, as his Lordship indicated, the rule would almost certainly have been invalid. This suggests then that a rule will be treated as ousting natural justice only if it operates so as to impose a sanction automatically without any action being taken by the relevant union committee. Once any discretion at all is left with the committee, even if it is limited to merely declaring that the rule has been infringed, then the courts will assume that the duty to exercise the discretion fairly will mean that the need to comply with natural justice is consistent with the rule.

A Valid Appeal

It is thus clear that in principle natural justice cannot be excluded by the rules of the union. Nor is it necessarily desirable that it should be. It does not follow, however, that the courts need require compliance in all circumstances. One issue which arises is whether a good appeal can cure an earlier decision which did not comply with procedural standards of fairness. The matter was considered in *Leary* v. *National Union of Vehicle Builders*[103] where Megarry J answered in the negative, holding that 'if there is a defect of natural justice, the proper course is for the body to which the jurisdiction is confided to rehear the matter de novo, rather than . . . let the matter be consigned to some appellate tribunal or other body'.[104] He continued by saying:

> That is not all. If one accepts the contention that a defect of natural justice in the trial body can be cured by the presence of natural justice in the appellate body, this has the result of depriving the member of his right of appeal from the expelling body. If the rules and the law combine to give the member the right to a fair trial and the right of appeal, why should he be told that he ought to be satisfied with an unjust trial and a fair appeal? Even if the appeal is treated as a hearing de novo, the member is being stripped of his right to appeal to another body from the effective decision to expel him. I cannot think that natural justice is satisfied by a process whereby an unfair trial, although not resulting in a valid expulsion, will nevertheless have the effect of depriving the member of his right of appeal when a valid decision to expel him is subsequently made. Such a deprivation would be a powerful result to be achieved by what in law is a mere nullity; and it is no mere triviality that might be justified on the ground that natural justice does not mean perfect justice. As a general rule, at all events, I hold that a failure of natural justice in the trial body cannot be cured by a sufficiency of natural justice in an appellate body.[105]

The matter has since been considered by the Privy Council which at least in part has qualified the approach adopted by Megarry J. In *Calvin* v. *Carr*,[106] the appellant was the part owner of a horse which had done less well than expected in a race in Australia. A stewards' inquiry found that the horse had been held back, and the appellant was disqualified from horse-racing and forfeited his membership of the Jockey Club. On appeal to a committee of the Jockey Club, the stewards' decision was upheld and the appellant claimed that he had been unlawfully penalized in the sense that there had been a breach of natural justice at the stewards' inquiry. The Privy Council rejected this argument and held for the Jockey Club on the ground that the appeal had cured the earlier defect, a decision which appears to fly in the face of *Leary* and the views expressed there by Megarry J.

Their Lordships held that there were cases, including the one before them, where defects could be cured on appeal. But the circumstances in which the appeal might have this potential effect were left vague. It was suggested that there are three different categories of cases. First, those where the rules provide for a rehearing by the initial body, or some enlarged form of it. Here it is possible to treat the first hearing as having been superseded by the second. Secondly, there are cases where, on examination of the whole hearing structure in the context of the particular activity to which it relates, there is a right to a fair hearing at both the initial and appellate stages. Finally, there is an intermediate situation where the court must decide whether, looking at the matter in the light of the agreements made and the course of proceedings, 'there has been a fair result, reached by fair methods, such as the parties should fairly be taken to have accepted when they joined the association'.[107] The present case fell into the last category: it related to the proceedings of a domestic body which overall had treated the appellant fairly. It was also said, however, that trade unions would fall into the second category — thereby endorsing *Leary*. However, it is not clear that convincing reasons were offered to justify this treatment of trade unions. It was said that 'movement solidarity and dislike of the rebel, or renegade, may make it difficult for appeals to be conducted in an atmosphere of detached impartiality and so make a fair trial at the first — probably branch — level an essential condition of justice'.[108] This may well be true, but in virtually all organizations there will be a tendency to confirm the original decision and support the committee's judgment. It is not clear why unions should be treated differently on this account, and perhaps it should not be assumed too readily that an initial defect in the trade union context can never be remedied on appeal. It is possible, for example, that where there is an appeal from a branch committee to a branch, a court would be prepared to place this in the first of the Privy Council's categories, particularly if there was no closed shop operating. But clearly the decision in *Calvin* v. *Carr*[109] provides little comfort to the unions, and in most circumstances Megarry J's approach in *Leary's* case is likely to be preferred.

Expulsion for Arrears

Although it thus appears that natural justice must be followed at all stages in the procedure, must it apply at all in the case of all expulsions? One area where the application of natural justice may be open to question is where the union seeks to expel automatically for non-payment of dues. The policy considerations which justify the courts in striking out other automatic forfeiture clauses are not as weighty here. This kind of forfeiture rule provides a valuable aid to organizational efficiency. In some unions the turnover of membership is extremely high, and it would prove administratively impossible to give all lapsing members a right to make representations before terminating their membership. At the same time it is inconvenient to retain such members on the books. No doubt the vast majority of lapsing members would not wish to make representations even if given the opportunity, since they are intending to leave the union. Consequently in practice compliance is unlikely to prove time-consuming. Nevertheless, as the TUC has commented, even giving written notice to each person in arrears to notify them of their possible exclusion would be expensive and extremely onerous administratively.[110]

There is therefore much to be said for the view that automatic forfeiture rules should be permitted where they relate to non-payment of union dues, even though they exclude natural justice. Indeed, the Industrial Relations Act 1971, which imposed natural justice as a statutory requirement in a whole range of contexts, expressly excluded it from such cases. However, it seems unlikely that a rule excluding natural justice even in this context will be considered lawful at common law. It is true that in *Fish* v. *NUGMW*[111] such a rule was held valid. The plaintiff appealed against the termination of his membership under a rule which provided that 'should any member, when in work, owe six months' contributions and not clear the books, his name shall be struck off'. He argued that the exclusion was unlawful as he had no opportunity to attend and explain the circumstances of his case. Romer J dismissed the action, observing that 'the rule did not confer a power of any kind, judicial or quasi-judicial, on anyone. It operated automatically when the event arose.'[112] But this approach was consistent with the contractual approach to natural justice then prevalent. Like the *MacLean* decision, the case was decided between the wars when the non-interventionist tendency of the judges was strong. More recently in *Edwards* v. *SOGAT*,[113] the Court of Appeal adopted a different view of rules of this nature. The plaintiff was excluded under a rule which stipulated that 'temporary membership shall terminate automatically if the member becomes over six weeks in arrears'. Lord Denning thought that the rule was invalid both because it infringed the right to work and because 'No union can stipulate for a power to expel a man unheard'.[114]

Like so many of Lord Denning's forays into the field of internal union affairs, this view is probably too widely stated. Lord Diplock's speech in *Cheall* v. *APEX*[115] suggests that there is no need for a hearing where it would make no difference to the outcome and where it would be 'a cruel deception'. However, this will not necessarily be true of all cases of automatic expulsion for non-payment of dues. First there may be a dispute of fact, and the member may thus wish to dispute that the rule has been broken.[116] Secondly, there may be a breach, but the member may wish to argue that it was caused by the fault of the union — as in *Edwards* v. *SOGAT* itself where the member fell into arrears because the union failed to operate a check-off agreement properly. In these circumstances the member might wish to argue that the rule should not apply where the breach is brought about by negligence or fault on the part of the union. Not only would such an argument be consistent with general contractual principles, it is supported by other authority, admittedly poorly reported. In the Scottish case *Connell* v. *NUDAW*[117] the union had deliberately caused the member to fall within a rule which provided for automatic forfeiture for non-payment of dues in order to comply with an award under a Bridlington type agreement. The Court of Session granted a declarator that the purported termination was unlawful. A third situation where members might deem that a hearing would make a difference is where they allege that they have been discriminated against in the operation of the rule. Here the case for a hearing may also be compelling. Although it may be *ultra vires* for the union to retain a person in membership once the rule is infringed, on the other hand there will now be a right to be heard before termination if because of established practice the members have a 'legitimate expectation' that they will not be expelled in such circumstances.[118] If, moreover, natural justice (or fairness as it is now called) is seen to embrace substantive as well as procedural safeguards, it may be possible for the aggrieved member to argue that in such cases the requirements of the rule book are to be qualified by considerations of fairness imposed by the general law.

The Bridlington Agreement

The other major area where the rules of natural justice might potentially have a limited impact is expulsion to comply with the Bridlington Agreement. This is an agreement, not intended to be legally enforceable, entered into by unions affiliated to the TUC. Its purpose is to prevent potentially divisive inter-union competition over members, and the 'poaching' of one union's members by another union.[119] The Agreement lays down a number of principles.[120] Principle 2 provides that 'No one who is or has recently been a member of any affiliated union should be accepted into membership in another without enquiry of his present or former union'. If after enquiries the 'transferring' union does not agree to the transfer, the 'transferee' must not accept the applicant into membership. The *status quo* must be maintained until the dispute is resolved, if necessary by the TUC. Principle 4 provides that the transferee must not accept an applicant where enquiries show that he or she is 'under discipline', 'engaged in a trade dispute', or 'in arrears with contributions'. Finally, Principle 5 provides that 'No union shall commence organising activities at any establishment or undertaking in respect of any grade or grades of workers in which another union has the majority of workers employed and negotiates wages and conditions, unless by arrangement with that union'. In the event of a dispute between affiliated unions about the operation of these principles, the matter will be referred to the TUC. If the parties are unable to reach a friendly settlement, the matter may be referred to the TUC Disputes Committee for adjudication. The Committee will usually consist of three senior union officials.

As we saw in Chapter 2, unions ran into trouble when they sought to expel members who had been recruited in breach of the Bridlington Agreement. In *Spring* v. *NASDS*[121] it was held that the defendant union had no implied power to expel a member to give effect to an award of the Disputes Committee. After this decision, the TUC introduced a model rule which it encouraged affiliated organizations to adopt. This gives express power to expel by providing that the union in question may 'by giving six weeks' notice in writing, terminate the membership of any member if necessary in order to comply with a decision of the Disputes Committee of the Trades Union Congress'. The leading case on the operation of the rule is now *Cheall* v. *APEX*[122] where the respondent resigned from ACTSS and applied to join APEX. Although APEX officers knew of Cheall's membership of ACTSS, they nevertheless accepted his application. Thereupon ACTSS alleged that the acceptance was a breach of the Bridlington Agreement, a claim which was ultimately accepted by the Disputes Committee, following which APEX was instructed to terminate Cheall's membership. APEX eventually complied with this instruction, for failure to do so would expose them to the risk of suspension and perhaps even expulsion from the TUC. The question before the House of Lords was whether this expulsion — which was made under the model rule — was unlawful, with one of several lines of attack being that it was in breach of natural justice. And this for two reasons: first because Cheall had not been permitted to attend before the Disputes Committee, and secondly because he had not been given a hearing before the executive committee of APEX before they took their action.

Both of these claims were rejected. So far as the first is concerned, it was held that 'the only parties to the dispute that was before the disputes committee were the trade unions concerned. They, and they only, were entitled to make representations written or oral to the committee'.[123] Lord Diplock continued by pointing out that 'Decisions that resolve disputes between the parties to them, whether by litigation or some other adversarial dispute-resolving process, often have consequences which affect persons who are not parties to the dispute; but the legal concept of natural justice has never been extended to give such persons as well as the parties themselves rights to be heard by the decision-making tribunal before the decision is reached'.[124] So far as the second point is concerned, Lord Diplock held that 'there was no legal obligation on APEX to give Cheall prior notice of their decision or grant him an opportunity to be heard'.[125] And adopting the words of Bingham J at first instance, Lord Diplock continued by saying that 'To have done so where nothing he said could affect the outcome would in my view have been a cruel deception'.[126] This thus provides a rather convincing and unequivocal statement that natural justice is not required to give effect to a disputes committee award. It does not follow, however, that all Bridlington expulsions can take place without natural justice being observed. There may be cases, for example, where two unions will settle their differences in accordance with the principles, without the need for a formal hearing of the Disputes Committee. The courts, it seems, will not accept in such cases an implied right to expel members in the interest of inter-union harmony.[127] In such cases, however, a breach of natural justice is not likely to be the major ground for challenging the decision. It is more likely to be challenged on the basis that there is no authority in the rule for an expulsion on this ground.

Natural Justice and Substantive Fairness

In administrative law, the application of the principles of natural justice has expanded greatly since the landmark decision in *Ridge* v. *Baldwin*.[128] One of the issues which has arisen is whether natural justice or fairness embraces substantive standards as well as procedural obligations. In other words, is there a duty not only to conduct a fair hearing, but also to take a decision which is in substance fair? If so, the duty to act fairly would be an important method of regulating the discriminatory application of discretionary powers, including decisions to discipline, decisions to activate automatic expulsion rules, and decisions to impose disproportionate penalties. The duty to act fairly would thus become a way of ensuring that union disciplinary committees acted consistently. This issue is, however, relatively underdeveloped. One reason for this perhaps is that administrative lawyers do not need to rely upon the duty to act fairly to impose standards of this kind. There is, for example, authority for the view that it may be a breach of the *Wednesbury*[129] principles for a public body to reach a decision which is unreasonable because, say, it is inconsistent.[130]

However, this is not to say that the matter has not been considered authoritatively at all. A judgment of immense significance is that delivered by Lord Denning in *Breen* v. *AEU*.[131] In that case, Lord Denning said that the principles of administrative law applying to statutory bodies apply also to domestic bodies. They do so on the basis that it is an implied term of the contract of membership that discretionary powers should be exercised fairly.[132] But by requiring fairness, Lord Denning appeared to import not only standards of procedural justice, but also the *Wednesbury* principles. That is to say the exercise of discretionary powers must not be unreasonable: the tribunal 'must be guided by relevant considerations and not by irrelevant. If its decision is influenced by extraneous considerations which it ought not to have taken into account, then the decision cannot stand.'[133] This is clearly of great significance — giving the courts the power admittedly not to challenge the reasonableness of a rule, but nevertheless the reasonableness of discretionary decisions made under the rules. It is to be noted that these principles have since been applied in a trade union context; and, further, that there is independent administrative law authority for the view that the duty to act fairly is strong enough to bear substantive burdens. In *HTV Ltd.* v. *Price Commission*,[134] Lord Denning said that the Price Commission were under a duty to act with fairness and consistency, and that if they regularly applied the words of a statutory code in a particular way, they should continue to do so unless there is good reason for departing from the practice.[135] He continued by saying 'It is not permissible for them to depart from their previous interpretation and application where it would not be fair or just to do so'.[136] The relevance for trade union disciplinary powers is clear and the dictum is made all the more relevant by the acceptance by Scarman LJ that a public body can act inconsistently and thus unfairly.[137]

The significance of the *HTV Ltd.* case is that it suggests an alternative method of importing substantive fairness into the exercise of union disciplinary powers. *Breen* suggests that it may be implied as a term of the contract. Insofar as *HTV Ltd.* suggests that it is part and parcel of the duty to act fairly as natural justice, then it operates as a requirement of public policy independently of contract. In practice, however, there is not likely to be any practical differences in the result secured, though theoretically the latter approach would restrict any ingenious contractual terms devised by unions to defeat *Breen*. The same considerations apply to the doctrine of proportionality which is beginning to appear in English administrative law. In *R.* v. *Barnsley MBC, ex parte Hook*,[138] the plaintiff had his licence to trade in the Barnsley Market rejected following an altercation he had had with a security officer who had upbraided him for urinating in the street. He successfully obtained an order of certiorari to quash the decision of the licensing committee on the ground that the principles of natural justice had not been observed. But, in addition, both Lord Denning and Sir John Pennycuick expressly relied upon what may be termed the proportionality principle which requires that the sanction inflicted should be related to the offence committed. Lord Denning explained the principle as follows:

> Now, there are old cases which show that a court can interfere . . . if a punishment is altogether excessive and out of proportion to the occasion . . . So in this case if Mr Hook did misbehave, I should have thought that the right thing would have been to take him before the justices under the byelaws, when some small fine might have been inflicted. It is quite wrong that the corporation should inflict on him the grave penalty of depriving him of his livelihood . . . On that ground alone . . . the decision of the corporation cannot stand.[139]

There seems no reason why this principle should not be applied to trade unions. If, however, it is imported through the contract, it could presumably be waived by an express term suitably drafted. However, if it is imported as a separate doctrine of public policy, such a maneouvre by the unions would not be effective.

STATUTORY REGULATION

A much more direct form of regulation and control than is provided by either the rule book or by natural justice are the statutory standards which override union autonomy. But as with admission, Parliament has traditionally played only a residual role in this area. The Trade Union Act 1913 required unions to have rules providing that members exempt from the obligation to contribute to the political fund were not to be placed at any disability or disadvantage by reason of their exemption (except in relation to the control and management of the political fund). Although this would operate to make it unlawful for a union to discipline or expel a contracted-out member, there are no reported cases where this has happened. Similarly, the Sex Discrimination Act 1975 and the Race Relations Act 1976 make it unlawful for a trade union to discriminate against members, by subjecting them to any detriment, or by depriving them of membership on the grounds of sex or race. Presumably the deprivation of membership in this context is intended to deal with an expulsion. But again there are no reported cases recently where a trade union has expelled a member on either of these grounds. Furthermore, it would be unlawful under European law to expel members simply on the ground that they are nationals of EEC member states, though discrimination on that ground would, as was pointed out in Chapter 3, be unlawful under the Race Relations Act in any event.

So far as more general restrictions on discipline and expulsion are concerned, these were recommended by the Donovan Commission in 1968, which proposed that 'any member of a trade union who considers that he has had some penalty unfairly inflicted upon him which amounts to a substantial injustice should have a right of complaint, in the last resort, to an independent review body'.[140] Such a right was in fact introduced by the Industrial Relations Act 1971 which provided by section 65(7) that union members were not to be subjected to any unfair or unreasonable disciplinary action. The Act also provided specifically that members were not to be disciplined for taking part in unlawful industrial action. TULRA also sought to regulate trade union discipline but was much narrower in its terms, providing that every member had the right not to be expelled from membership of a trade union 'by way of arbitrary or unreasonable discrimination'.[141] So not all disciplinary action was covered; not all unreasonable expulsions were covered (only those which involved unreasonable discrimination); and no attempt was made specifically to deal with the use of disciplinary rules during industrial disputes. However, this section was repealed in its entirety in 1976,[142] though statutory regulation of union expulsions reappeared with the introduction of sections 4 and 5 of the Employment Act 1980.

We have already discussed section 4 so far as it relates to exclusion from admission. The Act applies to expulsion in both pre-entry and post-entry closed shops, and the term trade union is widely defined to include a branch or section of a trade union. This means that the admission cases, such as *Kirkham, Howard* and *Goodfellow*, are also important in this context too. The provisions on expulsions are in fact identical. It is important to note that the section applies only to expulsions, and not other forms of discipline, but that the accompanying Code of Practice applies to all forms of discipline. So far as the statute is concerned, it is unlawful for a union unreasonably to expel a member in a closed shop situation.[143] Reasonableness is again to be determined in accordance with equity and the substantial merits of the case; and a union may act unreasonably even though it has acted in accordance with its rules, or reasonably where it has not.[144] Otherwise reasonableness is not defined, though some guidance on both procedural and substantive considerations is given in the Code of Practice. On procedural matters, paragraph 57 of the Code provides that in handling membership discipline, unions should adopt and apply clear and fair rules covering

   (a) The offences for which the union is entitled to take disciplinary action and the penalties applicable for each of these offences.

   (b) The procedure for hearing and determining complaints in which offences against the rules are alleged.

   (c) A right of appeal against the imposition of any penalty.

   (d) The procedure for the hearing of appeals against any penalty by a higher authority comprised of persons other than those who imposed the penalty.

   (e) Maintaining the *status quo* so long as a member is genuinely pursuing an appeal.

A breach of any of these procedural obligations could render an expulsion unreasonable even though it is in accordance with the rules of the union, and even though the union has cause for its conduct. However, these are not mandatory or inflexible requirements and some of them could no doubt be waived in cases of serious offences against discipline. As already pointed out in Chapter 3, the Code (paragraph 58) further provides that the procedures on expulsion should comply with the rules of natural justice. On the question of the grounds for expulsion, the Code addresses this too, though this is limited to the discipline of members who fail to participate in a strike. We deal with this question in Chapter 7. There has in fact been only one reported case relating to unreasonable expulsion under section 4. This is *McGhee* v. *TGWU*[145] where the appellant had been required by the terms of a union membership agreement to be a member of the respondent union. As time went on, McGhee became dissatisfied with the union's treatment and representation of him, and eventually he wrote to the general secretary alleging bias, favouritism and unfairness against local officers of the union. He was then fined by the branch committee for the tone of his complaint to the general secretary, which he refused to pay. Thereupon he received a letter from the union to the effect that the fine had been held against his union contributions and that he was now in arrears. Mr McGhee responded by resigning his membership of the union, as a result of which he was dismissed in accordance with the union membership agreement. He claimed, despite having resigned, that in fact he had been expelled. The very important question which arose in the case then was whether someone who had resigned from a trade union could claim to have been expelled.

The industrial tribunal answered in the negative, noting that there is no provision in the 1980 Act to provide for a constructive expulsion, whereas EPCA 1978 does specifically provide for a constructive dismissal. In these circumstances it was held that constructive expulsion was not something known to law and that, having resigned from the union, McGhee had no remedy against it. This view was supported by the EAT. The Appeal Tribunal noted that:

> When Parliament came to enact by the Act of 1980 the right (expressing it broadly) not to be unfairly or unreasonably excluded from membership of a union operating a closed shop, certain features already familiar under the 1978 Act and its predecessors were reproduced. Equity and the substantial merits are again stated as the criteria by which reasonableness has to be judged (s. 4(5)). The time limit is similarly defined by s. 4(6) (*sic*) and is subject to the same saving based on reasonable practicability . . . The basis of compensation for breach of the right is fixed by s. 5(4) (with certain variations) on lines very similar to the 1978 Act, and there is an almost identical provision for the reduction of compensation in the event of conduct by the union member causing or contribuing to any action of the union.[146]

The EAT noted, however, that despite the parallel, there is one feature of the 1978 Act which is not matched by any provision in the 1980 Act.[147] There is no attempt to provide any concept of constructive expulsion similar to the concept of constructive dismissal in section 55 of the 1978 Act. This led the Appeal Tribunal to conclude:

> The suggested implication into the 1980 Act of a concept of 'constructive expulsion' is, in our view, justified neither by the language of Parliament nor by the scheme of the legislation. If, in short, Parliament had intended to confer on closed shop union members who voluntarily surrender their membership a statutory right of complaint that resignation had been forced upon them by the conduct of the union or its officers, Parliament would have so provided in clear, express and appropriately specific language. It has not done so.[148]

It remains to be seen how the concept of unreasonable expulsion is developed by the tribunals and the courts. As one of the present authors has already pointed out:

> The crucial question is what the tribunals will consider to be unreasonable conduct. This is likely to be particularly controversial where the refusal to admit, or the expulsion, stems from the alleged misconduct or hostile attitudes of the applicant. Both union rules and discretions are brought under scrutiny, and difficult issues can arise. For example, is it reasonable to expel a member because he

votes for the National Front? Or because he publicly criticises union officials? In answering questions like these, preconceptions about the union's legitimate functions are likely to obtrude. For example, ought unions to seek to regulate political affiliation? Ought unions to be sufficiently democratic to permit outspoken criticism? However, the search for guidance as to how the tribunals will interpret reasonableness is not entirely fruitless. As with unfair dismissal cases, a whole range of factors are likely to be relevant such as the way in which similar cases have been treated in the past; the length of service in the union; whether the alleged misconduct justifies expulsion rather than some other, less onerous sanction; whether a proper investigation has been carried out; and — as a factor, but not a crucial one — whether union rules have been complied with. The tribunal should not substitute its own view for that of the unions but should ask whether a reasonable union could have reached the decision it did. So in theory rules and discretions should not be too closely regulated.[149]

In addition to the issues raised in the above passage, there is also the question of the Model Rule to comply with the Bridlington principles. It remains to be seen after *Cheall*[150] whether the rule will survive challenge on this ground, or whether it may need modification in any way. It is to be noted that in the Court of Appeal, Lord Denning struck down the rule on the grounds of unreasonableness.[151] This was overruled by the House of Lords, however. Although it is true that section 4 gives the courts a more direct basis for intervention, the reasoning of the Lords in the action under the rules would apply with equal force to one brought under the statutory jurisdiction.

But, however the courts decide to construe reasonableness in this context, a defendant union may not nevertheless be required to reinstate an expelled member, just as we have seen that it may not be required to admit an excluded member. Again, the union may 'buy off' an expelled member. The remedies and the procedures are the same as those which apply in exclusion cases, the details of which are considered in Chapter 3. An interesting procedural question which arises here, in view of the discussion earlier in this chapter, is whether a union could require members to exhaust internal disciplinary procedures before pursuing a claim. It is to be noted that in some cases the tribunals have required exhaustion as against employers. Between 1974 and 1980 a dismissal would be fair if it was because the employee in question was not a member of a trade union in circumstances where a closed shop operated.[152] Sometimes, however, union membership agreements would allow for non-members to appeal against an expulsion or dismissal, the industrial tribunals and the EAT taking the view that the dismissal would not be fair until these procedures had been exhausted.[153] It seems, however, that a similar duty will not be imported into the jurisdiction now under consideration. It is true that the time limit for bringing complaints under the 1980 Act is not the usual three months, but six months — in order to give voluntary procedures an opportunity to resolve the matter. It is true also that paragraph 60 of the Code of Practice on Closed Shop Agreements and Arrangements states that 'In general voluntary procedures are to be preferred to legal action and all parties should be prepared to use them'. Nevertheless, it appears that the tribunals have little discretion to require exhaustion, for despite the extended time limit and the sentiments expressed in the Code, the statute positively prohibits the ITs from imposing such an obligation, regardless of the fairness of the procedures. Thus, section 4(11) provides:

> Any provision in an agreement shall be void in so far as it purports to exclude or limit the operation of, or to preclude any person from presenting a complaint or making an application under [this section] . . .

We have already seen that the authors of the Code are not unqualified in their support for voluntary procedures. Together, the statute and the Code virtually prevent tribunals from requiring exhaustion as a matter of industrial relations policy. The only circumstances in which exhaustion might indirectly be provided is if tribunals accept that by failing to exhaust, the member has not taken every opportunity to mitigate his or her loss. This argument has been accepted in unfair dismissal cases where there is a similar statutory provision rendering void any agreement which seeks to exclude or limit the employee's right to claim for unfair dismissal.[154]

NOTES

1. *Industrial Relations Review and Report*, No. 272, May 1982, pp. 2–7.

2. Information is also drawn from a survey of union strike rules, published in *Industrial Relations Review and Report*, No. 279, September 1982, pp. 2–9.

3. See e.g. Summers, 'The Law of Union Discipline: What the Courts Do in Fact' (1960) 70 Yale LJ 175 at p. 207; and Grodin, *Union Government and the Law* (1961), ch. 4.

4. (1856) 5 HLC 811. See too *Czarnikow* v. *Roth, Schmidt & Co.* [1922] 2 KB 478.

5. [1952] 2 QB 329. See also *Baker* v. *Jones* [1954] 2 All ER 553.

6. *Ibid.*, at p. 342.

7. *De Smith's Judicial Review of Administrative Action* (4th edn, by J. M. Evans, 1980), p. 129.

8. See Wade, *Administrative Law* (5th edn, 1982), pp. 598–609.

9. [1951] AC 585.

10. *Ibid.*, at p. 600.

232 Trade Union Democracy, Members' Rights and the Law

11. [1968] Ch. 440.

12. [1980] AC 574.

13. *Ibid.*, at p. 590.

14. [1951] AC 585.

15. See *Annamunthodo* v. *Oilfield Workers' Trade Union* [1961] AC 945, and the decision of Ungoed Thomas J in *Lawlor* v. *UPW* [1965] Ch. 712, esp. at pp. 733-4. Both these cases narrowed the ratio of *White* v. *Kuzych* to where an express requirement was present. In *Lawlor's* case emphasis was put on the Court of Appeal decision in *Bonsor* v. *Musicians' Union* [1954] Ch. 479, where the court exercised jurisdiction even though a domestic appellate machinery was available. However, counsel for the defendants had not in fact strongly urged the argument that procedures should be exhausted in that case.

16. [1970] Ch. 326.

17. *Ibid.*, at p. 334.

18. [1972] ICR 484.

19. *Ibid.*, at p. 499.

20. [1965] Ch. 712.

21. Royal Commission on Trade Unions and Employers' Associations 1965-1968. *Report.* Cmnd. 3623, para. 663.

22. See note 1 above.

23. [1965] Ch. 712 at pp. 732-5.

24. [1981] IRLR 537.

25. *Hiles* v. *Amalgamated Society of Woodworkers* [1968] Ch. 440 at pp. 453-4.

26. (1976) 120 Sol. Jo. 780.

27. [1974] ICR 625.

28. [1980] IRLR 404.

29. The case is unreported at first instance.

30. [1975] AC 396.

31. Cf. *Cayne* v. *Global Natural Resources plc* [1984] 1 All ER 225 where it was held that the court must have regard to the merits of the dispute in deciding whether or not to grant an interlocutory injunction in cases where in practice the injunction would finally dispose of the matter.

32. [1976] ICR 473.

33. *Ibid.*, p. 494.

34. *Op. cit.*

35. At p. 407.

36. (1915) 31 TLR 632.

37. [1912] 2 Ch. 371.

38. *Burn* v. *National Amalgamated Labourers' Union* [1920] 2 Ch. 364.

39. *Bonsor* v. *Musicians' Union* [1954] Ch. 479 (CA); [1956] AC 104 (HL). For earlier examples of actions being rendered invalid on this account, see *Keely* v. *ETU*, *The Times*, October 17, 1919; *Walton* v. *Yorkshire Miners' Association*, *The Times*, March 8, 1921; *Wellard* v. *National Union of Printers, Bookbinding, and Paper Workers*, *The Times*, May 27, 1938.

40. See *Bonsor* v. *Musicians' Union* [1954] Ch. 479 at p. 486. It may be that in very exceptional circumstances the disciplinary power could be delegated: see *In re S* (a barrister) [1970] 1 QB 160.

41. See Citrine, pp. 267-9, and the cases there cited; *Payne* v. *ETU*, *The Times*, April 14, 1960; *Young* v. *Imperial Ladies' Club* [1920] 2 KB 523, approved by Megarry J in *Leary* v. *National Union of Vehicle Builders* [1971] 1 Ch. 34 at p. 53.

42. See *De Smith's Judicial Review of Administrative Action*, *op. cit.*, pp. 298-309.

43. [1953] 2 QB 18.

44. [1973] ICR 60.

45. (1966) 1 KIR 678.

46. *Ibid.*, at p. 698.

47. [1975] ICR 116.

48. [1929] 1 Ch. 602.

49. Unreported, but see the report of the CA at (1915) 31 TLR 632.

50. [1938] 4 All ER 51.

51. [1920] 2 Ch. 388.

52. [1952] 2 QB 329.

53. *Ibid.*, at p. 345.

54. [1952] 2 QB 329.

55. Notably *Mander* v. *Showmen's Guild of Great Britain, The Times*, November 4, 1966; *Silvester* v. *National Union of Printers, Bookbinding and Paper Workers, op. cit., Santer* v. *NGA, op. cit., Esterman* v. *NALGO, op. cit., MacLelland* v. *NUJ, op. cit.*, and *Porter* v. *NUJ, op. cit.*

56. *Evans* v. *National Union of Printing, Bookbinding and Paper Workers, op. cit.*, and *Wolstenholme* v. *Amalgamated Musicians' Union, op. cit.*

57. [1972] ICR 484.

58. (1966) 1 KIR 678.

59. [1974] ICR 625.

60. *Ibid.*, at p. 634.

61. Summers, *op. cit.* (footnote 3) at p. 180.

62. *Labouchère* v. *Earl of Wharncliffe* (1879) 13 Ch. D. 346, and *Dawkins* v. *Antrobus* (1879) 17 Ch. D. 615. These and other cases are discussed in *Lee* v. *Showmen's Guild of Great Britain*, [1952] 2 QB 329.

63. See *Leeson* v.*General Council of Medical Education and Registration* (1889) 43 Ch. D. 366 and *Allinson* v. *General Council of Medical Education and Registration* [1894] 1 QB 750; see also *Lee* v. *Showmen's Guild of Great Britain* [1952] 2 QB 329 at pp. 339–40 (Somervell LJ).

64. [1952] 2 QB 329 at p. 343.

65. *Ibid.*, at pp. 339–40 and 350–1.

66. *Ibid.*, at pp. 339, 341 and 350.

67. *The Times*, March 8, 1921.

68. *The Times*, November 4, 1966.

69. [1974] ICR 625.

70. [1965] Ch. 712.

71. [1952] 2 QB 329 at pp. 353–4.

72. [1977] AC 1014.

73. *Ibid.*, at p. 1047.

74. [1961] AC 945.

75. [1977] ICR 893.

76. See Citrine at p. 285 and the cases cited therein.

77. See *Pett* v. *Greyhound Racing Association (No. 1)* [1969] 1 QB 125.

78. Unreported, but noted in Industrial Relations Review and Report, *Legal Information Bulletin*, April 5, 1984, p. 12.

79. *Payne* v. *ETU, The Times*, April 14, 1960.

80. See generally on rights during the hearing, *R.* v. *Deputy Industrial Injuries Commissioner, ex parte Moore* [1965] 2 QB 456, per Diplock LJ.

81. [1969] 1 QB 125.

82. See *Enderby Town FC* v. *Football Association* [1971] Ch. 591 and *Maynard* v. *Osmond* [1977] 2 QB 240.

83. *R.* v. *Home Secretary, ex parte Tarrant* [1984] 2 WLR 61.

84. 1969 SLT 150.

85. *R.* v. *Rand* (1866) LR 1 QB 230; *R.* v. *Sunderland JJ* [1901] 2 KB 357; *R.* v. *Cambourne JJ, ex parte Pearce* [1955] 1 QB 41.

86. *R.* v. *Sussex JJ, ex parte McCarthy* [1924] 1 KB 256; *Metropolitan Properties (FGC) Ltd.* v. *Lannon* [1969] 1 QB 577.

87. *Jackson* v. *Barry Railway Co.* [1893] 1 Ch. 148.

88. [1978] ICR 676.

89. *Ibid.*, at p. 681.

90. [1951] AC 585.

91. *Ibid.*, at p. 596.

92. See also *Hamlet* v. *GMBATU* [1986] IRLR 293 where it was held that someone who sits at the first decision is not thereby disabled from sitting at the appeal.

93. [1978] ICR 676 at pp. 681–2.

94. [1929] 1 Ch. 602.

95. *Ibid.*, at pp. 623–4.

96. [1949] 1 All ER 109 at pp. 114–15; for other cases supporting the contractual basis of

natural justice, see Citrine, p. 284, n. 1. See also, the judgment of Ungoed Thomas J in *Lawlor* v. *UPW* [1965] 1 Ch. 712 at p. 729, where a very restricted view on the scope of natural justice was adopted; and *John* v. *Rees* [1969] 2 All ER 274 at pp. 306-8 per Megarry J, where the judge indicated that any contract excluding natural justice would be very strictly construed, and if on such a construction it excluded natural justice, the rule might be still void as contrary to public policy. See also the ambivalent dicta of Stamp J in *Hiles* v. *Amalgamated Society of Woodworkers* [1968] Ch. 440 at p. 452, who waivers between the contractual and public policy approach.

97. See also *Kahn-Freund's Labour and the Law* (3rd edn, by P. Davies and M. Freedland) (1983), p. 230.

98. To the extent that *Hamlet* v. *GMBATU* [1986] IRLR 293 suggests that natural justice may be excluded by the rules, it is, in our view, a straw in the wind.

99. See *Abbott* v. *Sullivan* [1952] 1 KB 189; *Lee* v. *Showmen's Guild* [1952] 2 QB 329, *Bonsor* v. *Musicians' Union* [1954] 1 Ch. 479; and *Edwards* v. *SOGAT* [1971] Ch. 354.

100. [1972] ICR 484 at p. 496.
101. [1982] IRLR 91.
102. [1964] AC 925.
103. [1971] 1 Ch. 34.
104. *Ibid.*, at p. 48.
105. *Ibid.*, at p. 49.
106. [1980] AC 574.
107. *Ibid.*, at p. 593.
108. *Ibid.*
109. [1980] AC 574.
110. TUC Annual Report 1971, pp. 46-7.
111. *The Times*, February 17, 1928.
112. *Ibid.* But see the contrasting, unreported decision of *Blore* v. *Goodwin*, May 29, 1966 (quoted in Citrine, p. 266), where a similar clause was held not to provide for automatic forfeiture and that, unless and until the member was struck off, he remained in membership.
113. [1971] Ch. 354.
114. *Ibid.*, at p. 376.
115. [1983] ICR 398.
116. As in *Gibb* v. *NUSMW*, unreported, but discussed in Industrial Relations Review and Report, *Legal Information Bulletin*, December 4, 1984, p. 9.
117. *The Times*, January 28, 1928.
118. *Council of Civil Service Unions* v. *Minister for the Civil Service* [1984] 3 WLR 1174.
119. Elias, Napier and Wallington, *Labour Law Cases and Materials* (1980), p. 333.
120. The principles are set out in Elias, Napier and Wallington, *ibid.*, pp. 333-4. For discussion, see Simpson, 'The TUC's Bridlington Principles and the Law' (1983) 46 MLR 635.
121. [1956] 1 WLR 585.
122. [1983] ICR 398.
123. *Ibid.*, at p. 404.
124. *Ibid.*
125. *Ibid.*
126. [1982] ICR 231 at p. 250.
127. *Walsh* v. *AUEW*, *The Times*, July 15, 1977. There may also be cases where a hearing will be required after a Disputes Committee award if there are reasons why the members should be given a special opportunity to make representations. See *Cheall* v. *APEX* [1982] IRLR 362 per Donaldson LJ at p. 369.
128. [1964] AC 40.
129. *Associated Provincial Picture Houses Ltd.* v. *Wednesbury Corporation* [1948] 1 KB 223.
130. See *R.* v. *Home Secretary, ex parte Findlay* [1984] All ER 301, especially per Lord Scarman.
131. [1971] 2 QB 175.
132. *Ibid.*, at p. 190.
133. *Ibid.*
134. [1976] ICR 170. See also *Preston* v. *IRC* [1985] 2 All ER 327.
135. *Ibid.*, at p. 185.
136. *Ibid.*

137. *Ibid.*, at p. 192.
138. [1976] 3 All ER 452.
139. *Ibid.*, at pp. 456–7.
140. Royal Commission on Trade Unions, etc., *op. cit.*, para. 631.
141. TULRA 1974, s. 5.
142. TULR (Am) A 1976, s. 1(1)(a).
143. 1980 Act, s. 4.
144. 1980 Act, s. 4(5).
145. [1985] IRLR 198.
146. *Ibid.*, at p. 201.
147. *Ibid.*
148. *Ibid.*, at p. 202. It is to be noted that although McGhee appealed to the Court of Appeal, his counsel dropped the 'constructive expulsion' issue, and he failed simply because he had not been expelled. See *McGhee* v. *TGWU*, IPS Brief 316 (1986), p. 16
149. Elias, 'Closing in on the Closed Shop' (1980) 9 ILJ 201 at pp. 209–10.
150. *Cheall* v. *APEX* [1983] ICR 398.
151. *Cheall* v. *APEX* [1982] IRLR 362.
152. EPCA 1978, s. 58.
153. *Jeffrey* v. *Laurence Scott Electrometers Ltd.* [1977] IRLR 466; *Curry* v. *Harlow DC* [1979] ICR 769.
154. *Hoover Ltd.* v. *Forde* [1980] ICR 239, and EPCA 1978, s. 140.

7

Discipline and Industrial Action

In Chapter 6 we saw how the courts have acquired considerable power to regulate the ways in which trade unions use their disciplinary rules. In this chapter we examine how that power is used in the crucial area of discipline for failing to take part in industrial action. The members may come into conflict with the union over the decision to take industrial action in three principal ways: they may wish to restrain the union from taking the action at all; they may seek to restrain the unauthorized expenditure of money, such as strike pay, in support of the action; and they may simply refuse to participate in the action thereby subjecting themselves to possible disciplinary sanctions. We considered the first two of these issues in Chapter 4, and it is only the last of them which will be dealt with here. The starting point in determining whether disciplinary sanctions may be lawfully imposed is that the union must have authority in its rules to expel, and it must have authority to do so on the ground of non-participation in a strike or other form of industrial action.[1] Typically all unions have such rules, authorizing discipline specifically in the event of strike-breaking, or on the more general ground of acting in a manner prejudicial to the interests of the union. It is to be noted, however, that occasionally there will be no such rule. Remarkably, at the beginning of the coal strike of 1984–5, the NUM had no such authority to expel. It is true that steps were taken to introduce a new rule (rule 51) to provide for the establishment of a National Disciplinary Committee with power to expel or suspend from membership any member who 'has done any act (which includes any omission) which may be detrimental to the interests of the union'. As we saw in Chapter 2, however, the validity of this rule is in some doubt in view of the circumstances in which it was introduced.[2]

THE *ULTRA VIRES* RULE

If there is authority to discipline for failing to strike, the first question which arises with regard to the disciplinary action is whether the strike is within the power of the union under the rules. If it is *ultra vires*, it will be unlawful for the union to discipline a member who fails to take part in the action. The point is illustrated by the cases arising out of the miners' strike which are discussed in Chapter 4. There is, however, a second point. Even if the action is within the rules, are there limits on the union's authority under the rules, imposed or implied by the general law? In particular, can the union take action under the rules if the action will lead to the commission of a criminal offence or a tort? The matter has been considered in three important cases. The first was in *National Sailors' and Firemen's Union of Great Britain and Ireland* v. *Reed* where Astbury J held that it would be unlawful for a union to call a strike which was not protected by the golden formula, and that the union would have no power to discipline a member who refused to participate in such an action:

> No member of the plaintiff Union or any other trade unionist in this country can lose his trade union benefits by refusing to obey unlawful orders.[3]

This case arose out of the General Strike, and Astbury J's conclusion that industrial action furthering that cause was not in contemplation or furtherance of a trade dispute has been much criticized. The judgment is also unsatisfactory in failing to make clear why the strike was unlawful. It is elementary labour law that there is no such animal as a 'lawful' or 'unlawful' strike. Admittedly the vast majority of strikes which do not attract the immunities will be unlawful in the sense that certain torts may be committed in the course of them, but this is not necessarily the case. However, the judge's analysis confirmed the views expressed in Parliament by two government spokesmen, both famous lawyers, Sir John Simon and the then Attorney-General Sir Douglas Hogg, who later became Lord Chancellor. But of course the government was bitterly hostile to the General Strike. Indeed, in an unprecedented interference in internal union affairs, the government pledged that those workers who had refused to participate in the General Strike and who had been disciplined as a consequence would be protected, and to that end it entered into discussions with individual unions to persuade them to expunge any disciplinary action already taken against members who had refused to strike. Subsequently, to deal with those unions who had refused to bow to such pressures, it redeemed its pledge by a provision in the Trade Disputes and Trade Unions Act 1927 which operated retrospectively. This made it unlawful for a union to discipline in any way members who refused to participate in industrial action which had been called in circumstances which were declared by the Act to be illegal, and which encompassed the General Strike.

The matter was also briefly considered in *Sherard* v. *AUEW*,[4] a case to which we shall return. Its importance for present purposes is the suggestion by Lord Denning that a union could not be restrained from calling industrial action where the action in question was tortious, in the sense that it was outside the golden formula. A similar approach appears to have been adopted in *Thomas* v. *NUM (South Wales Area)*[5] where it was argued that the organization of mass picketing was *ultra vires*, not because it was a breach of the defendant union's express rules but because it was unlawful in the sense that it was criminal and tortious. Although the rules of the area union plainly empowered the union to take industrial action and to organize picketing in support of the action, it was argued that the rules must be subject to an implied limitation restricting the authority of the union to that which was lawful. This is a crucially important argument with far-reaching implications. If it is correct, it would mean that every time a union organized a strike outside the immunities, it would be exposed to challenge not just by employers but by individual members, financed by organizations engaged mainly in the business of making mischief. And as the immunities contract, so the risk from these organizations expands. Scott J drew a distinction, however, between industrial action having criminal consequences and that which is tortious only. Thus he held that it must be *ultra vires* for a union deliberately to embark on a series of criminal acts. It is true that he was 'not clear' whether it was *ultra vires* to embark on a form of action which was bound to involve the commission of tortious acts, and that 'the answer might depend on the nature of the tort'.[6] He did, however, deal specifically with the economic torts, a point to which we shall return. Scott J also held that it was not *ultra vires* for a union to embark on a series of acts which carried the risk that criminal offences might be committed in the course thereof. So although it would be *ultra vires* for a union to embark upon a form of picketing that would be bound to involve criminal conduct, it would not be *ultra vires* for the union to embark on a form of picketing which was capable of involving crime. '*A fortiori* it would not be necessarily *ultra vires* for a union . . . to embark on a series of acts which carried the risk that torts might be committed'.[7]

The plaintiffs in *Thomas* had made three complaints. The first related to the picketing of five collieries which it was claimed involved the commission of torts against the plaintiffs, all of whom worked at the collieries in question. Injunctions were granted to restrain this conduct on the unprecedented ground that the 'unreasonable harassment' by the pickets amounted to a private nuisance. The second and third complaints related to picketing at other South Wales collieries (where none of the plaintiffs was employed), and to picketing at premises other than collieries (referred to by the judge as 'secondary picketing') such as power stations, steelworks and haulage companies. With regard to the second and third complaints, the plaintiffs unsuccessfully sought relief on the ground that the picketing was *ultra vires*. So far as the 'secondary picketing' was concerned, it was held that 'there is nothing necessarily *ultra vires* in the South Wales [Area] organising secondary picketing'. Such picketing is not inevitably tortious or criminal. It would, however, be *ultra vires* for a union 'to organise mass secondary picketing' for it would 'thereby be deliberately setting out to do something that would be bound to be criminal',[8] on the basis that mass picketing is an offence under section 7 of the Conspiracy and Protection of Property Act 1875. In this case, however, no injunction was granted to restrain such picketing because there was no evidence that any mass secondary picketing was organized by the South Wales union. Although Scott J accepted that the secondary picketing which had been organized by the union exposed it to liability in tort 'for, at least, interference with contract', in a profoundly important conclusion he also said that he was 'not prepared to hold that the picketing is, on that ground, *ultra vires* the [union]'.[9] This would appear to suggest that it is not *ultra vires* for a union to take action which may attract liability for interference with contract, because the action is outside the golden formula. It does not necessarily follow that the same would apply to the other economic torts (for example intimidation), though it is difficult in principle to see why not. For all practical purposes, it may well be then that the Astbury judgment is wrong and that it is not after all *ultra vires* for a union to call action which is tortious as against employers.

This is not to deny that *Thomas* has imposed an important limit on the power of unions under their rules. The restriction on criminal activity may be wider than is readily apparent. Apart from factory occupations and mass picketing, there are other more common forms of industrial action which will involve the commission of criminal action by the participants. Under section 5 of the Conspiracy and Protection of Property Act 1875, it is a criminal offence willingly and maliciously to break a contract of service or hiring, knowing, or having reasonable cause to believe that the probable consequences will endanger life, cause serious personal injury, or expose valuable property to destruction or serious injury. Since virtually every strike involves those participating in breach of their employment contracts, the scope of this liability is potentially very wide. This is particularly so since the phrase 'willingly and maliciously' means little more than intentionally or recklessly, and it seems that spite or ill-will are unnecessary. Theoretically, therefore, this section could render criminal industrial action by a very wide range of persons, including doctors, nurses, firefighters, ambulance staff and, because of the potential damage they can do to property, even dockers, certain transport workers, and those working in electricity generating stations. There are no reported prosecutions under this section even though it applies whether or not the action is protected by the golden formula, and the likelihood of any such prosecution is remote. Nevertheless, it could clearly become the basis of a very important restriction on the power of trade unions to take industrial action. Again, certain action by post office workers involving wilfully hindering the progress of the mail will at present constitute a criminal offence,[10] and therefore the union's disciplinary sanctions could not be imposed against a member refusing to comply with instructions which required him or her to take such action. It is also possible to envisage certain forms of industrial action constituting breaches of health and safety legislation. For example, workers who take part in a strike will sometimes be in breach of a duty imposed upon them by section 7 of the Health and Safety at Work Act to take reasonable care for the health and safety of others who may be affected by their acts and omissions.

JUDICIAL CONTROL OF DISCIPLINARY RULES

The effect of *Thomas* for present purposes would appear to be as follows: a trade union member may not be disciplined for failing to participate in industrial action which is criminal in its consequences. This is because the action in question is *ultra vires*. But a union member cannot defend his or her failure to participate in tortious action by the union on the ground that it is *ultra vires*. It does not follow, however, that the member may still be disciplined. It does not follow that because tortious action is not *ultra vires*, a member may therefore be disciplined for a failure to take part. This is a point to which we now turn. Is there industrial action which is lawful under the rules but with regard to which non-participants may not be disciplined? Will the courts interfere with union autonomy at the point where discipline and cohesion may be most fundamental? And, if so, which devices will they use to justify their intervention? A few possibilities seem obvious. For example, can the union discipline members who fail to strike because to do so would involve the breach of their contract of employment, or would involve them or the union in the commission of a tort, or would involve the breach of any other legal obligation? And can the union discipline members who refuse to strike because they have conscientious or other objections to so doing?

Breach of Contract

Most forms of industrial action will involve breaches of contract by those taking part. This is not inevitably so: overtime bans, for example, can frequently be instituted without the workers concerned breaching their employment contracts. Moreover, it is possible for workers to strike without such a breach by lawfully terminating their contracts, or even as a result of a specific agreement with the employer that strike action can be taken without a breach being thereby committed. However, as the Court of Appeal made clear in *Associated Newspapers Group Ltd.* v. *Wade*,[11] it will require very strong evidence indeed before a court is willing to conclude that the employer has agreed to such a term. In that case, the union had argued that where a closed shop exists it was an implied term of the union members' employment contract that they could obey instructions to take industrial action made in accordance with the union rules without thereby infringing their employment contracts. The court had no difficulty in rejecting this ingenious argument. They thought that the employer would never willingly cede such power to the union. Lawton LJ commented that if such a term did exist, it would be a recipe for social and economic disaster.

It follows, therefore, that frequently a member will be required to take industrial action in order to comply with his or her contract of union membership but will thereby be compelled to act in breach of his or her contract of employment. Can the union lawfully compel members to act in this way, or will public policy preclude it from acting on a rule or instruction which requires such a response? Essentially this raises the question of whether a contract to break a contract can be enforced in law. Surprisingly, English law gives no clear answer to this fundamental question. However, almost fifty years ago Lauterpacht expressed the opinion that such a contract was not enforceable.[12] Two reasons were given for the conclusion: the first was that such a contract is a contract to commit a tort since by its creation it involves an inducement of a breach of the original contract, and so falls under the general principle of rendering void contracts to commit a tort; the second was that since breach of contract is itself a legal wrong, the courts should not lend their support to uphold an agreement to enforce that wrong. However, whatever the justification for this approach in contract law generally, the application of this principle to the union contract of membership would make it virtually impossible for a union ever to discipline members who refused to obey a strike call. Nevertheless in the early years of this century, in *Amalgamated Society of Engineers* v. *Smith*,[13] the High Court of Australia left open the possibility that the common law might proceed down this path. After years of uncertainty, however, the English courts refused to adopt this approach. In *Porter* v. *NUJ*[14] the Court of Appeal rejected an argument that the union's power to demand obedience was limited to those situations where no breach of the employment contract was committed. Furthermore, it did so notwithstanding the fact that the union in that case did not expressly reserve to itself the right to discipline even where such breaches did occur. As Shaw LJ observed: 'A power to order "the withdrawal of any member or members from their employment" means, as I see it, a power to order a member to go on strike, and the power extends to requiring the member to strike although in so doing he may be in breach of contract with his employer. A power limited to ordering a member to terminate his employment by due notice would in practice be futile and inexpedient.'[15]

Liability in Tort

The mere fact, then, that members may be required to act in breach of their employment contracts does not justify in law their refusal to participate in industrial action. But what if they are required to commit a tort? Here the general principle in English law is more firmly established than in relation to a breach of contract: a contract to commit a tort is unlawful, save perhaps where the tort is wholly technical.[16] Consequently a rule which proposed to empower a union to compel its members to take industrial action, whether or not they thereby committed a tort, would be void. In practice, of course, rules do not take this form. Rather they will permit various bodies within the union to call industrial action in certain circumstances, and the rule will make no reference at all to any unlawful acts which might thereby be committed. In these circumstances the courts will construe the rule so as to permit the union to do what is lawful, and the rule itself will be valid. But if unlawful instructions are issued, they will not have to be obeyed. In practice, there are relatively few situations where an instruction to take industrial action will result in the members concerned committing torts. However, the position could well arise: for example, an order to 'sit-in' would constitute an order for the member to commit a trespass. More importantly, it is possible that picketing premises is inherently unlawful at common law as constituting the tort of private nuisance. If that is so, the instruction to picket will be unlawful and unenforceable, save where no illegalities are committed because the statutory immunities apply, i.e.

broadly where members are required to picket outside their own place of work in contemplation or furtherance of a trade dispute.[17]

The point so far is that the order to take industrial action may be unlawful where it requires the members themselves to commit a tort. But what is the position where the members are required to take action which will involve the union but not them in the commission of a tort? As has been pointed out, the members cannot defend their position on the ground that the union's conduct was *ultra vires*: for it is not. Yet it does not follow that the union can discipline strike-breakers where the conduct of the union is potentially tortious in the sense of being outside the golden formula. The matter was considered — albeit briefly — by Lord Denning in *Sherard* v. *AUEW*.[18] The defendant union had organized a one-day strike against the government's counter-inflation policy, and the plaintiffs were union members who sought a mandatory interlocutory injunction to order the union to withdraw these instructions to strike. They did so on two grounds. The first was that they alleged that the strike was essentially a 'political' strike and was thereby unauthorized by the union rules which, on their construction, permitted only industrial disputes. The court rejected this on the basis that the union constitution clearly did include the pursuit of political purposes, and in any event, as Roskill LJ pointed out, the phrase 'political strike' was one that 'did not readily lend itself to precise or accurate definition'.[19] The second argument was that the action was outside the golden formula and was therefore unlawful, and so could not be authorized by the union constitution. But this too was rejected, the Court of Appeal holding that it was at least arguable that the industrial action was one that fell within the golden formula, and that consequently no injunction could be granted. In addition, Lord Denning held that even if the immunity was inapplicable, it would not be open to members to complain providing they were personally subject to no disciplinary sanctions for refusing to participate. However, he made it clear that the imposition of any such sanctions would be unlawful:

> I would emphasise that no man should be victimised by the union and no steps should be taken against any man if he should think it right not to obey the call.[20]

Sherard suggests that there may be a distinction between the constitutional power of the union to call the strike and its legal right to discipline members who refuse to participate in it. The mere fact that the industrial action is *intra vires* does not mean that the union can automatically demand obedience to it. While the member may be unable to have the order to strike withdrawn, he or she may still be legally entitled to ignore the call. In effect, therefore, the power of the union to request the members to take industrial action will be greater than the power to instruct them to do so. Such a conclusion may not, however, be easily supported. It is difficult to know precisely what is the origin of this principle that a member cannot be compelled to participate in industrial action outside the golden formula. Presumably it has to be treated as a principle of public policy so that however widely union rules are drafted, they will be held inapplicable to enforce compliance with this kind of action. Admittedly, it would not be illogical for Parliament to say that the golden formula represents the boundaries of legitimate trade union activity and that members may not lawfully be disciplined for failing to go beyond the boundaries. Parliament did in fact take this stand in 1927 and again in the Industrial Relations Act 1971 which provided by section 65(7) that disciplinary action shall not be taken against any member of a trade union by reason of his refusing or failing:

(a) to take any action which, in accordance with any provision of this Act, would constitute an unfair industrial practice on his part, or

(b) *to take part in a strike* which the organisation, or any other person, has called, organised, procured or financed *otherwise than in contemplation or furtherance of an industrial dispute*, or in such circumstances as, in accordance with any provision of this Act, to constitute an unfair industrial practice on the part of the organisation or of that person, or

(c) to take part in any irregular industrial action short of a strike which the organisation, or any other person, has organised, procured or financed as mentioned in paragraph (b) of this subsection. (emphasis added)

This in fact may explain Lord Denning's remarks in *Sherard*. The reason why the unions could not discipline those taking action outside the golden formula is that it was forbidden by statute (the words in parenthesis) from doing so. If this is correct, the repeal of the statute took with it Lord Denning's point: to sustain the restriction in the light of the repeal of the IRA, would be to fly in the face of public policy as determined by Parliament. It is difficult to see on what other ground of public policy such a restriction could be justified. However, the matter remains to be settled authoritatively and the question must still be regarded as open.

Fiduciary Duties

One particular problem which is likely to become increasingly common with the expansion of professional and white-collar unions is the potential conflicts of loyalty that can arise in circumstances where the union demands obedience to a policy which conflicts with duties owed by its members to other organizations. The problem applies especially to managers who are executive directors and professional workers. One conflict arises because such workers may owe duties to their company as well as to their union. These duties may be both contractual and fiduciary. As we have seen, the courts may give priority to the con-tractual duties arising out of the contract of membership where these conflict with the duty arising out of the contract of employment. But will they also be willing to give priority to the contract of membership where the obligations arising out of that contract conflict with the equitable obligations which directors and perhaps other senior managers owe to the company? *Boulting* v. *ACTT*[21] suggest that they will not. Although it was held that there is no inherent conflict of duty when a director is also a union member, it was recognized that there was a potential conflict which could arise in this situation and, as Diplock LJ indicated, where this conflict crystallizes, priority will be given to the fiduciary obligations:

> It would be unlawful for the union or any of its members to induce the Boulting brothers to act inconsistently with their duty to Charter by threatening the coerce them in their capacity as members of the union by applying [disciplinary] sanctions.[22]

The implication of this would seem to be that not merely would the company have an action against the union in this situation, but in addition the member could prevent the union from disciplining him or her for the refusal to bend to any such unlawful coercion. Moreover, it is possible that the courts would take the view that this is not limited to executive directors but extends to the other senior managerial employees, embracing at least, to use Lord Denning's graphic phrase, those who constitute 'the directing mind and will' of the organization.[23] The courts might well take the view that the fiduciary content in their contracts would be sufficient to outweigh any union powers derived from the membership contract. The significance of this argument is that it reflects certain assumptions which, as Bain has shown,[24] are still com-monly held, particularly among managers (and no doubt many judges). These are that while trade unionism and even, perhaps, industrial action may be suitable for blue-collar workers, they are inappropriate for the white-collar worker who is expected to be more integrated into the organization and to be more involved in the realization of its goals. Consequently the courts may be particularly keen to insulate the employees of managerial rank from the disciplinary power of the union. And this is likely to be the case even where the fiduciary duties arise at a later point in time than the duties under the membership contract. So, for example, on this analysis, a union could be restrained from disciplining a member who was also a senior manager who thought it in the best interests of the company to pursue a company policy which directly conflicted with union policy, or who refused to disclose to the union certain confidential information which he or she possessed.

Procedure Agreements

There is some limited authority which suggests that at least in certain limited cases, it may be unlawful for a union to discipline a member who failed to strike in breach of a procedure agreement. In *Partington* v. *NALGO*,[25] a case decided by the Outer House of the Court of Session, the pursuer was expelled from the union for working during an official strike. However, the union had entered into a closed shop agreement with the employers, Scottish Gas, which provided *inter alia* that in the event of industrial action being taken, cover would be provided to ensure safety and to deal with emergencies. On its proper construction, the agreement provided that there would be prior discussions to determine which workers should provide the necessary cover but that if no agreement could be reached, Scottish Gas would have responsibility to determine the matter. In the event, no agreement was reached in this particular dispute, and Scottish Gas accordingly notified the pursuer that he should work to provide emergency cover. He did not obtain special dispensation from the union to do this work, despite the fact that the relevant union rule, 67(b), provided that any instruction to take industrial action was binding upon the member unless any such dispensation had been obtained. He was then expelled, and although there was some dispute as to which provision he was expelled under, the judge held that it was the rule which permitted expulsion for 'conduct which, in the opinion of the Executive Committee, renders him unfit for membership'.

In the circumstances, Lord Allanbridge held that the expulsion was unlawful. It was conceded that the relevant closed shop agreement was incorporated into the pursuer's contract of employment and, in the light of this, the judge found that the agreement, including the relevant paragraph relating to the provision of cover, was a tripartite agreement binding upon the union, the employer and the pursuer (though presumably, in the light of TULRA, section 18(1), it was not legally enforceable as between union and employer). His Lordship then held that in the circumstances of this case the pursuer's obligation to obey the instructions from the employer was paramount and transcended his duty to the union. So the question arises: how can this conclusion be reconciled with

Porter's case which held that priority should not be accorded to the contract of employment? His Lordship's judgment is a little obscure on this point. However, it appears that he treated the agreement as modifying the contract of membership — hence his description of it as a 'tripartite agreement'. So although under rule 67(b) specific dispensation would normally have been required before the member could attend work, that rule had been qualified by 'a specific and clear separate agreement . . . which could be frustrated by a strict application of [the] . . . rule'.[26] It appears, therefore, that his Lordship's view was that the contract of union membership had been modified, at least in relation to certain categories of union members, by a collective agreement which specifically dealt with the issue covered by the rules.

Possibly, however, his Lordship was intending to lay down a more general principle to the effect that the union cannot lawfully discipline a member who refuses to participate in industrial action which is in breach of a specific procedure agreement negotiated by his union, whether or not that agreement has modified the contract of membership. In other words, where a conflict arises between the terms of the procedure agreement and the contract of membership, priority will be given to the former. Admittedly it is not desirable that unions should simply ignore agreements, and it may well be that a member should consider it ethically unacceptable for a union to do so. But it is nevertheless difficult to construct a rule of law that the union cannot discipline its members in these circumstances, particularly where — as will almost always be the case — the procedure agreement is neither legally enforceable as between the collective parties nor, because of TULRA, section 18(4), incorporated into the individual contracts of employment of union members. Nevertheless, the courts may now be willing to develop a legal principle of this kind to reflect the provision in the Closed Shop Code. Indeed, even before *Partington* there was an obiter remark by Lord Denning in *Porter's* case where he hinted that this might be the law.[27] Even if it is not, it will still be difficult for a union to discipline a member in these circumstances unless it does so within a specific rule. If, as in *Partington's* case, the expulsion is made under a general disciplinary provision, the courts can readily conclude, as did Lord Allanbridge, that no reasonable union could discipline in these circumstances. Similarly with the statutory action alleging unreasonable expulsion.

Conscientious Objections

An additional restriction on the ability of a union to discipline strike-breakers arose in *Esterman* v. *NALGO*,[28] a case which we discussed in

Chapter 6. In that case, Templeman J appeared to import a conscience clause into the rule book, thereby disabling unions from disciplining any non-strikers who have a conscientious objection to the action in question. In *Esterman* the union was in dispute with local authorities about the level of the London weighting allowance. An agreement was in fact reached by the two sides but the Secretary of State for Employment refused to endorse it under the existing pay policy with the result that it could not become effective. Thereupon the Islington Branch Secretary, acting on instructions from the District Office, instructed his members to strike, subject to a number of excepted categories of members who included the plaintiff. The instruction was given despite the fact that in a ballot only 49 per cent of the members had voted in favour of strike action. In addition, members (including the plaintiff) were called upon not to co-operate with returning officers during forthcoming local government elections. The plaintiff refused to comply with the instruction and was subsequently given notice that she was to be charged with a disciplinary offence which authorized expulsion for conduct which in the opinion of the executive committee renders the member unfit for membership. As we have already seen, she successfully sought an injunction against the union to stop it from taking the action against her. And we have also seen that Templeman J purported to apply the Denning LJ test in *Lee* v. *Showmen's Guild of Great Britain*[29] — that the court should not interfere unless satisfied that no reasonable tribunal acting in good faith could reach a particular decision. In fact, however, if he did apply this test, he restricted its scope by saying that there are certain decisions under the disciplinary rules which may not reasonably be taken. In the first place, Templeman J held:

> when the national executive council take the serious step of interfering with the right of a member to volunteer or take work of any description outside his normal employment, the national executive council are only entitled to 100 per cent and implicit obedience to that order if it is clear that they have been given power to issue the order and if it is clear that they are not abusing that power. If a member disobeys an order of the national executive council which does not satisfy those tests, then it seems to me that he cannot be found guilty on that account of conduct which renders him unfit to be a member of NALGO.[30]

In this case, it was not clear whether NALGO had the power to take action against a returning officer with whom it had no quarrel, or whether it had the right to interfere with the spare-time activities of its members. But secondly, Templeman J held that even if the union did have the power:

the special circumstances in this case are such, in my judgment, that a member could very well come to the conclusion that this was an order to which the national executive council had no right to demand his obedience and it was an order which, as a person — a loyal member of NALGO — acting in its best interests, he felt bound to disobey.[31]

As suggested in Chapter 6, Templeman J appears thus to import a conscience clause into the rule book. Arguably, however, it would be a mistake to make too much of this. First, the initiative has never been followed nor applied in any subsequent case, and is supported only, if at all, by a rather cryptic dictum in *Porter* v. *NUJ*[32] — delivered again by Templeman LJ. Secondly, it is not clear that this limitation on a union's disciplinary powers is a universal privilege which could be claimed by all members in all cases. The following passage could be read as sustaining the view that the restriction is really something exceptional:

We have this background: although there was only 49 per cent support in the only ballot for selective strike action, the national executive council had already ordered the whole of the Islington branch to strike. A member could take the view that this 49 per cent might be a sufficient number to justify the national executive council in making a recommendation for a strike; it was no warrant for an order to strike with the threat in the background of expulsion for any member who had voted against the strike and thought that a strike was not in the interests of NALGO.

A member could take the view that action against the returning officers had never been submitted to a ballot and that whether or not a ballot was strictly necessary the national executive council, following the spirit as well as the letter of the instructions with regard to strikes, ought not to order, but rather — if they wished — to recommend, action against the returning officer. A member may have thought that such an order did not reasonably command obedience and that there was a possibility that it gave the appearance of coercing those who thought that action against the returning officers was not in the best interests of NALGO. He might take the view that, in all the extraordinary background of this case, he could not conscientiously accept an order given by the national executive council without a ballot or a fresh ballot against the wishes of the Minister and the secretary of the Trades Union Congress and in the existing national conditions, particularly since 100 per cent obedience to the order of the national executive council would seem to imply that 100 per cent of the members were firmly in support of the action which was being taken. A member might take the view that the national executive council order was an abuse of their powers, because, without any mandate by way of a ballot, it had the appearance some might think, of seeking to wreck the local elections which might be irreparably damaged. In brief in my judgment, a member was entitled to take the view that this was an order which he might be under a positive duty to disobey.[33]

The facts of this case might be contrasted with a situation in which the union pulled out its members clearly in accordance with the rules. In such a case, there is nothing in the above passages to suggest that a member of the union could confidently refuse to take part in the action without fear of being disciplined lawfully under the rules. And the points in the members' favour which do appear are to be read in the context of the rules of this particular association. Although Templeman J held that the plaintiff was entitled to resist because there was no ballot, it does not follow that a member would always be able to resist on this ground. Here the rules required a ballot to be held before an instruction to strike was given. Where there was no ballot, there was a power only to *request* members to take strike action. All the judge was saying in this case was that there was some doubt under the rules whether the union had the authority to give the instruction it did, and that for this reason the member was entitled conscientiously to resist. On this basis the case is not authority for the proposition that where the action is clearly within the rules the member has a right conscientiously to resist. This is not to deny the importance of the case. However, there is a significant difference between a conscience clause of universal application and one which can apply in very exceptional circumstances.

STATUTORY CONTROL OF UNION DISCIPLINE

It is clear from the foregoing discussion that the scope for judicial control of the application of trade union disciplinary rules in the area of industrial action is uncertain. In the absence of a well-developed common law basis for regulation, Parliament has also intervened to regulate the use of disciplinary rules against strike-breakers. The provisions in force at the time of writing are rather limited in their application, though there is a possibility of more direct and more sweeping measures.

The Closed Shop Code of Practice

At the time of writing, statute regulates the use of disciplinary sanctions for non-participation in a strike or other industrial action only indirectly through the Code of Practice on Closed Shop Agreements and Arrangements. The Code first came into effect in 1980, but it was amended in 1983, partly, according to the Secretary of State, in order to provide greater protection to the individual member who refuses to obey a union instruction to take industrial action, and is then subjected to, or threatened with, disciplinary sanctions. It is important to note that the Code is concerned only with the closed shop, though the relevant paragraphs apparently apply not merely to expulsion cases but also to any situations where any form of disciplinary action is taken or threatened by the union. It is important to note also that the Code is relevant not only where a statutory action is instituted under section 4 of the Employment Act 1980 for an alleged unreasonable expulsion, but also, as section 3(8) of the 1980 Act expressly makes clear, where proceedings are taken in the ordinary courts. However, the Code need only be taken into account by the relevant court or tribunal; it is a factor, but not necessarily the determining factor, to be considered in reaching a decision.

Indeed, in certain circumstances it is difficult to envisage how the Code will be able to have any effect at all. For example, if a union rule directly conflicts with the Code, it will nevertheless remain valid and binding at common law, notwithstanding the Code. So if a rule were to state, for example, that a member could be fined for refusing to participate in a strike, whether or not that strike was affirmed in a secret ballot, then it would seem that at common law the fine could lawfully be imposed even though the Code expressly and unequivocally states that disciplinary action should not be taken in these circumstances. However, if instead the rule provided for an expulsion and the member was expelled, then the Code could be taken into account in any proceedings brought by the member alleging an unreasonable expulsion under section 4 of the 1980 Act, since a tribunal would be able to hold that, in the light of the Code, the rule itself, and hence the expulsion, was unreasonable. Again, if the member were to be fined, under a general disciplinary rule, such as one specifying that he or she could be disciplined for acting to the detriment of the union, then, since the common law test for determining whether the imposition of the sanction is lawful is whether a reasonable union tribunal would impose it,[34] the court would be able to take the Code into account when determining what such a reasonable tribunal would do. In both these contexts the Code may colour the judicial perception of what is reasonable. So the Code is always potentially influential where a statutory action is taken to challenge an allegedly unreasonable expulsion, or where any disciplinary action is taken under a general disciplinary rule. In addition, it may be taken into account to help construe an otherwise ambiguous rule; if possible, it should be construed so as to be consistent with the Code. However, where the rule is clear and lawful, and some sanction short of expulsion is imposed, then it is hard to see how the Code can have any influence at all.

The key provisions of the Code for present purposes are paragraphs 61 and 62. Paragraph 61 contains four restrictions. The first is where the member had reasonable grounds for believing that the industrial action was unlawful in the sense that it fell outside the statutory immunities; or that it involved a breach of statutory duty or the criminal law; or that it constituted a serious risk to public safety, health or property. These are in fact sweeping restrictions. For example, it is not enough that the action is within the scope of the immunity: the members are protected where they failed to strike because they had reasonable grounds to believe that it was not, a crucial point in view of the 1982 amendments to the immunities which in many cases will lead to their application being very finely balanced, as was demonstrated by the decision of the Court of Appeal in *Mercury Communications Ltd.* v. *Scott-Garner.*[35] However, even if the action is clearly within the immunities, disciplinary measures may not be taken if the action involved a breach of statutory duty. The Code does not say, however, by whom the breach of duty must be committed: by the member, by the union, or by the employer? If the last, it would appear that public-sector unions would be unable to compel obedience to a strike call by the threat of disciplinary action where the closed shop operated. A strike in such cases will invariably involve a breach of duty (as was illustrated by *Hackney Borough Council* v. *Doré*[36] — where an electricity authority which was under a duty to supply electricity was unable to do so for the plaintiffs because its workers refused to connect the supply). This restriction is reinforced by the prohibition in cases of public safety and health which appear to preclude disciplinary actions against those engaged in public utilities such as the fire and health services. This in effect extends section 5 of the 1875 Act. Even if the industrial action is not a violation because, for example, there is no wilful breach of contract, discipline still may not be imposed if in fact the action endangers public health and safety.

The second restriction is where the members believed that the industrial action contravened their professional or other code of ethics. It is to be noted that this measure to some degree extends the earlier Code of Industrial Relations Practice, and is further strengthened by the Employment Protection (Consolidation) Act 1978, section 58(8), the relevant parts of which were inserted by the Employment Act 1982. Two paragraphs of the earlier Code are particularly relevant. Paragraph 23 stresses the need for unions and professional associations to co-operate in preventing and resolving any conflicts which arise. Paragraph 22 is more specific and provides:

> A professional employee who belongs to a trade union should respect the obligations which he has voluntarily taken on by joining the union. But he should not, when acting in his professional capacity, be called upon by his trade union to take action which would conflict with the standards of work or conduct laid down for his profession if that action would endanger:
> (i)   public health or safety;
> (ii)   the health of an individual needing medical or other treatment;
> (iii) the well-being of an individual needing care through the personal social services.

The 1978 Act provides that even if members are expelled, they may not be fairly dismissed by the employer, or subjected to any other detrimental action short of dismissal, where the expulsion occurred because the members refused to take part in the industrial action in breach of the Code of Conduct which applied to employees with their qualifications. However, this latter protection from unfair dismissal by the employer appears to be less effective than the protection from expulsion by the union in two ways: first, section 58(8) does not expresly apply where the employee simply honestly believes that participation in the industrial action would be in breach of the code. Secondly, the protection from the employer's action applies only where there is a written code of conduct applicable to persons with the same qualifications as the employee; in contrast, the protection against the union applies whenever the member is required to act in a manner which contravenes 'his professional or other code of ethics'. Arguably this need not be a formal written code at all, and possibly it could even be construed to include the member's set of personal ethical values. If so, it effectively protects members from disciplinary sanctions where they are acting in accordance with their consciences.

Occasionally, professional bodies and trade unions have given specific advice about how their members should resolve difficulties stemming from competing loyalties owed to the union and the professional organization. For example, the Law Society has laid down guidelines for solicitors in employment who may be required to take industrial action, e.g. those employed by local authorities. The gist of it is that it reluctantly recognizes that occasionally solicitors will have to respond to a call to strike and that it would accordingly be unfair to discipline members for unprofessional conduct in such circumstances. However, it strongly emphasizes that in order not to be in breach of his professional duties, the solicitor should take appropriate steps to see that 'so far as may be possible his employer's urgent interests will be protected and his urgent work dealt with', and that other members of the profession and the public suffer as little inconvenience as possible. A cynic might say that this is saying that to take industrial action will not be unprofessional conduct providing it is done without enthusiasm and so as to make the action as ineffective as possible! The problem for the member is that such a half-hearted response may well attract sanctions from the union. To be caught in this cross-fire is not enviable, not least because the law virtually leaves it to the parties to negotiate the cease-fire. Again, the rules of COHSE provide certain guidelines for members, such as nurses and midwives, who could face proceedings for professional misconduct arising out of industrial action. The General Nursing Council for England and Wales has expressed the view, which is consistent with paragraph 22 of the Industrial Relations Code of Practice, that it would constitute professional misconduct to put the health, safety or welfare of patients at risk. COHSE has sought to ensure that any industrial action it takes will not attract the wrath of the General Council by emphasizing in its rule book that 'when operating restrictive measures, a reasonable standard of patient care will be maintained and the respect of human dignity . . . will be observed'.[37]

The third restriction imposed by the Code applies to industrial action which is in breach of a procedure agreement. This is despite the fact that procedure agreements are not legally enforceable. This may represent Parliament seeking indirectly to enforce procedure agreements, a technique which is not unknown in Britain. For a few years, unemployment benefit was payable to people on strike where the strike was caused by the employer's breach of an agreement.[38] The fourth restriction is where the industrial action has not been affirmed by a secret ballot. When this was introduced, there was no duty on unions to ballot before strike action. As a result of the Trade Union Act 1984, however, a failure to ballot will make the strike 'unlawful' (to use the language of the Code) because it would be without immunity. However, it is to be noted that the Code is wider than the statute in the sense that the provisions of the Code apply to all strikes, whereas the statutory duty to ballot applies only to strikes 'authorized or endorsed' by responsible persons. It is likely, however, that a strike which has not been so authorized or endorsed will be in breach of the rules and, as we have seen, a union cannot discipline its members for failing to strike in breach of the rules, though this restriction is not dealt with in the Code. The fifth and final restriction relates to picketing. Paragraph 62 of the Code provides that disciplinary action should not be taken or threatened against a member on the ground that he or she has crossed an unauthorized picket-line or one that was not at the member's place of work. At common law it would already be difficult lawfully to discipline members in the former situation: they are under no obligation to comply with an unauthorized instruction, and an instruction not to cross an unauthorized picket-line is likely to fall into that category. However, the latter instruction is of a different category altogether. It is not even limited to preventing disciplinary action where a member crosses a picket-line which is formed outside the statutory protection afforded by section 15 of TULRA (as amended by the Employment Act 1980).

A picket-line may be within that section because the pickets are outside their own place of work and therefore attract the statutory immunities, and perhaps be perfectly lawfully conducted in every way. Yet still the union should not, according to the Code, discipline a member from another place of work, e.g. delivering supplies, who crosses that picket-line. This is tantamount to telling unions that they should not discipline strike-breakers. It is like telling employers that they should not dismiss an employee who works for a rival competitor. It is hardly surprising that this provision has been bitterly criticized for unfairly seeking to undermine union strength. It does not even require the members to take the view that they cannot in all conscience respect the picket-line. Partisan provisions of this kind undermine respect for Codes of Practice. If a controversial restriction of this nature is to be introduced, it is submitted that it should be a statutory provision and not operate as a quasi-legislative guideline.[39] The latter have almost the force of law: they will inevitably strongly influence the courts and tribunals which are finally responsible for implementing them. Admittedly the courts are not bound to give effect to the Code though, as we have seen above, the way in which the relevant provisions on union discipline are framed makes it very difficult for judges not to do so.[40] Constitutionally, therefore, the government is able to avoid direct accountability for these provisions; it can hide behind the judges' robes. This is an unacceptable way of seeking to regulate very important aspects of internal union government. It is true that in practice the provisions of the Code will become less relevant as the closed shop retreats, partly as a result of the attack mounted by the Employment Acts 1980–2. That, however, does not affect this important point of principle, though it does mean that we must look elsewhere to determine whether there are any limits on the power of unions to discipline their members for failing to strike. As we have seen, the judges appear to have developed the common law to meet this challenge, and it may be that Parliament may yet intervene to impose more direct restrictions of more general application.

A New Statutory Control?

As we saw in Chapter 1, more direct parliamentary intervention is not unprecedented in this country. The Trade Disputes and Trade Unions Act 1927 provided that:

> No person refusing to take part or to continue to take part in any strike or lock-out which is by this Act declared to be illegal, shall be, by reason of such refusal or by reason of any action taken by him under this section, subject to expulsion from any trade union or society, or to any fine or penalty, or to deprivation of any right or benefit to which he or his legal personal representatives would otherwise be entitled, or liable to be placed in any respect either directly or indirectly under any disability or at any disadvantage as compared with other members of the union or society, anything to the contrary in the rules of a trade union or society notwithstanding.[41]

The Act, however, applied only to a limited and exceptional range of activity, namely strikes or lock-outs such as the 1926 General Strike.[42] A more far-reaching limitation was provided by the Industrial Relations Act 1971 which sought to prohibit disciplinary action for failing to take part in a strike which was illegal or unlawful for a number of reasons, including the fact that it was an unfair industrial practice, or that it was not in contemplation or furtherance of an industrial dispute.[43] That, however, was repealed with the Industrial Relations Act in 1974 and little has been recorded about its impact. However, not only does British law provide precedents for more direct intervention in this area. Such constraints have also operated in other jurisdictions, and in some cases still operate. In Ontario, for example, the Labour Relations Act provides:

> No trade union shall suspend, expel or penalize in any way a member because he has refused to engage in or to continue to engage in a strike that is unlawful under this Act.[44]

There are suggestions that measures of this kind may well be introduced again into British law. Thus it has been reported that the government is preparing a fourth Bill on labour law, though it is likely that its introduction will be postponed until after the election.[45] It has also been reported that the government is concerned about four issues. One of these is 'the right to work despite a strike call', by which 'the Government would like to enable union members to protect themselves against what they saw as unfair action against them by their unions if they chose not to obey a strike call — even one sanctioned by a membership ballot under the 1984 Act'.[46] Under the proposals, unions would be prevented from taking disciplinary action against members. Such a measure would no doubt attract considerable support from Conservative backbenchers, one of whom has already criticized the Code of Practice as failing to give adequate protection to the individual worker.[47] It has been argued that as a purely practical matter, it is unrealistic to suppose that 'workers will sit down with the Code of Practice and go through its checklist of requirements in order to decide whether they come within the scope of its protection'.[48] As a result, what is needed 'is a clear and unambiguous statement that any expulsion from membership of a trade union for refusing to take part in industrial action will be regarded as unreasonable'.[49] It was also argued that such a measure could be justified on grounds of principle, on the basis that 'there is no reason why trade unions should not be able to persuade their members of the merits of their argument on any dispute without threatening loss of employment if workers fail to tow the line'.[50] Yet while such rhetoric will no doubt strike a political chord, the proposal is nevertheless difficult to justify.

In the first place, it is unlikely that inflexible union security arrangements of the kind permitted under TULRA (as amended by TULRA(Am)A 1976) will operate in this country again. The European Convention on Human Rights will clearly impose constraints, even though the scope of those constraints is not altogether clear. One effect may be a duty on Parliament to prescribe a wide conscience clause in union membership agreements. If this is done, it would be open to members to resign from the union rather than take part in strikes which are conscientiously offensive. The obligation would be on the unions to take action only if they have wide support — for to do otherwise would be to risk losing members. Secondly, if the concern is with protecting people's jobs, it is particularly difficult to justify an all-embracing measure which would apply regardless of whether a closed shop operates. Thirdly, by effectively postponing a right not to strike, the proposal denies to the union the ability to promote a dispute as effectively as possible and has the effect of strengthening the power of the employer to resist. If the jobs of individuals are not prejudiced by union sanctions, it is difficult seriously to justify this kind of intervention, particularly where the dispute is within the framework of legality determined by the state. This is not to deny that the state may have a role to play to protect individuals who refuse to strike where the strike is not in contemplation or furtherance of a trade dispute, or where it is unsupported by a ballot. Having set the frontiers of legitimate action, it would not be inappropriate to provide further that in closed shop situations a union which oversteps the frontiers may do so but may not discipline or expel members who decline to come along. However, if restraints of this kind are to be imposed on the exercise of trade union disciplinary powers, even-handed restrictions should be imposed on the disciplinary power of the employer. It would thus be unlawful for an employer to discipline and unfair to dismiss an employee who has participated in a strike supported by a ballot.

NOTES

1. *Luby* v. *Warwickshire Miners' Federation* [1912] 2 Ch. 379.
2. See *Clarke* v. *Chadburn (No. 2)* [1984] IRLR 350.
3. [1926] Ch. 536 at p. 00.
4. [1973] ICR 421.
5. [1985] 2 All ER 1.
6. *Ibid.*, at p. 29.
7. *Ibid.*
8. *Ibid.*, at p. 31.
9. *Ibid.*
10. See the Post Office Act 1953, s. 58.
11. [1979] ICR 664.
12. 'Contracts to Break a Contract' (1936) 52 LQR 494.
13. (1913) 16 CLR 537.
14. [1979] IRLR 404.
15. *Ibid.*, at p. 407.
16. Treitel, p. 324.
17. TULRA 1974, s. 15, as amended by the Employment Acts 1980.
18. [1973] ICR 421.
19. *Ibid.*, at p. 435.
20. *Ibid.*, at p. 433.
21. [1963] 2 QB 606.
22. *Ibid.*, at pp. 648-9.
23. *Ibid.*, at p. 624.
24. *The Growth of White-Collar Trade Unionism* (1970), pp. 135-40.
25. [1981] IRLR 537.
26. *Ibid.*, at p. 542.
27. [1979] IRLR 404 at p. 407.
28. [1974] ICR 625.
29. [1952] 2 QB 329.
30. [1974] ICR 625 at p. 632.
31. *Ibid.*, at p. 633.
32. [1979] IRLR 404.
33. [1974] ICR 625 at pp. 633-4.
34. See Chapter 6.
35. [1984] 1 All ER 179.
36. [1922] 1 KB 431.
37. See further, TUC, *Improving Industrial Relations in the National Health Service. A Report by the TUC Health Services Committee* (1981), pp. 160-4.
38. Unemployment Insurance (No. 2) Act 1924, s. 4(1).
39. See Elias, 'Closing in on the Closed Shop' (1980) 9 ILJ 201.
40. On the willingness of the courts to give normative effect to the Code of Practice on Picketing (1980), see *Thomas* v. *NUM (South Wales Area)* [1985] 2 All ER 1.
41. 1927 Act, s. 2.
42. 1927 Act, s. 1.

43. 1971 Act, s. 65(7).
44. RSO 1980, c. 228, s. 78.
45. *Financial Times*, June 20, 1985.
46. *Ibid*.
47. Howard, 'The Right to Refuse to Strike' *The Daily Telegraph*, October 5, 1983.
48. *Ibid*.
49. *Ibid*.
50. *Ibid*.

8

The Role of Law in
Trade Union Government

A proper assessment of the role which the law ought to play in the regulation of groups in society must depend largely on the public significance of the functions of these groups, and the methods they employ to pursue them. Inevitably an organization's legal status will influence both the nature and scope of judicial intervention — statutory corporations can be more fully controlled than registered companies, for example, as the unions discovered to their cost in *Osborne's* case[1] — but status should at best be no more than a minor factor in determining the appropriate legal controls. In particular, it is unpersuasive to argue that unions should not be subject to any legal control simply because they are in origin voluntary unincorporated bodies.[2] Churches, schools, clubs and unions may all lack formal incorporation, but this does not mean that they should be subject to similar legal regulation. Both Parliament and the courts should consider the particular needs and objectives of an organization before deciding what, if any, controls should be exercised over it. We begin our inquiry into the role of law in this area by considering the function of trade unions. We then ask why legal intervention can be justified and also to what extent the law should regulate trade union internal affairs.

THE BASIS FOR INTERVENTION

The Closed Shop

It has long been recognized that the power trade unions have over workers' job opportunities through the operation of the closed shop justifies some form of external control over union rules, though there is much debate about whether the control should be statutory or voluntary. This was the principal justification for the intervention proposed by the Donovan Commission.[3] In the view of the Report, the existence of the closed shop justified some regulation of trade union admissions with a view to some external review of complaints about arbitrary exclusions from membership.[4] The closed shop was also seen as the principal justification for some regulation of trade union disciplinary powers, on the ground that workers who consider themselves unfairly penalized by their union often cannot resort to resignation as a practicable course. If they did so, they would lose their jobs. But although the existence of the closed shop was raised as a justification for intervention both before and after the Donovan Report, and although it continues to be important, it is a much less forceful argument in 1986 than it was in 1968. For not only has the institution been the subject of far-reaching attacks by the Conservative government since 1979, it seems highly unlikely that we could ever return to a situation in which people could be compelled to join a specific trade union on pain of losing their jobs. This is because of article 11 of the European Convention on Human Rights, and the decision of the European Court of Human Rights in *Young, James and Webster* v *UK*.[5]

TULRA, as amended in 1976, provided that unions and management could enter into a union membership agreement requiring a specific class of employees to belong to one or more specified trade unions. Where such an agreement existed (and there was no obligation to conclude one), a dismissal for failure to belong to the union would be potentially fair,[6] with an exception being made for people who had genuine religious objections to trade union membership.[7] Dunn and Gennard have shown that by mid-1978, at least 5.2 million employees in Great Britain were known to be in closed shops, this amounting to 23 per cent of the total workforce.[8] Since then the numbers in formal union membership agreements has fallen sharply. The principal reason for this decline appears to have been the new legal environment which is hostile to the closed shop.[9] It is true that the closed shop may have been pushed underground in many cases, as it was during the period of the Industrial Relations Act 1971, when employers and unions colluded to maintain informally that which was prohibited by law.[10] However, the fact remains that save in those industries (mainly shipping and printing) where the pre-entry closed shop is still important, there are now few workers who can be lawfully dismissed or otherwise prejudiced in their employment because they are not union members.

The Employment Acts 1980–2 provided that a valid union membership agreement must be approved in a ballot of the workers affected by it. An agreement made for the first time must be approved by 80 per cent of those eligible to vote. In addition, all agreements must be approved in a ballot every five years by either 80 per cent of those eligible to vote or 85 per cent of those actually voting. Otherwise a dismissal for non-membership will be automatically unfair. However, even where a valid ballot has been held, there are a wide range of exemptions, whereby people may be permitted not to join even though they may have voted in the ballot. These include workers who were not union members at the time the agreement was introduced and who have never been members; workers who object to membership on grounds of conscience or some other deeply held personal belief;[11] and workers who have been unreasonably excluded or expelled from membership. Although it is quite likely that this legislation will be modified by an incoming Labour government,[12] there are limits as to how far it will be able to go. Article 11 of the European Convention safeguards the right to freedom of association, including the right to belong to a trade union.[13] Although the European Court has stopped short of holding that this embraces the right not to belong, it did nevertheless hold that the British legislation of 1974/76 was a violation of the Convention.[14] In particular, it held that in order to be lawful a union membership agreement must first allow for the protection of non-members at the time the agreement is signed; secondly, allow for objection to membership on grounds of conscience as well as religion; and thirdly, allow for a choice of unions to which the individual may be permitted to belong.[15]

Collective Bargaining

Although the closed shop is an important reason for limited intervention, it should not now be exaggerated. It now covers a rather limited area and it may not be possible to return to the legislation of the mid-1970s. In any event, the closed shop justifies only very limited intervention. It invites regulation on arbitrary exclusions and expulsions, and otherwise unjust treatment of a member. It also justifies some regulation of political action, such as that which is provided by the Trade Union Act 1913.[16] However, it is difficult to see that the closed shop can justify any more intrusive regulation. There is in fact a more powerful reason for subjecting unions to special legal rules. This justification for intervention lies in the main function of unions which is the regulation of jobs through collective bargaining. Collective bargaining is not simply concerned with the improvement of the material well-being of workers. Indeed, if this were its only achievement it might be difficult to justify the unions' continuing existence since economists continue to debate long and hard whether unions have historically made any significant impact on the level of wages in this country. However, collective bargaining does more than influence the material well-being of union members. It regulates labour management as well as labour markets and fulfils a vital function as a method of industrial democracy. Flanders has stated it thus:

. . . the value of a union to its members lies less in its economic achievements than in its capacity to protect their dignity. Viewed from this angle, employees — white collar no less than manual workers — have an interest in union organisation, however favourable their economic circumstances or the state of the labour market, for at least two reasons. They are interested in the regulation of labour markets and labour management because such regulation defines their rights, and consequently their status and security, and so liberates them from dependence on chance and the arbitrary will of others. Equally they are interested in participating as directly as possible in the making and administration of these rules in order to have a voice in shaping their own destiny and the decisions on which it most depends.[17]

On this basis an important function of trade unionism would be lost if the autocratic power of management was to be modified by the autocratic power of the union. Hughes has argued, 'Whatever form further developments in "industrial democracy" may take, they must rest heavily upon the representative character of the unions and on the arrangements for representation and accountability of representatives within them'.[18]

An argument which reinforces this particular justification for some form of intervention in union rules and practices is the fact that the process of collective bargaining now receives statutory support in a variety of ways. It is true that the statutory framework has been dismantled in several important respects since 1979. In particular, the right of unions to secure recognition through the medium of a third-party agency (ACAS) has been abolished,[19] as has the right to secure 'fair wages' for members by the use of the Fair Wages Resolution[20] and Schedule 11 of the Employment Protection Act 1975.[21] Nevertheless, unions can still take advantage of legislative provisions which will enable them to require employers to disclose information to their officials for the purpose of negotiation,[22] and also to permit their officials to take time off with pay to exercise their functions.[23] Moreover, it is possible in certain circumstances for collective agreements to be made which replace statutory rights. Agreements over such matters as redundancy pay,[24] guaranteed pay[25] or unfair dismissals[26] may have the effect of revoking the legislative provisions on these matters for the workers covered by the agreements, whether those workers are union members or not, and the negotiated terms are then substituted in place of the statutory provisions.[27] It is true that before this can occur the agreement generally has to be approved by the relevant Minister, and the likelihood of it being less satisfactory to the worker than the statute is very slim indeed. Nevertheless if unions are to take advantage of these provisions (and admittedly few do at present),[28] it seems unreasonable that the state should allow the decisions made by what might be termed a process of industrial democracy to be substituted for those made by the process of political democracy without securing for the individual worker at least the right not to be arbitrarily refused the opportunity of influencing that decision, however limited that influence might be. After all, once the agreement has been approved, the worker has no right to reject it and opt for the statutory provisions, even should he or she wish to do so. The argument that legal support for collective bargaining justifies some legal intervention will become more forceful should the Labour Party be elected to government again. In a policy document published in 1985, the Labour Party is committed to providing 'workers with positive rights to information, consultation and representation in company decisions'.[29] This seems to endorse the policies advocated before the 1983 general election when the following matters were described as 'key elements' in the party's programme:

(a) the *right to information*. A new right is needed on the disclosure of information to trade union representatives which would expand the range of issues covered and make the company's books available for inspection.

(b) the *right to consultation*. A right to be consulted in advance on actions and decisions affecting workers' interests would put trade unions in a stronger position to make use of information and play a more creative and responsible role in the decisions that shape industry's future. This role could be developed in workplace 'planning committees' made up of Joint Union Committee representatives and management.

(c) a *right to representation*. A right for workers to be represented through their trade union machinery, up to and including boards of management, would allow them to develop a permanent and continuous influence over all aspects of enterprise planning. Workers will be able to build up to 50/50 representation on the board of directors, or with a third element where this is mutually agreed.[30]

Freedom of Association

But although there may thus be a case for some intervention, there is a major obstacle. This is the doctrine of freedom of association, which is widely recognized as being essential for effective trade unionism.

Otherwise, trade unions could not exist and they would be unable to act in the interests of their members. Essentially, freedom of association has two dimensions. The first is the freedom of individuals to join and take part in the activities of trade unions without inteference by employers or the state. This is reflected in ILO Convention 87[31] which provides that workers and employers shall have the right to establish and to join organizations of their own choosing.[32] It is also reflected in ILO Convention 98[33] which seeks to guarantee to workers 'adequate protection against acts of anti-union discrimination in respect of their employment'.[34] In Britain the state does not impose sanctions — whether criminal or civil — on workers who join trade unions, though exceptionally the state as employer denies to civil servants the right to belong to them.[35] The notorious example of this is the withdrawal of the right to belong to staff employed at GCHQ, a decision taken ostensibly for reasons of national security and which has been held by the ILO Commitee of Experts to be a breach of Convention 87. In principle, however, the policy in recent years has been to recognize the importance of freedom of association and to intervene to protect it. The most visible manifestations of this are sections 23 and 58 of the Labour government's Employment Protection (Consolidation) Act 1978 which makes it unlawful for an employer to take action short of dismissal against an employee, or to dismiss an employee because the employee in question is a member of an independent trade union or has taken part in the activities of such a union at an appropriate time.

A second dimension of freedom of association is the right of the group to conduct its activities without the intrusive supervision of the state. This is also recognized by ILO Convention 87 which provides by Article 3 that:

> Workers' and employers' organisations shall have the right to draw up their constitutions and rules, to elect their representatives in full freedom, to organise their administration and activities and to formulate their programmes.

Article 3 then provides that 'The public authorities shall refrain from any interference which would restrict the right or impede the lawful exercise thereof'. If taken literally, this would appear to exclude any intervention in the internal affairs of trade unions. Perhaps the only form of legislative intervention in Britain which would be consistent with the letter of Article 3 is the Trade Union Act 1871 which sought to remove all judicial supervision of the affairs of trade unions. In fact, however, Article 3 has not been interpreted literally and indeed permits considerable scope for intervention in the internal affairs of trade unions. Perhaps the most relevant recent illustration relates to the complaint submitted by the Amalgamated Metal Workers' Union against the government of Australia in 1976.[36] In this case the union complained about the government's intention to require that union elections should be by postal ballot, the elections to be conducted by a government electoral officer. The union argued that such a procedure had been shown in the past 'to be wide open to gross interference by outside bodies financed and operated on behalf of corporations'.[37]

Between the making of the complaint and the decision of the Committee on Freedom of Association, legislation was in fact passed. This differed from the original proposal, however, in a number of important respects. The proposal that elections should be conducted by the Australian Electoral Officer met strong publicly expressed opposition from the trade union movement. As a result the government modified the legislation, dropping this requirement though retaining an option whereby unions could if they so chose request an officially conducted ballot at government expense. However, the Act did retain mandatory postal ballots, though it was also recognized that in special circumstances there may be other methods of election in which all members would be given an adequate opportunity to vote without intimidation and which would result in greater participation by members. A union which had rules making such provision could claim exemption from the statutory requirements. These measures in fact left the union with a rather hollow complaint, given that its own rules provided for postal balloting. Nevertheless, it was contended that mandatory postal balloting was a denial of fundamental rights and prevented the unions from determining their own structures on the basis of the industries they were associated with and the historical developments of their organizations. The case thus turned on a very important point of principle: is statutory regulation of the structure of government consistent with the requirements of Convention 87? The Australian government stoutly resisted the case against it, arguing that the fundamental objective of the legislation was to ensure a greater degree of industrial democracy and the fullest possible participation of members of employers' associations and union members in determining who should be their office bearers, and again to ensure that every member of a registered union or employer's organization had a real opportunity, without intimidation, to choose who should conduct the affairs of that organization.

The complaint was dismissed. It is true that the Committee of Freedom of Association did consider that any intervention by the public authorities in trade union elections 'runs the risk of appearing arbitrary and thus constituting interference in the operation of workers' organisations, which is incompatible with their right to elect their representatives in full freedom'.[38] In this case, however, the legislation was limited to imposing on organizations an obligation to elect their leaders by secret postal vote, without intervention from the administrative authorities except at the request of the organization concerned. The Committee concluded by noting that 'the government proposed these amendments in order to ensure the greatest possible participation of members in elections. Such procedural arrangements regarding elections do not appear to restrict the freedom of workers to elect their representatives. In these circumstances, the Committee recommends the Governing Body to decide that this case calls for no further examination.'[39] The approach adopted by the Committee suggests strongly that governments have a wide room for maneouvre in regulating the internal affairs of trade unions. Freedom of association does not mean complete autonomy *in* association, and would not appear to be an obstacle to any of the legislation operating in Britain to date. If the Australian case is a guide, then neither the Industrial Relations Act 1971 nor the Trade Union Act 1984 sailed remotely close to the frontiers of Convention 87. In fact, not only does freedom of association restrain intervention in internal self-government, it may indeed require intervention in some cases. In the constitutional law of other legal systems, freedom of association has been the basis and justification for intervention. For example, in the United States,[40] and now in Canada,[41] the right to freedom of association has been interpreted to require unions to operate plans to permit members to contract out of the obligation to finance political activity of the union. Freedom of association means that individuals have the right not to be forced into compulsory political association.[42]

THE SCOPE OF INTERVENTION

The function of job regulation and the methods employed by trade unions provide justification for a degree of legal intervention in the internal affairs of trade unions. An important point to note, however, is that these different issues justify different kinds of regulation. The closed shop and the promotion of political objects justify limited forms of intervention: the right not to be arbitrarily excluded or expelled from membership, and perhaps the right not to contribute to the financing of political activity to which the member objects, even though the majority perceive it to be in the interests of the union. Collective bargaining as a basis for intervention suggests, however, a case for a greater degree of intervention. If collective bargaining provides a right to participate in the rule-making process, trade union membership must permit access to this activity. As a result, collective bargaining suggests a need to protect not just the right to membership, but also the right of participation in the affairs of the union itself.

This inevitably raises very contentious issues, for it suggests a degree of regulation of union constitutions and interference with the right of a union autonomously to determine its own rules. The simple question then is this: how far should law go to protect or ensure the right to participate in the affairs of a trade union? Is it the function of law to impose some basic framework or standard of democracy with which all trade unions must comply? One problem about answering in the affirmative is that union democracy remains an elusive concept, and there are almost as many theories about it as there are writers on the subject. Nevertheless, an examination of the different concepts employed does reveal some interesting themes lying beneath the apparent confusion. Perhaps the most striking impression which emerges is the different approach adopted by the social scientist in contrast with the lawyer. To the former, the fundamental problem facing democracy has been, in the words of the Webbs, to reconcile 'a combination of administrative efficiency with popular control',[43] and discussion has centred mainly on the psychological, sociological and institutional conditions which enable this reconciliation to be achieved. It is the interrelationship between the union officials, both the full-time and lay officers, and the members which has provided the primary concern for the social scientist.

In contrast, lawyers have tended to emphasize a different aspect of union democracy. Generally they have not been so concerned to develop a comprehensive theory of union democracy but have focused on certain aspects of it only.[44] Their special concern has been with the individual, an almost instinctive response, perhaps, of their training in the traditions of the common law. It is the cry of individual oppression to which they are most carefully attuned. Consequently, they have stressed the rights and guarantees which will secure that the individual union member is fairly treated by his or her union.[45] This approach lays stress upon a different relationship within the union, that between the individual member and the organization. The lawyer then emphasizes member protection from abuse of power by the union, whereas the social scientist emphasizes member control. These two aspects of union democracy are obviously not entirely unrelated. It may sometimes be the case that the individual member or a minority within the union is unfairly treated precisely because the union officials are not sufficiently subject to control by the members. Furthermore, the protection of members from unfair treatment is a prerequisite of effective member control. Even the barest opposition to union policies cannot flourish if opponents can be arbitrarily expelled at the whim of union officials.

Union Democracy as Member Protection

If we see the function of union democracy as an instrument of member protection, what we are concerned with is union democracy as a concept of basic guarantees for union members, based upon the belief that unions should comply with certain standards of fair treatment and should not treat any member or minority group oppressively. It requires that unions should be justly governed. Inevitably in any organization there is tension between the powers of the governing body and its ability to take effective decisions on the one hand, and the rights of the individual to fair treatment on the other. The problem of reconciling the clash between the power of government and the interests of individual rights is perhaps most clearly and sharply defined in the realm of constitutional law. Here the solution, insofar as it is achieved, finds its expression in the constitutional principle referred to as the rule of law. While this is admittedly a vague concept, it can provide a suitable starting point for an analysis of membership rights in trade unions. Selznick has defined the essential purpose of the rule of law as 'the restraint of official power by rational principles of civic order'.[46] It is the application and adherence to the rule of law that provides the individual with some degree of protection from the naked power of the state.

These principles derived from the rule of law can equally be applied to the relation between the trade union and the member. To do so does not involve the general conclusion that the trade union can be compared with the state for all purposes. It is simply to recognize that the problem to which the rule of law is addressed, that is the attempt to find the balance between individual rights and official power, is common to both. What then are the principles that constitute the rule of law? This is a matter of some debate, though traditionally the notion extends purely to executive and not to legislative acts. Goodhart, for example, has described the rule of law as 'the machinery by which effect can be given to such basic rights as are recognised in any particular legal system'.[47] Such a concept requires merely strict and impartial adherence to the law. This will generally also involve adherence to adequate procedural safeguards, not as a prerequisite to the impartial and objective application of the law, but as an aid to that process. While this concept of the rule of law will provide some constraints upon the manner in which official powers are exercised, it need provide no protection against oppression at all, because it leaves untouched the content of the rules themselves; and, as Hart has pointed out, the notion of proceeding by the rules is compatible with the greatest injustice if the rules themselves are unjust.[48]

Consequently, if union members are to be fairly treated, it is necessary to establish not only strict conformity to the rules, but also that the rules themselves are just. It is not only the executive but also the legislative function of the union that must be closely scrutinized. But it is also necessary to go a stage further than this. Frequently a rule itself will be perfectly acceptable, but a policy or discretion made under a rule can be arbitrary or unfair. For example, a union could have a rule stipulating that it will admit into membership anyone it considers suitable and yet have an unwritten policy that it will not permit persons of a particular sex — just as the Jockey Club did in the case of *Nagle* v *Fielden*.[49] Likewise, the exercise of a discretion in a particular instance may be arbitrary or capricious, such as rejecting people because a union official has taken an irrational dislike to them. If misuse of power is to be controlled, then in those rare examples where it does occur it is not just the written rules which need to be subject to regulation but also the policies, both written and unwritten, and the exercises of discretion. The principles which are necessary to ensure fair treatment can therefore be broken down into three successive hurdles, each being more rigorous than its predecessor:[50]

(1) Members should be covered by general, clearly enunciated rules or policies. Unions should be governed in accordance with the rules.
(2) The rules and policies should be impartially and fairly applied.
(3) The rules and policies themselves should not be arbitrary or unjustifiably discriminatory; and discretionary powers should not be exercised in an arbitrary or unjustifiably discriminatory fashion.

These principles suggest that there will necessarily be some external regulation of union rules. The first consequence is that there may be some externally imposed requirement to have rules covering particular issues. The Donovan Commission also concluded that trade union rules should be clear and unambiguous, but that they generally fell far short of a satisfactory standard in these respects.[51] The Commission then pre-scribed a number of requirements with which union rules should comply 'with a view to ensuring better safeguards for individual members, but without impairing the freedom which trade unions ought to enjoy to frame rules to meet their own circumstances'.[52] The proposals covered five areas. First, the rules should state who is qualified for admission. Secondly, a separate rule should set out the disciplinary offences and the procedure for dealing with disciplinary charges. Thirdly, the rules should prescribe a procedure for settling disputes between a member and the union or an officer of the union. Fourthly, the rules should pre-scribe procedures for elections, dealing for example with the making of nominations, canvassing, and the issue and control of ballot papers in elections where a ballot is required. Finally, the rules should deal expressly with the position of shop stewards, prescribing their term of office and the manner in which they may be issued with credentials.[53] There is nothing particularly novel in these proposals. For example the Trade Union Act 1871, imposed requirements as to the subject-matter of union rules. Donovan merely proposed that these should be extended. Nor is there anything inherently dangerous in such a proposal. Unions would not be required to have rules on these questions; they would merely be required to specify them where they did exist.

The second consequence of the three principles outlined above is that there would be some external body ensuring that union rules were observed (principle one) and that powers under the rules were exercised in accordance with natural justice (principle two). Traditionally this function has been carried out by the courts — at least since the rejection of the self-government policy of the 1871 Act. The notion of some form of control which involves no more than an external agency requiring the union to stick to its own rules is not particularly controversial. Few trade unionists today would support the pure autonomy argument, the idea that there should be no external regulation of their affairs at all. Trade unionists are often dissatisfied with the way in which the judges interpret their rules, and also with the reluctance of the courts to recognize the advantages of internal disputes being settled by the unions' own domestic procedures where possible. As a result there is opposition to the principle of control according to the constitution where that role is left to the judges, opposition which was not likely to have been overcome by the performance of the judges in the miners' strike of 1984/85. Indeed, in 1986 the TUC expressed the view that:

> . . . remedies have always been available through the ordinary courts on the basis of the constitution and rules of the union being a contract of membership and the requirements of natural justice. Indeed over the years a number of judicial decisions adverse to unions' interests have resulted from such cases. The law in this area clearly needs rationalising and should be recast to take full account of the effective self-regulation practised by the Movement in this area and the need to strike a fair balance between unions' collective interests and the interests of the individual concerned which have traditionally been favoured by the law and the courts.[54]

However, the concern is not with the idea of external scrutiny to uphold the rules, but rather it is with the fact that the function is performed by the judges who are perceived as hostile to the interests of trade unions.

The third consequence of the three principles referred to above is much more controversial in the sense that it may mean that the substance of the rules will be subject to scrutiny. It also means that the exercise of discretionary power under the rules may also be subject to scrutiny. To some extent these controls can also be exercised through the traditional contractual mechanisms. Union rules themselves cannot be controlled in this way, save to the limited extent that public policy provides a narrow — though admittedly expanding — compass within which rules can be struck out. However, discretions are capable of being regulated by implying a term in the contract of membership that they should be exercised fairly. This is precisely what Lord Denning did in *Breen* v *AEU*,[55] when he held that a union committee which had the power to confirm or reject the election of a shop steward had to exercise its discretion fairly. On this basis, therefore, control over discretions can be subsumed under the principle of control according to the constitution. In practice, though, very few cases indeed have raised the question of how discretionary power within the union should be exercised. But if control is to be exercised over the rules themselves, this should be done by legislation rather than by the courts. Such intervention would, however, be required only to a modest degree. Indeed, the principle is already accepted by the unions with the application of the Sex Discrimination Act 1975 and Race Relations Act 1976 to trade union affairs. The Trade Union Act 1913 also makes it unlawful to discriminate against a member for non-contribution to the political fund. *It is difficult in fact to see how much further law ought to intervene in this respect*, though there is perhaps one possibility. It would be consistent with the arguments developed in this chapter to have a provision whereby workers should not be unreasonably excluded or expelled from a trade union, even where a closed shop does not operate. *It is unlikely, however, whether in practice such a law is necessary for reasons outlined at the beginning of Chapter 3.*

Union Democracy as Member Control

It is submitted then that there is a role for law in providing a floor of rights for union members to protect them from unfair or arbitrary treatment. The question which now arises, however, is whether there is a role for more intrusive intervention. Should the law lay down a framework of trade union democracy? The answer to this question depends to a large extent on perceptions of trade union function. If the function of unions lies primarily in improving the material position of workers, then the answer to both of these questions will be firmly in the negative. This perception of union function emphasizes materialism rather than idealism; it sees the union as a service rather than a movement, and as a means of achieving economic and social advantages *for* the member rather than *by* them. It is often referred to as 'business unionism'. Allen has argued that:

> Trade union organisation is not based on theoretical concepts prior to it, that is on some concept of democracy, but on the end it serves. In other words, the end of trade union activity is to protect and improve the general living standards of its members and not to provide the workers with an exercise in self-government.[56]

This stress on efficiency in materialistic terms often involves the corollary that the union should be run by officials.[57] Bargaining is seen as a skilled activity which should be left to the professionals. When this assumption is made, there is no apparent need for democracy at all. Indeed, democracy can be seen as positively undesirable if it is thought to have an adverse effect on union efficiency. For example, John L. Lewis, the former leader of the United Mineworkers of America, justified the presence of autocratic powers in the trade union by arguing that it was a question of 'whether you desire your organisation to be the most effective instrumentality . . . or whether you prefer to sacrifice the efficiency of your organisation for a little more academic freedom'.[58] And, indeed, there may well be substance in the view that a union's success or failure will lie in its ability to improve and safeguard the living standards of its members. In this context, the exercise in self-government is only a by-product, a safeguard against an entrenched oligarchy ignoring rank and file opinion.

It tends, nevertheless, to be assumed that unions ought to be democratic in some sense, if only because the democratic ethic is pervasive and it is difficult to defend an institution which lacks any pretension to being democratic. There is, however, a more compelling reason. The case for democratic government is related closely to the main function of trade unionism which, in the words of Flanders, is 'participation in job regulation'.[59] The case for democratic government is related also to the function of joint regulation and collective bargaining. As Summers has argued, the attempt to replace managerial prerogative by industrial democracy 'can be fulfilled only if unions which sit at the bargaining table are themselves democratic'.[60] In other words, collective bargaining as an activity — and the support of the state to that activity as a means of industrial self-government — justifies not just intervention to protect against arbitrary or unfair treatment. It also invites the requirement of a democratic and accountable organization for the fulfilment of that goal.

Yet it may be questioned whether law has any useful role in this context. The nature of government in a trade union will depend upon a wide range of factors. Turner has stressed the different characteristics of the members as an important factor.[61] Hughes has emphasized the importance of labour turnover and membership scatter,[62] while Hyman has emphasized the existence of rival factions within the union and the extent to which there is a tradition of democracy as factors which prevent the emergence of an oligarchic structure.[63] Again, Martin has argued that democracy exists where organized opposition is tolerated in a union, and gives twelve categories of factors which may constrain the leadership to tolerate opposition.[64] These include political culture, government attitudes and behaviour, pattern of membership distribution, union structure, and the collective bargaining system. What this indicates is that however democracy is defined, many of the relevant factors which help to promote it lie wholly outside the influence of the union itself. The inner workings of union government are significantly moulded by external factors over which neither officials nor members have any control. To take a simple example, union preference for decentralized bargaining may be wholly frustrated by such factors as high unemployment or the opposition of a strong employers' group favouring centralized negotiations. Second, it follows that many of these factors are likewise beyond the influence of the law. They are too diverse and too uncertain to be subject to legal regulation. The law can at best have but a modest role to play in furthering union democracy in the sense of member control.

But the law is not a wholly irrelevant force in fostering union democracy. In particular, the constitutional arrangements which a union adopts will inevitably be one of the factors which hinders or helps the creation of union democracy in the form of member control. There are perhaps a number of steps which might be taken in this direction. First, there seems no objection to require unions to make public certain information about their affairs, and in particular about the state of their finances. Such an obligation has in fact been in existence, at least for registered unions, ever since the Trade Union Act 1871, though the provisions have been modified and extended since then.[65] Secondly, there is no reason why a government should not seek to encourage unions to adopt one method of government rather than another. In particular, there is nothing intrinsically objectionable in the provisions of the Employment Act 1980 which made funds available to give free postal facilities to unions wishing to conduct postal ballots on certain matters. Indeed, such a source of finance may remove the economic constraints which would otherwise render this option impractical. Similarly in 1969 the then Labour government proposed in its White Paper

In Place of Strife[66] that money should be made available to promote union mergers. Of course, this means that the government is not then remaining wholly neutral and indifferent about the method of government which the members choose because clearly it thereby hopes that such ballots will be adopted. No doubt the particular proposal relating to postal ballots is often suggested by those who are not particularly concerned about union members' democratic rights but feel — and perhaps mistakenly — that union members are less militant than their officers, so that ballots for officers will tend to produce more 'moderate' union officials, and ballots on strikes will tend to lessen the incidence of industrial action. Distrust of the motives of government might well lead the unions to reject the offer of financial help, as many unions did in relation to the support provided by the Employment Act 1980. They saw this particular handout as the thin edge of a wedge which might lead to fuller regulation in time — a fear fully borne out by the Trade Union Act 1984. Moreover, there are some sound reasons why a union might choose not to hold a postal ballot despite the subsidy. However, providing the obligation to hold ballots is not imposed — and there is a chasm between imposing ballots and providing financial support — there seems no reason in principle why any government should not in this indirect way express a preference for the kind of government it would like a union to adopt, and the debate within the union can then take place on the merits of postal ballots, free from any economic considerations.

But is there a role for more active intervention by the state? Despite the initial resistance of the unions and the Labour movement to the 1984 Act, it is evident that attitudes have changed. Increasingly, it is being accepted that the state may in fact have a positive role to play in trade union internal affairs. In an important pamphlet,[67] Lord McCarthy (who led the opposition in the House of Lords to the 1984 Act) has argued that 'what is required is agreement on a set of "democratic guidelines", or "minimum rule-book standards" '.[68] These measures would be embodied in a Code of Practice, which would be taken into account in determining whether the different unions could take advantage of new but unspecified 'statutory participative rights at the place of work'.[69] In other words, to take full advantage of the statute, 'unions would have to show that their internal decision-making processes measured up to standards set out in the Code of Practice'.[70] This would provide 'both an incentive and the means to improve democratic practices'.[71] So far as elections are concerned, members of a trade union executive 'should emerge as the result of a process of *individual* voting — either by means of direct participation, or by a "mix" of direct and indirect methods'.[72] Indeed, McCarthy goes so far as to suggest that 'One result of guidelines of this kind would be the elimination of practices like branch block voting — where those who attend can commit the entire vote of the branch to the candidate they favour'.[73] These are important proposals simply because they represent an acceptance by a senior figure in the Labour movement of the legitimate role of the state in trade union government. Although McCarthy is far from clear on the status of the Code of Practice, it is to be produced after agreement with the TUC, thereby suggesting some corporatist initiative. And although it is not clear whether the Code would be statutory or voluntary in origin and status, it seems intended to have some legal force. Thus McCarthy also proposes that all union–member disputes should be transferred to industrial tribunals which would have regard to the Code of Practice.[74] The Code would thereby be given a legal status of sorts.

It is to be noted that Lord McCarthy is not alone in his willingness to embrace some form of state intervention in the government of trade unions. In 1986 the TUC engaged in a process of consultation with affiliated bodies about the future of labour law. As part of this process, it published a consultative document in January 1986.[75] In the document, the General Council repeated its opposition to the 1984 Act 'on the grounds that the legislation amounts to unwarranted state interference in unions' internal affairs, and overriding unions' constitutions and rules which are democractically determined by their members'.[76] It is now recognized, however, that it 'may be difficult to convince many trade unionists, let alone the wider public, that the present provision should be swept away without action being taken which would place strong emphasis on membership involvement and participation in union decisions. . . . To simply remove these provisions and not introduce some new measures in this area could lead to accusations that unions were diminishing the rights of members and were undemocratic.'[77] The General Council continued by asserting:

> It is clear that the trade union Movement and a future Labour Government would need to agree a balanced framework of measures to underpin the participative rights of union members. It is not envisaged that this would be exclusively or even predominantly legislative in form. Indeed, internal union affairs and detailed questions of workplace facilities for union democratic procedures are the proper responsibility of unions and would be more appropriately backed up by TUC guidance or an agreed Code of Practice setting out certain effective basic standards and safeguards for members while enabling the widest possible range of methods of membership participation.[78]

A number of affiliated unions did in fact make submissions in response to the consultative document. Those which addressed this question (in what was otherwise a wide-ranging document) divided into three groups. The first were those unions which favoured the retention of a statutory obligation to elect the national executive committee. These included EETPU, AUEW, UCW, UCATT and Equity, while CPSA made favourable noises. In each case the union either expressed unequivocal approval (AUEW) or a need for liberalization of the framework. The second category were those unions which favoured some form of Code of Practice, though it is unclear whether this would be drafted by the TUC alone, or in consultation with the government. The unions in this category included IPCS, NAS/UWT, USDAW, NUPE and ACTT. The third and final category of unions included TASS, NALGO, NUM and SCPS. They were against any form of external intervention in the internal affairs of their unions.

The consultative process of 1986 was not confined to the question of election to union executive committees. It also revealed interesting attitudes to strike ballots. The General Council remained critical of Part II of the 1984 Act on the ground that 'the provisions that the Conservative Government claims are designed to protect the interests of union members are in fact enforceable by employers, or customers, suppliers or other persons adversely affected by the industrial action, seeking an injunction or damages'.[79] On the other hand, however, it was acknowledged that 'many union members are coming to expect as of right a direct vote on decisions relating to industrial action'.[80] The General Council continued:

> If a Labour Government's policy was to encourage strike ballots in some form or other, enforcement of members' rights in this respect should not be linked to the lawfulness *per se* of the industrial action concerned (injunctions, damages etc) but should take the form of union members making a complaint about a failure to hold a ballot on the basis of union rules and/or the Code of Practice outlined above which if upheld might result in an order simply requiring that a ballot should now be held.[81]

A number of individual unions also addressed this matter in their responses to the Consultative Document. Again three different positions were adopted by those which tackled the question and in so doing were clear as to their intentions. The first were those unions — the EETPU and AUEW — which were in favour of retaining Part II of the 1984 Act. In the case of the EETPU, it was argued that the Act should be amended 'so that the failure to give a member a vote should not invalidate the whole ballot where the members' vote would not have made any material difference to the result'.[82] A second group of unions were those in favour of replacing the existing legislation with a different legal framework — with the emphasis on enforcement by the union member rather than by the employer. Unions in this category included UCW, APEX and NATFHE. In the case of UCW, it was argued that 'the precise procedure for balloting should be an internal matter for unions to determine — provided every member has a fair opportunity to participate in voting'.[83] Little detailed consideration was given to the question of enforcement, though various options included the courts, industrial tribunals and the TUC. The third group of responses were those in favour of repeal without replacement legislation. These included NALGO, NUPE and TASS.

The consultative process has thus revealed some support for the principles embodied in Parts I and II of the 1984 Act, though in some cases the support was conditional on fairly sweeping modifications to the content of the legislation. Perhaps unsurprisingly in view of the ballot results, the consultative process revealed also not inconsiderable support for Part III of the 1984 Act. On the question of political funding, the General Council set out three options.[84] These were:

(a) returning to the position under the Trade Union Act 1913 by removing requirements for periodic review;
(b) amending the law to enable a trade union to engage freely in whatever political activity it chooses. This would involve not only the repeal of Part III, but also the removal of the constraints imposed by the 1913 Act;
(c) retaining Part III but enacting similar provisions for companies.

The General Council appeared to favour the last of these options:

Of these, the latter (sic) option might well be the most desirable. Abolishing any legal regulation of union political activities is not without difficulty. Some members of unions who do not support the Labour Party might well drop out of union membership or seek to form alternative organisations if they had no individual option to contract out of payment of the political levy as there is now. Others might mount strong challenges to union executives at union conferences about the use of union funds for political purposes related to political parties. They might also campaign for union funds to be channelled to political parties other than Labour. The existence of separate political funds has, by and large, avoided these problems and, with careful organisation and thoughtful presentation of the issues, unions have so far without exception been successful in

retaining their political funds in the review ballots required by the
Act, and in doing so have strengthened support for their political
activities among their members.[85]

But as with the other issues discussed so far, no clear view emerged from
the affiliated organizations. There was support for option one from
ACTT, COHSE and USDAW; for option two from TASS, NALGO,
NUM and SCPS; and for option three from IPCS, AUEW, CPSA,
NATFHE, UCW and EETPU. It is to be noted, however, that a number of organizations were strongly opposed to imposing constraints on
company political spending which were comparable to those imposed on
unions. These included GMBATU, NALGO and UCATT with the last
claiming that 'The political fund requirement of the 1984 Act has so far
backfired on the Tories. The extension of the legislation to cover companies could similarly backfire on us. Indeed it might mean *increased* donations both to the Tories and to the SDP/Liberal Alliance.'[86]

The Means of Intervention

Having established the basis for intervention and the nature which that
intervention might take, the final question relates to the means of intervention. The crucial question, however, is whether the state should have
a hand in trade union affairs and, if so, how far it should intrude. As we
have seen, there is a growing awareness, in the Labour movement and
elsewhere, that the state does have a role to play, and a not inconsiderable
one at that. It does not follow, however, that the state should intrude by
means of legislation. The other option is for a system of self-regulation,
that is to say, for a system whereby the TUC and the government agree
to a series of guidelines, with these being embodied in a Code of Practice
issued by the TUC, and with the Code being policed and enforced by the
TUC. As already pointed out, such an option was favoured by a number
of unions in their submissions to the Consultative Conference on March
19, 1986.

The concept of self-regulation is by no means new. In 1968 the
Donovan Commission suggested the introduction of a number of legal
restrictions on trade union internal affairs. On admission, the rules
should be 'framed in such a way as to avoid discriminating arbitrarily
against any type of applicant, but unions must be allowed to retain
discretion in deciding whom they should admit'.[87] On discipline, the
rules should set out the disciplinary penalties, the disciplinary procedure, and provide for a right of appeal.[88] The rules should also lay
down a procedure for resolving disputes between a member and the

union,[89] and prescribe procedures for elections.[90] The rules would be supervised by a Registrar and a new statutory Independent Review Body would be established to deal with complaints between members and the union.[91] The TUC responded to these proposals by concluding that there was 'no convincing evidence that there was a serious problem',[92] but that they would 'give further consideration to the case for establishing certain basic principles to cover admissions, discipline and elections and would consider what machinery might be established under TUC auspices as a last resort for aggrieved individuals who had exhausted the unions' appeal machinery'.[93] In 1969 the General Council formulated a series of principles which it recommended trade unions to observe in their rules. Although they are lengthy, we set them out below. First, because they provide an interesting yardstick of the minimum rule book requirements which the General Council thought ought to govern trade unions, and secondly because they are not readily accessible.

ADMISSIONS

On admissions to membership the General Council recommended that union rules should observe the following principles:

1. A separate rule or section of the rule book should state clearly who is qualified for admission to the trade union or any separate section of the union.
2. A separate rule or section of the rule book should prescribe the procedures for admission and indicate when ratification of membership is complete.
3. A separate rule or section of the rule book should prescribe who has the power to consider and decide applications for admission.
4. A separate rule or section of the rule book should prescribe for what reasons an application for admission can be rejected.
5. The rules should provide that a rejected applicant should be informed of the reasons for his rejection.
6. The rules should provide for a right of appeal for an applicant who is refused admission.
7. The rules should provide that the right of appeal can be exercised by the rejected applicant himself.
8. Where the refusal is at branch, district, or regional level, the rules should provide that the appeal should be to a body which is:
    (a) of higher authority than the one which rejected the application, and
    (b) is comprised of persons other than those who rejected the application and who do not have a personal interest in the application.

9. The rules should provide that a rejected applicant should be informed at the time of his rejection of:
   (a) his right of appeal; and
   (b) the appeals procedures.
10. The rules should provide that the executive committee (or equivalent body) should have the power to admit applicants where an appeal is upheld.

DISCIPLINE

On discipline the members of the General Council recommended that union rules should observe the following principles:
1. A separate rule or section of the rule book should set out the offences for which the union is entitled under the rules to expel or take other disciplinary action and the penalties applicable for each of these offences.
2. A separate rule or section of the rule book should prescribe the procedure for the hearing of cases in which offences against the rules are alleged, such procedure or procedures to comply with the rules of natural justice. The General Council recommend that the rules of natural justice be taken to comprise the following:
   (a) The opportunity of being heard: this involves the following conditions:
       (i) a reasonably convenient time and place;
       (ii) a timely notice: the member concerned should be given sufficient notice to enable him both to prepare his defence and to get to the hearing;
       (iii) a sufficiently informative notice: the notice should be complete and not misleading.
   (b) A fair hearing and a bona-fide decision: this can be taken to comprise the following elements:
       (i) member's rights at a hearing: it is suggested that a member, should have the right to put his side of the case whether orally or in writing; to support his case by testimony, whether through witnesses or written statements; to hear the evidence against him; and to have an opportunity of answering it, and of questioning witnesses;
       (ii) a bona-fide decision: the adjudicating body should attempt to reach an honest decision, i.e. a decision which is unbiased and in accordance with the evidence presented and with the rules of the union.
3. The rules should provide for a right of appeal against the imposition of any penalty.

4. A separate rule or section of the rule book should prescribe the procedure or procedures for the hearing of appeals against the imposition of penalties, which should comply with the rules of natural justice (as stated above).
5. The rules should provide that an appeal should be to a body which is:
    (a) of higher authority than the one which imposed the penalty; and
    (b) is comprised of persons other than those who imposed the penalty and who do not have a personal interest in the case.
6. The rules should provide that an aggrieved member should be informed in writing of:
    (a) his right of appeal; and of
    (b) the procedure for appeals.
7. A separate rule or section of the rule book should prescribe the powers of reinstatement and reimbursement by the appropriate body.
8. The rules should provide that whenever practicable an expelled member should be allowed to remain a member so long as he is bona fide pursuing his appeal against the original decision.[94]

A circular setting out the recommendations was sent to all affiliated unions on June 27, 1969. Although the General Council 'fully recognised that reasonable time would be needed for any necessary amendments to be made'[95] to union rule books, it 'urged unions to take the appropriate steps as soon as possible'.[96] It must be said, however, that the response to the recommendations was disappointing. An important survey was published by Gennard, Gregory and Dunn.[97] The authors studied the rules of 79 unions affiliated to the TUC, with a combined membership of just under 12 million (at that time 99 per cent of the TUC's total membership). The survey covered all but three of the 81 unions in the TUC at that time with 5,000 or more members. It also included one union with fewer than 5,000 members. The authors revealed that 'with certain exceptions, the admission and disciplinary rules of most of the unions studied do not reach the standards of procedural elaboration . . . recommended by the TUC's 1969 proposals'.[98] On the question of admissions, 'only one-fifth of the unions studied provided notification of the reason for rejection to excluded applicants . . . and only two-fifths provided excluded applicants with a right of appeal'.[99] On the question of discipline, the 'rules tend to be more detailed'[100] and some unions 'provide extensive rights to members facing disciplinary action'.[101] There were, however, a number of significant differences between the rules of some unions and the TUC recommendations:

    (a) Many unions still rely primarily on general or 'blanket' clauses rather than a large range of specific offences.

    (b) Twenty-two unions (with 2.6 million members) merely named the body with disciplinary power, without providing any procedure.

    (c) Only 34 unions (with 5.4 million members) specified that notice of a charge must be given, and of these only 22 laid down a minimum period.

    (d) Only 19 unions (with 4.2 million members) expressly provided that the member had a right to attend the hearing and only a 'small number' of other unions mentioned disciplinary rights such as the calling of witnesses, producing documents and other evidence, and cross-examining the other side.

And apart from these shortcomings, it is unclear to what extent the *status quo* is maintained until the procedures are exhausted. According to Gennard, Gregory and Dunn, 'Such a rule would be very difficult to operate where appeal is made to the annual conference because of the length of time that might elapse before the final appeal is heard. However, of the unions where the appeal goes before the executive council or a permanent appeals body 21 with 2.4 million members provide that no disciplinary action be taken before the appeals process is exhausted.'[102]

The experience of the TUC recommendations as an exercise in self-regulation is far from encouraging. It suggests that if this route is to be adopted in the future, the TUC and its affiliated organizations will have to respond more enthusiastically and more effectively than in the past. Recommendations will have to be reinforced by some supervision to ensure that they are complied with. A second experiment in self-regulation, while apparently much more successful, is also not without difficulty. This is the TUC Independent Review Committee which, as we saw in Chapter 3, was formed in 1976 following the repeal of section 5 of TULRA. At the time of writing, the Committee has only a very limited jurisdiction, dealing with complaints of unreasonable exclusion or expulsion where a closed shop operates. So far as TUC Annual Reports are any guide, the workload of the Committee appears to have fallen significantly after a flurry of activity following its creation.[103] This may be due to a large extent to the decline in closed shop arrangements and also to the introduction of a statutory remedy in cases which would otherwise fall within the jurisdiction of the Committee. There are, however, proposals to breathe new life into the IRC. It is true that the question of enforcing members' rights was not tackled in detail by the TUC General Council in its Consultative Document. Nor was the matter dealt with by the unions which made written submissions in response. One exception to this is COHSE which suggested that 'to minimise hostile judicial intervention, all disputes between members and trade unions affiliated to the TUC should be referred, after the exhaustion of internal remedies, to the IRC'.[104] This is far-reaching in the sense that the jurisdiction of the Committee would be expanded to cover all rule-book disputes and would not be confined to closed shop exclusions and expulsions. COHSE also proposed that applications to the courts would not be permitted except to appeal against a decision of the Committee. And even then the body with jurisdiction to deal with the case would be the EAT (though for these cases composed of a lawyer and two TUC nominees). Thereafter an appeal would lie from the EAT to the House of Lords, bypassing the Court of Appeal 'which has shown itself so hostile to Trade Unions in the past'.[105]

As we pointed out in Chapter 3, the main problem with the IRC is the failure to maintain the *status quo* while a hearing is pending. This is not, however, a failing of self-regulation. It is simply a weakness of the present arrangements. It suggests that the TUC and affiliated organizations will have to be more willing to extend more powers to any review body in the future, if self-regulation is to work adequately. This is not to say that self-regulation is free from difficulty in principle. Although there is no doubt about the integrity or impartiality of the Independent Review Committee, one of the first principles of law is that justice must be seen to be done. This appears to be what Kahn-Freund was alluding to when he wrote that 'If one tries to look at it with the eyes of a worker rightly or wrongly believing himself to have been unjustly excluded or expelled from a union, one wonders whether he will believe in the impartiality of a body set up by the TUC.'[106] Such concerns will become more forceful and more relevant in view of the Labour movement's criticism of self-regulation in other areas and its demand for independent statutory supervision of the police and the city. Yet this is not to deny the value of the IRC or to suggest that the answer to the problem of dispute settlement is confined to a choice between non-legal self-regulation and enforcement by the High Court. It is doubtful anyway whether in fact such an option exists. As we saw in Chapter 6, the courts will readily interfere in trade union disciplinary cases and will not necessarily permit their jurisdiction to be postponed by an exhaustion of remedies clause. So the courts may restrain conduct even before the case gets to the IRC, and there is little prospect of awards of the IRC being immune from judicial scrutiny. It would be possible in principle to enact an exhaustion of remedies requirement and it might also be possible in principle to seek to exclude the courts from intervening in trade union internal affairs. In practice, however, the first could cause substantial injustice given the delay which might be involved.[107] And so far as exclusion is concerned, the experience of the 1871 Act and of ouster clauses in other areas of law suggest that it would be very difficult to achieve, even if it was desirable in principle to do so, a position which may not be readily tenable.

There is in fact a third option as to enforcement. This lies in the proposals of the Donovan Commission. As we have seen, the Commission proposed a series of minimum statutory requirements with which trade union rules should comply. In the words of the Commission, 'The requirements as to rules of registered trade unions will henceforth be rather more extensive, and will call for more supervision . . . than in the past'.[108] It was anticipated that the supervision would be conducted by the Registrar of Friendly Societies and that any disagreements between the Registrar and a union about whether the rules complied with the statute should be referred for settlement to an independent review body which Donovan proposed should be established. The review body would consist of three members, 'of whom two would be chosen from a panel of trade unionists appointed by the Secretary of State for Employment . . . after consultation with the TUC, and one would be a lawyer who would act as chairman'.[109] The Review Body would have jurisdiction over a wide range of issues:

   (i)   cases of alleged unfair imposition of penalties resulting in substantial injustice; and cases of alleged arbitrary rejection of an application for admission to a trade union, or a particular section of a trade union;

  (ii)   cases based on alleged breach of the rules of the union or violation of natural justice;

 (iii)   complaints of election malpractices; and complaints under the Trade Union Act 1913 and the Trade Union (Amalgamations, etc.) Act 1964;

 (iv)   cases in which disagreement arises between the Registrar and a trade union as to whether its rules comply with the requirements of the law.[110]

The procedure would be laid down in statutory instrument and would cover matters such as the attendance of witnesses and the production of documents. One important point is that appellants would be required to exhaust internal remedies before lodging a complaint with the review body, 'unless to do this would involve undue delay or damage'.[111] The Review Body would have power to award compensation, and its awards would be made enforceable by being registered in the county court — as is provided by the 1913 Act for awards of the Certification Officer in political fund disputes.[112]

If a statutory body of this kind was in fact created, it would not exclude the courts altogether. Indeed, the Donovan Commission proposed that in some cases the Review Body and the High Court should have concurrent jurisdiction.[113] At best, all that a body of this kind might secure is to postpone rather than prevent intervention by the courts. As a result, one of the benefits of such an arrangement would be lost, that being the need to find a system of adjudication which is not perceived as hostile to the interests of trade unions and in which both parties to a dispute have confidence. There are perhaps two ways of responding to this difficulty. The first, and possibly the least attractive, would be to make the decisions of the Review Body final, so that there is no appeal, and to seek to build into the statute an ouster clause to exclude judicial review. If this route was adopted, the ouster clause would have to be very widely drafted in order to defeat the presumption introduced by Lord Diplock in *re Racal Communications Ltd.*[114] There it was said that in the case of inferior tribunals, the presumption is that all errors of law amount to an excess of jurisdiction and consequently are not protected by an ouster clause. In order to meet this presumption and to overcome judicial resistance, it would be necessary to introduce something along the lines of the following remarkable provision which appears in the Labour Code of British Columbia:

> The [labour relations] board has and shall exercise exclusive jurisdiction to determine the extent of its jurisdiction under this Act . . . to determine a fact or question of law necessary to establish its jurisdiction and to determine whether or in what manner it shall exercise its jurisdiction.[115]

A similar, though not so explicitly sweeping, provision has since been used in British law. The Interception of Communications Act 1985 extends statutory regulation to the practice of telephone tapping. In so doing it creates a tribunal with powers to hear complaints that warrants to tap telephones have been issued improperly or irregularly. The statute also provides that 'the decisions of the Tribunal (including any decisions as to their jurisdiction) shall not be subject to appeal or liable to be questioned in any court'.[116] It remains to be seen, however, whether any government would have the courage to adopt a clause of this kind in a statute or in a jurisdiction which does not involve matters of national security or the investigation of crime.

The other option is to exclude the ordinary courts by providing an appeal to another specialist body, that is to say to use the courts in the adjudication of disputes in a more sensible and pragmatic way. This has wide implications for Labour law, extending beyond the question of trade union internal affairs.[117] It would be possible, however, to create a framework in which a few judges are permitted to develop expertise in labour law and some understanding of the policy goals of the legislation. This could be done in one of two ways. The first is to amend the Supreme Court Act 1981 as follows. There might be created a Labour Court as part of the Queens Bench Division, in the model of the Commercial Court. The judge or judges of the court would be puisne judges nominated by the Lord Chancellor, presumably having regard to a range of factors which would make the individuals in question suitable for work of this kind. The Labour Court would deal with all common law High Court actions in the field of labour law, including actions between employers and trade unions; employers and workers; and should they arise, actions for judicial review of the decisions of administrative agencies operating in labour law (such as ACAS and the CAC). It would also deal with appeals from the Review Body. In appropriate cases, the decision of the High Court would be final. Such a clause would operate to prevent appeal and to exclude judicial review, for the Court of Appeal has no inherent jurisdiction to review decisions of the High Court. It would also enable a specialist jurisdiction to develop, not constrained by the intervention of the Court of Appeal. It would also be possible, and perhaps desirable, for there to be lay assessors on the court, to advise the judge, rather on the model of the assessors in the county court in race relations cases, albeit that the practice of this jurisdiction is such that it is hardly a good precedent. An alternative to a Labour Court along these lines would be to build up a revamped EAT by giving it jurisdiction to deal with collective labour disputes. The EAT has, however, been a source of some disappointment in recent years, and some effort may be needed to convince potential litigants that it should be given this extended jurisdiction. However, if either approach was adopted, its success would depend on delicate handling by the Lord Chancellor and it would require a high priority — both politically and judicially — being given to labour law.

NOTES

1. *Amalgamated Society of Railway Servants* v. *Osborne* [1910] AC 87.
2. Trade unions are not corporate bodies, but they have many of the attributes of a corporation. See TULRA 1974, s. 2.
3. Royal Commission on Trade Unions and Employers' Associations 1965–1968. *Report*, Cmnd. 3623, paras. 606, 609–11.

4. *Ibid.*, para. 630.
5. [1981] IRLR 408.
6. TULRA 1974, Schedule 1(4). The law was later consolidated. See EPCA 1978, s. 58.
7. On this see *Saggers* v. *British Railways Board* [1977] ICR 809.
8. *The Closed Shop in British Industry* (1984), pp. 15–16.
9. See Employment Act 1980, s. 7 and Employment Act 1982, s. 3.
10. See Weekes, Mellish, Dickens and Lloyd, *Industrial Relations and the Limits of Law* (1975), pp. 33–63.
11. See on this *Home Delivery Services Ltd.* v. *Shackcloth* [1984] IRLR 470; cf. *Sakals* v. *United Counties Omnibus Co. Ltd.* [1984] IRLR 474.
12. See TUC, *Industrial Relations Legislation* (1986), pp. 20–1.
13. It is to be noted, however, that article 11(2) permits states to prohibit the exercise of the right where this is first prescribed by law and secondly necessary in a democratic society for the protection of the rights and freedoms of others. The TUC (*ibid.*, p. 21) appears to take the view that this still leaves some scope for arguing that the requirement that members be given a choice could be revised in the light of Bridlington. But this seems optimistic.
14. *Young, James and Webster* v. *UK* [1981] IRLR 408.
15. For comment, see Forde, 'The European Convention on Human Rights and Labour Law' (1983) 31 *American Journal of Comparative Law* 301.
16. See *Kahn-Freund's Labour and the Law* (3rd edn by P. L. Davies and M. Freedland) (1983), pp. 247–8.
17. Flanders, *Management and Unions* (1975), pp. 239–40.
18. Hughes, 'Trade Union Structure and Government'. Royal Commission on Trade Unions and Employers' Association 1965–68. Research Paper 5 (Part 2), para. 19.
19. Employment Act 1980, s. 19(b).
20. The resolution was revoked in 1983.
21. Employment Act 1980, s. 19(c).
22. Employment Protection Act 1975, s. 17.
23. EPCA 1978, s. 27. But see now 'Building Businesses . . . not Barriers'. Cmnd. 9794 (1986), paras. 7–9.
24. EPCA, s. 96.
25. EPCA, s. 18.
26. EPCA, s. 65.
27. See, generally, Bourn, 'Statutory Exemptions for Collective Agreements' (1979) 8 ILJ 85.
28. This procedure is most frequently used in the context of guarantee pay.
29. TUC — Labour Party Liaison Committee, *A New Partnership. A New Britain* (1985), p. 21.
30. TUC — Labour Party Liaison Committee, *Partners in Rebuilding Britain* (1983), p. 10.
31. Freedom of Association and Protection of the Right to Organise Convention, 1948 (No. 87).
32. *Ibid.*, Article 2.
33. Right to Organise and Collective Bargaining Convention, 1949 (No. 98).
34. *Ibid.*, Article 1(1).
35. See *Minister for Civil Service* v. *Council of Civil Service Unions* [1984] 3 WLR 1174.
36. *ILO Official Bulletin*, vol. LX, 1977, Series B, No. 2. Report of The Governing Body Committee on Freedom of Association. Case No. 846.
37. *Ibid.*, para. 47.
38. *Ibid.*, para. 56.
39. *Ibid.*, para. 57.
40. *Abood* v. *Detroit School Board*, 431 US 209 (1977).
41. *Lavigne* v. *Ontario Public Service Employees' Union, Toronto Star*, July 8, 1986.
42. See also *Rodgers* v. *ITGWU*, where the Irish court held that it is 'a necessary corollary to the right to join and become a member of a trade union that the right must extend to taking part in the democratic process provided by it and in particular to taking part in the decision-making processes within the rules of trade unions'. The case, which is unreported, is discussed by Kerr and Whyte, *Irish Trade Union Law* (1985), pp. 24–6.
43. *Industrial Democracy* (1897), vol. 1, p. 38.
44. Although there are a great number of articles relating to the protection of individual rights within trade unions, lawyers usually display little concern with the theory and meaning of union

democracy or with the relationship between individual rights and democracy. There are, however, several who do. See in particular the writing of Summers, notably 'Union Power and Workers' Rights' (1951) 49 Mich Law Review 805 and 'The Public Interest in Union Democracy' (1958) 53 North-Western Law Review 610. See also Cox, 'The Role of Law in Preserving Union Democracy' (1959) 72 Harvard Law Review 609 and Wellington, 'Union Democracy and Fair Representation: Federal Responsibility in a Federal System' (1958) 67 Yale Law Jo. 1327.

45. This is not to say that the lawyer will see union democracy solely in terms of the protection of members' rights. Summers argues, for example, that democracy involves participation by the members as well as the protection of minority and individual interests. In contrast, the latter aspect is rarely given any consideration by social scientists.

46. *Law, Society and Industrial Justice* (1969), p. 11.

47. 'The Rule of Law and Absolute Sovereignty' (1958) 106 *University of Pennsylvania Law Review*. 943 at p. 945.

48. *The Concept of Law* (1961), pp. 156–7.

49. [1966] 2 QB 633.

50. See further, Marshall, *Constitutional Theory* (1971), pp. 137–9.

51. Royal Commission on Trade Unions and Employers' Associations 1965–1968. *Report*, Cmnd. 3623, para. 648.

52. *Ibid.*, para. 649.

53. *Ibid.*, paras. 650–4.

54. TUC, *Industrial Relations Legislation* (1986), p. 21.

55. [1971] 2 QB 175.

56. Allen, *Power in Trade Unions* (1954), p. 15.

57. See Allen, *ibid.*, chapter 1.

58. Quoted by Summers, 'The Public Interest in Union Democracy' (1958) 53 *Northwestern Law Rev.* 610 at p. 619.

59. Flanders, *Management and Unions* (1975), p. 42.

60. Summers, 'Union Powers and Workers' Rights' (1951) 49 *Michigan Law Rev.* 805 at p. 820.

61. Turner, *Trade Union Growth, Structure and Policy* (1962).

62. Hughes, 'Trade Union Structure and Government'. Royal Commission on Trade Unions and Employers' Association 1965–68. Research Paper 5.

63. Hyman, *Industrial Relations: A Marxist Introduction* (1975), chapter 3. See also Hyman, *The Workers' Union* (1971), pp. 206–21.

64. Martin, 'Union Democracy: an Explanatory Framework' (1968) 2 *Sociology* 205. See also Undy and Martin, *Ballots and Trade Union Democracy* (1984), chapter 5.

65. It may be questioned, however, whether the present arrangements are adequate. See *Hughes* v. *TGWU* [1985] IRLR 382, where Vinelott J held that a trade union member has no right of access to union records in order to obtain information about the results of an election for general secretary in branches other than the one of which he was a member.

66. Cmnd. 3888 (1969).

67. 'Freedom at Work: Towards the Reform of Tory Employment Laws' (1985).

68. *Ibid.*, p. 40.

69. *Ibid.*

70. *Ibid.*

71. *Ibid.*

72. *Ibid.*

73. *Ibid.*

74. *Ibid.*, p. 41.

75. TUC, *Industrial Relations Legislation* (1986).

76. *Ibid.*, p. 11.

77. *Ibid.*, pp. 11–12.

78. *Ibid.*, p. 12.

79. *Ibid.*

80. *Ibid.*

81. *Ibid.*

82. EETPU, 'Industrial Relations Legislation' (1986), p. 11.

83. UCW, 'Industrial Relations Legislation' (1986), p. 6.

84. TUC, *Industrial Relations Legislation* (1986), p. 12.

85. *Ibid.*, pp. 12–13.

86. UCATT, 'A Response to TUC Consultative Document' (1986), p. 4.

87. Royal Commission on Trade Union and Employers' Associations 1965–1968. *Report*, Cmnd. 3623, para. 650.

88. *Ibid.*, para. 651.

89. *Ibid.*, para. 652.

90. *Ibid.*, para. 653.

91. *Ibid.*, para. 658.

92. TUC Annual Report 1969, p. 141.

93. *Ibid.*

94. TUC Annual Report 1969, pp. 142–4.

95. *Ibid.*, p. 144.

96. *Ibid.*

97. 'Throwing the book. Trade union rules on admissions, discipline and expulsion', *Employment Gazette*, June 1980, p. 591.

98. *Ibid.*, p. 599.

99. *Ibid.*

100. *Ibid.*

101. *Ibid.*

102. *Ibid.*, p. 597.

103. For a study of the Committee, see Ewing and Rees, 'The TUC Independent Review Committee and the Closed Shop' (1981) 10 ILJ 84.

104. COHSE, 'Comments on the TUC Document "Industrial Relations Legislation" ' (1986), p. 12.

105. *Ibid.*

106. See Kahn-Freund, *Labour and the Law* (2nd edn, 1977), p. 192.

107. A point recognized by the Royal Commission on Trade Unions and Employers' Associations 1965–1968. *Report*, Cmnd. 3623, para. 663.

108. *Ibid.*, para. 656.

109. *Ibid.*, para. 658.

110. *Ibid.*, para. 659.

111. *Ibid.*, para. 663.

112. 1913 Act, s. 3(2).

113. Royal Commission on Trade Unions and Employers' Associations 1965–1968. *Report*, Cmnd. 3623, para. 665.

114. [1981] AC 374.

115. Labour Code of British Columbia, RSBC 1979, c. 212, s. 33.

116. Interception of Communications Act 1985, s. 7(8).

117. The rest of this paragraph draws on Ewing, 'The Right to Strike' (1986) 15 ILJ 143.

Bibliography

OFFICIAL PUBLICATIONS

Certification Officer, *Annual Reports*, 1976–85. London, 1977–86.

Department of Employment, *Code of Practice on Closed Shop Agreements and Arrangements*, London, HMSO, 1983.

——, *Democracy in Trade Unions*, Cmnd. 8778, London, HMSO, 1983.

——, *Trade Union Immunities*, Cmnd. 8128, London, HMSO, 1981.

Department of Employment and Productivity, *In Place of Strife. A Policy for Industrial Relations*, Cmnd. 3888, London, HMSO, 1969.

Department of Labour (Republic of Ireland), *Outline of Principal Provisions of Proposed New Trade Dispute and Industrial Relations Legislation*, Dublin, 1986.

Eleventh and Final Report of the Royal Commission appointed to Inquire into the Organisation and Rules of Trade Unions and Other Associations, Parliamentary Papers, 1868–9, vol. XXXI.

House of Commons, The Employment Committee, Session 1982–3, *The Green Paper on Democracy in Trade Unions. Minutes of Evidence. Wednesday 2 March 1983*, HC 243-i, London, HMSO, 1983.

——, Session 1982–3, *The Work of the Department of Employment Group. Minutes of Evidence. Wednesday 13 April 1983*, HC 213-ii, London, HMSO, 1983.

Royal Commission on Trade Unions and Employers' Association 1965–68, Chairman: Lord Donovan, *Report*, Cmnd. 3623, London, HMSO.

BOOKS AND ARTICLES

Aaron, B., 'The Labor–Management Reporting and Disclosure Act of 1959', *Harvard Law Review* 73 (1960), 851.

—— and Komeroff, A., 'Statutory Regulation of Internal Union Affairs', *Illinois Law Review* 44 (1949), 425.

Abrahams, G., *Trade Unions and the Law*, London, Cassell, 1968.

Allen, V.L., *Power in Trade Unions*, London, Longmans, 1954.

——, *Trade Union Leadership*, London, Longmans, 1957.

Arthurs, H.W., Carter, D.D. and Glasbeek, H.W., *Labour Law and Industrial Relations in Canada*, Deventer, Kluwer, 1981.

Bain, G.S., *The Growth of White-Collar Trade Unionism*, Oxford, Oxford University Press, 1970.

——, ed., *Industrial Relations in Britain*, Oxford, Blackwell, 1983.

—— and Elias, P., 'Trade Union Membership in Great Britain: An Individual-level Analysis', *British Journal of Industrial Relations* 23 (1985), 71.

Ball, C., 'The Resolution of Inter-Union Conflict: The TUC's Reaction to Legal Intervention', *Industrial Law Journal* 9 (1980), 13.

Bealey, F., *The Post Office Engineering Union*, London, Bachman and Turner, 1976.

Beynon, H., ed., *Digging Deeper. Issues in the Miners' Strike*, London, Verso, 1985.

Biagi, M., *Sindacato Democrazia e Diritto Il Caso Inglese del Trade Union Act 1984*, Milan, 1986.

Bourn, C., 'Statutory Exemptions for Collective Agreements', *Industrial Law Journal* 8 (1979), 85.

Brown, W., ed., *The Changing Contours of British Industrial Relations: A Survey of Manufacturing Industry*, Oxford, Blackwell, 1981.

Campbell, A. and Warner, M., 'Changes in the Balance of Power in the British Mineworkers' Union: An Analysis of National Top-Office Elections 1974–84', *British Journal of Industrial Relations* 23 (1985), 1.

Carrothers, A.W.R., 'Case and Comment', *Canadian Bar Review* 34 (1956), 70.

Chafee, Z., 'The Internal Affairs of Associations Not for Profit', *Harvard Law Review* 43 (1930), 993.

'Chronicle. Industrial Relations in the United Kingdom', *British Journal of Industrial Relations* 22 (1984), 275, 411; 23 (1985), 153.

Citrine, N.A., *Trade Union Law*, 3rd edn by M.A. Hickling, London, Stevens, 1967.

Clarke, T. and Clements, L., eds., *Trade Unions Under Capitalism*, London, Fontana, 1977.

Clegg, H.A., *The Changing System of Industrial Relations in Great Britain*, Oxford, Blackwell, 1979.

——, *General Union. A Study of the National Union of General and Municipal Workers*, Oxford, Blackwell, 1954.

Coates, K. and Topham, T., *The New Unionism*, Harmondsworth, Penguin Books, 1974.

Cole, G.D.H., *Organised Labour*, London, Allen and Unwin, 1924.

Cox, A., 'The Role of Law in Preserving Union Democracy', *Harvard Law Review* 72 (1959), 609.

Creighton, W.B., *Working Women and the Law*, London, Mansell, 1979.

——, Ford, W.J. and Mitchell, R.J., *Labour Law Materials and Commentary*, Sydney, Law Book Company, 1983.

Crick, M., *Scargill and the Miners*, Harmondsworth, Penguin Books, 1985.

Crouch, C., *The Politics of Industrial Relations*, London, Fontana, 1979.

Davies, P., 'Refusal by Industrial Member to Follow Union Instructions', *Industrial Law Journal* 4 (1975), 112.

—— and Freedland, M., *Labour Law: Text and Materials*, 2nd edn, London, Weidenfeld and Nicolson, 1984.

de R. Foenander, O., *Shop Stewards and Shop Committees. A Study in Trade Unionism and Industrial Relations in Australia*, Melbourne, Melbourne University Press, 1965.

De Smith, S.A., *Judicial Review of Administrative Action*, 4th edn by J.M. Evans, London, Stevens, 1980.

Dickens, L. and Cockburn, D., 'Dispute Settlement Institutions and the Courts', in Lewis, R., ed., *Labour Law in Britain*, Oxford, Blackwell, 1986.

Drake, C.D., *The Trade Union Acts with Commentary*, London, Sweet and Maxwell, 1985.

Dubbins, A.D., Gennard, J. and O'Higgins, P., *Fairness at Work — Evenhanded Industrial Relations* [mimeo], 1986.

Dunn, S., 'The Law and the Decline of the Closed Shop in the 1980s', in Fosh, P. and Littler, C., *Industrial Relations and the Law in the 1980s: Issues and Future Trends*, Aldershot, Gower, 1985.

—— and Gennard, J., *The Closed Shop in British Industry*, London, Macmillan, 1984.

Edelstein, J.D. and Warner, M., *Comparative Union Democracy. Organisation and Opposition in British and American Unions*, New Brunswick, Transition Books, 1979.

Elias, P., 'Admission to Trade Unions', *Industrial Law Journal* 8 (1979), 111.

——, 'Closing in on the Closed Shop', *Industrial Law Journal* 9 (1980), 201.

——, 'Trade Union Amalgamations: Patterns and Procedures', *Industrial Law Journal* 2 (1975), 125.

——, 'Trade Unions — Expulsion — Damages — Right to Work', *Cambridge Law Journal* (1971), 15.

——, Napier, B. and Wallington, P., *Labour Law Cases and Materials*, London, Butterworths, 1980.

Elliott, J., *Conflict and Cooperation? The Growth of Industrial Democracy*, London, Kogan Page, 1978.

Evans, S., 'The Use of Injunctions in Industrial Disputes', *British Journal of Industrial Relations* 23 (1983), 133.

Ewing, K.D., 'The Check-off and the Problem of the Political Levy', *Modern Law Review* 44 (1981), 219.

——, 'Industrial Action. Another Step in the "Right" Direction', *Industrial Law Journal* 11 (1982), 209.

——, 'The Right to Strike', *Industrial Law Journal* 15 (1986), 143.

——, 'The Right to Strike Break', *Cambridge Law Journal* (1985), 374.

——, 'Secret Ballots', *Journal of the Irish Society for Labour Law* 5 (1986), 19.

——, 'The Strike, the Courts and the Rule-Books', *Industrial Law Journal* 14 (1985), 160.

——, 'Trade Union — Expulsion', *Cambridge Law Journal* (1983), 207.

——, 'Trade Union Political Fund Rules: A Note on Adjudication', *Industrial Law Journal* 9 (1980), 137.

——, 'Trade Union Political Funds', *Industrial Law Journal* 13 (1984), 125.

——, 'Trade Union Political Fund: The 1913 Act Revised', *Industrial Law Journal* 13 (1984), 227.

——, 'Trade Unions and Politics', in Lewis, R., ed., *Labour Law in Britain*, Oxford, Blackwell, 1986.

——, *Trade Unions, the Labour Party and the Law. A Study of the Trade Union Act 1913*, Edinburgh, Edinburgh University Press, 1982.

——, 'The TUC Independent Review Committee', *Industrial Law Journal* 8 (1979), 184.

—— and Napier, B.W., 'The Wapping Dispute and Labour Law', *Cambridge Law Journal* 45 (1986), 285.

—— and Rees, W.M., 'Democracy in Trade Unions — I: The Political Levy', *New Law Journal* 133 (1983), 100.

—— and ——, 'Democracy in Trade Unions — II: Secret Ballots', *New Law Journal* 133 (1983), 259.

—— and ——, 'Exclusion from Trade Union Membership', *Industrial Law Journal* 12 (1983), 106.

—— and ——, 'The TUC Independent Review Committee and the Closed Shop', *Industrial Law Journal* 10 (1981), 84.

Ferris, P., *The New Militants: Crisis in the Trade Unions*, Harmondsworth, Penguin Books, 1972.

Flanders, A., ed., *Collective Bargaining*, Harmondsworth, Penguin Books, 1969.

——, *Management and Unions*, London, Faber and Faber, 1975.

——, *Trade Unions*, 7th edn, London, Hutchinson, 1968.

Forde, M., 'The "Closed Shop" Case', *Industrial Law Journal* 11 (1982), 1.

——, 'The European Convention on Human Rights and Labor Law',

American Journal of Comparative Law 31 (1983), 301.

Fox, A., *Beyond Contract: Work, Power and Trust Relations*, London, Faber and Faber, 1974.

——, *History and Heritage. The Social Origins of the British Industrial Relations System*, London, Allen and Unwin, 1985.

——, *A History of the National Union of Boot and Shoe Operatives*, Oxford, Blackwell, 1958.

Gennard, J., Gregory, M. and Dunn, S., 'Throwing the Book. Trade Union Rules on Admissions, Discipline and Expulsion', *Employment Gazette* (June 1980), 591.

Goldstein, J., *The Government of British Trade Unions*, London, Allen and Unwin, 1952.

Goodhart, A.L., 'The Legality of the General Strike in England', *Yale Law Journal* 30 (1927), 464.

——, 'The Rule of Law and Absolute Sovereignty', *University of Pennsylvania Law Review* 106 (1958), 943.

Goodman, J.F.B. and Whittingham, T.G., *Shop Stewards*, London, Pan Books, 1973.

Gower, L.C.B., *Principles of Modern Company Law*, 4th edn by Gower, L.C.B., Cronin, J.B., Easson, A.J. and Lord Wedderburn of Charlton, London, Stevens, 1979.

Griffith, J.A.G., *The Politics of the Judiciary*, 3rd edn, Glasgow, Fontana, 1985.

Grodin, J.R., *Union Government and the Law: British and American Experiences*, Los Angeles, Institute of Industrial Relations, University of California, 1981.

Grunfeld, C., *Modern Trade Union Law*, London, Sweet and Maxwell, 1966.

Hadley, S.J., Hardy, T.S., Kwalwasser, H.J. and Tedeschi, L.L., 'Union Elections and the LMRDA: Thirteen Years of Use and Abuse', *Yale Law Journal* 81 (1972), 409.

Hart, H.L.A., *The Concept of Law*, Oxford, Oxford University Press, 1972.

Haslam, A.L., *The Law Relating to Trade Combinations*, London, Allen and Unwin, 1931.

Hepple, B., 'A Right to Work?', *Industrial Law Journal* 10 (1981), 65.

——, *Race, Jobs and the Law in Britain*, 2nd edn, Harmondsworth, Penguin Books, 1970.

—— and O'Higgins, P., *Employment Law*, 4th edn by Hepple, B., London, Sweet and Maxwell, 1981.

Hickling, M.A., 'The Right to Membership of a Trade Union', *University of British Columbia Law Review* 3 (1967), 243.

Howard, M., 'The Right to Refuse to Strike', *Daily Telegraph*, October 5, 1983.

Hughes, J., *Trade Union Structure and Government. Royal Commission on Trade Unions and Employers' Associations 1965–68*, London, HMSO, 1968. Research Paper 5, parts 1 and 2.

Hutton, J., 'Ballots before Industrial Action', *Industrial Law Journal* 14 (1985), 255.

——, 'Solving the Strike Problem: Part II of the Trade Union Act 1984', *Industrial Law Journal* 13 (1984), 212.

Hyman, R., *Industrial Relations: A Marxist Introduction*, London, Macmillan, 1975.

——, *The Workers' Union*, Oxford, Oxford University Press, 1971.

Industrial Relations Review and Report, 'The Independent Review Committee: The Success of Voluntarism?', No. 208, September 1979, p. 2.

——, 'Union Procedures on the Expulsion and Admission of Members — A Survey of Current Practice', No. 272, May 1982, p. 2.

——, 'Union Strike Rules: Part 2 — Strike Pay, Strike Committees and Disciplinary Rules', No. 279, September 1982, p. 2.

International Labour Office, *Freedom of Association. Report of Decisions and Principles of the Freedom of Association Committee of the Governing Body of the ILO*, 3rd edn, Geneva, ILO, 1985.

——, *The Public Authorities and the Right to Protection of Trade Union Funds and Property*, Geneva, ILO, 1974.

Jackson, P., *Natural Justice*, London, Sweet and Maxwell, 1973; 2nd edn, 1979.

Kahn-Freund, O., *Labour and the Law*, 2nd edn, London, Stevens, 1977.

——, *Labour and the Law*, 3rd edn by Davies, P. and Freedland, M., London, Stevens, 1983.

——, 'Trade Unions, the Law and Society', *Modern Law Review* 33 (1970), 241.

Kales, P., 'The Adjudication of Inter-union Membership Disputes: The TUC Disputes Committee Revisited', *Industrial Law Journal* 6 (1977), 19.

——, 'The Effectiveness and Utility of the Disputes Committee of the Trades Union Congress', *British Journal of Industrial Relations* 16 (1978), 41.

Kay, M., 'The Settlement of Membership Disputes in Trade Unions', in Carby-Hall, J.R.; ed., *Studies in Labour Law*, Bradford, MCB Books, 1976.

Kerr, A. and Whyte, G., *Irish Trade Union Law*, Abingdon, Professional Books, 1985.

Kerr, W.W., *The Law and Practice as to Receivers*, 16th edn by Walton, R., London, Stevens, 1983.

Kidner, R., 'The Bridlington Principles Under Attack', *Industrial Law Journal* 12 (1983), 38.

——, 'Implied Contracts Between Members and Unions', *Industrial Law Journal* 14 (1985), 124.

——, 'The Individual and the Collective Interest in Trade Union Law', *Industrial Law Journal* 5 (1976), 90.

——, 'Opening up the Pre-entry Closed Shop', *Industrial Law Journal* 15 (1986), 129.

——, 'The Right to be a Candidate for Union Office', *Industrial Law Journal* 2 (1973), 65.

——, 'Sanctions for Contempt by a Trade Union', *Legal Studies* 6 (1986), 18.

——, 'Trade Union Democracy: Election of Trade Union Officers', *Industrial Law Journal* 13 (1984), 193.

——, *Trade Union Law*, 2nd edn, London, Stevens, 1983.

——, 'Trade Union Political Fund Rules', *Northern Ireland Legal Quarterly* 31 (1980), 3.

——, *Trade Unions*, London, Sweet and Maxwell, 1980.

Lane, T., *The Union Makes Us Strong. The British Working Class, its Trade Unionism and Politics*, London, Arrow Books, 1974.

—— and Roberts, K., *Strike at Pilkingtons*, London, Fontana, 1971.

Lauterpacht, H., 'Contracts to Break a Contract', *Law Quarterly Review* 52 (1936), 494.

Lewis, R., 'Code of Practice on Picketing and Closed Shop Agreements and Arrangements', *Modern Law Review* 44 (1981), 198.

——, 'The Role of Law in Employment Relations', in Lewis, R., ed., *Labour Law in Britain*, Oxford, Blackwell, 1986.

—— and Simpson, B., 'Disorganising Industrial Relations: An Analysis of Sections 2–8 and 10–14 of the Employment Act 1982', *Industrial Law Journal* 11 (1982), 227.

—— and ——, 'The Right to Associate', in Lewis, R., ed., *Labour Law in Britain*, Oxford, Blackwell, 1986.

—— and ——, *Striking a Balance? Employment Law After the 1980 Act*, Oxford, Martin Robertson, 1981.

Lipset, S.M., Trow, M.A. and Coleman, J.S., *Union Democracy: The Internal Politics of the International Typographical Union*, Glencoe, The Free Press, 1956.

Lloyd, D., 'Damages for Wrongful Expulsion from a Trade Union', *Modern Law Review* 19 (1956), 121.

Lloyd, J., *Understanding the Miners' Strike*, London, Fabian Society, 1985 (Fabian Tract 504).

Lucas, J.R., *Democracy and Participation*, Harmondsworth, Penguin Books, 1976.

McCarthy, W., *Freedom at Work: Towards the Reform of Tory Employment Laws*, London, Fabian Society, 1985 (Fabian Tract 508).

McCarthy, W.E.J., *The Closed Shop in Britain*, Oxford, Oxford University Press, 1964.

——, *Trade Unions: Selected Readings*, 2nd edn, Harmondsworth, Penguin Books, 1985.

McCready, H.W., 'British Labour and the Royal Commission on Trade Unions 1867–1869', *University of Toronto Quarterly* 24 (1955), 390.

MacFarlane, L.J., *The Right to Strike*, Harmondsworth, Penguin Books, 1981.

McKendrick, E., 'Trade Unions and Non-striking Members', *Legal Studies* 6 (1986), 35.

Marshall, G., *Constitutional Theory*, Oxford, Oxford University Press, 1971.

Martin, R., 'Ballots and Trade Union Democracy: The Role of Government', in Fosh, P. and Littler, C., eds., *Industrial Relations and the Law in the 1890s: Issues and Future Trends*, Aldershot, Gower, 1985.

—— 'Union Democracy: An Explanatory Framework', *Sociology* 2 (1968), 205.

Michels, R.W.E., *Political Parties: A Sociological Study of the Oligarchical Tendencies of Modern Democracy*, London, Jarrold and Sons, 1915.

Miliband, R., *The State in Capitalist Society*, London, Quartet Books, 1973.

Miller, K., 'Trade Union Government and Democracy', in Lewis, R., ed., *Labour Law in Britain*, Oxford, Blackwell, 1986.

——, 'The Union Rule and the Miners' Strike', *Juridical Review* 31 (n.s.) (1986), 210.

Morris, G.S., 'The Regulation of Industrial Action in Essential Services', *Industrial Law Journal* 12 (1983), 69.

Mortimer, J.E., *A History of the Boilermakers' Society*, London, Allen and Unwin, 1973.

Musson, A.E., *British Trade Unions 1800–1875*, London, Macmillan, 1976.

Napier, B.W., 'Trade Union Discipline and Reluctant Strikers', *Scots Law Times (News)* (1982), 169.

——, 'Unions and Political Strikes', *Cambridge Law Journal* (1974), 71.

Newell, D., 'Lack of Jurisdiction and Contempt of Court', *Industrial Law Journal* 8 (1979), 44.

——, 'The Status of British and American Trade Unions as Defendants in Industrial Dispute Litigation', *International and Comparative Law Quarterly* 32 (1983), 382.

——, 'Trade Union Lay Representatives and Trade Union Rules', *Northern Ireland Legal Quarterly* 35 (1984), 52.

——, 'Trade Union Political Funds and the Check Off System', *Industrial Law Journal* 9 (1980), 122.

——, 'Trade Unions and Non-Striking Members', *Law Quarterly Review* 97 (1981), 214.

Oberer, W., 'Voluntary Impartial Review of Labor: Some Reflections', *Michigan Law Review* 58 (1960), 55.

O'Higgins, P., 'International Standards and British Labour Law', in Lewis, R., ed., *Labour Law in Britain*, Oxford, Blackwell, 1986.

Palmer, E.E., *Responsible Decision-Making in Democratic Trade Unions*, Ottawa, Privy Council Office, 1969 (Task Force on Labour Relations Study No. 11).

Pelling, H.M., *A History of British Trade Unionism*, 3rd edn, Harmondsworth, Penguin Books, 1976.

——, *A Short History of the Labour Party*, 5th edn, London, Macmillan, 1976.

Perrins, B., *Trade Union Law*, London, Butterworth, 1985.

Phelps Brown, H., *The Origins of Trade Union Power*, Oxford, Oxford University Press, 1983.

Poole, M., *Theories of Trade Unionism*, London, Routledge and Kegan Paul, 1981.

Pound, R., 'Equitable Relief Against Defamation and Injuries to Personality', *Harvard Law Review* 29 (1916), 640.

Pritt, D.N. and Freeman, R., *The Law Versus the Trade Unions*. London, Lawrence and Wishart, 1958.

Radice, G., *The Industrial Democrats. Trade Unions in an Uncertain World*, London, Allen and Unwin, 1978.

Richter, I., *Political Purpose in Trade Unions*, London, Allen and Unwin, 1973.

Riddall, J.G., *The Law of Industrial Relations*, London, Butterworth, 1981.

Rideout, R.W., 'Admission to Non-Statutory Associations Controlling Employment', *Modern Law Review* 30 (1967), 389.

——, 'The Content of Trade Union Disciplinary Rules', *British Journal of Industrial Relations* 3 (1965), 153.

——, 'Liberty of a Trade Union to Compel Breach of Legal Duty', *Modern Law Review* 26 (1963), 565.

——, *Principles of Labour Law*, 4th edn by Rideout, R.W. and Dyson, J.C., London, Sweet and Maxwell, 1983.

——, *The Right to Membership of a Trade Union*, London, Athlone Press, 1963.

——, 'Trade Union Membership, the 1890 Style', *Modern Law Review* 26 (1963), 436.

——, 'Upon Training an Unruly Horse', *Modern Law Review* 29 (1966), 424.

Roberts, B.C., *Trade Union Government and Administration in Great Britain*, London, Bell and Jones, 1956.

Rolph, C.H., *All those in Favour? The ETU Trial*, London, Deutsch, 1962.

Seifert, R., 'Some Aspects of Factional Opposition: Rank and File and the N.U.T. 1967–1982'. *British Journal of Industrial Relations* 22 (1984), 372.

Selznick, P., *Law Society and Industrial Justice*, New York, Russell Sage Foundation, 1969.

Simpson, B., 'The TUC's Bridlington Principles and the Law', *Modern Law Review* 46 (1983), 635.

Simpson, R.C., 'Judicial Control of A.C.A.S.', *Industrial Law Journal* 8 (1979), 69.

Slesser, H.H., *The Law Relating to Trade Unions*, London, The Labour Publishing Company, 1921.

Smith, I. and Wood, J.C., *Industrial Law*, 3rd edn, London, Butterworths, 1986.

Steele, M., Miller, K. and Gennard, J., 'The Trade Union Act 1984: Political Fund Ballots', *British Journal of Industrial Relations* 24 (1986), 443.

Stone, A.J., 'Wrongful Expulsion From Trade Unions: Judicial Intervention at Anglo-American Law', *Canadian Bar Review* 34 (1956), 1111.

Summers, C.W., 'Democracy in a One-Party State: Perspectives From Landrum-Griffin', *Maryland Law Review* 43 (1984), 93.

——, 'The Law of Union Discipline: What the Courts Do in Fact', *Yale Law Journal* 70 (1960), 175.

——, 'Legal Limitations on Union Discipline', *Harvard Law Review* 64 (1951), 1049.

——, 'The Political Liberties of Labor Union Members — A Comment', *Texas Law Review* 33 (1955), 603.

——, 'The Public Interest in Union Democracy', *Northwestern Law Review* 53 (1958), 610.

——, 'The Right to Join a Union', *Columbia Law Review* 47 (1947), 33.

——, 'Union Power and Workers' Rights', *Michigan Law Review* 49 (1951), 805.

Taylor, A.J.P., *English History 1914–1945*, Harmondsworth, Penguin Books, 1970.

Taylor, R., *The Fifth Estate. Britain's Unions in the Modern World*, London, Pan Books, 1980.

Thomas, T.C., 'Trade Unions and their Members', *Cambridge Law Journal* (1956), 67.

Thomas, A.W.J. and Engleman, S.R., *The Industrial Relations Act: A Review and Analysis*, London, Martin Robertson, 1975.

Tracey, R., 'The Legal Approach to the Democratic Control of Trade Unions', *Melbourne University Law Review* 15 (1985), 177.

Treitel, G.H., *The Law of Contract*, 6th edn, London, Stevens, 1983.

Turner, H.A.L., *Trade Union Growth, Structure and Policy*, London, Allen and Unwin, 1962.

Undy, R. and Martin, R., *Ballots and Trade Union Democracy*, Oxford, Blackwell, 1984.

Wade, H.W.R., *Administrative Law*, 5th edn, Oxford, Oxford University Press, 1982.

Webb, S. and Webb, B., *The History of British Trade Unionism 1666–1920*, London, 1919.

—— and ——, *Industrial Democracy*, London, Longmans Green & Co., 1897.

Wedderburn, K.W., 'The Bonsor Affair: A Postscript', *Modern Law Review* 20 (1957), 105.

——, 'Industrial Relations and the Courts', *Industrial Law Journal* 9 (1980), 65.

——, 'Ultra Vires: Out?', *Industrial Law Journal* 14 (1985), 127.

——, *The Worker and the Law*, 2nd edn, Harmondsworth, Penguin Books, 1971; 3rd edn, 1986.

——, Lewis, R. and Clark, J., eds., *Labour Law and Industrial Relations: Building on Kahn-Freund*, Oxford, Oxford University Press, 1983.

Weekes, B., Mellish, M., Dickens, L. and Lloyd, J., *Industrial Relations and the Limits of Law. The Industrial Effects of the Industrial Relations Act 1971*, Oxford, Blackwell, 1975.

Weir, J.A., 'Discrimination in Private Law', *Cambridge Law Journal* (1966), 165.

Wellington, H., 'Union Democracy and Fair Representation: Federal Responsibility in a Federal System', *Yale Law Journal* 67 (1958), 1327.

Whitmore, E.F., 'Judicial Control of Union Discipline: The Kuzych Case', *Canadian Bar Review* 30 (1952), 1.

Williams, P., 'The Political Liberties of Labor Union Members', *Texas Law Review* 32 (1954), 826.

Zamir, I., *The Declaratory Judgment*, London, Stevens, 1962.

OTHER PUBLICATIONS

Aims of Industry, 'Recommendations on the Green Paper "Democracy in the Trade Unions" ', London, 1983.

Amalgamated Union of Engineering Workers, 'Industrial Relations Legislation', London, 1986.

——, Technical, Administrative, and Supervisory Section, 'Industrial Relations Legislation', London, 1986.

Association of Cinematograph, Television and Allied Technicians, 'Industrial Relations Legislation', London, 1986.

Association of First Division Civil Servants, 'Industrial Relations Legislation: TUC Consultative Document', London, 1986.

Association of Professional, Executive, Clerical and Computer Staff, 'Industrial Relations Legislation: TUC Consultative Document', London, 1986.

Bakers, Food and Allied Workers' Union, 'TUC Consultative Document — Industrial Relations Legislation', London, 1986.

British Actors' Equity Association, 'Comments on the Consultative Document of the TUC: "Industrial Relations Legislation" ', London, 1986.

Civil and Public Services' Association, 'Industrial Relations Legislation: TUC Consultative Document', London, 1986.

Confederation of British Industry, 'Green Paper on Democracy in Trade Unions', London, 1983.

Confederation of Health Service Employees, 'Comments on the TUC Document "Industrial Relations Legislation" ', London, 1986.

Conservative Trade Unionists, 'Working Party Report on Consensus of Opinions Sought on the Green Paper "Democracy in Trade Unions" ', London, 1983.

Electrical, Electronic Telecommunications and Plumbing Union, 'Industrial Relations Legislation', London, 1986.

Engineering Employers' Federation, 'Response to Green Paper "Democracy in Trade Unions" ', London, 1983.

General, Municipal, Boilermakers and Allied Trades' Union, 'Industrial Relations Legislation: TUC Consultative Document', London, 1986.

Health Visitors' Association, 'Industrial Relations Legislation', London, 1986.

Institute of Directors, 'Democracy and Competitiveness — Further Steps Towards Trade Union Reform', London, 1983.

Institution of Professional Civil Servants, 'Industrial Relations: TUC Consultative Document', London, 1986.

National and Local Government Officers' Association, 'Industrial Relations Legislation. TUC Consultative Document', London, 1986.

National Association of Probation Officers, 'Industrial Relations Legislation', London, 1986.

National Association of Teachers in Further and Higher Education, 'Industrial Relations Legislation. TUC Consultative Document', London, 1986.

National Communications Union, 'Industrial Relations Legislation: Consultative Document', London, 1986.

National Union of Journalists, 'Industrial Relations Legislation: TUC Consultative Document', London, 1986.

National Union of Mineworkers, 'Industrial Relations Legislation', London, 1986.

National Union of Public Employees, 'Industrial Relations Legislation', London, 1986.

Society of Civil and Public Servants, 'Industrial Relations Legislation', London, 1986.

SOGAT 82, 'The Role of Law in Industrial Relations', London, 1986.

Trades Union Congress, Annual Reports for 1969, 1970, 1971, 1976, 1977, 1978, 1979, 1980, 1981, 1982, 1983, 1984, London.

——, 'Disputes Principles and Procedures', London, 1979.

——, 'Improving Industrial Relations in the National Health Service. A Report by the TUC Health Services Committee', London, 1981.

——'Industrial Relations Legislation', London, 1986.

——, Labour Party Liaison Committee, 'A New Partnership. A New Britain', London, 1985.

——, ——, 'Partners in Rebuilding Britain', London, 1983.

Transport and General Workers' Union, 'Comment on Major Review of Industrial Relations Legislation', London, 1986.

Union of Communication Workers, 'Industrial Relations Legislation', London, 1986.

Union of Construction, Allied Trades and Technicians, 'A Response to the TUC Consultative Document', London, 1986.

Union of Shop, Distributive and Allied Workers, 'Industrial Relations Legislation. An USDAW Response', London, 1986.

Table of Cases

Allen v. Flood [1898] AC 1   74
Amalgamated Metal Workers' Union
   v. Government of Australia (1976)   266
Amalgamated Society of Carpenters
   and Joiners v. Braithwaite [1922]
   2 AC 440   10
Amalgamated Society of Engineers v.
   Smith (1913) 16 CLR 537   242
Amalgamated Society of Railway
   Servants v. Osborne [1910] AC 87   35,
                 97, 115, 168, 260
American Cyanamid Ltd. v. Ethicon
   Co Ltd. [1975] AC 396   54, 158, 200
Annamunthodo v. Oilfield
   Workers' Trade Union [1961]
   AC 945   213
Associated Newspapers Group Ltd. v.
   Wade [1979] ICR 664   241
Associated Provincial Picture Houses
   Ltd. v. Wednesbury Corporation
   [1948] 1 KB 223   224, 225
Austin Rover v. AUEW (Engineering
   Section) (Unreported)   160, 166

Barnard v. National Dock Labour
   Board [1953] 2 QB 18   202
Bennett v. National Amalgamated
   Society of Operative House and Ship
   Painters and Decorators (1916)
   85 LJ Ch. 298   99–100, 101
Bonsor v. Musicians' Union [1956] AC
   104   12, 36, 44, 46–9, 50, 52–3, 202
Boulting v. ACTT [1963]
   2 QB 606   68, 73, 245
Bowers v. NGA (Unreported, 1984)   213
Breen v. AEU [1971] 2 QB 175   41–2,
               80–1, 225, 272
Brinks-Mat v. APEX (Unreported)   165,
               166, 167

British Actors' Equity Association v.
   Goring [1977] ICR 393; [1978]
   ICR 791   28, 36, 109–10
Brodie v. Bevan [1922] 1 Ch. 276   105
Brown v. AUEW [1976] ICR 147   34,
               110, 111–12
Byrne v. Kinematograph Renters'
   Society [1958] 2 All ER 579   76

Calvin v. Carr [1980] AC 574   196, 219,
               220
Carter v. United Society of
   Boilermakers (1916)
   85 LJ Ch. 289   101
Chapple v. ETU, *The Times*,
   November 22, 1961   103, 110, 111
Cheall v. APEX [1982]
   IRLR 362; [1982]
   IRLR 91; [1983] ICR 398   26, 36, 44,
            47, 217, 221, 223, 230
Clark v. NATSOPA [1985]
   IRLR 494   84
Clarke v. Chadburn (No. 2) [1984]
   IRLR 350   53–4
Clarke v. NUFTO, *The Times*,
   October 18, 1957   71
Coleman v. POEU [1981] IRLR 427
               171, 172
Connell v. NUDAW, *The Times*,
   January 28, 1928   222
Cotter v. NUS [1929] 2 Ch. 58   101,
       103, 104, 105, 113, 116, 123, 129
Cox v. National Union of Foundry
   Workers of Great Britain and
   Ireland (1928) 44 TLR 345   115–16
Crofter Hand Woven Harris Tweed
   Company v. Veitch [1942] AC 435   75

Davies *v*. Carew-Pole [1956]
1 WLR 833   76
Dodd *v*. Amalgamated Marine
Workers' Union [1924] 1
Ch. 116   17
Drake *v*. Morgan [1978] ICR 56   98
Duke *v*. Littleboy (1880) 49 LJ Ch. 802   9
Durham Miners' Association, *In re*.
(1900) 17 TLR 39   123, 130-1

Eastham *v*. Newcastle United Football
Club Ltd. [1964] Ch. 413   73
Edwards *v*. Halliwell [1950] 2 All ER
1064   33, 107, 113-14
Edwards *v*. SOGAT [1971] Ch. 354   38,
39, 40, 41, 55-7, 78, 221, 222
EETPU *v*. Times Newspapers Ltd.
[1980] QB 585   14-15
Elliott *v*. SOGAT 1975 [1983]
IRLR 3   180
Esterman *v*. NALGO [1974] ICR
625   199-200, 207, 210, 211, 247-50
Evans *v*. National Union of Printing,
Book Binding and Paper Workers
[1938] 4 All ER 51   204
Express and Star Ltd. *v*. NGA (1982)
[1985] IRLR 455; [1986]
IRLR 222   160-2

Faramus *v*. Film Artistes' Association
[1963] 2 QB 527; [1964] AC 925   36,
37, 38, 41, 70, 71-2, 217
Fettes *v*. NUM (Scottish Area), *The
Scotsman*, September 25, and
November 3, 1984   121-2
Fish *v*. NUGMW, *The Times*,
February 17, 1928   221
Forster *v*. National Amalgamated
Union of Shop Assistants, Ware-
housemen and Clerks [1927]
1 Ch. 539   46
Foss *v*. Harbottle (1843) 2 Hare 461   100,
103, 104, 107, 110, 112-14,
123, 129, 131

Goodfellow *v*. London and Provincial
Union of Licensed Vehicle Workers,
The Times, May 22, and June 5,
1919   115
Goodfellow *v*. NATSOPA [1985]
IRLR 3   86

Greig *v*. Insole [1978] 1 WLR 302   73
Guaranty Trust Co. of New York *v*.
Hannay and Co. [1915] 2 KB 536   73

Hackney Borough Council *v*. Doré
[1922] 1 KB 431   252
Harington *v*. Sendall [1903]
1 Ch. 921   130
Heatons' Transport (St Helens) Ltd. *v*.
TGWU [1972] ICR 308   28, 32
Hiles *v*. Amalgamated Society of
Woodworkers [1968] Ch. 440   196, 199
Hilton *v*. Eckersley (1855) 6 El. &
Bl. 47   3-4
Hodgson *v*. NALGO [1972] 1 WLR
130   25, 106, 114, 118, 129
Hopkins *v*. NUS [1985] IRLR 157   127-8
Hornby *v*. Close (1867) LR 2 QB 153   5
Howard *v*. NGA (No. 3) [1983]
IRLR 445   86, 89
Howard *v*. NGA (No. 4) [1984]
IRLR 250   93
Howard *v*. NGA (No. 5) [1984]
IRLR 489   91
HTV Ltd. *v*. Price Commission
[1976] ICR 170   225
Huntley *v*. Thornton [1957] 1 WLR
321   49

Institution of Mechanical Engineers *v*.
Cane [1961] AC 696   130

Jordan *v*. UCATT (Unreported)   102

Kelly *v*. National Society of
Operative Printers (1915)
84 LJ KB 2236; (1915)
31 TLR 632   52, 201, 204
Kelly *v*. Wyld (1937) 81 Sol. Jo. 179   102
Kimberley *v*. Showmen's Guild of
Great Britain, *The Times*,
November 25, 1953   33, 104, 111
Kruse *v*. Johnson [1898] 2 QB 91   36,
41, 44

Lawlor *v*. Union of Post Office
Workers [1965] Ch. 712   197-8, 210
Leary *v*. National Union of Vehicle
Builders [1971] 1 Ch. 34   219, 220
Lee *v*. Showmen's Guild of
Great Britain [1952]

2 QB 329   24, 38–9, 62, 194, 205–6, 207, 208, 209, 210, 248
Leigh v. NUR [1970] Ch. 326   25, 31, 196
Liptrott v. NUM (Notthingham Area), Industrial Relations Review and Report, July 23, 1985   31
Lonrho Ltd. v. Shell Petroleum Co. Ltd [1981] 2 All ER 456   74
Losinka v. CPSA [1976] ICR 473   200
Luby v. Warwickshire Miners' Association [1912] 2 Ch. 371   201–2

Macdougall v. Gardiner [1907] 1 KB 361   115
McGahie v. USDAW (1966) SLT 74   11
McGhee v. TGWU [1985] IRLR 198   228–9
McInnes v. Onslow-Fane [1978] 1 WLR 1520   42–4, 80, 88
MacLean v. The Workers' Union [1929] 1 Ch. 602   204, 217
MacLelland v. NUJ [1975] ICR 116   105, 203–4
McNamee v. Cooper, *The Times*, September 8, 1966   106–7, 116–17, 118
Manders v. Showmen's Guild of Great Britain, *The Times*, November 4, 1966   209–10, 211
Martin v. Scottish Transport and General Workers' Union 1952 SC (HL) 1   70, 71
Mercury Communications Ltd. v. Scott-Garner [1984] 1 All ER 179   252
Merkur Island Shipping Corporation v. Laughton [1983] IRLR 218   159
Metropolitan Borough of Solihull v. NUT [1985] IRLR 211   158
Milton v. Nicolson 1965 SLT 319   45

Nagle v. Fielden [1966] 2 QB 633   39, 40, 42, 76, 77, 78–9, 80, 82, 270
National Sailors' and Firemen's Union of Great Britain and Ireland v. Reed [1926] Ch. 536   237
NATSOPA v. Kirkham [1983] IRLR 70   84–5, 86
Nisbet v. Percy 1951 SC 350   44–5
Norey v. Keep [1909] 1 Ch. 561   17, 18

NUGMW v. Gillian [1946] KB 81   14–15
NUM (Kent Area) v. Gormley, *The Times*, October 20, 1977   99, 105–6, 109

Oram v. Hutt [1914] 1 Ch. 98   98
Osborn, *see* Amalgamated Society of Railway Servants [1911] 1 Ch. 540   21 (note 30)

Padfield v. Minister of Agriculture, Fisheries and Food [1968] AC 997   81
Partington v. NALGO]1981] IRLR 537   199, 246–7
Paterson v. NALGO 1977 SC 345   108–9
Pett v. Greyhound Racing Association (No. 1) [1969] 1 QB 125   214
Porter v. NUJ [1979] IRLR 404   200, 242, 247, 249

R. v. Barnsley MBC, *ex parte* Hook [1976] 3 All ER 452   225–6
Racal Communications Ltd, *In re.* [1981] AC 374   286
Radford v. NATSOPA [1972] ICR 484   31, 197, 206, 217–18
Reeves v. TGWU [1980] IRLR 307   180
Richards v. NUM [1981] IRLR 247   171
Ridge v. Baldwin [1964] AC 40   224
Rigby v. Connol (1880) 14 Ch. D. 482   23
Roebuck v. NUM (Yorkshire Area) (No. 2) [1978] ICR 676   215, 216
Rothwell v. APEX [1976] ICR 211   71
Russell v. Duke of Norfolk [1949] 1 All ER 109   217

Sansom v. London and Provincial Union of Licensed Vehicle-Workers (1920) 36 TLR 666   125
Santer v. NGA [1973] ICR 60   203
Scott v. Avery (1856) 5 HLC 811   194
Secretary of State for Education and Science v. Tameside MBC [1977] AC 1014   212
Sherard v. AUEW [1973] ICR 421   238, 243, 244
Shipping Company Uniform Inc. v. ITF [1985] IRLR 71   155–6
Shotton v. Hammond (1976) 120 Sol. Jo. 780   199
Silvester v. National Union of

Printing, Bookbinding and Paper
Workers (1966) 1 KIR 678   203, 206
Spring v. NASDS [1956]
1 WLR 585   31,223
Steel v. UPW [1978] ICR 181   19
Steele v. South Wales Miners'
Federation [1907]
1 KB 361   114–15
Stevenson v. URTU [1977] ICR 893   213

Taff Vale Railway Co. v. Amalgamated
Society of Railway Servants [1901]
AC 426   12
Taylor v. NUM (Derbyshire Area)
(No. 1) [1985] IRLR 440   120–1, 122
Taylor v. NUM (Derbyshire Area)
(No. 2) [1985] IRLR 65   17–18
Taylor v. NUM (Derbyshire Area)
(no. 3) [1985] IRLR 99   123
Taylor v. NUM (Yorkshire Area)
[1985] IRLR 445   121, 122, 124–5
Thomas v. NUM (South Wales Area)
[1985] 2 All ER 1   238–40
Tierney v. Amalgamated Society of
Woodworkers [1959] IR 254   72

Torquay Hotels Co. Ltd. v. Cousins
[1969] 2 Ch. 106   159

Walker v. AUEFW 1969 SLT 150   214
Walton v. Yorkshire Miners'
Association, *The Times*, March 8,
1921   209
Watson v. Smith [1941] 2 All ER 725   25
Weakley v. AUEW, *The Times*,
June 12, 1975   34
Weinberger v. Inglis [1919] AC 606   72,
77, 80
White v. Kuzych [1951] AC 585   195–6,
197, 199, 215–16
Wolfe v. Matthews (1882) 21 Ch. D.
194   9
Wolstenholme v. Amalgamated
Musicians' Union [1920]
2 Ch. 388   204–5

Yorkshire Miners' Association
v. Howden [1905]
AC 256   9, 11, 20, 97, 123
Young, James and Webster v. U.K.
[1981] IRLR 408   261

Index

abstention, 14–19
ACAS, 263, 287
acts by a trade union, 159–62
  tortious, 157–9
ACTSS, 223
ACTT, 181, 182, 277, 279
adherence, contract of (Selznick), 26
administrative law, 41, 212, 224–6
admissions
  applications for, 64–5
  and the closed shop, 62–95
  and eligibility, 68–72
  invalid, 70–2
  legitimate expectation cases, 80–1
  procedures, 63–7
  re-admission, 77, 78
  rejected, 62
  and statutory regulations, 82–93, 226–7
  TUC proposals on, 280–1
AEU, 29
Aims of Industry, 140
Alderson, Baron, 4
Allanbridge, Lord, 199, 246–7
Allen, V.L., 273
amalgamations, 174; see also mergers,
      union; Trade Union (Amalgama-
      tions) Act
APAC, 63
APEX, 63, 64, 141, 192, 223–4, 278
appeals, 191, 192–3, 198–9
  validity, 218–20
arrears, expulsion for, 220–2
ASLEF, 199
Astbury J, 116, 237, 239
ASTMS, 63, 64, 151, 181
audi alteram partem principle, 212–14
AUEW, 64, 168, 198, 277, 279
Australia, 169, 266
AUT, 168

authorization of official action, 160–2
autonomy, principle of union, 6–11, 136,
      138, 271
  and admission rules, 89
  and contract, 27–8, 131
  courts and, in disciplinary affairs,
      193–201, 206, 226, 240

Bain, G.S., 245
Bakers' Union, 168
ballots before industrial action, 152–68
  implications, 165–8
  requirements, 162–5
  rigging, 138
  secret, 137, 139, 164, 254
  subsidies for, 136–7, 143–4
  see also merger ballots; postal ballots,
      strike ballots; triggered ballots;
      workplace ballots
BALPA, 143, 168
Bankes LJ, 77
Bentham, Jeremy, 2
bias, rule against, 214–16
  establishment, 215
  ideological, 215–16
  personal, 216
BIFU, 167
Bingham J, 217, 224
Birkenhead, Lord, 77
Blair, Tony, 145–6, 163–4
Blastfurnacemen, 181
Boilermakers' Society, 63
Boreham J, 98
branch block elections, 141, 142, 151, 276
breach of contract, 52–7, 130–2
  see also employment contract; member-
      ship, contract of
Bridlington agreement, 64, 73, 79, 222–4,
      230

Bristow J, 86
British Columbia: Labour Code, 286
British Institute of Management, 152
Browne-Wilkinson J, 86, 92
Bruce, Mr., 7
Buckley J, 57
Buckmaster, Lord, 10
Budd J, 72
business unionism, 273

CAC, 287
Cameron, Lord, 109
Canada, 169, 256, 267, 286
candidates for office, 145–7
CBI, 140, 154
Certification Officer (CO), 15, 16–17, 30,
    142, 147–9, 169
  Annual Report (1983), 176
  and ballots, 137, 174
check–off agreements, and political levy,
    170, 177–8, 179–81
Chief Registrar of Friendly Societies, 4, 5,
    12, 15, 30, 169, 285
civil servants, 265
  unions, 182–3
Clark, Alan, 172, 173, 177
closed shop, 65, 181, 255
  admissions and the, 62–95
  basis for intervention in, 260–2
  post-entry, 84, 227
  pre-entry, 83, 84, 227, 261
  right to work and, 40
  and threat to livelihood, 208, 210, 211
  see also Code of Practice on Closed Shop
    Agreements
clubs, 208–9, 260
Code of Industrial Relations Practice,
    191, 199, 227–8, 252–5, 257
Code of Practice proposed for 'democratic
    guidelines', 275–9
Code of Practice on Closed Shop
    Agreements and Arrangements
    (1980)
  amended (1983), 251
  exclusion and natural justice, 81, 87–8,
    89, 92, 231
  on industrial action, 155, 247, 251–5
COHSE, 254, 279, 284
collective bargaining, 43, 273, 274
  and basis for intervention, 262–4,
    267–8

Combination Acts (1799–1800), 1
  repeal (1824), 2–3
Communists: ban in EETPU, 29, 145,
    146–7
Companies Act (1985), 14
company law, 96, 102, 112
compensation claims for unreasonable
    exclusion or expulsion, 91
complaint, right of, 227, 261, 270, 279
  time limit for bringing, 231
compliance, substantial, 111–12
conference, 105, 107–9
conscience clause in contract of
    membership, 207, 248, 257,
    262
conscientious objections in strike-
    breaking, 247–50, 253
Conservative governments, 12, 83, 257,
    261, 277
consistency, 224–6
conspiracy, action for, 74–5
Conspiracy and Protection of Property
    Act (1875), 239
constitution, union's, 96, 97–8
  interpreting, 99–101
  limitations, procedural and substantial,
    104–7
  members' rights, limits to enforcement
    in, 110–19
contract, 23–8
  action based on, 75–7
  and constitution, 96–7, 130
  principle of freedom of, 212
  see also breach of contract; employment
    contract; membership, contract of
Cortonwood Colliery, S. Yorkshire, 119
County Court, 3
Court of Appeal, 284, 287
Courts, the
  and control of disciplinary rules,
    240–50
  and election exclusion rules, 145–6
  ousting the jurisdiction of, 194, 211
  role in domestic disciplinary proce-
    dures, 193–201, 204–7, 208–12
  trade union government and, 96–135,
    136, 271, 284–7
CPSA, 150, 165, 277, 279
craft unions, 63
criminal activity, industrial action as,
    238–40

CTU, 140
custom and practice, 32–4

damages, 55–7
Danckwerts J, 33
Darling J, 115
De Smith, S.A., 194
decision, 195–6
declaration, interim, 53–5
democracy, 274
  direct and representative, 110
  and statutory formulae, 138
  see also industrial democracy; union democracy
Democracy in Trade Unions, Green Paper (1983), 138–40, 145, 153–4, 157, 169–70
'democratic guidelines', 275–6
Denman J, 9
Denning, Lord
  on admission, 69, 73, 78, 81
  on ballot, 99, 106
  on contract, 24, 26
  on damages, 56–7
  on discipline, 194, 202, 205, 206, 208, 210, 247
  and duty to act fairly, 41–2, 272
  on internal relations of union, 109
  on proportionality, 226
  on right to legal representation, 214, 217, 221
  on right to work, 38–9, 248
  on tortious conduct, 159, 238
  on union rules, 28, 35–6, 44, 76, 230
  on victimization, 243–4
  on voluntary association aspects of trade unions, 130
Derbyshire miners, 120
Dilhorne, Viscount, 28, 110
Diplock, Lord, 36–7, 159, 200–1, 221, 223–4, 245, 286
directors, 68–9, 244–6
discipline
  and breaches of *ultra vires*, 104, 107
  and expulsion, 191–235
  and industrial action, 236–59
  judicial role in, 208–12, 240–50
  rules and procedures, 191–3
    breach of, 111, 203
    enforcing, 202–3
    reviewing the decision, 203–7

TUC proposals on, 281–2
discrimination, in union admission, 79, 83, 136
  direct and indirect, 18–19
  and expulsion, 226–7
  national, 83
  see also Race Relations Act; Sex Discrimination Act
dismissal, unfair, 40, 230–1, 253
domestic procedures, and the Courts, 193–201
Donovan Commission, 11, 12, 57, 260–1, 279–80, 285–6
  on admissions, 62, 72, 83, 88, 92, 261, 270, 279
  on elections, 270, 279
  on exhaustion policy in disciplinary proceedings, 198, 261, 270, 279
  on legislation on trade union government, 152, 153
  proposed independent Review Body, 285–6
  and right of complaint, 227, 261, 270, 279
  on shop stewards, 271
  on Trade Union Act (1913), 183
  on trade union rules, 138, 270–1
Doughty, George, 65
Dunn, S., 261, 282–3
duty to act fairly doctrine, 41–4
  and right to work, 78–82
  see also fairness, substantive; natural justice

EEC Regulation 1612/68 on admission, 83
EEF, 140, 154–5, 183
EETPU, 168, 192, 193, 277, 279
  ban on Communists, 29, 145, 146–7
efficiency, administrative
  and popular control in unions, 268, 272–3
elections of officials, 138–52
  case for legislation, 138–9
  conduct of, 142–5
  direct, 139–40, 141
  exclusion rules, 145–7
  indirect, 139, 141, 150
  proposals for, 275–6
  re-election, 150–1
  subsidies for, 137

eligibility rules, 63
  admissions and, 68–72
  declaration of, 72–4
employers, 257–8
  disclosure of information, 263
  and freedom of association, 265
  and political fund ballots, 175
  and strike ballots, 154–5, 165
  subsidized ballot re terms and
    conditions of employment, 137
Employment Act (1980), 20, 44, 53
  on admission, 67, 83–6, 227, 251,
    261–2
  on exclusions, 87–8, 251
  on public money for ballots, 137–8,
    139, 143–4, 274
  time limit for complaints, 231
Employment Act (1982), 40, 44, 82, 159,
    252, 261–2
Employment Appeal Tribunal (EAT), 15,
    67, 284, 287
  on admissions, 84–6, 89–90
  on unfair dismissal, 229–31
employment contract, 43
  breach of, 158, 164, 239, 241–2
Employment Protection Act (1975), 15,
    263
Employment Protection (Consolidation)
    Act (EPCA) (1978), 15, 228, 229,
    252–3, 265
endorsement of official action, 160–2
entitlement to vote, 143, 164, 175
Equity, 168, 277
estoppel, doctrine of, 72
ethics, breach of, 208–9, 252–4
European Assembly, 171
European Convention on Human Rights,
    257, 261, 262
European Court of Human Rights, 261
European law, 227
Eve J, 46, 205
Evershed, Lord, 37–8
evidence, in disciplinary proceedings,
    204–5
executive committee, 105, 107–9, 150,
    165–7
exhaustion doctrine, 194–8, 230–1, 284–5
express terms, 29–30
expulsion from union, 80–1, 87–90
  constructive, 228–9
  discipline and, 191–235

remedies, 90–3
  statutory regulation and, 226–31
  unreasonable, 227–31

fact, issues of law and, 194, 221
Fair Wages Resolution, 263
fairness, substantive, 224–6
FDA, 63, 199
fiduciary duties, 96
  conflicts of loyalty and, 244–6
  of directors in unions, 69
  of union officials, 96, 113
Flanders, A., 262–3, 273
forfeiture, automatic, 217–18, 220–1
Foster J, 71
Fraser, Lord, 45
fraud, 114
freedom of association, 3, 262, 264–7
  Committee on, 266–7
Friendly Societies Act (1985), 4–5
Fry J, 9
funds, union, 123–4
  see also political fund

GCHQ, 265
General Nursing Council for England and
    Wales, 254
General Strike (1926), 237–8
Gennard, J., 261, 282–3
GMBATU, 63, 174, 193, 279
  indirect elections, 139, 141, 150
Goddard CJ, 204
Goff J, 31, 117, 197, 203, 206–7
good faith, in disciplinary proceedings,
    204
Goodhart, A.L., 269
Goulding J, 106–7, 114
government intervention in union affairs,
    1–6, 138–40, 146, 237, 255–8,
    274–9
Gower, L.C.B., 130
Gowrie, Earl of, 147, 162
grade unions, 63
Gregory, M., 282–3
Grunfeld, C., 113, 183
guaranteed pay, 263
Gummer, Selwyn, 139, 146–7, 163

Harman J, 76
Hart, H.L.A., 269
Havers, Sir Michael, 127

Health and Safety at Work Act (1974), 240
hearing
  appellate, 219–20
  initial, defects in, 195–6
    forestalling the, 199–201
  right to a, 212–14
Heathfield, Peter, 125
High Court, 147–9, 287
Hogg, Sir Douglas, 237
Hosiery Workers, 182
Hughes, J., 263, 274
Hutton, J., 165–6
HVA, 168
Hyman, R., 274

ILO Conventions, 265–6
immunities, 139, 154, 156, 252, 254
  removing, 157–9
implied terms, 30–2, 201
In Place of Strife, White Paper, (Labour), 12, 275
incorporation, trade unions and, 128–32
individual rights, protection within trade unions, 268
industrial action
  ballots before, 152–68
  discipline and, 227, 236–59
  see also overtime bans; strikes
industrial and professional unions, 63
industrial democracy, 262–3
Industrial Relations Act (1971), 11–14, 20, 136, 261
  and automatic forfeiture, 221
  and disciplinary action, 244, 256
  mandatory ballots, 153
  registered unions as incorporated bodies, 12–13, 47
  on rejected admissions, 83
  repeal (1974), 14, 97, 256
  and right of complaint, 227
  sequestration of union funds, 125
  on union rules, 29–30, 191
Industrial Relations Review and Report (1982), 62–5, 87, 191–3, 198–9
industrial tribunals, 91–3
information disclosure
  by employers, 263
  by unions, 274
injunction, 53–5
  in breach of *ultra vires*, 97, 118, 129

interlocutary, 54–5, 199–201
Inland Revenue Staff Federation, 182
Institute of Directors (IOD), 140, 157
Interception of Communication Act (1985), 286
intervention in trade union government
  basis for, 260–7
  means of, 279–87
  scope of, 267–79
intimidation, 3, 239
  questions on ballot paper, 164
intra vires action, 113, 243
IPCS, 277, 279
Ireland, 126
irregularities, insubstantial, 111
ISTC, 193

Jackson, P., 79
Jauncey, Lord, 122
Jessel, Lord, 23
jobs, regulation of, 262, 267, 273
Johnston, Lord, 108
Joyce J, 130
judiciary, relationship with unions, 23–61, 271
  see also Courts, the

Kahn-Freund, O., 27, 284
Keith, Lord, 50
Kent miners, 106
Kidner, R., 148
King, Tom, 182

Labour Governments, 11, 169, 183, 274
labour law, proposals, 276–87
labour management and markets, 262–3
Labour Party, 182
  membership of union officials in, 31, 146
  and political fund, 168, 170, 183
  worker's rights to information, consultation and representation, 264
Lauterpacht, H., 241
law, role in trade union government, 260–89
Law Society, 253–4
Lawrence LJ, 116
Lawton LJ, 241
Lewis, John L., 273
liability
  in tort, 242–4

union contractual for acts of officials, 48–51, 160
Liberal Government (1911), 168
listing, 15
litigation under Trade Union Act (1984)
  Part I, 151–2
  Part II, 166 Table 1
livelihood, threat to, 208, 210, 211
loyalty, conflicts of professional, 244–6, 252–4
Luxembourg, 126
Luxmoore J, 102

McCarthy, Lord, 65, 275–6
MacDermott, Lord, 47, 50
McGahey, Michael, 125
Macnaghten, Lord, 10, 11
magistrates, 215
majority rule principle, 110, 112–17
  application, 103, 104
  desirability, 117–19
  exceptions, 113–14, 129–30
  see also Foss *v.* Harbottle
majority vote, no requirement, 162
Manchester, 5
Martin, R., 274
  Ballots and Trade Union Democracy, 140, 150, 165, 167
Master and Servant Acts, 2
Maugham, Lord, 75, 204, 217
meetings
  branch for disciplinary action, 192
  inadequate notice of, 104–5, 114
Megarry, Sir Robert, 40, 41, 42–3, 53–4, 57, 106, 219–20
  on rejected admission, 73, 80
Melford Stevenson J, 203
members' rights, 198
  to exemption from political levy, 169, 183
  to a hearing, 212–14
  infringement of personal, 114, 131–2
  to legal representation, 213–14
  limits to enforcement, 110–19, 130–2
  and rule of law, 269–70
  to vote, 143, 164, 175
membership, 72, 107–10
  exclusion from, 72–7, 87–90
    right of appeal against, 64, 81
membership, contract of, 23–61
  breach of, 130–2, 241–2

conscience clause, 207, 248, 257, 262
  and disciplinary powers, 201
  enforcing the, 44–51
  modification by tripartite agreement, 246–7
  and natural justice, 217–18, 225
  nature of, 25–7
  parties to the, 46–8
  terms of, 29–34
    judicial control of, 34–44
mergers, union, 275
  ballots, 137
Mervyn-Davies J, 126
Miner, The, 120
miners' strike (1984–5), 31–2, 53–4, 162, 271
  contempt of court in, 124–6
  financial support, 126–8
  sequestration of funds, 125–8
  ultra vires rule and, 119–28, 236
  unlawful, 120–4
Misrepresentation Act (1967), 71
moderation assumption, 140, 152–3, 275
Mortimer, J.E., 3
Morton, Lord, 12, 48–9
Musicians' Union, 197

NACO, 168
NALGO, 141–2, 168, 277, 278, 279
  campaign against cuts, (1983), 172
NALHM, 168
NAS/UWT, 277
NATFHE, 278, 279
National Coal Board, 119
National Industrial Relations Court, 153
nationality, discrimination on grounds of, 83
natural justice, 41, 80–1, 88, 212–26, 271
  defects of, 218–20
  exclusion of, 216–18
  see also duty to act fairly doctrine
NCU, 151, 193
negligence on part of the union, 222
negotiations, and strike ballots, 163–4
nemo judex in re sua principle, 212, 214–16
Neville J, 105, 201–2
News International, 165, 166
NGA, 63, 77, 165, 166, 181, 192
  Stockport Messenger dispute, 125
Nicholls J, 120–1, 122–3, 124
Nolan J, 32

norms of union behaviour, 209
Nottinghamshire miners, 120, 162
NUFLAT, 101
NUGMW, 63, 64
  see also GMBATU
NUJ, 63, 64, 192
NUM, 105-6, 143, 150, 151, 277, 279
  strike (1984-5), 119-32, 236
NUPE, 64, 277, 278
NUR, 63, 64, 146, 160
  branch block voting, 142, 150, 151
NUS, 127-8, 143, 167
NUT, 63, 64, 192

officials, union
  control of powers, 96
  election of, 138-52
  union contractual liability for acts of,
    48-51, 160
Oliver J, 199
Ontario: Labour Relations Act, 256
open unions, 63
overtime bans, 241

Parker, Lord, 98
Pearson, Lord, 28, 110
Pennycuick, Sir John, 103, 226
Peterson J, 115
Phillimore J, 115
picketing, 238-9, 242
  and crossing the picket-line, 254-5
  secondary, 239
Pickford LJ, 73
Pilcher J, 76
Place, Francis, 2
plaintiff, 'proper', 100, 112-13
Plowman J, 31, 197, 206, 217
political fund
  assets and liabilities, 175-8
  ballots, 30, 168-83
  proposals on, 278-9
  right of exemption, 178-81, 226
political levy of action by union, 114-15
  contracting in, 169, 181
  contracting out, 169, 181, 183, 267
  refund of, 178
political objects, 170-3
  periodic review, 173-5, 181
political party membership and union
    elections, 146-7
Polmaise Colliery, 119

Porter, Lord, 12
post office, 182-3
postal ballots, 144-5, 167
  half, 167
  mandatory, 266
  subsidy for, 137, 274
  TUC boycott of (1980), 139
powers
  discretionary, 272
  implying, 98-9
  limits on disciplinary, 255-8
  location of industrial action, 165-7
  restraint of union, 96-132
  subjectively worded, 208-12
prejudice, *see* bias
presidents, 141
Prior, James, 154
procedure agreements, 246-7
  breach of, 254
professional unions, 244-6
professional bodies, 208, 252-4
property rights, and members' interests,
    23-8
proportionality, doctrine of, 225-6
public policy, union rules and, 196-8
  and admissions, 68-9
  and discipline, 194, 210-12, 244
  and natural justice, 217-18, 225
public sector unions, 64
public utilities, and industrial action, 240,
    252-3

quorum in disciplinary procedure, 202

Race Relations Act (1976), 18, 74, 79, 83,
    226-7, 272
railway workers' dispute (1972), 153
receiver, appointment of, 125
referendum, 109-10
registration
  of members, 145
  of union, 4, 12-13, 15, 274
  see also listing
religious objections to union membership,
    261, 262
remedies
  dual re Trade Union Act (1984), 147-9
  for rejected admission, 74-5, 82
  for unreasonable exclusion from union
    membership, 90-3

representation, right to legal, 213–14
repudiation of acts of union officials by the union, 160–2
resolutions omitted from agenda, 115
right to work
  despite a strike call, 256–7
  and duty to act fairly, 42, 44, 78–82
  and judiciary intervention in union affairs, 37–40
right-wing organizations, 151
Romer LJ, 205–6, 208, 209, 210, 221
Roskill LJ, 28
Rossendale Union of Boot, Shoe and Slipper Operatives, 168
Royal Commission on trade unions (1867), 5–6, 7
Royal Commission on Trade Unions and Employers' Associations (1965–8), *see* Donovan Commission
RSC Order 45, 125
rule book, union
  control through the, 201–12
  election changes not recorded in, 151
  'minimum standards' proposed, 275–6
  and terms of contract, 29–30, 97
rule of law, 269–71
rules, union, 26–7, 76, 269–71
  ambiguous inter-relationship between two, 109–10
  ballot subsidies for amendment, 137
  custom and practice and, 32–4
  disciplinary procedures, 191–2
    subjective, 208–12
  on election procedures, 138
  as 'legislative code', 35–7
  and public policy, 196–8
  and scope for judicial control, 27–8
Russell CJ, 44, 113, 209

Sachs LJ, 38, 40, 56–7, 78
Salmon, Lord, 28, 40, 76, 80, 110
Scargill, Arthur, 124, 125, 151, 216
Scarman, Lord, 28, 110
Scotland, 178
  miners, 119, 121
  NALGO strike (1977), 108
Scott J, 128, 238–9
Scottish Gas, 246
Scottish Typographical Association, 77
SCPS, 151, 277, 279

SDP (Social Democratic Party), 182
secretaries, general, 140, 141
Select Committee of the House of Commons on Employment (1982–3), 183
Select Committee of the House of Commons on Industry Report (1824, 1825), 2–3
Selznick, P., 26, 269
Sex Discrimination Act (1975), 18, 19, 74, 79, 83, 226, 272
Shaw LJ, 242
Sheffield, 5
shop stewards, 271
Simon, Sir John, 237
Simon, Viscount, 216
Skinner J, 160
SLADE, 167
Slade J, 73, 200, 201
social scientists' view of union democracy, 268
SOGAT, 165, 166, 181
Somervell, Lord, 47, 208, 209
South Wales miners, 106, 238–9
Stamp J, 196, 199
state as employer, 265
status quo arrangements 198–9, 284
statutory regulation of union affairs, 11–14
  admission, 82–93
  control of discipline re industrial action, 250–8
  discipline and expulsion, 226–31
  government, 136–90, 266
  limits of contractual enforcement, 44–6
Staughton J, 156
STE, 63, 151
strike ballots, 137, 152–5, 162–4, 277
strikes
  non-participation in, 236–59
  period between ballot and, 163
  unlawful, 130–1
subjective rules, 208–12
subsidies for trade union ballots, 136–7
Summers, C.W., 208, 273
Supreme Court Act (1981), 287
Sweden, 169
Swinfen Eady LJ, 201
Switzerland, 126

TASS, 277, 278, 279

Tebbit, Norman, 182
Templeman J, 199, 210, 215, 216, 248–50
terms of contract, judicial control of, 34–44
see also express terms; implied terms
TGWU, 29, 63, 64, 165, 167, 182, 192
  indirect elections, 139, 145–6, 150, 151
Thatcher, Margaret, 83, 146
time limit.
  on applications to court re election procedures, 151–2
  for bringing complaints, 231
Times, The, 182
tort
  economic, 238, 239
  liability in, 242–4
  of maintenance, 98
  remedies in, for rejected applicant, 74–5
tortious acts
  duty to hold a ballot re, 157–9
trade, restraint of, 3–5, 7, 37–8
Trade Disputes and Trade Union Act (1927), 169, 238, 256
Trade Union Act (1871), 6–14, 168, 265, 271, 274
  restraint of trade (Section 3), 7, 37, 38, 39, 71
  restraint on court intervention, 7–11, 52, 125, 136
  repeal, 11–14, 45
  on union rules, 29
Trade Union Act (1913), 53, 174
  on admission, 82
  ballot for political fund, 30, 35, 168–9, 183, 226, 262, 272
  breach of rules, 46, 97
Trade Union Act (1984), 20, 53, 136, 141–52
  Part I, elections, 141–52
  Part II, ballot, 30, 155–68, 173, 254
  litigation under, 166 Table 1
  Part III, political fund, 169–83
  resistance to, 275–9
Trade Union (Amalgamations, etc.) Act (1964), 30, 45, 137, 174
Trade Union and Labour Relations Act (TULRA) (1974)
  amended (1976), 14–18, 20, 55, 136, 227, 257

on admissions, repealed (1976), 65, 83, 283
  duty to ballot, 158, 159
  on injunctions, amended (1975), 55
  membership agreements between unions and management, 261
  picketing, 255
  procedure agreements, 246–7
  restraint of trade, 38, 39
  on statutory objects, 35
  trade union not a corporate body, 52
  and ultra vires use of union funds, 123, 125, 128–32
Trade Union Immunities, Green Paper (1981), 154
transfer of members between unions, 222–4
tribunals, 194, 230–1
  see also Employment Appeal Tribunal; industrial tribunals
triggered ballots, 154–5
Truck Acts (1831–1940), 179
trusteeship of union funds, 125
TUC (Trade Union Congress)
  -affiliated unions, 88, 150, 191
  boycott of Industrial Relations Act, 13, 139, 140, 144, 222–4
  Disputes Committee, 223–4
  General Council consultative document (1986), 276–84
  Handbook on the Industrial Relations Act, 32
  Independent Review Committee (IRC), 16–17, 65–7, 193, 283–5
  on self-regulation, 271
  Statement of Guidance on exemption from political funds, 181
Turner, H.A.L., 274

UCATT, 151, 192, 277, 279
UCW, 199, 277, 278, 279
ultra vires doctrine, 35–6, 97–102, 128–32
  action, 45, 71
  awards of Disputes Committee re eligibility issues, 73–4
  breaches, 102–10
  re discipline for failing to strike, 237–40
  evading the challenge, 101–2
  and the miners' strike, 119–28
Undy, R.

Ballots and Trade Union Democracy, 140, 150, 165, 167
unemployment
  and admissions, 89
  and collective bargaining, 274
Ungoed Thomas J, 197, 198, 210
union democracy, 268
  as member control, 272–9
  as member protection, 269–72
union government
  and the Courts, 96–135
  nature of, and democracy, 273–5
  role of law in, 260–89
  self-regulation in, 271, 273, 279–84
  statutory regulation of, 136–90
unions, trade
  acts by, 159–62
  and application of Trade Union Act (1984) Part II, 155–6
  function of, 260–3, 267, 272–3
  legal status, 1–3, 168, 260
  problems of illegality, 97–8
  relationships within, 107–10, 268
  and *ultra vires*, 128–32
  unincorporated status, 3–5, 52, 128
  as voluntary associations, 129–32
  see also craft unions; grade unions; industrial and professional unions; open unions; white-collar unions
United States of America, 208, 267
Upjohn LJ, 54, 69, 71, 73
USDAW, 277, 279

Vinelott J, 18, 123–4
voluntary associations, trade unions as, 129–32
voting
  entitlement, 143, 164, 175
  turn-out, 138

Walton J, 34, 112
Wapping dispute (1986), 165
Warner J, 158
Warrington J, 100
Watkins J, 106
Webb, B., 2, 268
Webb, S., 2, 268
Wedderburn of Charlton, Lord, 50, 65, 128, 147, 149
Wednesbury principles, 224, 225
white-collar unions, 244–6
Whitford J, 105
Wilberforce, Lord, 28, 73, 212
work, right to, *see* right to work
workers
  franchise (1854), 5
  rights to information, consultation and representation, 264
  status and security of, 263
workplace ballots, 137, 144–5, 150, 167
Wrenbury, Lord, 10

Yorkshire miners, 106, 119, 121
Younger J, 101